Your
Questions,
Scripture's
Answers

John F. Brug

D1166742

NORTHWESTERN PUBLISHING HOUSE
Milwaukee, Wisconsin

Second printing, 2014

Photo: Shutterstock
Art Director: Karen Knutson
Designer: Pamela Dunn

Northwestern Publishing House
1250 N. 113th St., Milwaukee, WI 53226-3284
www.nph.net
© 2013 Northwestern Publishing House
Published 2013
Printed in the United States of America
ISBN 978-0-8100-2542-4
ISBN 978-0-8100-2576-9 (e-book)

Contents

Foreword v

Resources vii

1 The Bible.. 1

2 Biblical Doctrines... 45

3 Ministry 79

4 The Sacraments 107

5 Church Fellowship... 145

6 Last Things (Eschatology) 191

7 Other Churches and Religions 213

8 Creeds and Confessions.. 251

9 Christians and Government... 261

10 Sexual Morality, Marriage, and Divorce 289

11 Adiaphora 315

Scripture Index... 357

Subject Index 365

Foreword

Questions and answers have always been an important format for Christian teaching. In catechisms, students carefully study a set of questions and well-tested answers to those questions. In Bible classes the opportunity for students to ask questions is an important part of the learning process. In recent years the question-and-answer columns in *Forward in Christ* (formerly *Northwestern Lutheran*) and the Q & A section on the WELS Web site have been quite popular and widely used. This book is offered as a response to that interest in the question-and-answer format. It is a compilation from the questions that I answered for the "Your Questions, Please" column in the *Northwestern Lutheran* during the 1990s and more recently for the WELS Q & A site. It is hoped that these discussions will still be interesting and helpful now in book form.

Both the questions and answers have been edited—sometimes expanded, sometimes shortened, occasionally combined. They do not present a systematic or comprehensive treatment of any of the topics discussed, but simply provide a cross section of the questions that are on people's minds. Both the questions and answers vary greatly in length. Sometimes long questions have short answers and vice versa. Part of the reason for the shortness of some answers is that the *Northwestern Lutheran* format allowed for only three hundred to four hundred words. The answers had to get right to the point quickly. In general, in the Q & A format, longer answers are given when the information is not readily available elsewhere. If a more comprehensive answer is readily available elsewhere, the questioner is often referred to that source. I have tried to arrange the questions so that the answers in a series complement one another.

As you read, give as much attention to the questions as to the answers. They are a window into how people see our church and its teachings. They reveal some of the sources of spiritual distress and show how people seek to deal with that stress. Often they express eagerness to learn and understand; sometimes, pain or sorrow; and occasionally, anger or hostility. Often for those answering the questions, the most challenging part of the job is trying to determine what exactly the questioner is asking and why. It is often hard to read the attitude and motive of the question, though this is one of the most important factors in determining the best response to the question.

Many of the questions are ones that Scripture answers directly. Others call for opinions or subjective evaluations on the basis of scriptural principles. When WELS has official statements on the issue, I usually refer to them. If there seems to be a general consensus on an issue in WELS, the answer often includes *we* or *our*. When I give a personal opinion, I use *I* or phrases like "it seems to me."

My hope is that this book will serve more as a question book than as an answer book. By that I mean that I hope reading this book will raise as many questions as it answers and lead readers to further study—above all, to check out the Scripture references provided. Interest in finding answers from Scripture should lead to further, regular searching of the Scriptures, including a plan for regular cover-to-cover reading of the Bible. Many other resources for further study are suggested in this book, both in the list of resources that follows immediately after this foreword and scattered throughout the chapters of the book.

John F. Brug

Resources

Below is a list of resources for further study. The first list is of general sources about Christian doctrine, arranged from easier to more difficult. The second listing is subject specific. The most important items are marked with an asterisk. These resources will be mentioned at appropriate places in the discussions that follow.

General Sources

*Armin Schuetze, *Basic Doctrines of the Bible*, Milwaukee: Northwestern Publishing House, 1969. A clear, concise overview of biblical doctrine.

*WELS Conference of Presidents, *This We Believe*, Milwaukee: Northwestern Publishing House, 1999 edition. Official doctrinal statement of WELS with theses and antitheses. Covers all major doctrines.

Richard Gurgel, *This We Believe: Questions and Answers*, Milwaukee: Northwestern Publishing House, 2006.

Doctrinal Statements of the WELS, Milwaukee: Northwestern Publishing House, 1997 edition. A collection of formal doctrinal statements of WELS on selected issues.

*The People's Bible series, Milwaukee: Northwestern Publishing House. A series of 41 commentaries for laypeople, covering every book of the Bible.

*People's Bible Teachings series, Milwaukee: Northwestern Publishing House. A series of 20 doctrinal studies for laypeople on all of the main teachings of the Bible.

Mark Paustian, *Prepared to Answer* and *More Prepared to Answer*, Milwaukee: Northwestern Publishing House, 2004. Provides a helpful model for sharing the Christian faith by supplying Scripture-based responses to common objections to Christianity.

God's People series, Milwaukee: Northwestern Publishing House. Twelve volumes on the lives of key Bible people.

*Lyle Lange (ed.), *Our Great Heritage*, 3 vols., Milwaukee: Northwestern Publishing House, 1991. Essays on doctrinal topics, many of which originally appeared in the *Wisconsin Lutheran Quarterly* or as pastoral conference essays.

Wisconsin Lutheran Quarterly, WELS theological journal for pastors. Makes frequent use of Hebrew and Greek in exegetical articles, but many articles are valuable also for laypeople.

*Wisconsin Lutheran Seminary Online Essay Collection: www.wls. wels.net/library/Essays/essayindex.htm A huge collection of doctrinal essays from WLQ and other sources.

*WELS Q & A. Go to www.wels.net. Then go to Q and A. A large collection of questions submitted by readers to receive answers from WELS pastors. You can browse the archives or submit your own questions.

Theodore Laetsch (ed.), *Abiding Word*, 3 vols., St. Louis: Concordia Publishing House, 1946. Doctrinal essays for laypeople in celebration of the LCMS centennial.

Adolf Hoenecke, *Evangelical Lutheran Dogmatics*, 4 vols., Milwaukee: Northwestern Publishing House, 1999–2009. A dogmatics for pastors. The English translation is not yet complete.

Francis Pieper, *Christian Dogmatics*, St. Louis: Concordia Publishing House, 1950. A dogmatics for pastors.

*Paul McCain, et al., *Concordia: The Lutheran Confessions*, St. Louis: Concordia Publishing House, 2005. A new translation of the Lutheran Confessions.

Ewald Plass, *What Luther Says*, 3 vols., St. Louis: Concordia Publishing House, 1959. Selected quotations from Luther's writings arranged topically.

On Specific Subjects

John Schaller, *Biblical Christology*, Milwaukee: Northwestern Publishing House, 1919. A detailed study of the person and work of Christ.

John Brug, *Church Fellowship: Working Together for the Truth*, in the People's Bible Teachings series, Milwaukee: Northwestern Publishing House, 1996.

John Brug, *A Bible Study on Man and Woman in God's World*, Milwaukee: Northwestern Publishing House, 1992.

WELS Conference of Presidents, *A Study of Marriage, Divorce, Malicious Desertion, and Remarriage in the Light of God's Word*, Milwaukee: Northwestern Publishing House, 1990.

David Kuske, *Biblical Interpretation: The Only Right Way*, Milwaukee: Northwestern Publishing House, 1995.

Brian Keller, *Bible: God's Inspired, Inerrant Word*, in the People's Bible Teachings series, Milwaukee: Northwestern Publishing House, 2003.

1
The Bible

We begin with questions concerning the Bible itself, because the Bible, as God's inspired, errorless Word, is the only source of guidance from God which we have for answering the questions on other topics which follow. A good introductory study of this topic is the volume *Bible: God's Inspired, Inerrant Word*, by Brian Keller in the People's Bible Teachings series.

The Bible as a Book

Your Question **Why do we believe that the Bible is God's inspired Word?**

The primary biblical passage describing the inspiration of Scripture is 2 Timothy 3:16: "All Scripture is God-breathed and is useful for teaching, rebuking, correcting and training in righteousness." The NIV does a good job of rendering in a literal fashion the term that describes the inspiration of the Bible. The words of the Bible were "breathed out by God." That is, the Holy Spirit did not merely inspire the apostles to give their own view of religion. He actually gave the content and words of Scripture. Another passage is 2 Peter 1:19-21: "We have the word of the prophets made more certain, and you will do well to pay attention to it, as to a light shining in a dark place, until the day dawns and the morning star rises in your hearts. Above all, you must understand that no prophecy of Scripture came about by the prophet's own interpretation. For prophecy never had its origin in the will of man, but men spoke from God as they were carried along by the Holy Spirit." The writers were moved by the Holy Spirit to write the Bible.

The words of Scripture were inspired in that they were breathed out from God; the writers were inspired in that they were carried along by the Holy Spirit.

Your Question What was Paul's definition of "Scripture" at the time of his writing this passage (2 Timothy 3:16), and how do we verify what he meant? Might he not have been simply referring to Old Testament writings?

It is very clear his definition includes both Old and New Testaments. See 1 Timothy 5:18, which quotes both Moses and Luke as inspired writers of Scripture. Luke's gospel could not have been much more than five years old at this point. Also 2 Peter 3:16 clearly refers to Paul's letters as Scripture. Paul also applies the concept of inspiration to his own writing: "This is what we speak, not in words taught us by human wisdom but in words taught by the Spirit, expressing spiritual truths in spiritual words" (1 Corinthians 2:13).

In short, his definition of Scripture is all of the inspired books that had been written at the time when he was speaking.

Your Question How do we know that all of the books that were yet to be written and compiled to make up the New Testament were in fact considered by the above writer (Paul) to be "Scripture"? Many of the New Testament letters had not yet been written and certainly the New Testament compilation was only carried out some considerable time after the writer lived.

Almost all of them were written by the time of 2 Peter. Revelation was the last written and specifically says it was received by inspiration. In chapters 21 and 22, Revelation echoes Genesis 1–3 and closes with the same admonition not to add or subtract, which is found in Deuteronomy (compare Deuteronomy 4:2; Revelation 22:18).

Compiling the books into one volume has nothing to do with determining which books are canonical. During the whole time of the Old Testament, the canonical books were circulated as separate scrolls.

Your Question When the books of the New Testament were compiled, who determined what writings were to be included? Where is it stated in the Bible, or anywhere else for that matter, that the men

(as indicated above) who compiled the books of the New Testament as we know it today were inspired by God when performing this compilation? How did they know how to identify and select only those writings that were "inspired"?

Inclusion was not based on a later human decision but on the immediate recognition of inspiration. The books were recognized immediately when given. John knew he was inspired, as did Paul. See 1 Timothy 5:18 and 2 Peter 3:16 cited previously. Binding the books together in one volume simply made them easier to use, it did not make them canonical. Inspired and noninspired books were sometimes bound together, as they are in many German Bibles. Nobody ever compiled the books to make them canonical. That recognition was given when they were first received. Later lists of canonical books did not create the canon; they simply recognized it. The WELS doctrinal statement on Scripture calls this "a quiet historical process." "The Canon, that is, the collection of books which is the authority for the Church, is not the creation of the Church. Rather the Canon has, by a quiet historical process which took place in the worship life of the Church, imposed itself upon the Church by virtue of its own divine authority" (*Doctrinal Statements of the WELS*, pp. 10,11). This is discussed in Volume 1 of *Our Great Heritage*, pp. 98-125. This article also appeared in the *Wisconsin Lutheran Quarterly* (April 1972), pp. 94-119.

Your
Question **I believe that there is a God. But how do I know that the Father, Son, and Holy Spirit of the Bible are the true God? To accept the words of the Bible as truth, I need to know that the Bible comes from the true God. How exactly do we know that the 66 books of the Bible are God's Word, and not just another man-made religious code? What criteria were used to select these writings?**

The books of the Bible are not God's Word because someone selected them or because someone believes them, but because God gave them by inspiration of the Spirit. No human authority or arguments can demonstrate this to you. The only "proof" is that the Holy Spirit uses the law of God revealed in the Bible to convict us of our sin, and he uses the gospel to convince us that Christ is the Savior from sin. We do not believe that Christ is our Savior because rational arguments have convinced us that the Bible is God's Word. But because the Holy Spirit has used the Bible to give us faith in Christ, we are convinced it's God's Word.

Your
Question **In order for something to be Scripture it must be inspired by God, efficacious, and be absolute truth. Given that the Bible, as it contains the Scripture, is the only complete source of God's revelation to man what would prevent other written works from being Scripture provided their roots were found in the Bible? Of course, no one could make that claim of being inspired by God, yet there have been many works of the word that have had great impact. Could man alone write something that is efficacious and absolute truth? Could God still be speaking to us today through the Word and the word?**

When a pastor preaches a sermon based on the Word of God as found in the Bible, we say he is preaching the Word of God to us. The same is true when someone presents the message of the gospel drawn from Scripture in his or her own words. The Holy Spirit can work faith through those words. We would call such messages scriptural, but we would not call them Scripture. This distinction preserves the unique character of the words inspired by God in the Bible, which are the standard or norm by which all other messages are judged. The essence of the Word of God is the message that God wants to convey to us. The material form of the Word of God is the words he gave by inspiration.

The gospel works with power not only when it is quoted verbatim from the Bible, but when its true meaning is given in different words. If this were not true, the Bible could not be translated. The essence of the Bible is its divinely intended meaning. Where that meaning is correctly presented, the Holy Spirit works through the power of the Word.

Originally and primarily, we today can find these truths only from the Bible, but they can be passed on in a secondary way using other words that correctly summarize the truths of the Bible.

Your
Question **Peace and greetings to you in the Name of Our Lord and Our Mother. My question is, why do Lutherans believe the Bible to be the only and sole source of infallible authority for the Christian, when the Bible nowhere makes that claim that it alone is the only infallible authority. It seems that if we judge that claim by the Bible itself, it refutes itself. I can't understand how a Protestant can believe in the nonhistorical theory of *sola scriptura*. If it were not for the infallible Catholic Church, then we would not know what the inerrant written Word of God is. If *sola scriptura* is true, then who's right? The Baptist?**

The Lutheran? The Methodist? The Calvinist? All claim to go by God's Word alone, all claim to be inspired by the Holy Spirit, and yet all teach totally different things. If the Bible alone could tell us all we need to know, then why hasn't it yet? *Sola scriptura* is a historically bankrupt system. Of course we need a Church to teach us what Scripture means. It would be like writing the U.S. Constitution and giving it to the people to interpret itself. That seems dubious.

It is relatively simple to dismiss your claim of an infallible Roman church. The Bible says that we are saved by grace alone through faith alone not by works (Ephesians 2:8,9). The Catholic church says we are saved by faith and works. One of these claims is false. This means that Christians must either believe that the Roman church is infallible and the Bible is false, or that the Bible is infallible and the Roman church is false. The Lutheran church holds to an infallible Bible and recognizes that the Roman church is false. If the Bible is our standard, it is historically absurd to say that the Roman church is infallible since it contradicts the Bible on so many points.

Your statements illustrate the reasons why we recognize the Roman papacy as the Antichrist. It condemns the two most important doctrines of the Bible—Scripture alone and by grace alone through faith alone. Paul condemns those who deny these teachings in his letter to the Galatians, which we would encourage you to read. Rome throws its anathemas (curses) against those who follow Scripture, Paul anathematizes the false teachings of the Catholic church and those who promote and defend them. It is clear which side you have chosen.

Your
Question **What hermeneutical method (method of Bible interpretation) is used in the Wisconsin Evangelical Lutheran Synod, and what does the method entail?**

Our method is called grammatical-historical. We study the text grammatically and syntactically and interpret it in light of the immediate and wider context of Scripture. The basic rule is let Scripture interpret Scripture. We may study the historical context of a certain passage of Scripture to see if there is any information from historical records or archaeological finds which may help us to understand the events and the language of the text, but no human science such as archaeology or literary criticism can sit in judgment on Scripture. You will find a detailed discussion of this in *Biblical Interpretation: The Only Right Way* by David Kuske.

Your Question I'm not sure what category this fits in, most likely the end of time? Anyways, my question is this: I have heard more and more about a "secret code" in the Bible. This code seemingly has all the answers to future, past, and present events. This "code" has even found its way to the big-screen in the movie entitled *The Omega Code*, which by the way, has received many endorsements from Christian TV Networks. So, I'm wondering if there is any truth to this or is this just wishful thinking?

The most publicized Bible codes are based on the sequence of letters in the Hebrew Old Testament. The alleged codes are discovered by copying letters from the Hebrew Old Testament at specified intervals—every 5th letter, every 10th letter, every 17th letter, etc. The resulting sequences of letters are then read to see if they spell out a message. Occasionally one of the sequences forms a readable string of Hebrew words.

These alleged "codes" are not valid for three reasons. (1) The spelling of words in the various texts of the Old Testament that we have is not consistent. Words are spelled differently in different manuscripts. It would be like spelling the word *through* in one copy and *thru* in another. This means that every biblical manuscript would produce a different set of messages. No biblical manuscript that we possess has the exact spelling and number of letters of the original. (2) The resulting messages are very vague, like horoscopes. The connection between them and alleged fulfillments is very subjective and arbitrary. (3) God's Word communicates to us clearly in terms we can understand, not in codes that can only be figured out by a computer.

Your Question Sometimes when I am reading the Bible it seems to me that the chapter divisions are in the wrong place. For example, the end of Isaiah 52 really seems to be the beginning of chapter 53. How did we get the chapter and verse divisions in our Bible? How reliable are they?

The chapter and verse divisions as we have them are not an original feature of the biblical text. In the oldest Hebrew manuscripts of the Bible, the text is divided into verses and paragraphs by little dividing signs and by spaces, but these divisions are not numbered. The numbering of the verses and the dividing of the text into chapters originated in the Latin Vulgate Bible. Our present chapter divisions were established by Archbishop Stephen Langton of Canterbury, England, in the 13th century. This method of division was then incorporated into the Hebrew Bible, although the chapter and verse divisions of the Hebrew Bible do not always match those of the English Bible.

In short, the chapter and verse divisions as we have them are the interpretations of a later editor. In general, they are quite well done and help the reader follow the author's line of thought, but readers should not feel too bound by them in reading and interpreting the text. The same is true of the headings that have been inserted into many modern study Bibles. In some cases, these modern headings are an improvement over the traditional chapter divisions. In my NIV study Bible a new division begins at Isaiah 52:13, not at Isaiah 53:1. This is an improvement over the traditional division.

When you read the Bible, use the chapter divisions and the editor's headings as a help in following the train of thought, but do not feel too constrained by them. Remember the books of the Bible were written to be read as books, not as chapters and verses.

Your Question **There are so many Bible translations out there. I don't know which one to use anymore. One pastor has said that the NIV has a "Reformed slant." What does that mean? Should we Lutherans be more concerned that we have the most faithful translation available, instead of just throwing in with the rest of Christendom in using the NIV?**

It certainly was much simpler to select a translation when the King James Version (KJV) was the predominant Bible for English-speaking Christians. Whether it was a better situation for Bible students is another question.

The King James is a fine translation. Its one major shortcoming is that much of its beautiful English has become outdated. Many passages have become very difficult for readers to understand. As a result many contemporary English translations were undertaken in recent decades. Although the Wisconsin Synod has never had a mandatory Bible translation, in recent years the NIV has been accepted for general use.

It is confusing to refer to the NIV as a *Reformed* translation. Strictly speaking, only the Calvinist branch of Protestantism should be called Reformed. Much of what people categorize as "Reformed" theology is actually Arminian theology, which represents the opposite pole of

Protestant Christianity from Calvinism. In passages such as Jude 4, the King James Version, which we used for many years, is actually more Reformed than the NIV, which we are now using. The NIV was translated by a panel of scholars representing the whole spectrum of evangelical Protestantism, including a few Lutherans. They naturally served as a check against one another and prevented narrowly biased translations to a considerable degree. Some years ago, about the time that WELS members began using the NIV, I received a tract from a well-meaning member of one of our congregations. It vehemently denounced the NIV as doctrinally unreliable. The irony was that the Baptist author's main objection to the NIV was that it was too Lutheran and that there was a danger that readers of the NIV might get the impression that Baptism was a means of grace which worked regeneration in those who received it. Perhaps if some Lutherans call the NIV too Reformed and some Baptists call it too Lutheran, the translators did a better job of avoiding denomination bias than some critics have given them credit for.

This is not to say that the NIV translation is a perfect translation or that there are no passages in it which we would like to see improved. There are some passages that could be translated better and that may reflect a doctrinal slant on the part of the translators, but there are none that cannot be understood correctly. Almost all doctrinal disagreement between Lutherans and other Christians is due not to differences of translation but to disagreement about the interpretation of passages.

Perhaps the best example of such a problem passage is Acts 3:21, which the NIV renders, "[Jesus] must remain in heaven until the time comes for God to restore everything." The KJV translates, "Whom the heaven must receive until the times of restitution of all things." Luther translated, "He must receive heaven." Both the NIV and KJV have been quoted by the Reformed as evidence against the real presence of Jesus' body and blood in the Lord's Supper. However, the NIV rendering can be understood correctly as a restatement of Jesus' words in Luke 13:35, "You will not see me again until you say, 'Blessed is he who comes in the name of the Lord.'" The problem with the Reformed view of the Lord's Supper is not so much due to the translation of Acts 3:21 as to the application of the passage to the Lord's Supper. Acts 3:21 has nothing to do with the Lord's Supper. It is about Christ's visible, bodily presence, not his sacramental presence.

There would be some advantages to having a translation prepared by confessional Lutherans, but even if such a Lutheran translation becomes available, there would still be advantages in using the commonly accepted English translation for witnessing and instruction of people from other denominations. The NIV appears to be the translation that has the best chance of gaining and holding such status, at least among evangelical Christians.

In 2001, the publishers of the NIV produced a revision called the TNIV. One of the chief reasons for this revision was gender inclusive language in all passages where this is the original intention of the authors. While this edition improves some renderings of the NIV, it also introduces new problems and cannot be considered a significant improvement over the 1984 NIV. (This answer does not consider the NIV 2011 edition.)

Your
Question **Some churches that my friends go to use the New American Standard Bible. I heard that it was the most faithful translation when compared to the original. Is that true? And, if so, why don't we use it?**

Both the NIV and the New American Standard Bible (NASB) were produced by Protestant Bible scholars who were committed to upholding the inspiration of Scripture. The main differences between the two versions is that the NASB is more literal (that is, more word for word) in its rendering of the Hebrew and the Greek and that it remains somewhat closer to the style and language of the King James Version.

More literal is not necessarily more faithful. The goal of a translator is to say the same thing in his language that the writer said in the original. Sometimes a word-for-word rendering is not the best way to do this, because the idioms of different languages cannot be matched up word for word. Sometimes a rendering that is less word for word does a better job of transferring the meaning of the text into the translator's language. Every translator is constantly wrestling to find the right balance between sticking as close as possible to the original language of the Bible while at the same time conveying the meaning of the text in the idioms of his own language.

A good example of this problem is found in Acts 2:27. The NASB translates rather woodenly, "You will not abandon my soul to Hades."

This confuses the reader, since Jesus' soul was not in hell after his death but with God in heaven. The NIV renders into more idiomatic English: "You will not abandon me to the grave." This is the correct idea. In this case the less literal translation is better than the more literal rendering.

My own personal assessment is that the NASB translators at times err in the direction of being overliteral and that the NIV translators at times would have been wise to stay with a more consistent, literal rendering than they did. So it is pretty much a standoff on the issue of faithfulness. The NIV has an edge in readability, but the NASB or one of the recent revisions of it would be an excellent choice for Bible students who are looking for a more literal version to compare with the NIV. The New King James (NKJV) would serve the same purpose. The NIV, NASB, and NKJV can all serve a valuable purpose in the Bible student's library.

Your Question **Recently I was reading through John in the NIV. I noticed that several verses at the beginning of chapter 8 are prefaced by a warning that these verses are not in the best copies of the Bible. I noticed the same thing near the end of Mark 16. What's going on? Are these verses God's Word or not? Can we rely on our NIV Bibles?**

We have many handwritten Greek manuscripts for all of the books of the New Testament. Some of them have fewer words than other copies of the same book. In all such cases, translators face the question, "Did the longer text add words, or did the shorter text leave some out?" In some cases the evidence is heavily weighted in one direction, and the translator's decision is relatively easy. In other cases the decision is less clear. I believe that in such cases the wiser choice is to print the longer reading in the main text and to use a footnote to indicate that the words are missing from some manuscripts.

At times the NIV relegates such words to the footnotes or omits them entirely. In the two cases you cite, the NIV has chosen the less drastic solution of prefacing the questioned verses with a warning that they do not appear in all Greek manuscripts. The decision to tag them as suspect is a subjective judgment made by the NIV editors. At times the NIV editors place too much weight on certain Greek manuscripts from Egypt as the "earliest and most reliable." These manuscripts happen to be missing the longer readings in John 8 and Mark 16. The NIV should have given greater attention to weighing all of the manuscripts from all geographic areas of the church rather than placing so much weight on a few favored manuscripts.

The TNIV also marks these verses as dubious.

Your Question **I have been reading a book entitled *From God to Us* by Norman L. Geisler and Wm. E. Nix, in which they speak of the *Textus Receptus.* The TR is something new to me having heard about it just within the last few months, and then from someone of the Reformed persuasion. In the book, the authors seem to disparage the TR, at least, they don't seem to be too wild about it. What's the story here?**

At the time when the King James Version was translated, the so-called *Textus Receptus* was the available, commonly accepted text of the Greek New Testament. In the Western church, knowledge of the Greek text was just being reestablished at this time. The Roman Catholic Church had made the Latin Vulgate the official text of the Bible. As a result, from about 600 to A.D. 1500 the Greek text of the New Testament was not widely copied and distributed in the Western church. In the 1500s, after the printing press was invented, a Dutch printer got the humanist scholar Erasmus to edit a Greek text of the New Testament. The dozen or so copies of the Greek New Testament that Erasmus used had been made in Byzantium (Constantinople, Istanbul) from about 1200 to 1400. Over the next one hundred years, several other publishers also printed Greek New Testaments based on about a hundred copies made in Byzantium from 1100 to 1400. One of these publishers boasted in an advertising blurb that the Greek New Testament that he published was the *"textum ab omnibus receptum"* ("the text accepted by everyone"). Thus the title *Textus Receptus*.

Between 1600 and the present, several hundred copies of the Greek New Testament were found that date back to 200 and 600. Many of these are from other areas of the early church, such as Egypt. More than two thousand additional copies of the text copied in Byzantium from 900 to 1400 (most of which are similar to the *Textus Receptus*) also were found.

This has led to two theories about which copies of the New Testament should be used in editing a text of the New Testament. Some insist that the thousands of copies made in Byzantium are the "best" copies to use. Others insist that the "best" copies to use are those early copies made from 200 to 600 rather than those made later in Byzantium from 900 to 1400. The arguments used to support each of these two theories have proven to be very subjective. The only objective approach is to compare and weigh all of the evidence from all of the copies of the New Testament that are in existence (both those from the early centuries and the later ones from Byzantium).

It's also important to know that real differences between all these copies involve less than 1 percent of the verses of the New Testament. And none of the verses that are different in these many copies affect doctrine in any way. No doctrines would be lost by the omissions since these doctrines occur in other passages. Thus it is quite evident that God has carefully preserved his inspired Word for us down through those centuries when the New Testament was being copied by hand.

Old Testament Passages

Your
Question **Can you help me to understand in detail the sale of the birthright in Genesis 25:29-34? Thanks.**

In Old Testament culture, the firstborn son had a right to a double inheritance from his father. In the case of the patriarchs through whom the line of the Savior was being passed, it would be natural for the firstborn to assume that this included the promise of the Savior (though God did not, in fact, follow the right of the firstborn in carrying on the line of the Savior).

We do not know if Esau had the right to sell his birthright or if it was a sin or crime for Jacob to try to buy it. At any rate, Isaac did not intend to honor the deal his sons had made. The story is told to show us the attitude of the two sons. Esau valued his special right in the family and presumably also the promise of the Savior so little that he was ready to sell them for a bowl of bean soup to gratify his hunger. For this reason Scripture calls him a "godless" man (Hebrews 12:16). Jacob, on the other hand, valued the promise greatly but tried to obtain it in a wrong way. He took advantage of his brother's need and weakness and later deceived his father. Jacob had to learn the hard way to trust in the Lord and not to rely on his own tricks.

Neither Esau nor Jacob deserved the blessing, but God graciously bore with Jacob's weaknesses and taught him to be an "Israel" who prevailed with God.

**In Exodus 4:24, why was God going to kill Moses? Why
wasn't Moses' son circumcised? Why did Zipporah circumcise him? Was
Jethro, Zipporah's father, a Hebrew priest?**

The questions you ask have puzzled commentators for centuries.
Since neither the context of the verses nor other parts of Scripture
provide us with any additional information, the only answers are those
we can deduce from the text.

The failure of Moses to circumcise his son was an act of negligence
and disobedience. The penalty for neglecting circumcision was to be
"cut off" from God's people (Genesis 17:14). This explains why God
threatened Moses with death. The apparent reason why Zipporah had
to quickly circumcise their son was that Moses was unable to do so
because he was incapacitated by the blow the Lord had sent against
him. By touching Moses with their son's foreskin, Zipporah was
demonstrating that the offense which threatened Moses' life had been
removed. Her quick action may also have been due to the fact that she
realized the threat to her husband's life was her fault.

Most commentators believe that Moses' failure to circumcise his son
was due at least in part to the objections of Zipporah. Her comments
after she had circumcised their son imply that this ritual was disgusting
to her. She said to Moses, "You are a bridegroom of blood to me"
(Exodus 4:25). This suggests that she thought her marriage to Moses
was forcing her to subject her son to a rite she found repulsive, yet this
was the only way she could keep Moses as her husband. The opinion
that Zipporah was not in agreement with all that God was requiring of
Moses receives some support from the fact that Moses sent her away
during the time that he was confronting Pharaoh (Exodus 18:2).

Although much about this incident remains a mystery, the basic
lesson is clear: God expected that a man who was going to be the leader
of his covenant people would be faithful in observing the regulations
of that covenant within his own family.

We probably wouldn't call Jethro a *Hebrew* priest since he was not a
member of the Israelite priesthood descended from Levi and Aaron. He
was, however, apparently a worshiper of the true God like Melchizedek.
He was perhaps a descendant of Abraham through his wife Keturah
(Genesis 25:4). In that sense, he could be called a Hebrew.

Your
Question In the People's Bible Study Guide on Joshua there are a
number of "agree-disagree" statements concerning the story of Rahab
and the spies. They are:

- **Rahab was justified in lying to protect the spies.**
- **The author's aim was to justify her lies.**
- **Hebrews 11:31 and James 2:25 show that her lies were okay in God's eyes.**
- **All forms of deception are morally wrong.**
- **It is sometimes right for governments and their agents to lie, but never for individuals.**

I think there can be only one right answer to these questions. I await your answer.

The key statement is the fourth: "All forms of deception are morally wrong." If there is agreement that this statement is false, the significance of all the other statements becomes minimal. Does all deception fall into the category that the Bible condemns as "lying"? Can a Christian, for example, be an undercover officer or a spy?

Luther believed that not all withholding or denial of the truth is morally objectionable "lying." Luther did not condone lying, but he defined *lying* as withholding the truth from someone who is entitled to it or telling a falsehood to hurt someone. The midwives in Egypt did not have an obligation to tell Pharaoh where the Hebrew babies were so he could kill them. An undercover police officer trying to apprehend drug dealers does not tell them who he is before he has the evidence on them. A pastor cannot betray information that was confessed to him in confidence. Luther said that such withholding of the truth to protect the innocent is not properly called lying.

If Rahab was convinced that the cause of Israel was the cause of God and that the cause of the Canaanites was evil, she did not have a responsibility to help the Canaanites thwart Israel's invasion plans.

If Rahab's behavior was not lying in the sense condemned by the Eighth Commandment, then the first three statements become moot. It is possible to debate whether the authors of Joshua, James, and Hebrews were trying to condone her action since they make no specific statement about this, but if her action was not a lie condemned by the Eighth Commandment, it really makes no difference.

14

If Rahab's action was not lying, the fifth statement also becomes moot or at least irrelevant to the situation in Joshua. The question does, however, point out that if Rahab was lying, so were Joshua and the spies, since they were party to the same deception. There seems to be no grounds for evaluating the actions of Joshua and the spies by one set of criteria on the grounds that they were government officials and Rahab's actions by a different standard since she was a private citizen.

If the fourth statement is true and all deception is always lying and morally wrong, then it becomes impossible to defend the other four statements. The key to all four statements is a clear definition of what lying is.

The situation is somewhat parallel to the Fifth Commandment. The Fifth Commandment forbids all murder, but it does not forbid all killing. The Eighth Commandment forbids all lying, but it does not forbid all withholding of the truth.

Your Question

Why is the book of Judges called Judges? It doesn't seem to be a very good name since the heroes in the book are more fighters than judges.

It is true that the only "judge" in Judges who is described as exercising judicial functions is Deborah (Judges 4:5). Some of the other heroes of the book may have exercised such functions, but certainly their main activity described in the book was serving as military leaders and deliverers for Israel. Samuel, whose "judgeship" is described in 1 Samuel, frequently held court, so he certainly deserves the title "judge." He too, however, served as a military deliverer and political leader.

The Hebrew name of the book, *Shophetim*, means "rulers" or "deliverers." When the Old Testament was translated into Greek in the 2nd century B.C., the translators chose a Greek word that means "judges" as their rendering for *shophetim*. The Latin Bible, which was the standard Bible of the church for many centuries, simply followed the Greek. The earliest English translations followed the Latin, and most contemporary English translations have retained the translation.

"Deliverers" would be a better translation of *shophetim* than "judges," but translators are very hesitant to try to undo more than two thousand years of tradition when it comes to naming a book of the Bible.

15

Your Question Why are many biblical persons who commit sins not condemned in the Bible? Samson visits a prostitute with no effect, but God takes his power for allowing his hair to be cut. Lot's daughters have sex with him and no punishment is mentioned.

Much of the Bible is descriptive. It tells us what happened, not what should have happened. The acts described are not evaluated. The reader should be able to analyze whether the acts are good or bad by knowing God's law.

In the case of Samson, the judgment that came upon him before the end of his life was a result of his unfaithfulness, of which his meeting with the prostitute was just a part. When God does not punish immediately, this does not mean he lets the person get away with it. The judgment may come later, as it did in this case. For an Israelite reader, the judgment on the act of Lot's daughters would be implicit in the history of the nations descended from them, Moab and Ammon. An Israelite would read Genesis 19:37,38 as a negative statement of the outcome of this act.

In many cases the judgment on unrepented sin will not come until eternity.

Your Question I remember my pastor saying the Bible never contradicts itself. We believe women should not have authority over men. This does not explain Deborah. Deborah led an army because Barak didn't. Deborah had authority over many men. God praised her. I would expect him or Scripture to say this was wrong in keeping with 1 Timothy 2 and not contradicting itself. I would expect Deborah to refuse the position and make another man take it. The WELS position makes the Bible contradict itself, whereas the Missouri Synod, which interprets that women should not be pastors instead of women suffrage, would not make the Bible contradict itself. Please clarify. For the first time in my life, I am considering the Missouri Synod.

Since Deborah served as judge of Israel, doesn't this show that women can and should act in leadership positions among God's people? The reasons why we cannot make Deborah's example a model for us is outlined briefly in the previous answer about Samson.

The first point to keep in mind is that we cannot derive our principles from descriptions of what some person did during biblical times. We must derive our principles from biblical prescriptions, that is, direct commands that are applicable to us. The Bible often describes something someone did without judging the propriety or motivation of the action. For example, we are not told if Joseph acted with good, bad, or mixed motivation when he reported his brothers to their father. The Bible does not judge the compromises of her faith that Esther had to make to become queen of Persia. It simply reports them. Even the example of Christ does not apply to us, unless we have a scriptural command to follow his example. For instance, Jesus' violent expulsion of the money changers from the temple does not give us license to smash bingo games and bazaars in churches today. For this reason, we cannot use the description of what Deborah did to overrule the prescriptions that are given to us in Paul's letters. Judges tells us what happened. Paul tells us what should happen. There is no contradiction between them.

Furthermore, there are clear indications in the text of Judges that although there may have been nothing blameworthy in Deborah's conduct, the circumstances that compelled Deborah to act as she did were far from ideal or exemplary for us. During the dark days of the judges, the people of Israel by and large had lost their moral sense of direction. In the book of Judges, we find Samson consorting with prostitutes, Gideon setting up an idolatrous shrine, and Jephthah fulfilling his rash vow to sacrifice his own daughter. It is highly dangerous to take the actions of the judges as exemplary for us without the scriptural command to do so. God did not tell Deborah to lead Israel into battle but to tell Barak to do so. No other judge was urged to tell someone else to take command as Deborah was. It is perhaps also significant that Othniel, Ehud, Gideon, Jephthah, and Samson are explicitly said to have been raised to judgeship by the Lord. Of the prominent judges whose stories are featured in Judges, only Deborah is introduced without such an explicit statement.

Deborah herself recognized that all was not as it should be in this situation. She privately rebuked Barak for failing to exercise leadership and said that it would reflect negatively on him when the glory for victory went to a woman and not to him (Judges 4:8,9). All of these factors make it clear that it is not sound interpretation to set the actions of Deborah against the explicit commands of Paul. Deborah is not rebuked because she is not the one guilty of misconduct. It is Barak who is guilty and who is rebuked.

The reason we cannot accept the attempts of the LCMS to limit the application of Paul's teaching only to the pastoral office is that this is not what the passages say. In the relevant passages, Scripture does not focus on what offices women may hold but on what activities or roles they may fill. First Timothy 2 does not deal directly with the issue of whether a woman can be ordained or can be a pastor or an elder. What it does say is that she should learn in a submissive way and that she should be silent in the church. It also says she should not teach or have authority over a man. It would not matter whether she did these things as a pastor or elder or without holding any specific office. It would be equally wrong in either case. The proper question for us to ask is whether a woman can serve the whole congregation in the position of pastor or elder without acting in a way that would place her in violation of the scriptural commands cited above. The principles that man is to be the head, that woman should submit, and that woman is not to have authority over man clearly forbid a woman to exercise the office of pastoral leadership over the whole congregation since that office involves the exercise of authority over men. But the application of those principles is not limited to the pastoral office. However, many of the functions performed by a pastor, such as Baptism, may be performed by women under some circumstances. Women can share the Word with others privately as part of the priesthood of all believers. Women can share the Word as called evangelists, especially with other women. In some cultures, such as many Islamic cultures that practice strict separation of the sexes, it may be necessary for most or all of the catechetical instruction of women to be done by women with final responsibility for the acceptance of members with the pastor and elders. When the church enters such a culture, it might for a time be necessary to have a separate women's service conducted entirely by women. Women can lead the devotions for women's groups. There are many ways in which women can serve with the gospel, but they should not do it in a way that goes against what Paul teaches.

Your
Question Just was surfing around the Web this afternoon and clicked on Hamas, the terrorist group, for I wanted to see what they had to say about the killing in Jerusalem. Led to other Web sites, I found out that Palestinians believe they were founded from the Jebusites, who were first attacked by Israel, and that Jerusalem was theirs originally.

They have some weird beliefs, but having another bible (Koran) what would you expect? Anyhow, they claim there was no Solomon's temple and that there never has been one iota of evidence that there was any temple by Solomon or Israel. What does Scripture say of this? I think it says that Jerusalem was destroyed and that the ark of the covenant will never "come to mind" or be in their possession again. (Ezekiel?) So that would rule out any excavations of the ruins, wouldn't it?

Every reputable historian or archaeologist agrees that the temple built by Zerubbabel, rebuilt by Herod, and destroyed by the Romans in A.D. 70 stood on the site of the so-called Temple Mount in Jerusalem, which is now occupied by the Al-Aqsa Mosque and Dome of the Rock shrine. It is very clear in the book of Ezra that this second temple, as it is called, was a rebuilding of the temple built by Solomon. Solomon's temple was completely destroyed by the Babylonians in 586 B.C., just as the second temple was completely destroyed by the Romans. All that would be left would be underground foundations and terrace walls. Since Herod greatly enlarged the Temple Mount, it is possible that some of these ruins could be found if the Temple Mount could be excavated. On the eastern wall of the Temple Mount, one can see the seam where the Old Testament enclosure ends. Digging in from this point would seem to be the best place to find such remains. The Muslims who control the Temple Mount will not allow such excavations. There is much evidence for Israelite presence in both Old Testament and New Testament Jerusalem. One can discard Solomon's temple only by discarding Scripture. In this point at least, the Palestinian version of the history of Jerusalem is as you say "weird."

Some Palestinians may indeed be descendents of Canaanites who lived in the land, but many more are descendents of other peoples living in the land at the time of the Muslim conquest or later arrivals in the land of Israel. Probably more of them are ethnic Jews than Jebusites.

Your
Question **In Psalm 104:4, the NIV says, "He makes winds his messengers, flames of fire his servants," but the quotation of this verse in Hebrews 1:7 says, "In speaking of the angels he says, 'He makes his angels winds, his servants flames of fire.'" Why this discrepancy?**

The Hebrew of Psalm 104:4 could be translated either "He makes winds his messengers" or "He makes his angels (messengers) winds." The first means that God uses natural forces like the winds as his messengers. The second means that God's angels are swift as the wind. Both of these statements, of course, are true.

The NIV translators chose to go with the first translation in Psalm 104, apparently because they thought that it fit best with the context of the psalm, in which verse 3 says, "He makes the clouds his chariot and rides on the wings of the wind." In Hebrews 1 they were forced to go with the second translation because it is the only translation permitted by the Greek and by the context of Hebrews 1.

Although the NIV translation of Psalm 104:4 is grammatically and doctrinally possible, it was not a wise choice, because it suggests that the author of Hebrews was misquoting the psalm. Since the Hebrew of Psalm 104:4 permits the translation adopted by the author of Hebrews and since it is not uncommon for Scripture to speak of the natural and supernatural forces of the heavens side by side (Psalm 148:1-4), the NIV translators should have translated Psalm 104:4 so that it agrees with the inspired writer's use of the passage in Hebrews 1:7.

Your
Question In some of the psalms, the title includes the name of the tune. Do we have any of these tunes? What was their musical accompaniment like?

Notice that in these psalm headings (see for example Psalm 75) the words "To the tune of" are in half brackets, indicating that they are not in the Hebrew text. In other words, we do not know for certain that these phrases are the titles of tunes, although this seems to be the most likely explanation. Although musical notation was known at the time of David, we do not have a record of any of the original melodies of the psalms. The present Hebrew text of the psalms includes musical signs above and below the letters that have been given varying musical interpretations, but we do not know how ancient these melodies are or if any of the various interpretations successfully recovers the original meaning of these signs. These signs yield a type of music similar to medieval Christian chants. These Hebrew chants may preserve chants that originated in ancient synagogues. In the temple, the psalms were performed with orchestral accompaniment, so the original melodies may have been quite different from those used in synagogue worship. The musical settings used with the psalms in *Christian Worship* (CW) are of recent origin.

Your
Question   **My question concerns a passage in Ezekiel 28. My friend (Baptist) and I (converting from Baptist to WELS) have been having a very drawn-out discussion over this. He believes that the references to the King of Tyre are actually references to Satan. He believes that this passage points out that Satan was in charge of music while he was in Heaven (specifically verse 13's references to timbrals and pipes), that when Satan fell he corrupted music on this earth, and that any music that isn't specifically God-worshiping is evil.**

My questions are these:

1. **Does Ezekiel 28 refer to Satan or to the King of Tyre or to both?**
2. **Does this passage (or any other passage) indicate that Satan was in charge of music in heaven?**
3. **Does this passage (or any other passage) indicate that music has been corrupted by Satan, that ANY nonchurch music is evil?**
4. **Why are the words in Ezekiel 28:13 translated as "settings and sockets" in some translations and "tabrets and pipes (tambourines and flutes)" in others?**

If you could help us, this would be great. My friend, a talented musician, has given up playing his guitar, etc., because of his concern that he might be doing something evil. I thought that what music he played, as long as it wasn't anti-God, would come under adiaphora and to relax about it, but I also don't want to encourage him to do something that might violate his conscience. Thank you for taking the time to answer my questions!

The Bible says very little about the fall of the evil angels other than stating the fact (2 Peter 2:4). Exactly what their crime was we are not told. First Timothy 3:6 seems to hint at pride as the original sin of the evil angels. Paul says that an overseer should not be a recent convert "or he may become conceited and fall under the same judgment as the devil."

Some point to Ezekiel 28:12-19 as also referring to the fall of Satan because of the figure described there having some similarities to Satan. The passage, however, says very clearly that the text is primarily about the king of Tyre. This agrees also with the surrounding context, which is a table of nations.

Why then is the king of Tyre described in satanic terms? Because he is a henchman of Satan, who is conforming himself to Satan. He has the same arrogant attitude toward God that Satan had when he fell and that he still has. Like Satan he abused the position of trust into which God had placed him. A similar comparison occurs in Isaiah 14 where the king of Babylon is described in satanic terms (see below).

There is little reason to believe that Ezekiel 28:13 has anything to do with music. There are two difficult expressions near the end of the verse, but since all the other terms refer to gems, the context indicates that these words too refer to gems in some way. A large majority of the English translations I checked support the idea that these terms refer to settings for jewels. The first of the two words occurs only here. It is similar to the word for tambourines, but that meaning does not fit the context here. The second word means something hollowed out. Round settings and sockets for jewels fit the context best. The most that could be said for the idea that these terms refer to musical instruments is that this interpretation is very doubtful. We do not formulate teaching on the basis of unclear passages.

Even if we would grant that the terms refer to instruments used by Satan, it would not follow that all music is bad. Satan misuses many good things; that does not make the things in themselves bad. The Bible often refers to music of joy at a wedding and sadness at a funeral (Matthew 11:17) without suggesting that the music or dancing are in themselves bad. There are, however, also negative references to music that marks a lifestyle of indifference to God, including the role of Cainites in developing music (Genesis 4:21).

Your friend's conscience is being burdened by claims based on uncertainty and obscurity. First of all, Ezekiel 28 does not refer directly to Satan. Second, it is doubtful that verse 13 refers to music. Third, there is no indication in Scripture that music had anything to do with Satan's role in heaven or his fall. Fourth, the fact that Satan can misuse something does not mean that the thing in itself is bad.

We can only say that secular music is inherently evil if Scripture says so. It does not. Your Baptist friend is wrong to burden his own conscience or someone else's conscience in uncertain things. Read Romans 14.

What you have advised your friend is correct, but he needs to become convinced of it in his own conscience. We should not go against our own conscience even when it is misinformed. We do need, however, to correct an erring conscience with the Word of God.

Can music be misused in the service of Satan? Certainly. Can music be used to praise God? Certainly. Is it proper to use music to express joy and sorrow in everyday life? Certainly. "Test everything. Hold on to the good. Avoid every kind of evil " (1 Thessalonians 5:21,22).

Your
Question **I'm confused about the name Morning Star and to whom Isaiah 14:12 refers: the king of Babylon or Satan. Last week in church we sang a hymn written by a layperson. It was praising God, then began to praise the Morning Star. Whoa! Time-out! I remembered our pastor last spring discussing Satan in Bible class. He mentioned that Satan was a fallen angel and named him as the "morning star" with reference to Isaiah 14:12. It's clear that Jesus is referred to as the Morning Star (Revelation 22:16) so the hymn was fine. I grew up in another faith that was a bit "wishy-washy" on Scripture. I love the simple clarity of truth WELS gives. I do not micro-analyze Scripture but just accept it as it's written, simply, as a child. On this one, I'm confused though. My question is: to whom does Isaiah 14:12 refer? To conclude that Isaiah refers to the king of Babylon whereas Genesis and Revelation refer to Satan, the only possibilities I see would be (a) a striking coincidence of sins, (b) figurative language rather than literal—I'd guess in Isaiah as it was perhaps a part of an "oracle concerning Babylon" that Isaiah saw, or perhaps (c) the sins of Adam and Eve (desire to be like God) were man's sins exclusively and not necessarily Satan's as well. Making me even more confused is the translation issue. The KJV, in Isaiah 14:1 names "Lucifer" as the one fallen from heaven; the NIV does not; it names the "morning star." The KJV's naming of Lucifer certainly appears to clarify who the fallen is (Satan rather than the king of Babylon).**

It is clear that the primary reference in Isaiah is to the king of Babylon. However, since he is Satan's henchman, he is described as being like Satan, in Satan's image, so to speak. The terminology is appropriate to describe Satan, but here it is applied to one of his assistants.

As far as the double use of "morning star" to refer to two different people—this is not unusual. Scriptural imagery is not wooden. The same imagery can be used for more than one person or thing. For example, both Satan and Christ are called lions. The point of comparison with Satan is that he prowls around like a lion; with Christ, it is that he is majestic and powerful.

Lucifer is simply the Latin translation of this passage, which was carried over by some English translations. It means "light bearer." It was adapted from the Greek rendering of the passage, which also means "light bearer." Both of these terms can refer to Venus, the morning star. So this is simply a matter of choosing a different English translation. They all mean the same thing. On the basis of a misinterpretation of this passage, Lucifer became a traditional name of Satan (it was not originally). By its translation "morning star," the NIV is perhaps trying to avoid giving the impression that Isaiah 14 refers directly to Satan.

Your
Question Can we consider the faithful of the Old Testament to have been Christians? Is it correct to say that Christianity didn't begin until Jesus' earthly ministry? A lot of people say that, but it sounds dispensationalist.

We can speak of the Old Testament faithful as Old Testament Christians because they were saved by faith in the Christ who was to come. The Hebrew word for the coming Savior was Messiah. It means exactly the same thing as Christ. Anyone who was a "Messiahian" was also a "Christian." The name Christian, of course, did not come till later, but the substance was the same. Romans 4 is a chapter that stresses this.

Your
Question What is the 70 weeks of Daniel? I heard a Reformed preacher teaching about it and am not sure what it is about. I heard him talking about the prophesy of the freedom of the Jews not yet having been proclaimed and will be in the seven years of peace? Please explain!

Daniel 9 is one of the more difficult prophecies. The 70 weeks seem to represent the time from the days of Daniel until Christ's first coming and the beginning of the New Testament era. The first seven weeks are the time from Daniel to Ezra and the next 62 weeks from Ezra to Christ. The last week is the arrival of the Savior and the beginning of the church. The rejection of Jesus by most of Israel led to the

24

destruction of Jerusalem by the Romans in A.D. 70. Some Lutheran commentators have suggested that the first seven weeks are the time from Daniel until Christ's first coming and the 63 weeks are the New Testament era.

Millennial interpreters think these verses refer to trials the Jews will face before the beginning of the millennium, but this teaching has no support in Scripture.

The People's Bible commentary on Daniel discusses these verses in more detail. See also the section on end times in chapter 6.

Your
Question In church yesterday we read Isaiah 65:17-25. A few parts I did not understand. I thought this passage was talking about life after death. What does it mean in verse 20: "he who dies at a hundred will be thought a mere youth, he who fails to reach a hundred will be considered accursed"? Death does not happen in heaven, does it?

A characteristic of Isaiah's prophecy is that he often describes eternal things with pictures taken from Old Testament daily life. Another example is in chapter 66:18-24 in which events that take place in the New Testament church and in the new heavens and new earth are described in terms of horses and wagons and Sabbath days. Hell is described as worms. Because of the other passages that state very directly that there is no death in heaven, we understand verse 20 as a reflection of the poetic language of Isaiah. He sometimes describes heavenly things in earthly language. On the other hand, he sometimes describes earthly judgments with language appropriate to judgment day. See the description of Jesus' ministry in Isaiah 35:1-7 for another example of mixing literal and poetic language.

Your
Question My other question is about verse 17: "the former things will not be remembered nor will they come to mind." My mother died recently. From this am I to understand that she doesn't remember that she was a mother on earth and our whole relationship will not be remembered? I know I caused her a lot of pain and I would prefer she forget that, but she was a wonderful mom, truly a gift from God, and I would prefer not to forget that gift. It doesn't seem to make sense to me (God's thoughts are above my thoughts) that everything on earth would be forgotten. How does this tie in with Matthew 17:3 in that somehow Peter, James, and John recognized Moses and Elijah?

This verse from Isaiah that you cite is about being freed from all of the sorrows of this life. Verse 17 means essentially the same thing as verse 19. It does not address the issue of whether or not we will know people in heaven. In 1 Thessalonians 4 we read about meeting our loved ones at Christ's return. In some accounts there are recognizable people in heaven, such as Abraham in Luke 16. We have no details of what these relationships will be like in heaven, but it appears that we will have relationships with those whom we knew on earth and with those we did not. Whatever caused pain in those relationships here will no longer be present there.

New Testament Passages

Your Question **Does the Word of God in the first several verses of John's gospel come from the natural knowledge of God?**

A quick reading of John 1:1-18 makes it clear that these verses convey information about Jesus that is revealed only through the gospel, not through the natural knowledge of God. The Word (that is, Jesus) existed already in eternity with the Father. He was present at creation. He is the one through whom the world is saved. None of this information can be obtained from nature. It is learned only through the revelation given by the Holy Spirit. (Read 1 Corinthians 1 and 2.)

There are, however, two statements in these verses that might lead a reader to wonder whether the natural knowledge of God is in the picture here. Verse 4 says, "In him was life, and that life was the light of men." Verse 9 tells us, "The true light that gives light to every man was coming into the world." If Jesus was the light of men already before he was born into the world and if he gives light to all men, some might say that this must refer to the natural knowledge of God, since "every man" does receive the natural knowledge of God, but neither the gospel nor saving faith are received by "every man."

It is true that since Jesus is the Creator-God, the natural knowledge of God, received by all, does come from Jesus. Such an interpretation, however, does not fit the context here. Jesus was the light of men, that is, the Savior for the whole world, also during Old Testament times. As the promised Savior, he was revealed to the world at the time of Adam and again at the time of Noah, but the world did not want him.

He gives light to all people by winning salvation for each of them and offering this salvation to them, but those who prefer to live in darkness reject this light. These verses, therefore, are not talking about the natural knowledge of God but about mankind's rejection of the revelation of salvation God has given to them. "The light shines in the darkness, but the darkness has not understood it. . . . His own did not receive him." The damnation of so many of the world's people is not the result of God's hiding the light of salvation. It is the result of the world's rejection of the light that was there for all. This is the message John emphasizes throughout his gospel.

Your
Question **During this Christmas season a question has occurred to me. In the Old Testament, the prophets foretold that the Messiah would come from the line of David. And in the first chapter of Matthew the genealogy of Jesus is presented, culminating with verse 16: "Jacob the father of Joseph, the husband of Mary, of whom was born Jesus, who is called Christ." But Joseph was not Jesus' actual father. He was, for lack of a better way to put it, our Lord's stepfather or foster father. The genealogy of Matthew's gospel is valid for Joseph, who obviously was of David's line. But genealogy is traced through human ancestry, which is determined by paternity. If I adopt a son, I can give him my surname and treat him as I would a biological son, but that boy is not of my genealogy. My ancestors are not really his. How does one apply the genealogy of the line of David to Jesus? Was Mary, his mother, also of David's line? (She was, in effect, his only human parent.) I know that one could say that God is the Father of Adam, and that since we all are descended from the first man, we are all of the same lineage as David. But it seems the genealogy outlined in Matthew's gospel was of a more specific nature.**

Biblical genealogies were often based on legal descent as well as on physical descent, especially in cases of a levirate marriage in which the child of a man was counted as the legal descendent of his deceased brother in the family genealogy (Deuteronomy 25:5,6). Matthew 1 seems to provide Jesus' legal descent from David through Joseph. Luke 3 apparently provides his physical descent through Mary, who was also a descendent of David. Not all commentators are agreed on the interpretation of these two genealogies, but it is clear that they give Jesus' ancestry from two perspectives, both of which were valid for Jesus' contemporaries. Jews may well have been most interested in the legal genealogy, which is provided by Matthew. On the other hand,

Luke's gentile readers may have been more interested in the physical descent as the questioner was.

Your Question **First, during Jesus' time on earth, how was the marriage ceremony performed? Was Jesus' mother (Mary) considered married to Joseph as soon as Joseph said he would take her as his wife (before Jesus was conceived)?**

At the time of Jesus, the legally binding marriage was the signing of the papers by the parties or more likely by their representatives. Some translations call this betrothal, but it was the legal marriage, not a conditional engagement. From this point on, the couple was legally bound and the marriage could be ended only by divorce. They did not have the right to live together or have sexual relations until the time of the wedding celebration, which was similar to our wedding reception. This was often quite far removed from the betrothal date. From the account of Scripture, it seems clear that Joseph found out about Mary's pregnancy after they were legally married (betrothed) but before they had begun to live together.

Your Question **Did Mary have other children?**

There are three theories about Jesus' brothers and sisters who are mentioned in the gospels. One is that these were actually Jesus' cousins. Another is that these were children of Joseph, whose first wife had died before he married Mary. Both of these theories were motivated at least in part by the desire to preserve Mary's virginity even after Christ's birth. The third idea is that these were children of Mary and Joseph born in a natural way after Christ's birth. This is the most natural understanding of the passages in which Jesus, Mary, and these brothers and sisters appear together. See, for example, Matthew 12:46 and 13:55,56: "While Jesus was still talking to the crowd, his mother and brothers stood outside, wanting to speak to him" and "Isn't this the carpenter's son? Isn't his mother's name Mary, and aren't his brothers James, Joseph, Simon and Judas? Aren't all his sisters with us?"

Your Question **I have a question about the baptism of Jesus since we just had it as a theme of a recent service. The minister mentioned that the sins of the world were washed from Jesus at his baptism—not his own**

sins since we know Jesus is perfect and without sin—but that he was washed clean of all people's sins. I did research in any available commentaries [i.e., People's Bible series] but could not find that as an aspect of Christ's baptism. The authors of the commentaries noted that Jesus identified with us at his baptism and that God the Father anointed Christ with the Holy Spirit to begin his public work of saving sinners. Were our sins washed from Jesus at his baptism? Weren't our sins washed away on the cross at Calvary by the blood of Jesus? If so, is there a double washing away?

Jesus' baptism was part of his work of fulfilling all righteousness for us and, in a way, validates our baptism, but it was Jesus' death on the cross that made the payment for our sins. Scripture repeatedly emphasizes this fact. Even John's baptism drew its power to forgive sins from Christ's death. John pointed to Jesus as the Lamb of God who would die for sin.

Your Question Did the devil not know that Jesus is God and that God cannot be tempted to sin? If he did know, why did he attempt to tempt Jesus in the wilderness?

The only answer we can suggest is that in spite of his great craftiness, Satan is incredibly stupid. How could he think that by inciting men to kill Christ on the cross, he could destroy God's plan? How could he imagine that God would allow him to take over heaven? His blindness and stupidity is mirrored in every sinner who imagines he can disobey God and get away with it. Obeying God is wisdom; working against him is stupidity.

Your Question What is the sin against the Holy Spirit? Can you be forgiven of that sin or not? If someone is an unbeliever, are they blaspheming against the Holy Spirit? (Mark 3:29) If an unbeliever becomes a believer, are they forgiven of that sin of being an unbeliever?

"The sin against the Holy Spirit" is used as a special name for a malicious rejection of the Holy Spirit's testimony to Christ, from which one can no longer turn back. It is the last stage of hardness of heart. Because the very nature of this sin is rejection of the forgiveness won by Christ, a person who has committed this sin has no forgiveness.

All unbelief is sin, all resistance to the Holy Spirit is sin, but not all unbelief and resistance to the Holy Spirit is "the sin against the Holy

Spirit." A person who repents of these sins of unbelief and resistance has forgiveness.

A person who is rejecting the gospel should be warned of the danger of committing the sin against the Holy Spirit if he persists in his unbelief.

Your
Question **In Matthew 12:32, Jesus says speaking against the Son of Man will be forgiven but against the Holy Spirit will not. Father, Son, and Holy Spirit are one, so what is Jesus' point here?**

"Speaking against the Son of Man" refers to taking offense at the humble appearance of the carpenter of Nazareth and doubting if he could really be the Son of God. Jesus' humble appearance might leave some excuse for questioning his claims. "Speaking against the Holy Spirit" is rejecting his testimony in our hearts that Jesus really is God's Son. A person who rejects the Holy Spirit's testimony is without excuse and without salvation.

Your
Question **My question is regarding the Lord's Prayer. Did Jesus really mean for us to repeat it as a memorized prayer, which becomes meaningless words because it is memorized and not thought about? Wasn't he just giving us a guide to pray like?**

Jesus taught the Lord's Prayer on two different occasions (Matthew 6 and Luke 11). On these two occasions he taught the same basic prayer in different words. From this it is clear that he did not intend that we must always use exactly one verbatim formula for prayer. He was teaching us how to pray.

Nevertheless, the Lord's Prayer is a model prayer. We would be presumptuous to think that we could do better by writing our own. For that reason it is very appropriate for us to use it as a prayer we can share with others. We should, of course, think about the meaning of the words we are speaking. That is why one of the chief parts of Luther's Catechism is devoted to explaining the Lord's Prayer and so many other devotional books have been written about it. People can daydream during a prayer that is being read as well as during one that is memorized, so the need for thoughtful praying applies to every prayer.

Your
Question **Please explain why we do not hear more about our obligation to repent when we consider and pray for the people suffering disasters around the world. God forgives us, but are we really looking at the major factor causing disasters? (Luke 13:1-5)**

I have difficulty answering your question because I don't think it is true as a general statement that we do not hear about the need for repentance. I do not know what specific situation you have in mind. It has always been my experience that we regularly teach that every disaster is a warning to us to repent, and I have often used Luke 13 to make that point. The issue comes up very often in connection with the AIDS crisis and natural disasters.

It may be rather natural that when we are praying for the victims of a specific disaster that we focus more on the victims' needs for relief than on our own need for repentance. Both subjects—repentance and helping those in need—should be before us all the time, not just when we are praying for a specific disaster.

Your
Question **In *The Poisonwood Bible* (a good novel about a Baptist mission in Africa gone wrong), p. 248, a comment is made that the Hebrew word for "camel" is the exact same word as the one for "a coarse piece of yarn," and that when Jesus is talking about a camel going through the eye of a needle, he could also have been talking about a piece of yarn. However, since the New Testament isn't in Hebrew, this seems fishy to me.**

I think this explanation arises from the misguided notion that if the Bible is inspired, Jesus could not use figurative language or hyperbole. Jesus uses the same kind of language in Matthew 23:24, where he says that in their hypocritical way of carrying their efforts to avoid any unclean food, the Pharisees strained out a gnat but swallowed a camel. Everyone understands that such language is not literal but is expressing emotion, as we might do if we say, "I told you a million times."

My Hebrew dictionary does not list any word for yarn under the root *gml*, which means "camel," but even if it did, I don't think it would have anything to do with Jesus' intention in this passage.

31

Your Question In John 10:33 the Jews threaten to stone Christ because they claim he was calling himself God. Jesus answers that God's Word calls men "gods." The Mormons and New Age people use this to say we are all gods. What are they not understanding?

Jesus is not putting himself on the same level with us, nor is he putting us on the same level as God. He is turning his enemies' charges back on them by comparing the lesser with the greater. On rare occasions in the Old Testament, those who were God's spokesmen were called "gods" (Psalm 82:6; and perhaps Exodus 22:8, where the NIV translates "gods" as "judges"). If mere men who served as God's spokesmen could be called gods, how could the Jews object if the true God, who came from heaven to obey his Father's will, called himself the Son of God?

Your Question In Matthew 24:15,16 Jesus states, "So when you see standing in the holy place 'the abomination that causes desolation,' spoken of through the prophet Daniel—let the reader understand—then let those who are in Judea flee to the mountains." Has this prophecy been fulfilled? If not, then assuming the holy place means the temple, does the temple need to be rebuilt?

This verse refers to the events that preceded the destruction of the temple in Jerusalem by the Romans in A.D. 70. The temple has never been rebuilt and does not need to be rebuilt, since the animal sacrifices formerly made there are not needed now that Christ has completed his work. The tearing of the temple veil at the time of Jesus' death symbolized this fact, and the epistle to the Hebrews states this fact directly and repeatedly.

The events of A.D. 70 do, of course, serve as a type of the events of the Last Day.

Your Question Matthew 24:21,22. What kind of distress is Jesus talking about that would cause no one to survive unless those days were cut short? Has that time happened or is it yet to come?

The first event that Jesus is talking about in Matthew 24 is the destruction of Jerusalem in A.D. 70 by the Romans. This event was a result of Israel's rejection of Christ. It produced incredible suffering in

Israel. But in this chapter the terrible events that take place during the last days of Jerusalem are also a type that points to the last days of the world, when much of the Christian world turns its back on Jesus as Israel did. The distress refers to the apostasy in the church and the persecution of those who wish to remain faithful. We, of course, cannot say with certainty if we are in those days right now because we cannot predict the day of Christ's return. We can observe, however, that the world seems to be on a course to greater wickedness and unbelief.

Your Question I recently read in an article that Gethsemane was not a garden but a cave. Is this some new idea?

The name Gethsemane apparently means "oil press." In biblical usage "garden" includes what we would call an orchard. Gethsemane thus was a "garden," that is, an olive orchard. This "garden" apparently had an oil press, which gave the place its name. The press could have been either outside or inside a building. Since caves were often used the way we would use a barn or farm shed, it is possible that Gethsemane's oil press was in a cave. The cave identified with Gethsemane today is only a very short distance from the "Rock of Gethsemane," which is inside the Church of All Nations. Both of them, either of them, or neither of them may have been part of Jesus' Gethsemane. Although it is not correct to say that the cave was Gethsemane as the article did, the cave may have been in Gethsemane, and the oil press could have been in the cave. There is no indication that any of the events at Gethsemane took place inside a cave (Luke 22:41).

Your Question Was Judas present at the Last Supper? If he was, do we have the right to keep anyone away from Communion?

We do not know for sure whether Judas received the Lord's Supper since the evangelists do not always relate events in strict chronological order. When subjects overlap, they sometimes finish one subject before beginning the next.

Matthew 26:23; Mark 14:20; and John 13:26-30 seem to place the identification and departure of the traitor during the Passover supper, which preceded the Lord's Supper. Luke 22:21 seems to have Judas present during the Lord's Supper. Since Luke frequently departs from chronological order, I favor the interpretation that Judas left before the

Lord's Supper. This debate is discussed in Ylvisaker, *The Gospels*, pp. 654-658.

It makes no difference to our practice whether or not Judas received the Lord's Supper. At the time he was still a hypocrite, not a known sinner. If Judas received the Supper, he is an example of the person who eats and drinks judgment to himself when he receives the sacrament in an unworthy manner.

The administrator of the Lord's Supper has no responsibility to prevent the attendance of hypocrites who ignore the warnings of Scripture. We do, however, have the duty to try to protect people from unworthy reception by refusing the Supper to the openly impenitent, to those who do not recognize the presence of Christ's body and blood, and to those who cannot examine themselves (1 Corinthians 11:26-32). We also have the duty to preserve the oneness expressed by the Supper by attending only with those who are united in doctrine with us (1 Corinthians 10:16,17).

Your Question Was Judas Jesus' brother?

Judah was one of the most common names in Jesus' time (Judas and Jude are forms of the same name like Robert, Rob, and Robby), so there are several Judases in the New Testament. There were two apostles named Judah/Judas/Jude. One of them was the traitor. Judas the traitor was not Jesus' brother. He seems to have been from Keriot in Judah, not from Galilee. We know little about the other apostle named Judas. For this reason he is sometimes called Jude the Obscure. He was also known as Thaddeus or Lebbaeus, perhaps to avoid the name Judas. The third Judas, Jesus' brother Judas/Jude (Matthew 13:55), seems to be the same Jude who wrote the epistle of Jude. The James who wrote the epistle of James was another brother of Jesus. The apostle James, the brother of John, was probably Jesus' cousin. James is an English form of the name Jacob, so it too was a common name in Israel.

Your Question What do we know about the method of Jesus' crucifixion? One reads conflicting accounts of how crucifixion was done and the kind of crosses used.

Crucifixion, the most horrible form of execution in the ancient world, was not a Roman invention, but had been used by the Persians,

Carthaginians, and Greeks before them. The Jewish leader Alexander Janneus had on one occasion crucified eight hundred Pharisees who opposed him. Among the Romans, this shameful penalty was especially reserved for slaves and rebels.

Although there are many crucifixion accounts by ancient writers, they are generally hesitant to describe the act in much detail because it was so horrible. Romans didn't even like to think about the idea.

There was no set method for crucifixion; the torments and forms of mockery were limited only by the sadistic imagination of the executioners. The "cross" could be anything from a plank to a pole, a T-shaped cross, or the cross familiar as a Christian symbol. Sometimes the victim carried only the crossbeam to the execution site. He was tied or nailed to the beam, and it was raised up to the pole. The victim's body weight was supported by a peg under his crotch to keep him from dying too quickly of suffocation. Crucifixion was designed to be a slow death.

The descriptions of Jesus' crucifixion make it clear that he was nailed to the cross through his hands and feet. The title above his head makes it likely his cross was the traditional form. Study of a skeleton of a crucified man, excavated in Jerusalem, indicates that his feet were nailed to the side of the cross through the heel bones. It is likely that the arms were nailed to the cross through the wrist to better support the weight. This does not contradict the gospels since the Hebrew and Greek words for "hand" may include the lower arm.

How did Jesus' contemporaries view a death like his? The Roman writer Seneca argued that any sane man would choose suicide rather than crucifixion. "Can anyone be found who would prefer wasting away in pain, dying limb by limb, or letting out his life drop by drop, rather than expiring once for all? Can any man be found willing to be fastened to the accursed tree, long sickly, already deformed, swelling with ugly welts and shoulders and chest, and drawing the breath of life amid long-drawn out agony? He would have many excuses for dying even before mounting the cross." Amazingly, a man willing to go to the cross was found. Even more amazing this man was God come from heaven to be our Savior. He died a death that noble Romans considered unspeakable.

Certainly to the people of Jesus' day, the horrible nature of crucifixion was well-known and needed no description. Perhaps today when the cross has become a beautiful symbol rather than a horrible instrument of execution, we need to be reminded of its real nature. Yet the gospels are not very interested in dwelling on the cruel details of that death. They rather matter-of-factly record its reality and point us to its meaning. Scripture directs our attention to the love of the victim, rather than to the cruelty of the executioners. It is not so much the *how* of that death but rather the *completeness* of the payment for sin, which was rendered there, that should seize and hold our attention. The important truth about Jesus' crucifixion is that his death was for me.

Your Question

I recently read, "the sun stopped shining" at the moment of the Savior's death. Punctuation in some translations of Luke 23:44,45 seems to connect "the sun stopped shining" with the tearing of the curtain of the temple at the moment of Jesus' death; others with the darkness from noon to three. Is there an answer from the Greek of exactly when the sun stopped shining?

All three of the synoptic gospels mention the darkness from noon till 3:00 (the sixth to the ninth hour) (Matthew 27:45; Mark 15:33; Luke 23:44). All three mention the tearing of the temple curtain (Matthew 27:51; Mark 15:38; Luke 23:45). Only Luke places these two events side by side in his account. Neither Mark nor Matthew mentions an intensified darkness among the signs occurring at the moment of Jesus' death, signs that they discuss in more detail than Luke. It seems most likely, therefore, that Luke is giving a condensed summary of the supernatural signs which accompanied Jesus' crucifixion and that his statement "the curtain of the temple was torn" is the conclusion of his description of the three hours of darkness.

The punctuation and the grammatical construction followed in the latest edition of the United Bible Society Greek text supports this interpretation. Other manuscripts of the Greek New Testament, however, have a different grammatical construction in the Greek, which makes it more possible to join together the darkening of the sun with the tearing of the temple curtain. These manuscripts were the ones used by the editors who inserted the verse numbers into our New Testament.

Of the 16 translations of Luke 23 I consulted, 12 clearly join the entire reference to darkness into one sentence that refers to the whole three hours. Only one (the New King James) clearly joins the darkening of the sun and the tearing of the temple curtain. Three allow either understanding.

The evidence is, therefore, quite strong that "the sun stopped shining" refers to the whole three hours. The significant point, however, is that the three gospel writers all agree that three hours of darkness and the tearing of the temple curtain were important signs that occurred at the time of Jesus' crucifixion.

Incidentally, since Jesus' death occurred at the full moon of Passover, the darkness could not have been an ordinary solar eclipse.

Your Question

Jesus appeared to Mary of Magdala and said, "Do not touch me. I have not yet ascended to my Father." Why was she not allowed to touch him and shortly after other women were allowed to? And also other people including doubting Thomas?

The usual explanation is that he wanted Mary to realize that he was not back to stay with them, but after appearing briefly to his followers, he would return to heaven and they would not see him again until they entered heaven. This interpretation is the basis for the NIV translation, "Do not hold on to me" (John 20:17).

Your Question

My question is on the statement that Jesus descended into hell. In our WELS services, sometimes it is presented that Jesus descended into hell while on the cross, thus it would have been a spiritual descent. Other times, it is said that Jesus descended into hell after he is risen from the dead. Which one is it? Where does this theology come from? And is this idea a carryover from the Roman Catholic church? Now, it is not impossible for the Son of God to descend into hell because he has power over all things. But, when Jesus was crucified he said, "Father, into your hands I commit my Spirit" (Luke 23:46). So, I believe that while he was dead Jesus' spirit was with God the Father in heaven. I think that perhaps the spirits in prison are demons in bodies on earth. Do you have a better explanation for this statement in an area where we know so little about?

There is only one passage that gives us specific information about Jesus' descent into hell, that is 1 Peter 3:18-20, literally translated: "having died in flesh and having been made alive in spirit in which he went and made a proclamation to the spirits in prison, who disobeyed long ago when God waited patiently in the days of Noah." This tells us that Jesus descended to hell after he had risen from the dead but probably before he began his resurrection appearances. It is clear from many places (Jude, 2 Peter 3, Luke 16) that the prison of spirits is hell, not bodies on earth. When Jesus cast out demons, they wanted to stay in the bodies so that they would not have to go back to the prison of hell (Matthew 8:29). The spirits were in the prison of hell when Jesus preached to them. These spirits were the disobedient people who perished in the flood, not demons. Though demons certainly were present, and Jesus' descent showed his victory over them. Colossians 2:15 appears to allude to the descent into hell.

Your
Question **In *Meditations* on 23 February 2002 and on 24 March 2002 the author(s) stated that Jesus knew he would suffer hell (24 March) and that Jesus suffered the agony of hell (23 Feb.). Are the authors just being carried away in their enthusiasm to show the depths of Jesus' suffering on our behalf, or are they representing a departure in doctrine? My understanding is that Jesus' exaltation begins with the descent into hell and my understanding is that this is based on Scripture, 1 Peter 3:18ff.; Formula of Concord, Epitome, Art. 9; Pieper, II, pp. 314 ff.; Hoenecke, III, pp. 132ff.; *Our Great Heritage*, II, pp. 572ff.**

On the cross Jesus suffered the torments of hell for us, but this is not his descent into hell. As you correctly point out, Jesus did not descend into hell to suffer but to display his victory over Satan after he was alive again and to testify to the lost in hell. The devotions refer to Jesus' suffering on the cross in which, as our substitute, he suffered the punishment of hell for us. This is what led him to cry, "My God, my God, why have you forsaken me?" (Mark 15:34). As the essence of being in heaven is joy in the presence of God, the essence of hell is being under the wrath of God, separated from his forgiveness. Preachers should be careful that their language does not confuse these two things by calling Jesus' suffering on the cross a descent into hell. It is, however, correct to say he suffered hell for us.

Your
Question **In a sermon the pastor spoke of blind Bartimaeus being able to use his new sight to see Jesus ascend to heaven. Is it clear from the gospels and Acts who was present at the Ascension? Was it only the Eleven or could it have included more people like Bartimaeus?**

The events of Jesus' Ascension are described only in Luke 24 and Acts 1. In Luke 24 the Ascension account follows without any further introduction after Jesus' appearance to "the Eleven and those with them" (Luke 24:33). This certainly permits and perhaps even suggests the presence of others besides the Eleven at the Ascension. The verses of Acts 1 explicitly mention only the apostles, but Acts 1:4 seems to refer back to Luke 24:42-48, which describes events that were witnessed by more people than just the Eleven. Other disciples were present at the events immediately following the Ascension in Acts 1. The brief allusion to the Ascension in Mark 16:19 does not add any additional evidence to the discussion.

Even though the presence of others beyond the Eleven is not explicitly mentioned in the accounts of the Ascension, it is not safe to conclude that no disciples except the Eleven were present, since the gospels frequently omit mention of some of the participants of events. (For example, compare John 19:39 and Mark 15:43). In short, it seems possible that there were other witnesses of the Ascension beyond the Eleven, but there is no specific evidence concerning who those may have been.

Your
Question **The following questions arise from Acts 16:37-40. What distinguished a Roman citizen from other people? How could Paul prove his citizenship?**

A more significant discussion of Paul's citizenship occurs in Acts 22:23-28. There we learn that Paul was born as a Roman citizen. This means that either his father or grandfather had been awarded a grant of Roman citizenship either for some service rendered or through good connections with important people. Such citizenship was recorded in official lists and census documents. People who traveled a lot, like soldiers, had documents, similar to our passports, called *diplomas*, which they carried with them as proof of citizenship. As a frequent traveler, Paul may have had such a document. Roman citizens also had distinctive dress, but it does not seem likely Paul would have worn this, especially when working among the Jews. In all of the cases where this issue comes up, Paul's questioners are surprised by his claim of citizenship. The main reason the issue comes up is that a Roman citizen had greater legal rights and protections than other subjects of the empire.

In his book *Roman Law and Roman Society in the New Testament,* A. N. Sherwin-White comments that many of the questions about Paul's Roman citizenship cannot be answered definitively from the Roman historians. For some aspects we are dependent largely on the comments in Acts.

Your Question **We recently had some Mormon missionaries come to our door. They believed that "works precede faith" and cited the book of James. I've read that James was writing to people who believed you could have faith without it showing itself in works. How do we know that the people he was writing to believed this?**

Many of the New Testament books were written at least in part to correct errors that were threatening the church. Normally the New Testament writers do not describe the errors of the false teachers in much detail. They focus on setting forth the truth that will counter the error. We must deduce the nature of the error from their positive presentation. In only a very few instances do we have some additional information from one of the church fathers.

Since James is very concerned to show that true faith will always produce works, we deduce that at least some of his opponents were downgrading the importance of works as a fruit of faith.

The Mormon view you cite shows that they have no understanding of what a good work is. Their view is impossible because nothing can be a good work without faith as its motive. To be a good work, a deed needs two characteristics: it must be according to God's law and it must be done for the right motive—faith that is thankful for forgiveness. These are just a few of the passages that state these principles: Hebrews 11:6; Romans 8:7,8; Galatians 5:6; Philippians 2:13; and John 15:5.

The Mormon view is especially strange, since most people who mix faith and works as causes of salvation do not teach that works precede faith but that they follow it.

Your Question **Recently I have been comparing different versions of the Bible. I noticed in the NIV version that 1 John 2:18 contains "the" before the word *antichrist*. I didn't find this in the New American Standard, the King James Version, the Authorized Standard Version,**

the Revised Standard Version, and the New King James Version. What accounts for the difference?

Although both Greek and English have the definite article *(the)*, the use of it is not the same in both languages, so one cannot simply place *the* into the English translation wherever the Greek has the definite article. Sometimes English requires the article where Greek does not have it and vice versa. One must be familiar with the idioms of both languages to make a decision.

In 1 John 2:18, the definite article does not occur in the Greek text, but in the context it is clear that this first reference is to the great Antichrist, not to a minor antichrist. In English we can render this in one of two ways: "you have heard that the antichrist is coming" or simply by capitalization, "you have heard Antichrist is coming." I prefer the second, but the NIV's approach is acceptable. The English translation should make it clear that the great Antichrist is the one referred to.

In verse 22 the Greek has the article with *antichrist* and the NIV retains it in the English translation. This is misleading, since John is not talking here about the Antichrist but about antichrists in his own time. This article is what is called "the article of previous reference." John is talking about the antichrists he had first mentioned in verse 18. In this verse, "the antichrist" could better be translated as "the kind of antichrist I mentioned previously."

This is an especially interesting example of Greek grammar because it provides both an example of a passage in which the Greek does not have the article and the English needs it and one in which the Greek has the article and the English does not need it.

Your
Question **How do you fit in 1 Peter 1:23 with the idea that we can lose our salvation? Why does 1 John 3:9 say that we cannot sin after we come to faith when Paul constantly urges us to turn from our old life and not be deceived by false preachings?**

First Peter 1:23 says nothing about the question of whether we can fall from faith. The "imperishable seed" in this verse is the Word of God as the next verse shows. "Imperishable" here is an attribute of the Word, not of our faith.

The issue of falling from faith is addressed in other passages. The Bible teaches very clearly that it is possible to fall from faith

(1 Corinthians 10:12). It also assures us that God will protect us from falling (1 Corinthians 10:13). The first passage warns about being complacent. The second comforts us when we are troubled. Among the other passages that deal with this are Matthew 13:18-23; Hebrews 10:26,27; and John 10:27-29.

First John 3:9 says that those who belong to God cannot continue to sin by living impenitently in sin. In 1 John 1:8-10, John clearly says Christians still sin and have sins to confess, but these are sins of weakness, not sins they cling to.

Your
Question **Regarding 1 Timothy 5:8, I have heard that the original language speaks to outcome rather than intent, and if one follows the language exactly, anyone who attempts but does not succeed in providing for his family is worse than a unbeliever (the context makes clear that providing is in the material sense). I also have heard rationalizations that try to make the case that even though the original language speaks to outcome, the language should be interpreted as speaking only to intent and action, rather than outcome. My question is this: Can we ignore the original language in this fashion, while holding to Luther's interpretation of "is" with regards to real presence? If we do ignore the original language in 1 Timothy 5:8, are we being inconsistent in our interpretation of the real presence?**

First Timothy 5:8 says, "If anyone does not provide for his relatives, and especially for his immediate family, he has denied the faith and is worse than an unbeliever." The Greek verb rendered "provide for" can mean either to "care about" and "be concerned about" or to "provide for." The word itself does not determine whether intent or successful provision is the point of the passage. The context of Scripture, however, does. In both the Old and New Testaments, the Bible is filled with passages that make it clear that God does not condemn the victims of oppression or disaster who cannot provide for their families because of injustice, war, or famine. Rather, he is concerned about their needs, is responsive to their prayers, and will punish those responsible for injustice. The explanation that the original language speaks to outcome rather than intent is clearly wrong. It ignores both the meaning of the word and the context. The explanation that the passage is speaking about intent and action, rather than outcome, is correct. The passage condemns those who through their own negligence and indifference fail to provide for their families. (Naturally, where there is lack of intent and action, there will also be a lack of outcome.) This interpretation is not ignoring the meaning of the original language but correctly interpreting it in its context. In the same way 2 Thessalonians 3:10 is not condemning a person who cannot work because of health or age or lack of opportunity but one who is unwilling to work. The interpretation you cite above wrongly burdens consciences.

Your Question

I am WELS discussing "decision theology" with my Baptist cousin. What would be the best response to my cousin's statement below: "So using all of scripture"—How about Revelation 3:20? "Here I am! I stand at the door and knock. If anyone hears my voice and opens the door, I will come in and eat with him, and he with me." These are the direct words of Jesus. This passage "clearly" indicates that we have a choice. We have the choice to open the door and then begin our fellowship with him. But he won't open the door for us, we have to cooperate before the fellowship begins, i.e., free will. He doesn't say, "I'm going to open the door, invite myself in, and sit down to eat with you, and you with me. You can kick me out and reject me if you want but I'm going to just let myself in because I want you to be saved."

The first problem with the Baptist use of Revelation 3:20 is that they do not carefully note to whom it is addressed. It is not addressed to the unconverted, but to Christians who are beginning to slide away from Christ and are, therefore, being called to repentance. Note verse 19 and the whole context of the letters to the churches. We do cooperate with the Holy Spirit after our conversion but not before our conversion.

Even if this passage would be addressed to the unconverted, it would not teach that our free will is responsible for our conversion. It would simply be proclaiming the gospel in the form of an invitation as is often done in Scripture. The question as to where the power comes from to accept that invitation must be answered by the passages that directly address that question, such as Jeremiah 31:18: "Cause me to turn and I will turn" (literally translated) or John 6:44: "No one can come to me unless the Father who sent me draws him." Lutherans do not question that we come to Christ or turn to him, but they accept the statements of Scripture which teach that the power for that conversion comes from the Holy Spirit, not from our free will.

2
Biblical Doctrines

Your
Question I was reading a commentary by John Mueller, and I believe he correctly states: "In view of these facts (referring to the natural knowledge of God) the anti-theistic theories held by men are NOT the results of sound reasoning, but rather the effects of man's perverse, willful suppression of the natural knowledge of God, which He has implanted into the human heart, Rom 1:18. They do not represent progress in human religious thought, but rather spiritual and moral decadence." I think he is saying the heart of the problem with the unbeliever is not in his thinking, but rather in his resistant will toward God. However, on the next page Mueller speaks of the natural knowledge of God as being of great value, because from it we can construct so-called rational proofs for God's existence. To me this does not seem to make sense. First Mueller states unbelief is from the willful suppression of the natural knowledge of God. Mueller then claims it is of value to use rational proofs for God's existence to combat unbelief. My questions are: Cannot only the Word of God change a person's stubborn will from hostility toward the love of God's will? Are rational proofs such as cosmological proof or historical proof stronger than the natural knowledge of God even though they are not constructed by God, but by man?

The so-called proofs for the existence of God are simply intellectual, sophisticated statements of the natural knowledge of God. They have no more value than any other form of the natural knowledge of God. That is, they can serve as a point of contact for discussion, but they cannot convert a person or give him knowledge of the true God. In this sense, they are pre-evangelism, not evangelism proper, which comes only through the gospel.

Mueller's point is that atheism is not based on sound logic, as if atheism was logical and faith was illogical. Atheism reflects a corruption of every inner part of man, his intellect, his will, and his emotions. One cannot reason a person out of such corruption. Pointing out gaps in his logic will not convert such a person. On the other hand, people who are troubled by doubts raised by atheists and critics of the Bible, but who are not suppressing the natural knowledge of God, may find some reassurance in rational and empirical evidence. We are not necessarily talking about the same individuals when we talk both about the limitations and the use of the so-called proofs and other forms of the natural knowledge of God.

Your
Question Is it necessary to believe in the Trinity to be saved? I live in Sweden, and after being involved with different Pentecostal and "faith movement" churches I have started going to LBK ("Lutheran Confessional Church," a Scandinavian church in fellowship with WELS). On their Web site they teach that those who don't believe in the Trinity believe in a false God, and that if you "deny the divinity of one of the persons in the Trinity, you deny all of them." What does the Bible teach?

It teaches that those who don't believe in the Trinity believe in a false god, and that if you deny the divinity of one of the persons in the Trinity, you deny all of them. One of the clearest statements of this is in John 5:19-23. See also 1 John 2:23. One cannot deny the Son without denying the Father who sent him to be our Savior. Judaism and Islam, for example, believe in one god, but he is not the God of the Bible. They are seeking God in the wrong way (Romans 10:1-3). We are baptized in the name of the triune God—Father, Son, and Holy Spirit. We can't tear the Trinity apart and have the work of one without the other, since they all work together in the one plan of salvation.

The orthodox church confessed this truth in the Nicene and Athanasian Creeds. Belief in the Trinity does not require that a person have a knowledge and understanding of all the technical terms used to express the doctrine of the Trinity in the theological writings of the church but that one must believe in all the persons of the Trinity as they are revealed in the Bible.

Your Question I've heard people say that God rested on the seventh day because he was tired. I thought that the word for "rested" (sha-bath) could also mean simply to "cease." But Exodus 31:17 says that God rested and "was refreshed" (na-fash). Did God actually grow weary from his "work"?

God never gets tired. He never needs a break from upholding the world (John 5:17). Isaiah 40:25-31 says, "'To whom will you compare me? Or who is my equal?' says the Holy One. Lift your eyes and look to the heavens: Who created all these? He who brings out the starry host one by one, and calls them each by name. Because of his great power and mighty strength, not one of them is missing. . . . Do you not know? Have you not heard? The LORD is the everlasting God, the Creator of the ends of the earth. He will not grow tired or weary, and his understanding no one can fathom. He gives strength to the weary and increases the power of the weak. Even youths grow tired and weary, and young men stumble and fall; but those who hope in the LORD will renew their strength. They will soar on wings like eagles; they will run and not grow weary, they will walk and not be faint."

The Bible does sometimes describe God's actions by using terms from similar human experience: terms like *awake, remember, forget,* etc. These terms are called anthropopathisms—ascribing human emotions and actions to God. These terms are not literal descriptions of the unchanging, tireless God, but they describe him as he appears from our perspective.

Your Question Can prayer change God's mind? I read an article in *Watchman of the Wall* that stated, "One of the most amazing truths in the Bible is that our prayers can change God's mind. As intercessors, we have the privilege of shaping history before the throne of God." The article made reference to Exodus 32:9-14 as proof.

The Bible says two things that are hard for our reason to fit together.

The first is that God in his essence is not subject to change. He knows everything even before it happens. He has known his plans from eternity. He cannot be manipulated or influenced into doing something that is not truly the best course of action.

The Bible also tells us (James 5:16) and shows us with many specific examples that the prayer of a righteous man is powerful and effective. God hears and answers prayers.

Our prayers are one of the factors God considers in determining his course and timetable of action. He will remain true both to his law and his gospel, but he truly hears our prayers and acts upon them. He urges us to pray and promises to hear our prayers.

We can pray confidently, though we may not understand all the mysteries of God's will and actions.

Your Question I have been a member of a WELS congregation in Minnesota all of my life. Ever since I was 16 years old, I have been praying to God that I could have a girlfriend and, ultimately, a wife. Now I am 40 years old. I have no wife, no girlfriend, not even a first date! What's wrong with me? Why won't God help me?

God often answers our prayers through actions he leads us to take. In Matthew 9 he told the disciples to pray for laborers for the harvest. In Matthew 10 he sent them out in answer to their prayers. You say nothing about what actions you have taken to seek a girlfriend or why such actions may have been unsuccessful. This is something we should not try to guess. If you truly have the desire to find a life partner, you should seek counsel from wise and trusted Christian friends, both men and women. They can help bring you into contact with a suitable life partner and can offer you advice and help if you are unwittingly raising barriers that have prevented this.

You should continue to seek to know and understand God's will for you. You should also read 1 Corinthians 7 and consider ways in which you can serve him though unmarried if that is his will for you. Also recognize the advantages an unmarried person has for such service. We wish you God's blessing in your search for a wife and for an understanding of his will.

Your Question What is the difference between "the theology of the cross" and "the theology of glory"? What are some good sources to read on this subject?

The theology of the cross reflects Jesus' teaching that we must deny ourselves, take up our cross, and follow him. As long as we are still in the world, we Christians as individuals and the church as a whole will face much tribulation and suffering. The church will often suffer persecution and scorn. The theology of glory looks for success now that can be measured in worldly terms. Our lives now are expected to be a triumph. Our lives are indeed already a triumph in Christ, yet it remains true that we must through much tribulation enter the kingdom of God.

A book-length treatment of the topic is Daniel Deutschlander's *The Theology of the Cross* (Northwestern Publishing House, 2008). Two good articles about this in the *Wisconsin Lutheran Quarterly* are "The Development of Luther's Theology of the Cross" by James Kiecker (Summer 1995) and "An Optimistic Theology of the Cross" by Richard Gurgel (Spring 1998). Several books have been written with the title *Luther's Theology of the Cross*. Two of the better known are by Walter von Loewenich and Alister McGrath. Most major works on the theology of Luther will have treatments of this topic, and encyclopedias of religion and church history will often have briefer treatments. You should find much material on this in any religious library.

Your Question **Could you briefly summarize how the Protestant view of prayer (Baptists, Assemblies of God, etc.) sometimes deviates from the biblical description of prayer? Thank you very much.**

In general, there are not any specific doctrinal problems with the view that such churches have of prayer. The main problem of practice is that they sometimes view prayer as a means of grace. When people are troubled or feel weak in faith, they might be advised to pray harder or more often as a way of working their way out of the problem and building greater strength. Lutherans would emphasize the importance and power of prayer but would direct the weak above all to the Word and sacraments. God may strengthen us as an answer to our prayers, but he uses the Word as the instrument through which he strengthens us. Prayer is essentially the opposite of the means of grace. In prayer we talk to God. In the means of grace, God talks to us. When we are weak, we need to put the greatest emphasis on God's talk, not ours.

Your Question **I would like to know why the WELS prohibits prayers for the dead when the Lutheran Confessions permit (but do not command) the practice. I refer to Article XXIV of the Augsburg**

Confession, "We know that the ancients spoke of prayers for the dead. We do not forbid this" (*The Book of Concord,* Tappert translation, p. 267).

Your quotation appears to be a reference to Article XXIV 94 of the Apology (pp. 416,417 of the *Triglotta*).

We don't forbid all prayers for the dead but only prayers to the dead. Article XXI of the Augsburg Confession says, "Of the worship of saints they teach that the memory of saints may be set before us, that we may follow their faith and good works, according to our calling, as the Emperor may follow the example of David in making war to drive away the Turk from his country. For both are kings. But the Scripture teaches not the invocation of saints or to ask help of saints, since it sets before us the one Christ as the Mediator, Propitiation, High Priest, and Intercessor." Our prayers for the dead are not to include prayers for their forgiveness or their salvation. For those who died in the faith such prayers are unnecessary. For those who died without faith, such prayers do no good. Article XXI of the Apology makes it clear that prayers for the dead are prayers of thanksgiving not prayers of intercession or invocation.

Your
Question When were the angels created? Is it possible that they existed prior to the Genesis account? Job 38:6,7 says the angels shouted for joy when God laid the earth's foundation.

The Bible does not say when the angels were created, but it must have been within the six days of creation, since only God existed when he began the work of creation on the first day, and he created no new things after he rested from his work at the end of the sixth day.

Bible scholars have suggested three possible times for the creation of angels: on day one with light; on day four along with the sun, moon and stars, the visible "hosts of heaven"; or on day six with man. These are all plausible guesses, but there is no scriptural proof for any one of them.

There are a number of difficulties with Job 38:6,7. Literally translated it says, "The morning stars sang together and the sons of God shouted for joy" when God laid earth's cornerstone. It is likely that the NIV is correct when it interprets the name "sons of God" as a reference to the angels, but it is possible that this is a figurative name for the stars since it is parallel to the term "morning stars." On the other hand, it is possible that "morning stars" is a name for angels. It is most likely, however, that this passage says that both the stars and the angels were present when God laid the earth's foundation.

Some scholars have, therefore, quoted these verses as proof that the angels were created on day one with light and, therefore, were present when the world's "foundation" was laid on day two. However, since Job 38 mentions both the stars and the angels as being present when the earth's foundations were laid, it does not seem to be distinguishing the days of creation. It is treating the days of creation as a whole. It is simply saying that the angels and the stars, unlike short-lived Job, were present at the time of creation. The passage is not intended to pinpoint the time of God's creation of the angels, but simply to teach Job humility.

This leaves us where we began: we cannot specify on which of the six days angels were created.

Your Question **When was Satan, along with his followers, cast out of heaven? In 1 Kings 22:20-22 it sounds as if the evil angels are still serving in heaven long after the fall. Did Satan remain in heaven until Jesus' resurrection?**

Satan and his evil angels were thrown into hell immediately after they rebelled against God. They did not maintain their place in heaven (2 Peter 2:4; Jude 6). They immediately lost their glorious and privileged position.

Although he is now a resident of hell, Satan and his angels can still attack Christians on the earth (1 Peter 5:8; Revelation 12:13,17; Matthew 8:28-32).

Satan is also pictured in Scripture as appearing before God in heaven. In addition to the passage you have mentioned, Job 1 and 2 and Zechariah 3 provide noteworthy examples of this. With God's permission, Satan and his angels mislead unbelievers (1 Kings 22), slander and attack God's saints (Job 1 and 2), and accuse God's people of sin (Zechariah 3). These passages are intended to show that although Satan no longer enjoys life in heaven, he still must serve God. God uses even Satan's evil schemes to serve his own good purposes of judging unbelievers and testing and strengthening his saints. God restricts and limits Satan's activities so that they will serve the ultimate good of God's people.

Before Jesus' death and resurrection, Satan could with some degree of plausibility claim that all sinners, like Abraham, Moses, and David, belong in hell with him. On this basis he could accuse them before God and say that God was unjust in allowing sinners like Moses and David to be in heaven. When Jesus died and rose from the dead, the payment for sin, which makes it just for a holy God to allow redeemed sinners to live with him in heaven, was put on open display for everyone to see. Jesus displayed this victory over Satan during his descent into hell (Colossians 2:15). Scripture also describes this victory of Christ as a fall of Satan from heaven (Luke 10:18; John 12:31; Revelation 12:7-10). Satan can no longer plausibly accuse us.

Satan was cast down from heaven, that is, he was deprived of the privilege of enjoying life in heaven immediately after he fell into sin. He was also "cast down" when Christ died and rose from the dead, because it was then that Satan's ability to accuse God's people of sin was forever destroyed. Passages like 2 Peter 3 speak of the first casting down of Satan. Passages like Revelation 12:7-10 speak of the second "casting down" of Satan.

Your
Question **At what time in art history did angels change to having a feminine appearance or even to the form of an infant? Although the angels as spirits have no sex, in the Bible they seem to have appeared as men.**

For hundreds of years, the form of angels in Christian art was constant—dignified young men with great feathered wings and flowing robes, surrounded by light. Angels project an air of authority. This form continued to be prominent in Christian art until in the Renaissance paintings of the 15th and 16th centuries, other forms became common—angels that are more feminine in appearance and even baby angels called cherubs. These angels often appear with Mary and other female saints. Some art historians connect this shift in style with the intensification of the cult of Mary. The angels around friendly Mother Mary take on some of her traits, but they are not referred to as "she." The angels that seem more feminine in appearance are still intended to represent young men. The baby angels that often appear with the Christ Child are similar to the cupids in paintings of mythological scenes. When Christian art no longer had a clear purpose of instructing the people, the artist had the opportunity to express the new interest in antiquity and the more humanistic spirit of the new age more freely.

Your
Question **Please explain the difference between spirit, soul, and body. Hebrews 4:12 says, "For the word of God is living and active. Sharper than any double-edged sword, it penetrates even to dividing soul and spirit, joints and marrow; it judges the thoughts and attitudes of the heart." I always believed that the soul and spirit were the same. Also, what does it mean when the soul contacts the intellectual realm?**

The Bible has two sets of words that refer to the soul, which is the nonmaterial part of a person, which gives life to the body and is the center of spiritual, emotional, and intellectual life, and which continues to exist even when the body dies. The first set (Hebrew *nephesh* and Greek *psuche*) is usually translated "soul" in English. It can also be translated "life." The second set (Hebrew *ruach* and Greek *pneuma*) is usually translated "spirit." Either set can refer to the soul as defined above. The *nephesh-psuche* set is especially fitting when the relationship of the soul to the body is under consideration. The *ruach-pneuma* group is especially fitting when the relationship of the soul to God is under consideration.

In the Bible then, *soul* and *spirit* are synonyms with a difference of connotation. The point of the Hebrews passage is that God can separate and understand what man cannot investigate or fathom. We can't explain how the soul interacts with the body via the brain.

Your
Question **I have three questions. Actually, it is the same question asked in three different ways: How does the conscience, in terms of good or bad, relate to the absolute sinful nature of man at birth? How does the law, understanding that the law is perfect and that God places the law into us via our consciences, affect the totally sinful nature of man at birth? Does man have anything good in him prior to coming to faith?**

We have to distinguish three things: the natural knowledge of God, the natural knowledge of the law, and conscience.

The natural knowledge of God is a natural awareness that there is a Creator-God and that we are responsible to him. You can read about this in Romans 1:18-32.

The natural knowledge of the law is a partial knowledge of God's moral law that remains in all people. We are now like people who look at the world through dirty glasses. Our vision of the natural law is now obscured. Some have a blind spot here, some have a blind spot there. But people everywhere in the world have knowledge of many basic points of the law. They know that they should do certain things, like obey their parents, but they do not.

Conscience is not a norm or standard for behavior. It is not a source of law but a reaction to the law. It is the faculty in human nature that accuses us of doing good or bad. Conscience may use the natural knowledge of the law, the revealed law of God, or learned human standards of behavior in making its judgments. It may use either correct or incorrect standards in making its judgments.

All that the natural knowledge of the law and conscience can do is to make people aware that they are guilty of sinning against God. They can influence outward conduct, but they cannot improve the sinful human nature. They cannot enable a person to do true good works, which must be motivated by the gospel.

Read Romans 2:12-15.

Your Question **After the death of Jesus, how long was he in hell? The implication in the Apostles' Creed is that it was till his resurrection.**

There is only one passage that gives us specific information about Jesus' descent into hell, that is, 1 Peter 3:18,19, "made alive by the Spirit . . . he went and preached to the spirits in prison, who disobeyed long ago when God waited patiently in the days of Noah." This tells us that Jesus descended to hell after he had risen from the dead, but probably before he began his resurrection appearances. During the time between his death and resurrection, his soul was in heaven as his words on the cross revealed. Thus, we see that the wording of the Apostles' Creed does not give a clear indication of the time of his descent. This point must be clarified by a comparison of several passages of Scripture.

The order in the creed may, however, reflect the unclarity of many in the early church about the purpose of Jesus' descent. Many of them thought that Jesus descended to a region of hell called limbo in order to rescue the Old Testament believers, who had to wait there until Jesus had died for sin. Others thought he went there to give unbelievers another chance. Some thought he went there to suffer. All of these views contradict Scripture. The purpose of Jesus' descent into hell was not to preach the gospel, but to declare his victory over Satan and his forces. Colossians 2:15 seems to refer to this aspect of Jesus' descent into hell.

Though Scripture gives us little information about Jesus' descent into hell, we rightly classify it as part of his exaltation since it was a declaration of his victory over sin, death, and the devil. This victory was complete and declared as such by his resurrection.

Your Question **What is the WELS position concerning the doctrine of election as found in the Holy Bible?**

We believe that God has elected some people to salvation through faith in Christ (see Ephesians 1). He does this purely by his grace, not because of anything in the person who is elected. God has not predestined anyone to damnation. Christ died for all, and the Father has declared all forgiven in Christ.

The reason we do not believe in predestination to damnation is that Scripture very clearly says that God wants all men to be saved (1 Timothy 2:4). This same truth is also taught in other passages of Scripture. It might seem logical to conclude that if God elects some to salvation, he must elect the rest to damnation. But the statements of Scripture that Christ died for all, that God is the Savior of all, and that God wants all to be saved do not permit such a conclusion. Therefore, we simply let all the words of Scripture on this matter stand side by side without trying to reconcile them by our reason. For a full study, see the book *Predestination* by John Moldstad, which is part of the People's Bible Teachings series.

Your Question **I have often wondered if the term "the very elect" implies there were others not elected by God. Since the Bible clearly states that it is the will of God that all men be saved, please clarify election.**

The Bible tells us that God elected specific individuals to be saved. Paul told the Ephesians, "In love [God] predestined us to be adopted as his sons through Jesus Christ" (Ephesians 1:4,5). The fullest description of this election to salvation is found in Ephesians 1:3-14.

As you note, the Bible also tells us, "God our Savior . . . wants all men to be saved and to come to a knowledge of the truth" (1 Timothy 2:3,4) and that "the man Christ Jesus . . . gave himself as a ransom for all men" (verses 5,6). The Bible, in fact, goes a step further and says Christ is the Savior of all people (1 Timothy 4:10 NIV 2011). We, therefore, cannot accept the Calvinist claim that God predestined some people to be damned and that Christ died only for the elect.

Our reason tells us that if God elected some people to be saved, he must have elected the rest to be damned. But Scripture does not allow this conclusion. Scripture says it is entirely due to God's grace if a person is saved, but it is entirely due to a sinner's unbelief that he or she is lost. How this can be is a mystery to our reason, but we simply let both statements of Scripture stand.

Your
Question Do Lutherans believe that one can know if they are one of the elect? How would you understand Paul when he says, "Make your calling and election sure"? In what way is election a doctrine of comfort in Lutheran theology? If I am currently a believer, can I be assured that, while I may fall away like David in the Old Testament, ultimately I will be brought safely home to heaven?

The Bible says two things that seem to be contradictory to our reason. On the one hand, it warns us of the danger of falling. On the other hand, it assures us of the security of God's elect. It is hard for our reason to put these two things together, but we must let both statements of Scripture stand.

The Bible teaches very clearly that it is possible to fall from faith (1 Corinthians 10:12). In the next verse it also assures us that God will protect us from falling (1 Corinthians 10:13). The first passage is a real warning. As God's law it warns us when we are complacent. The second comforts us with the gospel when we are troubled. We must preach both truths.

Among the other passages that deal with this are Matthew 13:18-23; Luke 8:11-15; Hebrews 6:4-6; Hebrews 10:26; and John 10:27-29. Luke 8:13 clearly speaks of those who believe for awhile and then fall away. Hebrews 6 is perhaps the strongest statement because it speaks of those who fall as ones who have been enlightened and having shared in the Holy Spirit. It may refer to those whose fall becomes final because they commit the sin against the Holy Spirit. We also have the example of David, who fell from faith and was restored.

We, therefore, cannot endorse the idea "once saved always saved," which claims a person can never permanently fall from faith and often looks at our past experience as our chief source of assurance. We must warn the complacent, careless Christian of the danger of falling, as Scripture does. But in times of doubt, we should not look at our feelings to see if we ever felt saved but at the truths of objective justification that proclaim what Christ has done for us once and for all. Our works, which testify to the presence of faith in us, are a secondary assurance of our calling and election, but for our chief confidence we should look outside ourselves to the verdict of God (1 John 3:20). The faith the Holy Spirit has worked in us assures us of our election (Ephesians 1:11-14).

Knowing when to preach either of these two teachings is a matter of recognizing the difference between the law and the gospel. The law is to warn the complacent; the gospel is to comfort the troubled.

Our WELS writings emphasize both of these truths. On page 17 of *This We Believe* (1999), we reject the idea that people who have come to faith can never fall, but we also emphasize the security of God's elect, since Scripture does both. I hope this clarifies our position for you and shows why it is scriptural to preach both warning and comfort.

Your Question

Psalm 5:5 says God hates sinners. Since we are all sinners, this means God hates us. John 3:16 and so many others say that God loves us. I've read two explanations. Some say the love verses refer only to the elect. God loves them because he knows they will accept Christ and so he loves them through Christ. This is the Calvinist "TULIP" explanation. My own pastor says that Psalm 5:5 and a lot of other verses that talk about God hating mean to disapprove or have disdain. That's what the Hebrew word in Psalm 5:5 means. He said the verses that say God loves us use the word "agape," meaning unconditional love. It says nothing about approving. God loves us because of who he is, not because of who we are. *Agape* and *hate* are not contradictory; God hates the sin but loves us. *Hate* and *phileo* are contradictory, but the Bible never says that God likes us or approves of us. Thus God *agapes* us but hates our sinfulness. I read a couple of posts here, and it seems Lutherans take the Calvinist view. Can you clarify? Thanks!

The Calvinist solution is wrong. God's love in sending the Savior was not limited to the elect.

It is true that God's love of sinners does not imply approval of their sinful ways. There is, therefore, some truth in the second explanation, but we need to go a little further. God's hatred of sinners is the verdict of the law. God's love for sinners is the gospel. Law and gospel are reconciled only at the cross of Christ, which displays both God's holy hatred of sin and of those guilty of sin and God's love for sinners. This is explained in the last part of Romans 3, in which God is revealed both as the just upholder of the law, who punishes the guilty, and as the justifier of sinners by grace.

Your Question What is fatalism, and how do we oppose it?

Fatalism is the belief that everything that happens is inevitably predetermined. All these predestined events will happen, just as foreordained, no matter what a person does. A fatalist will, therefore, face life with a "whatever will be will be" attitude. In some Asian religions, fate is determined by a blind, irrational, impersonal cosmic power. In some forms of Islam, fate is determined by God.

During the Gulf War there were reports that some Muslims did not take cover during Scud missile attacks since whatever God has determined will happen no matter what precautions a person may take. Such an attitude is contrary to Scripture. Such conduct is very similar to the "testing of God," which Satan suggested when he urged Jesus to jump off the temple roof.

The doctrine of divine providence does teach us that all things are controlled by the will of God, but his rule is wise and it is fair. It is neither blind nor arbitrary. As he determines what will happen in this world, God considers people's good and evil conduct and the prayers of his people. Although the scales of justice will not be perfectly balanced until judgment day, God rewards the righteous and punishes the wicked already during this lifetime. Good and evil conduct influence a person's "fate." The doctrine of God's providence does not eliminate people's responsibility for their conduct.

It, nevertheless, is true that many things in life remain outside of our control—natural disasters, accidents, and violent crime. They seem to occur in a pattern that is arbitrary and unfair. Scripture assures us, however, that God controls and uses even these evils so that they work for the ultimate good of his people. The story of Job is a prime example of this truth in operation. Although Job never learned exactly what was going on behind the scenes, we see how God protected Job and used even Satan's evil schemes for Job's ultimate good.

Knowing that God is in control of everything does not lead us to the pessimism of fatalism. We remember three truths: (1) God wants us to live as his children who realize that they are responsible to him for their actions. (2) God considers our actions and our prayers as he determines the course of our lives. (3) God will direct everything in life for our good.

Your Question

Psalm 19:13 says, "Keep your servant also from willful sins. . . . Then will I be blameless, innocent of great transgression." Am I correct in believing that before birth a child does not willfully sin and is innocent until he willfully sins against conscience?

When David claimed innocence in Psalm 19, he was not claiming sinlessness. He was saying that as a believer who has not committed malicious sins that would lead to a fall from faith, he stood under the grace of God and had complete forgiveness of sins. As a child of God, he was innocent of any charges that Satan or his enemies could bring against him.

An unborn child has a sinful nature. We assume that an unborn child does not commit sins, but we do not know this with certainty. Whether or not a child commits sins before birth and during infancy, we know that both before and after birth a baby is guilty of sin—the original sin inherited from its parents. In Psalm 51:5, David says, "Surely I was sinful at birth, sinful from the time my mother conceived me." There is no age of innocence.

We do not know how God deals with an unborn child. From special cases like John the Baptist (Luke 1:44), we know that God can work in an unborn child.

The fact that every child is guilty of sin already at birth emphasizes the importance of bringing babies to be baptized.

Your Question

I have been given an article to show that I am wrong in my beliefs that all babies are not necessarily saved and that the age of

accountability is not a biblical doctrine. Can you help me defend my position against this error?

Many passages of Scripture teach that we are born in sin and that we sin from the time of our birth. A few of them are Psalm 51:5; Ephesians 2:3; Romans 5:12; and Genesis 8:21.

The strongest refutation of the false notion of an "age of accountability" is death. Death is the wages of sin, yet children die even before they are born. There can be no death except where sin has been charged to a person. Follow Paul's argument through Romans 5.

Passages that speak of children not being held responsible for parents' sins refer to earthly judgment for actual sins, not to accountability for original sin. It is very clear, for example, that the subject of Ezekiel 18 is actual sin not original sin. Read verses 5 to 18. Passages which show that God judges each of us for our own actual sins do not serve as evidence that he does not judge us for original sin. Passages concerning these two categories cannot be jumbled together.

We can assume that a person who dies is sinful. We cannot conclude that a person who dies young is a worse sinner than anyone else or that he or she is being punished for a specific sin. This is covered in Luke 13.

Your
Question   I was raised in a Christian family, confirmed, and attended an ELS church. My faith was strong, but I slipped into the ways of the world and certain disbelief during my 20s. I am now 57 years old and desperately want to regain the faith that I knew as a child. I am extremely concerned about the fact that I am possibly guilty of the "unforgivable sin" and pray each day that I can regain my faith. Have I slipped too far in avoiding Christ over the last several years to return to his good graces? I admit, through prayer, that I have fought against his Word and am having difficulty regaining my faith. Is this possible? Now I often become despondent while considering the fact that there may be no hope for me—can he forgive me? Can the Holy Spirit again return to my heart?

Can God forgive you? He already has. Can the Holy Spirit return? He already has. The Holy Spirit has returned to your heart (if, in fact, he ever left it). Your feelings of repentance for your sins and your desire for Christ cannot come from your own sinful flesh. They are the promptings of the Holy Spirit working within you. If you had committed the sin against the Holy Spirit and driven him finally from your heart, there would be no struggle in you—there would be only spiritual death. The battle is the battle of the flesh against the Spirit.

It is very possible that you never lost your faith entirely, but that you passed through a time of weakness or of not being very conscious of your faith. We should all certainly pray that God strengthens our faith, but the means that God uses to do that is the gospel. Your salvation does not depend on how saved you feel (though feeling that confidence is good). Your salvation depends on what Jesus has done. Jesus lived, died, and rose for everyone in the world. That means Jesus lived, died, and rose for you. Jesus paid for every sin of everyone in the world. That means Jesus paid for every sin of yours. God the Father has declared the sins of the entire world forgiven. That includes yours. Jesus died for you. That is a fact when you feel it and when you don't. God declared that Christ paid for your sins in full. That is a fact when you feel it and when you don't. In your baptism God declared that you are his child. That is a fact, and God never breaks his word. Focus on these facts, not on your feelings.

Read the beautiful passages of the Bible that assure us of the reality of forgiveness. Read in 2 Corinthians 5 of how God has reconciled the world (and that includes you) to himself in Christ. Read in Romans 5 of the peace we have with God through our Lord Jesus Christ. Listen to the words of forgiveness in the confession and absolution in church. If you feel the need and have the desire, you can receive private, personal confession and absolution from the pastor. In the Lord's Supper you receive very personal assurance in the body and blood of Christ given and shed for you. A very good book that can lead you to many of the most comforting passages of the Bible is *Answer to Anxiety* by Herman Gockel. Perhaps you can find a copy of it.

In all of this, focus on the facts, not on your feelings. If you focus on the facts of what Christ has done, your feelings will become strong again.

Your
Question   **As a WELS member I find lots of people don't see things as I do! Sometimes I wonder if I understand. I believe that Jesus died for all my sins not just the ones I repented for. And if I do the sin over and over, I still will be forgiven. I believe there are sins we all repeat every day and don't repent of for one reason or another (like smoking, or what we think, etc.). If we truly believe that Jesus died**

for our sins, is that not what he said gets us to heaven? Please help me understand.

There is no forgiveness for any sin for which we remain impenitent, but we do not have to be able to list every sin we commit in order to be repentant for all of them. We confess all our sins, known and unknown (Psalm 19:12). In this way we do repent of every sin, not just those we can list. The grace of God is a condition in which we stand all of the time so long as we have faith (Romans 5:1,2). We are standing under a constant shower of God's forgiveness. In weakness we may fall into the same sins over and over again (Romans 7:14-25), but again and again God forgives us. We do, however, need to be warned that deliberate sins, which we do against conscience, can destroy our faith and deprive us of forgiveness (Psalm 19:13). We should never carelessly or deliberately continue in sins because of God's generosity in forgiving us. Living deliberately in sin leads to loss of faith, to loss of forgiveness, and to loss of salvation (Hebrews 10:26). Someone who is carelessly sinning needs to hear the strong warning against sin. One who is troubled by his or her sins of weakness needs to hear the assurance of the gospel.

Your
Question It has often been said, "While we cannot make the Word any more efficacious, surely we can remove human obstacles that we put in the way of the Word," usually in reference to the preaching of the pastor or performance in the Divine Service. Are there any Scriptures which teach such an idea?

It is not clear what you are asking since there are two ideas, not one, in the question you ask.

The first is that the efficaciousness, that is, the power to convert, lies in the Word alone not in our style of presentation. The gospel when presented less than eloquently does not lose its power to save. A very fluent presentation does not convert by its style. Only the Holy Spirit working through the gospel converts. I assume you are not questioning this, but that you are asking about the second part, which says that we can put obstacles in the way of the Word and that we should be careful not to do that.

There are a lot of passages for both points, but I will emphasize mainly the second point: we can do things that hinder the hearing of the gospel and we can remove such hindrances. All you have to do is read Paul's two letters to the Corinthians and you will find passages for both points. Look, for example, at the context of these passages:

2 Corinthians 4:7: But we have this treasure in jars of clay to show that this all-surpassing power is from God and not from us.

2 Corinthians 3:4-6: Such confidence as this is ours through Christ before God. Not that we are competent in ourselves to claim anything for ourselves, but our competence comes from God. He has made us competent as ministers of a new covenant—not of the letter but of the Spirit; for the letter kills, but the Spirit gives life.

2 Corinthians 6:3-10: We put no stumbling block in anyone's path, so that our ministry will not be discredited. Rather, as servants of God we commend ourselves in every way: in great endurance; in troubles, hardships and distresses; in beatings, imprisonments and riots; in hard work, sleepless nights and hunger; in purity, understanding, patience and kindness; in the Holy Spirit and in sincere love; in truthful speech and in the power of God; with weapons of righteousness in the right hand and in the left; through glory and dishonor, bad report and good report; genuine, yet regarded as impostors; known, yet regarded as unknown; dying, and yet we live on; beaten, and yet not killed; sorrowful, yet always rejoicing; poor, yet making many rich; having nothing, and yet possessing everything.

1 Corinthians 9:12,19-23: On the contrary, we put up with anything rather than hinder the gospel of Christ. . . . Though I am free and belong to no man, I make myself a slave to everyone, to win as many as possible. To the Jews I became like a Jew, to win the Jews. To those under the law I became like one under the law (though I myself am not under the law), so as to win those under the law. To those not having the law I became like one not having the law (though I am not free from God's law but am under Christ's law), so as to win those not having the law. To the weak I became weak, to win the weak. I have become all things to all men so that by all possible means I might save some. I do all this for the sake of the gospel, that I may share in its blessings.

Even a halting or hesitant presentation does not make the gospel incapable of converting a person, but we can do things that prevent a person from even hearing it. Among these things are alienating people by a sinful lifestyle, speaking in a language people don't understand, mixing false teaching with the gospel, etc. Paul made a very conscious effort to avoid doing these things. Every Christian should in every way make the teaching about God our Savior attractive (Titus 2:10).

Your
Question **Some of my friends admonish me about the need for a "new birth." The way they speak implies that I have to do something to receive this new birth. What do I do to be "born again"?**

The same thing you did to be born the first time. Nothing. The baby does not do anything to be conceived and born. Or to use another comparison, what does a dead person do to be made alive again? Nothing. Those who are by nature dead in sin cannot do anything to make themselves alive. So little can we do anything to be born again or raised from spiritual death. To be sure, a change takes place in us just as it does in birth or resurrection, but the power does not come from us.

In his first letter John says, "Everyone who believes that Jesus is the Christ is born of God" (1 John 5:1). To be born again means to come to faith in Christ. We come to faith in Christ when the Holy Spirit creates faith in us. He does this through the preaching of the gospel or through Baptism. "You have been born again, not of perishable seed, but of imperishable, through the living and enduring word of God" (1 Peter 1:23). "No one can enter the kingdom of God unless he is born of water and the Spirit" (John 3:5).

When a baby is born, the initiative and power do not come from the baby but from the mother. When we are born spiritually, the initiative and power do not come from us but from God. Sometimes we hear people say, "Your part is to believe what God says and to receive Jesus as your Lord and Savior." This is misleading since it implies that although God has done almost everything, our one contribution is to believe. Our faith, however, is a gift from God. It is not our contribution to salvation. It is true that God does not believe for us, but God does create faith in us. We do not come to faith by our own power but by the power of God. We receive Christ the way we receive a gift. All the credit for the gift goes to the giver, not to the receiver.

When you know someone who needs to be "born again," the thing to do is not to keep telling him how much he needs to be "born again."

The thing to do is to tell him about his sin and his Savior, so that the Holy Spirit will work faith in him through the gospel.

Your
Question Being raised in a nondenominational Christian church, I have tried to understand your views on salvation, specifically, you stress that when we are saved, we do not make a decision to accept Christ into our lives. When I first read some Q. & A. about this topic from your Web site I was astounded, because the concept you stated made no sense to me. The more that I have read, however, leads me to believe that maybe it's all just a misunderstanding. As I understand it, you believe that stating, "I accepted Jesus Christ into my life, as my personal Savior," is in effect taking part of the credit for what Jesus accomplished on the cross. This, of course, would be wrong, because we can only be brought to faith through the work of the Holy Spirit in our lives. (We are born dead in sin, and our natural being is opposed to God, so we cannot come to Christ by our own ability.) I agree with all of these statements. So where are the differences? My question to you is, do you believe that having faith in Christ, we make decisions for (or against) him in our everyday lives? (Many times we must decide whether to do things our own way, or to follow the will of God.) God did give us free will to choose whether to do what is right or wrong, did he not? When I prayed to the Lord, confessed my sins, asked for forgiveness for them, and asked him to be Lord and Savior of my life (what some call the "sinner's prayer"), I already had faith in Christ or I would not have prayed. I was certainly not taking any credit for what the Lord did for me. One of the questions on your Web site was in regards to a play at an Assembly of God church that this person attended after which the pastor emphasized that the congregation should "Be saved, and accept Jesus Christ into their lives." I don't believe that the pastor was in any way saying that these people would be saved by their abilities, but that the Holy Spirit was working faith in people's hearts through the play, and/or through the pastor's spoken words of God. The pastor was stressing what the Bible says we need to do in order to be saved: Believe. Somewhere in the Bible it says, "Those who accepted his message were saved." This is not saying that these people did it on their own or took credit for it. Just that they accepted, not rejected, the message of Christ. Please comment. Thank you.

From the way you explain your belief, it seems you have the correct understanding of conversion. We cannot cooperate in our conversion because we are dead in sin. After we have been converted by the Holy

Spirit, we do cooperate with him in our sanctification, our everyday Christian living (though not perfectly).

When the Bible describes our coming to faith, it describes it from two viewpoints. We can say, "He turned to God." We observe the change in the person. But if we want to describe what really happened, we say, "The Holy Spirit changed his heart." We can use the same kind of language in daily speech. I can say, "I saw the car turn at the corner." Speaking more precisely I would have to say, "I saw the driver turn the car."

We do turn to God, but the key question is, Where does the power come from? We object to the statement that we have the power either "to decide for Christ or against him," as if we were in kind of a spiritual neutral and have in us the power to go either way. Our natural mind is completely opposed to God and cannot decide to obey him (Romans 8:6-8). We cannot believe in Christ by our own powers (1 Corinthians 12:3). We do turn to Christ, but the power to turn to him comes from the Holy Spirit, not from us. Our will is changed, but it is God the Holy Spirit who works in us to will and to act according to God's good purpose (Philippians 2:13). One of the best expressions of this truth, that we turn to God but that the power comes from God, is Jeremiah 31:18. Literally translated it says, "Cause me to turn and I will turn." (The NIV is not very good in this verse.)

What we object to is the synergistic* view, which says that the reason "some are saved and others are not" is that there was something different in those who were saved, which enabled them to decide for Christ. This is the way conversion is explained by many Arminian or synergistic theologians, including some Lutherans who have strayed from the Lutheran view.

Concerning your question: "God did give us free will to choose whether to do what is right or wrong, did he not?" Before conversion we had no free will in spiritual things, only a limited freedom of choice concerning external or civic morality. After conversion we have free will in spiritual choices, but it is still limited by our battle against our sinful nature, which remains (Romans 7).

---

*Synergism is any belief that man can cooperate in his conversion or that his works play a role in obtaining forgiveness.

You said, "When I prayed to the Lord, confessed my sins, asked for forgiveness for them, and asked him to be Lord and Savior of my life (what some call the "sinner's prayer"), I already had faith in Christ or I would not have prayed." What you say is correct. When you prayed this prayer, you may have reached a greater awareness of your faith, but you already had faith before. And when you came to faith, you had complete forgiveness of sins. The confusing thing about this prayer is that it suggests to some people that "accepting Jesus as Savior and Lord of my life" is a higher stage of Christianity than simply believing in him as my Savior. Anyone who has faith has been born again and has accepted Jesus as Savior and Lord. A person may grow in sanctification and display his faith more fully in his life, but his sanctification is something he received at the moment he came to faith. When we come to faith, justification (forgiveness of sins) is complete; sanctification (our good works) continues to grow.

Your
Question   **When the Bible uses the word "repent," is this a law or gospel teaching? I was told during a study that when we have to do something, it is law. So if we repent that is law. I was confused and questioning this doctrine. Can you give me an answer and Bible passages for this teaching?**

The underlying idea behind the biblical words for repentance is to "turn" or to "change one's mind." A person turns from sin to God. Turning from sin involves sorrow over sin (contrition). This is worked by the law. True repentance includes trust in God's promise of forgiveness as its most important part. This is produced by the gospel. Both the law and the gospel thus have roles in working true repentance. It is the role of the gospel, however, which is of highest importance because there can be no true, God-pleasing repentance without faith worked by the gospel.

When it follows the preaching of the gospel, the imperative "repent" is not really a command of the law that we must fulfill. It is an invitation to believe the gospel promise that accompanies it. It is like the invitation given to a starving man as he is being fed, "Eat some of this food." The power to accept the gospel invitation does not lie in the unconverted recipient of the invitation but in the gospel promise through which the Holy Spirit works. The gospel works that faith which it calls for. The Scriptures clearly tell us that we are saved by grace alone and that salvation is a gift of God, worked in us through his unfailing grace (Ephesians 2:8,9). Yet we are directed to hear (and read and study) his Word, to obey his commands, to seek his forgiveness with a contrite heart, and to lead a sanctified life as the natural outcome of our reciprocating love of God.

Your Question

"God's gift of grace in justification remains independent of human cooperation. . . . The Christian cannot and should not remain without works. But whatever in the justified precedes or follows the free gift of faith is neither the basis of justification or merits it." Perhaps you recognized this as a quote from the Joint Declaration between the Lutheran World Federation and the Roman Catholic Church. If you didn't know the source, would you still consider it erroneous or inadequate? Doesn't this suggest that the Catholic teaching on justification, while ambiguous or incoherent at times, is more nuanced than "faith and works together," as it is often characterized on this site?

No, the doctrine of justification in Roman Catholic theology is not ambiguous. It is clearly faith and works together as many Catholic sources plainly declare.

The first sentence you quote does not deal with the issue at stake because it does not define *grace*. Catholics and Lutherans agree we are justified by grace. The disagreement is what is the nature of justifying grace. Is it only a verdict of God (the biblical view), or is it an ability God puts in us that enables us to complete our justification by the works we do?

The second sentence could be understood correctly if it were not undone by what follows it. If by "nuanced" you mean are there some sentences in the Catholic presentation of justification that can be understood correctly, the answer is yes. If you mean is it unclear whether the Catholic church teaches salvation by faith and works, the answer is no.

For example the treatment of justification by the Council of Trent says:

Chapter VII "What the Justification of the Ungodly Is, and What Are Its Causes"

This disposition, or preparation, is followed by *justification itself, which is not only the remission of sins but also the sanctification and renewal of the inner man through voluntary acceptance of grace and of the gifts by which an unjust person becomes a just one and an enemy becomes a friend,* that he may be an heir according to the hope of eternal life. *The causes of this justification are these:* the final cause is of course *the glory of God* and of Christ and life eternal; the efficient cause is the merciful God, who gratuitously washes and sanctifies, sealing and anointing with the Holy Spirit of promise, who is the pledge of our inheritance; *the meritorious cause, however, is His most beloved, only-begotten Son,* our Lord Jesus Christ, who, when we were enemies, because of the exceeding love with which He loved us, through His most holy suffering on the tree of the cross merited justification for us and made satisfaction to God the Father for us; again, *the instrumental cause is the Sacrament of Baptism,* which is the sacrament of faith, without which no one is ever justified; *finally, the single formal cause is the righteousness of God, not that by which He is Himself righteous but that by which He makes us righteous, or that by which we, being endowed by Him, are renewed in the spirit of our mind and are not only reputed to be, but are truly, called and are righteous, receiving the righteousness in us, everyone his own. . . .*

In this section what is said about the meritorious cause is undone by what is said about the formal [essential] cause of justification. This makes the change in us the formal cause of justification. That faith is only the beginning of justification is treated in the next chapter and the following canons.

Chapter VIII "How It Should Be Understood That the Ungodly Is Justified, by Faith and Gratis"

When the apostle says that a man is justified by faith and gratis, these words are to be understood in that sense which the perpetual consensus of the Catholic Church has held and expressed, namely, that we are said to be justified by faith because *faith is the beginning of human salvation,* the foundation and root of all justification, without which it is impossible to please God and to come to the fellowship of His children. But we are said to be justified gratis because none of those things which precede justification, whether it be faith or works, merit the grace of justification. "For if it is grace, it is not by works, otherwise [as the same apostle says] grace is not grace."

Canon XI "If anyone says that a man is justified either solely by the imputation of Christ's righteousness or solely by the remission of sins, to the exclusion of the grace and charity which is poured out into their hearts by the Holy Spirit and stays with them, or also that the grace by which we are justified is only the favor of God; let him be anathema."

Canon XII "If anyone says that justifying faith is nothing else than trust in divine mercy, which remits sins for Christ's sake, or that it is this trust alone by which we are justified, let him be anathema."

Canon XXIV "If anyone says that the received righteousness is not preserved and also not increased before God through good works but that the works are only the fruit and signs of the justification obtained, not also a cause of its increase; let him be anathema."

The Catholic teaching is very clear. Justification is by faith and works. A complete treatment of the topic is found in Martin Chemnitz, *Examination of the Council of Trent,* Vol. 1, pp. 465-664.

Your
Question **Are not hearing, obeying, seeking and sanctified living "works"? Not hearing prevents the Holy Spirit from working in us; not obeying is to defy God; not seeking forgiveness is to be excluded from God's grace; not attempting to live a God-pleasing life is to have a faith that is but a hollow shell. Aren't these necessary works to be saved?**

A Christian does good works as a result of his faith, but he or she is not saved by them. They earn nothing. Our good works are something we do as a result of our forgiveness; they are not a cause of our forgiveness.

Our faith is a "work" in the sense that we do it. The Holy Spirit does not believe for us. But our faith is a work of the Holy Spirit in that he works it in us. Our faith is not the cause of our forgiveness. It simply receives the gift Christ won for us. We are saved *by* grace *through* faith.

Good works are not necessary as a cause of forgiveness. They are necessary as a natural result of our new life in Christ. A branch attached to Christ bears Christlike fruit. Good works are not optional, but they are not "necessary" in the sense that we feel them as a burden.

The misleading phrase "good works are necessary for salvation" is discussed extensively in Article IV of the Formula of Concord. Study this document for further insight into this question.

Your
Question In justification, the terms *objective* and *subjective* justification are confusing. Objective justification to me borders on universalism. It states that when Christ died, forgiveness was pronounced to all and is an accomplished fact and that everyone is declared forgiven. If everyone is declared forgiven, to me that means that all are saved. I believe when Christ died He made forgiveness possible (the offer of forgiveness is there). But, you are not forgiven until repentance and faith is wrought by the Holy Spirit. Please comment. This is confusing for me.

The teaching of objective justification is that God the Father declared the sins of the whole world forgiven because Christ had paid for all sin. To benefit from that payment and that declaration, it is necessary that a person be brought to faith in Christ as his Savior (subjective justification). Read 2 Corinthians 5:18-21, where both of these points are clearly stated.

Objective means that God's verdict of forgiveness for the world does not depend on my feeling. It is an accomplished fact even before I hear about it or respond to it. *Subjective* means I joyfully apply this verdict to myself: The world's sins are forgiven, therefore my sins are forgiven.

The Bible says the very thing that you seem hesitant to say, that Christ is the Savior of everyone, even of those who do not believe (1 Timothy 4:10). Though they have been saved from sin by Christ, those who do not believe will never enter salvation because they throw away Christ's payment. If I put money in the bank for you, it is legally yours. Your debt has been paid. If you do not believe me when I tell you about it and you never use the money that is yours, you never benefit from it. It is the same with justification. Christ has made the payment for us and God the Father has credited it to our account (objective justification). If I don't believe that it was given for me (subjective justification), I will never benefit from it. Though God's forgiving grace is universal, salvation will not be universal because many spurn God's grace.

My faith is not a cause of my justification. It simply receives the gift God gives. Our faith does not complete justification. It simply accepts it. Even this acceptance is a gift that the Holy Spirit works in me.

What is the WELS teaching on objective justification? My friend and I have had a discussion, and he pointed me to the Kokomo articles, or theses, as an example of what WELS teaches. Being just a layman I was wondering if I should use these to teach others who may have the same question, as he did for me.

The teaching of objective justification is that God the Father declared the sins of the whole world forgiven because Christ had paid for all sin. To benefit from that payment and that declaration, it is necessary that a person be brought to faith in Christ as his Savior (subjective justification) (2 Corinthians 5:18-21). See the preceding question.

The so-called Kokomo Statements should not be taken as representative of WELS teaching. Much that has been put out and circulated about the Kokomo Statements has been a misrepresentation of the WELS position by those who falsely accuse WELS of universalism. Three of the statements are lifted from WELS sources but taken out of context; they caricature the WELS position and should not be taken as an adequate presentation of WELS teaching.

A brief evaluation of the so-called Kokomo Statements is contained in a 1982 paper by Siegbert Becker, "Objective Justification," which is available from the Wisconsin Lutheran Seminary library. Papers on objective justification also appear in volume 3 of *Our Great Heritage*, available from Northwestern Publishing House. The people who made the Kokomo Statements were defenders of the views of an LCMS seminary professor who denied objective justification (the LCMS did not accept his view).

Professor Becker was addressing a controversy that had arisen concerning statements Professor John Meyer had made in his commentary on 2 Corinthians, in which he had referred to "saints in hell." By this term Professor Meyer was trying to express in a striking way that there will be people who end up in hell even though Christ paid for their sins and God the Father declared their sins forgiven. They have lost the benefit of Christ's death for them because they did not believe Christ died for them. This phrase of Professor Meyer's was pounced on by people who denied the doctrine of objective or universal justification as their way of ridiculing the doctrine. Since the Bible uses the term "saints" only of believers, it is best not to use the term for anyone but believers. Professor Meyer was trying to say in a striking way that the fact that people end up in hell is not due to a failure on God's part to provide them with forgiveness but to a failure on their part to believe in that forgiveness. Luther made very similar statements, which Professor Meyer was simply echoing. Professor Meyer's doctrine of objective or universal justification was correct, but we might not want to use his term. Professor Becker's aim was to defend Professor Meyer's teaching of the doctrine without being tied to his term. There have never been any saints in hell in the common understanding of the term *saints*—believers who have benefited from Christ's death through faith. Those to whom Jesus made a proclamation in hell were not believers but unbelievers who died in the flood. Old Testament believers went to heaven when they died.

Your Question   I am WELS, but have relatives in LCMS. How does the LCMS differ from WELS in the Third Use of the Law?

I am not aware of any difference between WELS and the LCMS in this question. Both believe that Christian people still need to use the law as a mirror, curb, and rule. Only Christians can use the law as a rule or guide to God-pleasing conduct since only they have the right motive to do good works, namely, gratitude to God for forgiveness. There was however a group in the LCMS who denied the third use of the law. They have sometimes been called the Valparaiso theologians. They were aligned with the Seminex movement. The LCMS did not accept their view.

A Christian person needs the law for three purposes. Like a mirror it shows us our sins and our daily need for forgiveness. This could be called the first use of the law, since for sinners it is the most important use.

As a curb the threats of the law hold us back from sin. If our sinful nature tempts us to steal, but fear of apprehension and punishment holds us back, this is not a God-pleasing motive for refraining from sin, but it does prevent harm to me and my neighbor. This is the civil function of the law in society, but it is also a benefit to Christians because it deters others from harming us and us from harming them. It does not produce godly conduct, but only outward, civic righteousness.

Christians use God's law as a guide. It tells us what he wants us to do or not to do. If we had no sinful nature, we would need no written code and could live by the basic principle, "Love your neighbor as yourself."

But our sinful nature often tries to disguise its selfishness as love. God's law tells us what real love is. Only the gospel can provide us with the motivation to obey the law out of love for God. Conduct pleasing to God is guided by the law and motivated by the gospel.

First Corinthians 9:19-21 explains a Christian's relationship to God's law. Christians are not under God's law, that is, they are not burdened by it nor motivated by its threats. Christians are not without God's law. They live in Christ's law. They are still guided by God's law. (The NIV does a poor job of reflecting the difference between the prepositions in the Greek text of these verses. The Greek says the Christian is not under the law, but lives in the law).

Your
Question **Do we still have to obey the Ten Commandments?**

That depends on what you mean by "the Ten Commandments" and "have to."

If by "the Ten Commandments" you mean the moral law of God that is embodied in the Ten Commandments, the answer is yes. They still apply to Christians. The Third Commandment as given to Israel does, however, also embody principles about the Saturday Sabbath, which were part of the ceremonial law for Old Testament Israel. The New Testament states clearly that these Sabbath regulations as such do not apply to us (Colossians 2:16,17). That is the reason we do not observe a Sabbath on Saturday. We do have Sunday as a regular day of worship, but this day was freely chosen by the church.

We "have to" keep the commandments since they are the will of God for us. They are not optional or an extra-credit part of Christianity. We "have to" keep them in that it is natural for a branch attached to Christ to produce Christlike fruits. A good tree produces good fruit.

We do not "have to" keep them as a way of obtaining forgiveness. Good deeds are not a cause of our forgiveness but a result of forgiveness. We do not "have to" keep them as if they are a burden imposed upon us, which we reluctantly must carry. In so far as we have been made new by the Holy Spirit, we gladly and willingly obey God's commandments. My "old man" still fights against the Holy Spirit, but he is no longer the "real me."

When it comes to sanctification, I understand that the good works come only from the power of the Holy Spirit and it is not of my own power that I can do anything good.

My question is that how can a person do anything good when he is consumed with false guilt as his motivator for doing the good works? False guilt, as I understand it, is when a person is motivated to do good works because it makes him look like a good person or out of obligation, etc. True guilt is looking within the self, admitting the sin, asking for forgiveness and doing what is right in a similar situation. This could be a good work or this could be just simply godly living.

In teaching sanctification why doesn't WELS teach people about understanding true guilt and false guilt? Especially false guilt? We live in a society that glamorizes self and reinforces false guilt. Why aren't there workshops or educational Bible studies that help struggling Christians with this difficult daily struggle with themselves? Many people have the faith but they don't know what to do with it. They don't know how to put their faith into action because they are not being taught. How do we deal with this issue at a synodical level? I appreciate any thoughts you have on this issue as well as your answers.

To understand the problem we need to begin by distinguishing between guilt and guilt feelings. We often fail to do this in English and use the word *guilt* both for guilt and for guilt feelings. You are talking primarily about guilt feelings, not about guilt.

Guilt is not a subjective feeling. Guilt is liability to punishment because we have broken God's law. It is an objective reality that is there whether we feel it or not.

There are two kinds of unhealthy feelings in relation to guilt. The first occurs when a person is guilty but does not feel guilty. He does not recognize or he denies his sin. This is unhealthy because if he remains impenitent, he will be condemned by his sin. In a sinful world a proper awareness of guilt is as necessary as a sense of pain. Pain warns us to pull away from the hot stove. Proper feelings of guilt warn us to turn from sin. The way we are to address this problem of the lack of guilt feelings where there is guilt is by preaching the law of God to the impenitent.

The second unhealthy kind of guilt feelings is feeling guilty when you are not guilty. This may occur when a person is misinformed about God's law and thinks that something is a sin when it is not. This is overcome by a correct teaching of God's law. False guilt feelings also may occur when a person feels guilty even though God's forgiveness has removed his guilt. This is overcome by preaching the gospel. When a person realizes that his guilt has been removed, his heart is free and he can serve God in the love and joy that comes from forgiveness.

The proper way to deal with guilt feelings is to deal with the guilt. Many approaches to therapy try to remove the feelings without dealing with the guilt. This is like treating cancer with aspirin. The only true therapy to deal with guilt is the proper preaching of law and gospel. We teach this as the central point of all preaching, teaching, and counseling.

This cannot be reduced to a simple formula or a set of standard answers. Like a doctor, a pastor must diagnosis the individual who is troubled by inappropriate guilt so that he can dispense the right formula of law and gospel to the individual needs. We teach this as the most important skill of a pastor. While there is a need for special counseling with individuals and there can be special classes on the issue of guilt, the best treatment and preventative for wrong feelings of guilt is a steady diet of properly balanced preaching of law and gospel. Every church service is addressed to the issue of dealing with guilt.

In encouraging sanctified living, we use the gospel as the source of motivation and power. The law does serve as a guide for Christian living (third use of the law) by identifying the acts of love that are pleasing to God. In teaching sanctification, we need to stress the following points that are explained in the essay "The Lutheran Doctrine of Sanctification and Its Rivals," which is available in the collection of essays accessible on the Web site of the library of Wisconsin Lutheran Seminary.

- True Lutheran teaching emphasizes the importance and necessity of sanctification, Christian living, and good works in the life of every Christian.

- True Lutheran teaching emphasizes the distinction of justification from sanctification.

- True Lutheran teaching concerning sanctification clearly distinguishes the roles of the law and the gospel in sanctification.

- Lutheran teaching emphasizes the priority of the means of grace as the tools God uses in producing sanctification in the lives of his people.

- Lutherans emphasize the means of grace in their efforts to help Christians grow in sanctification, since only the means of grace produce the proper motivation for sanctification. Nevertheless, in our preaching and teaching, we should also refer to other means God may use in a secondary way to strengthen and encourage us in our sanctification, such as the examples of others.

- Lutheran teaching of sanctification emphasizes God's power, rather than human effort, as the source of sanctification. Lutheran teaching, nevertheless, emphasizes also the importance and necessity of our cooperation and effort in our sanctification. Unlike Christ's work in justification, the work of the Holy Spirit in sanctification does not substitute for our efforts.

- Lutheran teaching of sanctification also warns of the struggle and difficulty that every Christian will face in sanctification.

- Lutheran teaching recognizes that sanctification will never be perfect in this life.

- Lutheran teachers thank God for progress in sanctification and commend Christians for the gains that they make.

- Lutheran teaching of sanctification urges people never to rest on their laurels but to keep striving to improve.

- Lutheran teaching of sanctification keeps believers' eyes on the goals of sanctification.

We cannot directly address what is troubling you about this issue because we do not know what it is. The things you are asking for are what we teach and do. If you feel the proper application of law and gospel as it is outlined above is missing from the spiritual care you are receiving, this is an issue you need to discuss with your pastor.

3
Ministry

The doctrine of the ministry has been one of the most debated doctrines in American Lutheranism. In the 19th century, C. F. W. Walther upheld the confessional Lutheran view against the Romanizing views of Grabau and Loehe. In the 20th century, there was considerable discussion of so-called Wisconsin Synod and Missouri Synod views. Echoes of both of these discussions continue today and will be referred to in the discussions that follow. A summary of the main issues is found in the essays "Current Debate Concerning the Doctrine of the Ministry," *Wisconsin Lutheran Quarterly* (Winter 1994) and "The Doctrine of Church and Ministry in the First One Hundred Volumes of the *Wisconsin Lutheran Quarterly*" (Fall 2003). Many essays on this topic are available in the online essay collection of the Wisconsin Lutheran Seminary library.

Your Question

Paul seems to distinguish two offices of the ministry: elder or overseer and deacon or deaconess. What responsibilities or characteristics distinguish the one from the other? How does this apply to the life and ministry of the church today?

In the only place where Paul discusses the two offices side by side (1 Timothy 3), he lists the qualifications for holding these offices, not the duties of the office holders. Since the same Christian character is required for both offices, this description does little to help us distinguish the offices. The main characteristic that distinguished the elder/overseer from the deacon was the ability to teach. (The office of deaconess was not discussed separately. Women referred to may have been the wives of deacons.)

A comparison of such passages as Acts 20:17 and 28 indicates that *elder* and *overseer* were interchangeable terms. A consideration of all the passages in which the terms *elder* or *overseer* occur suggests that this office was roughly similar to our office of pastor, but that the responsibilities of the office were often divided among several men so that a given elder might have been more of a specialist and less of a generalist than our pastors normally are. Among the duties of elder/overseers were shepherding the flock (Acts 20:28), teaching and preaching the Word and directing the affairs of the church (1 Timothy 5:17), encouraging sound doctrine and refuting error (Titus 1:9), praying for the sick (James 5:14), and laying hands on candidates for the ministry (1 Timothy 4:14). First Timothy 5:17 implies that not all elders were directly involved in preaching and teaching the Word.

It is generally believed that the duties of deacons and deaconesses were similar to those of the men appointed to be in charge of the charitable work indicated in Acts 6. Those men, however, were not called deacons, nor are the duties of a deacon or deaconess described anywhere else in the New Testament. At times the church has applied the term *deacon* or *deaconess* to people who assist the pastor in the ministry of the Word.

A survey of the relevant passages indicates that the New Testament congregations established by the apostles were not bound to rigid terminology or forms of ministry but were free to make the arrangements that would best serve the changing needs of the congregations. We may do the same if we observe the qualifications that Scripture sets for those serving in the public ministry and we remember the one mission the Lord has given to the church—to preach the gospel.

The terminology and the arrangement of the ministry in our congregations have undergone numerous changes since the time of the apostles. We use the title *pastor* for the office that is closest in scope to the elder of the early New Testament church, although the title *pastor* occurs only rarely in the New Testament. We use the term *elder* for church councilmen who have a narrower assignment than the elders of the early church. Our Lutheran elementary school teachers have an assignment different in scope from that of any of the ministers who appear in the pages of the New Testament. We do not regularly use the term *deacon*, though some sister churches do. Though some of the externals have changed, the substance of the ministry established by Christ remains the same.

Your Question

I am trying to understand the ecclesiastical structure of Lutheranism and the biblical basis for it. Could you please describe the basic government, hierarchical structure, and relationship of the local church, including pastors, elders, and deacons? Also could you please comment on the relationship of the local church and its leaders to that of the synod and its leaders?

Since Scripture does not command any specific form of church government, we do not insist on any particular form of church government as a biblical form.

In practice, WELS has a congregational form of government. Each congregation calls its own pastor or pastors, owns its own property, and governs its own affairs. It does so through its voters' assembly and its boards and officers. There is no prescribed form for the boards and the number of officers. These are determined by the congregation and vary considerably depending on the size and programs of the congregations. New congregations may choose to work together with the synod as mission congregations that are subsidized by the synod. In this case, they agree to cooperate with the synod home mission board in determining their financial plans, building programs, etc.

Congregations may join the synod to support joint efforts in missions, worker training, and other programs. The synod program is adopted by the synod convention, which meets every other year. Voting delegates are chosen from among the pastors, male teachers, and congregational delegates. In the interim between conventions, synodical business is managed by elected and called officials and department heads. Various entities within the synod also have elected governing boards. Doctrinal discipline is the responsibility of the district presidents and their assistants.

More information can be found in the constitution and bylaws and in the constitutions and bylaws of individual congregations.

Your Question

When I was growing up, it seemed like everybody knew that "minister" meant the same as "pastor." Now it seems like we call everyone ministers. Is this a change in our idea of what a minister is?

The English words *minister* and *ministry* were borrowed from Latin. They originally meant "servant" and "service." In the King James Version, they were used with a wide range of meanings, but in recent centuries they came to be used almost entirely as technical terms for two types of service. My English dictionary lists "clergyman" or "pastor" as the number one meaning of *minister*. The other main meaning of *minister* is a government official, like the prime minister of England.

What complicates this seemingly simple situation is the fact that the King James used *minister* and *ministry* as the translation for nearly every occurrence of a group of words in the Greek New Testament (*diakon-*), which more recent translations, such as the NIV, sometimes translate as "ministry" and sometimes as "service." In the New Testament this word group is not limited to describing the service rendered by men whose work corresponded to that of our pastors. It was also used to describe other kinds of service, such as that provided by the men in Acts 6 who managed the distribution of help to the widows and performed secular service as well, such as waiting on tables.

When we use the words *minister* and *ministry* to refer to other forms of service in the church besides that of the pastor (such as the service provided by Christian teachers), we are simply returning to this wider usage of the terms *service* or *ministry*, which was common in the New Testament. This wider usage of the term *minister* still occurs in contemporary English but has grown much less common. My English dictionary also defines *minister* as "one who acts as the agent of another." In this sense everyone who is called by the church to carry out some service in its name is a "minister." This is what we often call public ministry.

If we are going to use *ministry* in this wider sense, a number of cautions are necessary. Since the wider usage of *ministry* is called archaic (outdated) by the dictionary, to avoid confusion we must make it clear to our hearers that we are returning to a wider usage of the term *minister* than that which has been common in the recent past. We must be careful that we do not confuse the service or ministry that Christians do on their own initiative as part of the priesthood of all believers (private ministry) with the ministry that they carry out in response to a church's call and in the name of a church (public ministry). We must also be careful that we do not diminish respect for the pastoral ministry, the most comprehensive form of the public ministry of the Word, which was established by Christ.

Your
Question   My question has to do with the divine call and my concern that WELS is starting to seriously blur the distinction between the call to public ministry with the gospel ministry that is given to all Christians. I have read several papers about ministry and the divine call posted on the seminary Web site's online essays. I am a subscriber to the weekly call reports and recently found these two calls listed: 1. A call was issued for "VP of Institutional Advancement" and then in the next call report it was amended to read "VP of Institutional Advancement & Church Relations" at Wisconsin Lutheran College. 2. Next was "Chief Executive Officer" for Wisconsin Lutheran Child and Family Services. These sound more like job offers than calls. Please clarify for me how a VP and a CEO are called positions. If you can, please be specific about how the handling of the means of grace unique to the public ministry is going to be used in these jobs.

I understand that the church has freedom to make a divine call as it sees fit to meet its needs, and that the men called to these positions should have a strong spiritual background (Acts 6). I still think it causes confusion when the WELS increasingly uses the terms *minister* and *ministry* to apply to almost any task no matter how far removed from the means of grace it is. What you end up with is a huge array of jobs that have been given a cloak of spirituality by deeming them "called positions."

The ELS is struggling with the wording of its doctrine of church and ministry partly because they see how the WELS has watered it down. This is of great concern to many individuals like me.

The first part of your question you are addressing to the wrong place. It needs to be addressed to Wisconsin Lutheran College (WLC) and Wisconsin Lutheran Child and Family Service. They are the ones who have established the scope of these two offices. Either of these positions probably could be designed to include more or less "pastoral" or "executive," "administrator," aspects. The fact that WLC included church relations in the scope of the call seems to indicate why they wanted to call for the position. The synod has no handbook or guidelines for groups to use as a template in describing such calls. This is the responsibility of the local group.

But before you conclude that there is a WELS/ELS difference here, you should also inquire how organizations affiliated with the ELS, such as Thoughts of Faith and the Schwan Center, have handled similar positions in the past. You may find cases in which they too called pastors for such positions. I think you are seeing a difference between the two synods in this matter that does not exist in reality. In both synods, calling bodies of affiliated organizations can use the same freedom to analyze and define their needs and to call or hire individuals to serve those needs accordingly.

The kind of situation you are discussing here has nothing directly to do with the distinction between the call to public ministry and the gospel ministry that is given to all Christians. It is rather a question of the relationship between different kinds or forms of public ministry in the church. The gospel ministry that is given to all Christians is exercised, for example, when a mother teaches her children or shares the gospel with an unchurched neighbor, not when a church asks her to undertake similar activities on its behalf. Under no definition or arrangement would the two positions you asked about be examples of the gospel ministry that is given to all believers.

In each case, the question is what kind of public ministry or service of the church is attached to this position. The closest parallel is Acts 6, which you cite. In addition to their gospel duties, the apostles had been occupied with administrative duties. To free them from this overload, other men were called and installed (we might even say "ordained" with the laying on of hands) to take up these administrative duties. As far as we know, at first their offices were purely administrative. If such division of responsibility and such calling and "ordaining" were done by the apostles, what makes such calls wrong today?

As noted previously, the wide use of the term *ministry* comes directly from Scripture, which uses the term for a wide range of services both within and outside the church. This can be easily seen simply by looking at all the uses of the word in the King James Bible. Also in the Old Testament, the called Levites filled a wide variety of offices— pastoral, musical, educational, financial, and administrative.

What is really in danger of being "watered down" in the present discussion is the public ministry of those who serve in some capacity other than pastor. If one says that what a Sunday school teacher does is only a function of the priesthood of all believers, this is a real watering down. To say that others can help the pastor by serving in a limited or even part-time, voluntary form of ministry does not water down the ministry of the pastor any more than the ministry of the deacon watered down the ministry of the apostles. There is no blurring of the distinction between public ministry of the Word, other forms of ministry, and the priesthood of all believers in our teaching. All these distinctions are maintained.

Your Question

Why do pastors have automatic tenure at their churches? Why don't they have periodic performance reviews like people in other positions?

Pastors cannot have "tenure" because they are not employees. They are not hired nor do they serve under a contract. Pastors are called by Christ through the church. The arrangement between a pastor and a congregation is not to be thought of as a business deal, which stipulates a certain amount of work for a certain amount of pay. The pastor is to freely give the spiritual treasures he has received from Christ to those whom he serves; they in turn are to freely give to him from the earthly treasures they have (Galatians 6:6; 1 Corinthians 9:11).

An employee's performance has to satisfy the person who hires him. Unless protected by terms of a contract, he or she can be dismissed for rather arbitrary reasons. A pastor's duty, however, is not to satisfy the desires of the congregation but to be faithful to God, who has called him (1 Corinthians 4:1-4). This means a pastor must often tell members of the congregation truths that they do not want to hear. He must confront sin even when people are offended by his words of warning from God's Word. His "performance" therefore cannot be judged by the same standards used by worldly businesses.

A pastor can be removed from his position for holding to false doctrine, for immoral conduct, for inability to perform the duties of his office, or for willful neglect of his duties. A pastor and the leaders of the church should regularly discuss and evaluate the work of the church and ways in which they can serve its members better, but this should be done in the spirit of Christian cooperation, not with an employer-employee mentality.

At the seminary where I teach, professors are regularly visited by members of the board, they visit one anothers' classes on a regular rotation, and they may seek feedback from the students at various intervals. Similar things can be done on a parish level to help the pastor evaluate the way in which he is carrying out the various elements of his ministry.

Your
Question **I am disturbed by ads in the *Northwestern Lutheran* that request services of a vacationing pastor. Generally the use of the parsonage is offered in exchange for preaching. The requesting congregation is usually in a popular vacation area. Isn't this tantamount to a pastor selling his services as a minister of God? Where does the doctrine of the call come in? Does the requesting congregation extend a formal call to the vacationing pastor?**

What should a congregation do when their pastor is going to be absent? They could arrange to have one of the councilmen or perhaps the principal of the school conduct a worship service. In such circumstances the worship leader often reads a sermon provided by the pastor. Most congregations, however, prefer to arrange for another pastor to substitute for their pastor in his absence. They normally do not call this person formally or directly but delegate the responsibility for obtaining a substitute to the pastor. The invitation extended by the pastor to his substitute, extended with the congregation's authorization, is, in effect, a limited call on behalf of the congregation. The guest preacher is normally paid for his services.

In the Midwest, where congregations are close together, neighboring pastors, professors from a nearby school, or seminary students are often available as substitutes. In other areas of the country where our congregations are far apart, it is not so easy to obtain a substitute. The practice of inviting a vacationing pastor as a substitute has been found to be a workable and mutually beneficial arrangement by some pastors and congregations under such circumstances.

The relationship between one who teaches the Word and those who receive it is described in Scripture as a mutually beneficial exchange. The preacher shares his spiritual knowledge with the congregation. They share material blessings with him (Galatians 6:6; 1 Corinthians 9:11). The arrangement you describe in your letter is simply one form of such a sharing and exchange. For the pastor, in addition to whatever material benefits there may be, there is the benefit of becoming acquainted with another congregation of our synod, which may be quite different from his own congregation. For the host congregation and pastor, there is the benefit of having their services continued without interruption and the secondary benefit of having the parsonage taken care of in the pastor's absence. Even if you consider the benefits offered to the visiting pastor to be wages for services rendered, there would be nothing objectionable about this arrangement since Scripture clearly states, "The worker deserves his wages" (1 Timothy 5:18). When you called your pastor, didn't you tell him what his salary would be? How is this any different?

Scripture states both the principle that the worker deserves his wages and that no one should publicly preach in the church without being called. It leaves the church much freedom as to how it will carry out these principles in particular cases.

Your Question **Does John 20:23, "If you forgive anyone his sins, they are forgiven; if you do not forgive them, they are not forgiven," apply to the church or to the priesthood of all believers? Does the ministry of the keys contradict the Fifth Petition as far as whether we should always forgive anyone who sins against us?**

Christians exercise the ministry of the keys, the power of forgiving or not forgiving sins, in two ways. Publicly, that is, in the name of a congregation, the keys are exercised by the called pastor, by other leaders, and by the assembly of the church. Privately, the keys are exercised by individual Christians in their personal dealings with other Christians. James 5:14 and 16 seem to refer respectively to the public and private assurance of forgiveness: first, by the elders of the church; second, by private individuals. The general principles and the nature of the forgiveness offered is the same in the private and public use of the keys.

The frequent statements of Scripture to the effect that we should always forgive those who wrong us do not deny the necessity of using the locking key, "If you do not forgive them, they are not forgiven." These statements refer to two different senses of forgiveness. As far as our personal attitude toward those who have wronged us, we should always have a forgiving attitude, not holding a grudge or hatred even against enemies who are not sorry they have wronged us. But if those who have wronged us are not repentant, we cannot assure them of God's forgiveness. We must apply the locking key and warn them that their impenitence is excluding them from eternal life. To the impenitent we should say, "I am not holding a grudge against you for the wrong you have done me. I am willing to forgive you. But unless you repent of the wrong you have done and confess your sin, your sin is not forgiven. It will condemn you before God's judgment." Such a statement is not an expression of an unforgiving spirit. On the contrary, it is motivated by a loving concern for the offender and by the hope that he will repent and be forgiven.

Your Question

In the summer I attend a mission congregation on weekends. Sometimes the pastor can't get a substitute, so a layman will conduct the service and read a sermon. This works well, but I get a little disturbed when the layman gets to the part of the service which reads, "As a called servant of the Word and by the command of my Lord Jesus Christ, I forgive you all your sins." Don't you think we should have an alternate reading recommended for the layman to use? Or is there no problem with this?

In the Communion service of the *Lutheran Hymnal*, the pastor announced, "By virtue of my office as a called and ordained servant of the Word . . . I forgive you." This statement was confusing to some people, since it gave the impression that only an ordained pastor can announce the forgiveness of sins authorized by Jesus when he established the ministry of the keys. The ministry of the keys, however, was given to the whole church, and any believer may assure other penitent sinners that their sins are forgiven. To prevent this misunderstanding the reference to ordination was not retained in *Christian Worship*.

But what about the reference to a "called servant of the Word"? This remains because although any believer may exercise the ministry of the keys privately, no one may exercise this ministry publicly without a call from the church to do so. A vicar, teacher, or layman who leads the service in the pastor's absence has a call from the congregation to do so. This is a very limited call, especially in the case of the lay leader, but it is a call nevertheless. They may, therefore, read this section of the liturgy without violating any doctrinal principle of Scripture.

Such a practice, however, could easily cause confusion since many people undoubtedly understand the phrase "called servant of the Word" as another name for "pastor," or at least as a reference to a full-time, fully trained servant of the Word. This confusion could be avoided by having the lay leader omit the words "called servant of the Word." A better solution, however, would be to explain to the congregation the sense in which the lay leader is a "called servant of the Word." His call is much more restricted than the pastor's. He does not have the training to assume responsibility for all of the duties of the ministry. He has, however, been asked to assist the regularly called pastor in carrying out some of the duties of the ministry in a very limited way. No one should be permitted to do this without adequate training and a call from the congregation. Although this call may be rather informal because of its limited scope, to avoid confusion it should be recorded by the voters' assembly and publicly announced in some way.

If this is carefully explained, the congregation will understand that although the lay leader is a "called servant of the Word" for the limited purpose of conducting the service in the pastor's absence, he has not been trained or called to assume the responsibilities of the pastoral ministry.

Your
Question   **A question has arisen at our church council meetings and recently at a voters' meeting. Is it proper for a called worker to use "titles" which may imply that he is doing something different than what he was called for? More specifically, is it proper for a called worker to take on duties that fall outside of his original call? In our case, this deals mainly with staff ministers, not pastors. However the question remains of how a called worker can "redefine" his call without the congregation approving such a change. It seems appropriate that the church council and voters should approve any changes and the call in question be re-issued to conform to the change in duties.**

The titles and scope of duties of a called worker are defined by the calling body, not by the worker. This does not mean that called workers cannot do things that any Christian may do, such as talking to their neighbors about Christ, even though they are not specifically called for evangelism. This limitation applies only to what they do in the name of the congregation, not to private actions not done in the name of the congregation.

As needs change, both the called worker and the congregation should be open to making adjustments to meet a different situation, for example, shifting to a different grade in the school to deal with a new enrollment situation.

We cannot comment further on a specific situation about which we have no information, but the general principle is that the scope of the call is set by the calling body. A worker who becomes aware of new needs can, of course, bring them to the attention of the congregation

Your Question **The church that I belong to is about to lose its fifth minister since about 1972. Something doesn't feel right about this. I am beginning to question that something might be wrong with our church because God keeps taking away the ministers. All of the ministers who God has called away are exceptionally good. I know most of the members are feeling just as confused as I am. I can't help but wonder if my church is not "God-pleasing" and so the Lord moves these shepherds to apply to, transfer to, or be "called" to a different church. Perhaps we, the members, should also be looking for a different church. Maybe this is God's way of warning us that our church is not a place where the grace of God can keep us. I know I plan to start trying different churches, ones where the ministers stay. Are there any "God-pleasing" WELS churches out there where the ministers stay?**

Why do you focus on the taking away of pastors instead of on God's continuous giving?

You say that for more than 25 years the Lord has always supplied your church with "exceptionally good" ministers. Why then would you conclude that there is anything wrong with your congregation or with God's care for your congregation? If God has provided your congregation with good pastors for 25 years, why does it matter if he has done it with one pastor or with five? If what you say is true, it seems to me that his grace is keeping you very well.

Five changes of pastors in 25 years is more frequent change than we would normally like to see. I recently heard of a congregation that had only five pastors in one hundred years. These two cases are probably close to the two extremes, with the average falling somewhere in between. But long or short pastorates are not in and of themselves proof that a congregation is a "good" or "bad" congregation. A pastor may leave after a short time for either good or selfish reasons. A pastor may stay for a long time for either good or selfish reasons. We cannot jump to conclusions.

Generally speaking, we would encourage pastors to stay in a call a minimum of five years, and your congregation's experience is close to that minimum. But there may be valid reasons for such exceptional cases. Therefore, it would be wrong to draw any conclusions either about the congregation or the pastor after a short pastorate.

When a pastor leaves a congregation, it is not necessarily because he is in any way unhappy with that congregation. On the contrary, a pastor and his family often leave with great sadness and with tears because of the love that has grown between them and members of the congregation. He may wish he could stay, but he has been convinced that God is calling him to serve in another place where his special gifts are urgently needed. Or he may have reached the conclusion that another man with different gifts could serve his present congregation better than he could. He may even leave with the conviction that things are going to be much more difficult for him at the place to which he is being called.

On the other hand, it may happen that a pastor leaves for selfish reasons or because of dissatisfaction with faults of the congregation, but it would be wrong to jump to such a conclusion without clear evidence for it. If there is such evidence, the congregation should seek to correct those problems with the help of the circuit pastor or district president. If there is in fact some situation that is making it difficult for pastors to work in a given congregation, this should be considered in calling a new pastor, so that a man can be called who has the gifts to work with the congregation in resolving the problem in a God-pleasing way.

I am sure that most of the congregations that had Paul as their founding pastor would have been happy to have him stay for many years, but God had a purpose in having him move on to found new congregations in other places. Though you may not always see clearly what God's purpose was for your congregation and for the pastors who served you for a short time, you can be sure that in every case he had a purpose, which would ultimately work for the good of his kingdom.

Your
Question Can a call for a pastor, a divine call, for some reason not be by God? Why I am asking is that my church recently called a new pastor, and this new pastor is really hurting our church. Our membership has dropped, no new members have come. He doesn't

make his calls on people. Most of the members are "upset" with him and his family. The list goes on and on, but I cannot say too much as to give away whom I am talking about as he reads this site too. I was just wondering if a call could ever be a bad thing. Also, if you can email me directly I would love to ask you some more personal questions about this matter that I do not feel I can post without someone figuring out whom I am speaking of. Thank you.

A call is "divine" when the church uses the authority God gives to it to call someone to be its pastor on the basis of the qualifications and duties set forth in Scripture. Such a call is always "valid," that is, both the pastor and the congregation should be faithful to the duties established by the call. Such a call may have been extended in an improper way if someone "pulled strings" or used improper influences to receive the call or to manipulate people to call a certain person. If there were such a case, the call would still be valid, but the guilty parties should recognize and repent of their improper actions.

Even when everything was done properly in extending the call, either the pastor or the congregation may be unfaithful in carrying out their responsibilities. In such a case, they should be admonished about their neglect and given the opportunity to correct what is wrong. If the pastor is neglecting his duties, the first responsibility for admonishing him is with the council and the congregation. If this is unsuccessful, the congregation can ask the circuit pastor for help in dealing with the pastor. Talking about the pastor behind his back will not do anyone any good.

In such a case there is nothing wrong with the call. The fault lies with the person who is not faithful to the duties of the call. Not everyone who receives a call faithfully carries it out, just as not every confirmed or married person is faithful to his or her vows. There is nothing wrong with the confirmation or the marriage vow in such a case—the fault is with the person who does not remain faithful.

If you feel the present pastor does not come up to the standards of the former pastor, this may be due to negligence on his part, but it may be that he is being faithful in using limited gifts that do not match the exceptional gifts of the former pastor. You need to be careful in judging whether the fact that some people have left is the fault of the pastor or of those who left. Did they leave because he was unfaithful or because he was faithfully saying things they did not want to hear? Or perhaps a combination of the two? Have you considered the possibility that the present problems are at least in part the fault of the congregation? These are some of the questions that the circuit pastor can help you address. Be careful not to jump to conclusions.

God may at times allow us to suffer trials to test and strengthen us; at others, to warn us against sin. Sometimes in hindsight we may be able to see his purpose clearly; at other times not. In every case we can be sure that in all things God will work for the good of those who love him.

Your Question Recently I have been influenced by persons of the Anglo-Catholic following. They maintain that for a ministry to be valid it must follow the "Apostolic Succession" by the special rite of the "laying on of hands" by bishops, thus conferring an "unbroken" line of ministry dating from the time of the apostles. Is there any scriptural basis for this position, and if not, where did this doctrine originate?

The idea of apostolic succession is followed by the Roman Catholic and Orthodox churches and the Episcopal Church of England (Anglican, hence Anglo-Catholic). The Roman Catholic church insists on the role of the pope over the bishops in the hierarchy. The others do not. The Evangelical Lutheran Church in America (ELCA) has agreed to reestablish apostolic succession with the help of the Episcopal Church of America and Swedish Lutherans. See also the description of Romanizing Lutherans below, according to which neither pope nor bishops are necessary, but only ordination by a ministerium of pastors.

The tendency to rely on hierarchical bishops began already in the second century of the church's history, but there is no support for it in Scripture. The "bishops" or "overseers" (*episkopoi*) in the New Testament are pastors or overseers of congregations not territorial bishops exercising authority over other pastors.

Christ has given the right to call pastors to the church, not to a hierarchy. One becomes a pastor through the call of the church, not through the laying on of hands by a bishop. Ordination and installation recognize the validity of the call. Our pastors are ordained by other pastors, but there is no need for a succession of bishops or for a certain rite of ordination. Real "apostolic succession" is to follow the doctrine of the apostles. If you want to read more about this, you might want to read the volume on church and ministry in the People's Bible Teachings series available from Northwestern Publishing House.

Your
Question In a recent answer the writer speaks of Romanizing Lutherans and a revival of their views within the Lutheran church today. What are these views and where are they showing up?

As noted above, the Roman Catholic church maintains that the ministry (priesthood) depends on apostolic succession passed on through the pope and bishops and given through ordination.

Romanizing Lutherans base the ministry on a succession of pastors back to the apostles (without the pope), and they see ordination as a means of conferring the ministry rather than as a rite confirming that the ministry has been given through the call of the church.

The term "Romanizing Lutherans" is explained by both Adolf Hoenecke and Franz Pieper in their dogmatics. Both of them supported Walther in his dispute with the Romanizing Lutherans (especially Grabau and Loehe). See Hoenecke, *Evangelical Lutheran Dogmatics* (ELD), IV, pp. 204-207,214,215; and Pieper, *Christian Dogmatics* (CD), III, pp. 447,448,454-459.

Hoenecke says, "Many Lutherans walk in the footsteps of the papists when they take away from the church the right to call and have the preacher become a preacher through ordination as a sacrament" (ELD, p. 204). He points out that another trait of Romanizing Lutherans is to interpret Augsburg Confession V as a reference to the public ministry rather than to the means of grace (ELD, p. 207).

On the same subject Pieper says:

One is inclined to judge Hoefling [who made the pastoral ministry simply a practical necessity] less severely because his opponents (Muenchmeyer, Loehe, Kliefoth, etc.) taught a strongly Romanizing doctrine of the ministry, namely, that the office of the public ministry is not conferred by the call of the congregation as the original possessor of all spiritual power, but is a divine institution in the sense that it was transmitted immediately from the Apostles to their pupils, considered as a separate "ministerial order" or caste, and that this order perpetuates itself by means of the ordination. Some also spoke as if the means of grace exerted their full power and efficacy only when they were administered by men of this "order." Against this caricature of the public ministry Hoefling correctly argues that it makes the officiant a "means of grace" alongside Word and Sacrament: "The believers might see themselves with their spiritual needs referred not so much to Word and Sacrament as rather to the organ (the minister) divinely privileged to administer and distribute them. The full efficacy of the means of grace appears dependent on an external legal institution; the Holy Ghost now operates not so much in and through the means of grace as rather through the nomistic organs of their administration." (CD, III, p. 447)

Among the frequent indicators of Romanizing tendencies in the doctrine of the ministry that Hoenecke and Pieper list are (1) taking the right to call from the congregation, (2) regarding ordination as a sacrament in the proper sense, (3) seeing the institution of the pastoral ministry in Augsburg Confession V, and (4) making the pastoral office a means of grace alongside the Word and sacraments. The most serious indicator of a Romanizing view is the idea that absolution or the means of grace are more effective or complete when given by an ordained pastor.

Though this view opposes the view Walther contended for, it has appeared in some elements of the Missouri Synod and its sister churches.

- Grabau and the Buffalo Synod, the opponents of Walther: Ordination is a part of the divine ordinance by which a person is legitimately taken into the ministry ("Third Synodical Report," p. 7).

- David Scaer, LCMS seminary professor: "I personally find it very difficult to designate as a human rite or adiaphoron any ceremony in which God is the Giver and the Holy Spirit is the recipient [sic], which can only be administered under certain stringent conditions, which carries with it a threat, which makes the acting participant in the rite responsible for the activities of the recipient of the rite, and which gives the recipient a gift which remains" (*Ordination: Divine Rite or Human Ordinance*, p. 12).

- Independent Evangelical Lutheran Church (SELK) in Germany: In ordination, the ordinand receives the gift of the Holy Spirit through the laying on of hands to equip him for ministry. This petitioned gift is effectively given, not simply prayed for (*LOGIA*, X 3, p. 23).

Your
Question I have heard that some congregation leaders are calling themselves "Reverend Father." I am curious as to why they would be doing this. I realize this question's answer is an opinion and am not strictly looking for the truth. However that would be the ultimate goal. I am, however, as a youth of this synod, looking for another more experienced perhaps more educated opinion. A reply would be wonderfully and prayerfully appreciated.

Jesus summarizes the attitude we should have toward titles in the church in Matthew 23:7-12:

> "[The Pharisees] love to be greeted in the marketplaces and to have men call them 'Rabbi.' But you are not to be called 'Rabbi,' for you have only one Master and you are all brothers. And do not call anyone on earth 'father,' for you have one Father, and he is in heaven. Nor are you to be called 'teacher,' for you have one Teacher, the Christ. The greatest among you will be your servant. For whoever exalts himself will be humbled, and whoever humbles himself will be exalted."

Jesus warns against a love for honorary titles in the church, in which all Christians are brothers and sisters. In their letters the apostles often referred to their office (Paul often introduced himself as "Paul, an apostle of Christ Jesus"), but they did not refer to themselves by honorary titles, though such titles were common in their society.

It is not the titles in themselves that are a problem, but the attitude that underlies them. Paul could call himself a father to those who came to faith through his preaching. When he spoke this way, he was expressing the bond of love between them and the zeal with which he cared for them. He was not suggesting a general title for all pastors. "Even though you have ten thousand guardians in Christ, you do not have many fathers, for in Christ Jesus I became your father through the gospel" (1 Corinthians 4:15).

Paul had a father's love and concern for the Corinthians, especially for those who were brought to faith through his ministry. Paul could refer to his apostolic authority when it was appropriate to do so, but his emphasis was on being a faithful servant of Christ who declared to them the whole will of God. Paul was concerned that his hearers would submit to God's authority not to his. Paul told the Thessalonians: "As apostles of Christ we could have been a burden to you, but we were gentle among you, like a mother caring for her little children. . . . For you know that we dealt with each of you as a father deals with his own children, encouraging, comforting and urging you to live lives worthy of God, who calls you into his kingdom and glory" (1 Thessalonians 2:6-12).

If "father" is a title lovingly and thankfully offered and humbly received, it could be good. If it is expected or demanded as evidence of rank or superiority, it would be bad. Many Lutherans feel uncomfortable with the title "Father" because of its use in hierarchical churches like the Roman Catholic church. It can easily reflect the attitude that Jesus warns us against in Matthew 23, "Do not call anyone on earth 'father,' for you have one Father, and he is in heaven."

The same could, however, also be said of the title "Reverend," which we often use in formal address. According to my dictionary, *reverend* means "worthy of or entitled to reverence, honor, respect, veneration, or adoration." Certainly the pastoral office and those who hold it should receive honor and respect, but the word *revere* often has connotations that go beyond that.

You asked for an opinion, so I will offer you mine. I do not particularly care for the titles "Reverend" or "Father" for the reasons outlined above, but I do not make a big point of telling someone not to call me that. Occasionally at the door of the church someone will call me Father, and I don't jump in and correct them. I also have worked in a church body in our fellowship in which the people do not customarily address their pastors by any title, but only by their names. I have not noticed that they have any less respect for the ministry than members do where some title is customary. So what is important is not so much the title in and of itself but the attitude that lies behind it.

All that being said, if a title is going to be used, many, or I believe most, of our pastors prefer "pastor," which simply means "shepherd." It has scriptural precedent and reminds the pastor of the attitude he should have—he is a servant under Christ the chief Shepherd. He is to care for the flock, even if it means sacrificing himself for the flock.

He is not there to be served but to serve. If he understands that and practices it, he will have the respect of God's faithful people. The specific title he has will not be that important.

When Paul faced the problem of disrespectful members in the congregation at Corinth, he addressed the problem by reminding them of the calling he had from God and that their disrespect for him and his message was disrespect for God. This is the best way for us to address this problem when it occurs in our churches today.

Your Question **In a previous answer you mentioned that Luther talked hypothetically about female pastors. What was the occasion, and what did he say on this subject?**

Your question does not cite the previous answer correctly. The answer did not refer to women serving in the pastoral office. It said that many of the functions performed by a pastor, such as a baptism, may be performed by women under certain circumstances. It also said that Luther hypothetically discussed women preaching in a congregation consisting entirely of women. Though he talked about women preaching and administering the sacraments in certain situations, he does not discuss this as a formal pastoral office, though he does refer to authorization to preach:

> You must not say, "This is a man or a woman. . . ." They are all priests. All may proclaim God's Word, except that, as Paul teaches in 1 Cor. 14:34, women should not speak in the congregation. They should let the men preach, because God commands them to be obedient to their husbands. God does not interfere with the arrangement. But he makes no distinction in the matter of authority. If, however, only women were present and no men, as in nunneries, then one of the women might be authorized to preach. ("Sermons on First Peter," *Luther's Works* [LW], 30:55)

> Therefore order, discipline, and respect demand that women keep silent when men speak; but if no man were to preach, then it would be necessary for the women to preach. For this reason we are firmly convinced on the basis of Holy Scriptures that there is not more than one office of preaching God's Word, and that this office is common to all Christians. ("Misuse of the Mass," LW, 36:152)

The second function, to baptize, they themselves [the Catholics] have by usage allowed in cases of necessity even to ordinary women, so that it is hardly regarded any more as a sacramental function. Whether they wish or not we deduce from their own logic that all Christians, and they alone, even women, are priests, without tonsure and episcopal "character." For in baptizing we proffer the life-giving Word of God, which renews souls and redeems from death and sins. To baptize is incomparably greater than to consecrate bread and wine, for it is the greatest office in the church the proclamation of the Word of God. So when women baptize, they exercise the function of priesthood legitimately, and do it not as a private act, but as a part of the public ministry of the church which belongs only to the priesthood. ("Concerning the Ministry," LW, 40:23)

Luther clearly says "ministry of the Word" is done by women. Luther's point is that Rome despised Baptism and made a false distinction when they said anyone may baptize, while at the same time reserving the rule of the Lord's Supper to their priests. We would not call baptisms performed by women "public ministry" as Luther did, since we use the term "public ministry" only in reference to people who have received a distinct public call. Luther's point in calling such a baptism "a public ministry" seems to be that the child has entered the church through the baptism performed by the woman. The church accepts this baptism performed by a woman as its own and does not rebaptize the child as it would have to do if there were something missing from the baptism performed by a woman. In the first statement he says that the authority of the Word is not less when spoken by a woman than it is when spoken by a man, but the order of creation does not permit her to exercise authority over a man by preaching in the congregation.

Your
Question **I'm a very active member and officer of a conservative LCMS congregation, and I'm interested in learning more about WELS. I strongly believe that Scripture forbids women from exercising authority within the congregation, and we do not allow women to serve on our council. My question, however, concerns lay readers. I've always questioned our practice of not allowing such readings. I've read Walther's *Church and Ministry* very carefully, and Walther's discussion (and theses) on the doctrine of the universal priesthood of believers has convinced me that lay readings of Scripture (as opposed to**

preaching) by both men and women is a vital affirmation of this doctrine which Luther championed. Even if lay reading were deemed to be authoritative teaching, it would appear to me that at the very least men (particularly elders) should read Scripture during worship services. After all, isn't this what the Reformation was all about, that the Word doesn't just belong to the clergy but to the universal priesthood? What is the position of WELS on the issue of lay readings by the universal priesthood of believers, and is this position memorialized anywhere so that I can read it?

Strictly speaking, when laypeople assist the pastor during the service or in teaching classes or making calls, this is not an exercise of the priesthood of all believers since they are acting publicly in the name of the congregation. People cannot take this work upon themselves without a call from the congregation to do so (limited and informal as that call may be). The priesthood of all believers is what we do on our own initiative as Christians, teaching our children, witnessing to our neighbors, and so on. It is possible for a person to energetically practice the priesthood of all believers without ever holding a formal office in the church. If there was no priesthood of all believers, we could not have lay readers in the service, but the priesthood of believers does not require such a practice.

Leadership of the worship service should rest in the hands of the pastor or, in his absence, of another male called by the congregation to lead. Preaching in a Christian congregation is to be authoritative teaching (Titus 2:15) and therefore should not be done by a woman. Such preaching would also conflict with the command of silence set forth in 1 Corinthians 14, where the situation that called forth this application of the principle seems to be parallel to the public preaching in our services.

Most of our congregations normally have the pastor read the Scripture lessons as part of his role of leading the worship service. We are not insistent on this, in so far as we permit even children to present portions of Scripture in special services. If we accept this practice and the presentation of musical solos by women, it would be inconsistent to claim that reading Scripture inherently and inevitably involves authoritative teaching. Nevertheless, I believe that under present conditions we should not adopt the practice of having women as lectors. From a practical point of view this practice would be a source of confusion and offense, since some churches have used and are using such roles for women as stepping stones toward the assumption of the pastoral ministry by women. Such a practice would also be doubtful from a doctrinal point of view.

The regular use of lay readers is not the practice of most of our congregations, but there is no command of Scripture or policy of the synod that forbids it. It is left up to the freedom of the congregation to determine its practice. If lay readers are used, they should be well trained and well prepared to do the readings fluently and expressively. One reason to have the pastor do the readings is that if he is preaching on the pericope texts, he has studied the texts and understands how they fit together to emphasize the theme of the Sunday, and he can make this clear either by notes in the bulletin or by brief introductory statements. There is more to "reading the lessons" than simply reading them.

Your Question **The official LCMS position is that God has instituted only one ministry *(Predigtamt)*, namely, the pastoral ministry *(Pfarramt)*. Their official Web site declares: "With respect to the doctrine of the ministry . . . our Synod has held that the office of the public ministry (the pastoral office) according to the Scriptures is the one divinely established office in the church." How do you evaluate this LCMS statement?**

Following Luther, WELS agrees that "Christ instituted one office in his church," but that one office or ministry is not simply the pastoral ministry; it is first of all "the ministry of the gospel" held in common by all Christians.

The LCMS statement creates confusion because it does not adequately recognize the twofold use of the terms *ministry* and *office* as terms that refer first to functions and then to positions occupied by persons who carry out those functions. *Predigtamt* often refers to a function: preaching the gospel. *Pfarramt* refers to a public position held by a man who preaches the gospel. Though the *Pfarramt* is a form of *Predigtamt*, the two terms cannot simply be equated as the LCMS tends to do. When the confessions and Luther talk about the one office in the church, they are talking about the one function, preaching the gospel, not about the pastoral ministry, a position held by a person in the church. Most of the confusion in the LCMS position revolves around the failure to deal with this distinction adequately. Recognizing the two senses of "office" (*Amt* and *Predigtamt*) is the key.

Luther very clearly says that in the wide sense of the term, the "ministry of the Word" (*Predigtamt*) is a right entrusted to all Christians. This includes the right to proclaim the Word, to use the sacraments, and to judge teaching. He repeatedly makes it clear that when he refers to the ministry of the Word as the one office in the church, he is not referring to the pastoral office (as some today falsely claim) but to the entrusting of the means of grace to the whole church. As the following statements clearly say, he believed this highest office is entrusted to all Christians:

These passages very strongly and clearly corroborate that the ministry of the Word is the highest office in the church, that it is unique and belongs to all who are Christians, not only by right but by command. The first office, that of the ministry of the Word, therefore, is common to all Christians. This is clear, from what I have already said, and from 1 Pet. 2:9, "You are a royal priesthood that you may declare the wonderful deeds of him who called you out of darkness into his marvelous light." I ask, who are these who are called out of darkness into marvelous light? Is it only the shorn and anointed masks? [that is, ordained Catholic priests] Is it not all Christians? And Peter not only gives them the right, but the command, to declare the wonderful deeds of God, which certainly is nothing else than to preach the Word of God. But some imagine a twofold priesthood, one spiritual and common to all, the other external and limited, and say that Peter here speaks of the spiritual one. But what is the function of this limited and external office? Is it not to declare the wonderful deeds of God? But this Peter enjoins on the spiritual and universal priesthood. In truth these blasphemers have another, external, ministry in which they declare, not the wonderful deeds of God, but their own and the pope's impious deeds. So, as there is no other proclamation in the ministry of the Word than that which is common to all, that of the wonderful deeds of God, so there is no other priesthood than that which is spiritual and universal, as Peter here defines it. (LW, 40:21-22)

Walther agreed with this position:

One can also recognize very clearly what those of old frequently understood by office of the ministry (*Predigtamt*), namely, that they often took "office of the ministry" as entirely synonymous with "Gospel." The Apology does not have Grabau's understanding according to which the office of the ministry (*Predigtamt*) is always equivalent to the office of pastor (*Pfarramt*). . . . No, when our old teachers ascribe such great things to the office of the ministry, they thereby mean nothing else than the service of the Word (*den Dienst des Wortes*) in whatever way (*Weise*) it may come to us. ("The True Visible Church," in *Essays for the Church*, Vol. 1, p. 102)

Your
Question I have been studying the differences between the WELS and the LCMS and I am confused as to the differences and the scriptural support for the understanding of the office of ministry between the two. I quote from the question and answer section of the LCMS Web site: "The doctrine of the ministry. With respect to the doctrine of the ministry, since the days of C. F. W. Walther our Synod has held that the office of the public ministry (the pastoral office) according to Scripture is the one divinely established office in the church, while the church possesses the freedom to create other offices, by human institution, from time to time to assist in the carrying out of the functions of the pastoral ministry. The WELS' *Theses on Church and Ministry*, however, expressly deny that the pastoral ministry is specifically instituted by the Lord in contrast to other forms of public ministry (see Doctrinal Statements, pp. 9-11; cf. the Commission on Theology and Church Relations' 1981 report on *The Ministry: Office, Procedures, and Nomenclature*)."

Could you please elaborate on the differences, specifically, scriptural support for or against each position? If I understand it properly, the LCMS states that the pastoral office is the only divinely established office in the church and as such is a "called" office. If this is the case, then why in *The Lutheran Witness* (official publication of the LCMS) do I read of calls extended to people in other forms of ministry? Further, doesn't Scripture tell us of different "jobs" that people are called upon to do through their gifts thus indicating that there are other divinely instituted offices within the church?

Along the same lines, I know that in the LCMS there are district presidents as part of the organizational structure of the synod. I don't seem to hear of any of these in the WELS. Is that correct and if so, why is that? Thank you for all of your help.

You have already anticipated most of the answer to your question. The reason that WELS does not limit the ministry of the Word to one form, namely, the parish pastor, is that Scripture does not. Various forms of ministry existed in the New Testament churches. There is no indication that they were derived from the office of pastor, or even that the office of pastor existed in the exact form in which we have it today. The New Testament explicitly says there are "different forms of ministry" (1 Corinthians 12:5). Numerous examples show that this is true not only of ministry in the wide sense but of public ministry of the Word as well (1 Timothy 4:13; 4:11; 3:2; 6:2; 3:5; 5:17; Ephesians 4:11; 1 Corinthians 12:28; Romans 12:6-8, etc.).

It is true that a congregation may need no other form of the ministry than one pastor to fulfill everything Christ has commanded it to do. But it is free to establish other forms, and such forms, when established, are parts or forms of the one ministry of the Word established by Christ. A congregation may have one pastor who has responsibility for everything, two pastors who divide all the duties, several pastors who specialize in different aspects of the ministry, or one or more pastors assisted by other types of called workers. The church at large can also establish other forms of ministry such as missionary or seminary professor or district president. Workers called to any of these positions are serving in the ministry of the Word established by Christ. Christ has given the church authority to call people to different forms of ministry. Those who are called to a limited or specialized form of the ministry are nevertheless a part of the ministry authorized by Christ. The ministry of the Word cannot simply be equated with the office of parish pastor, as Walther also recognized (see p. 102). The pastoral ministry is the most common and comprehensive form of the ministry, but it is not the only form.

If a person follows the so-called Missouri Synod position in a strict and consistent way, he would have to say that a district president is not serving in the ministry of the Word established by Christ but in a human office, that he is, essentially, a minister of the law not a minister of the gospel. The WELS has district presidents too, but they continue to serve congregations as parish pastors (with help from another pastor or vicar) at the same time that they serve as district presidents. We certainly could call them to serve full-time as district presidents and believe that they would still be serving in the ministry of the Word if we did. It does seem to us to be ironic and inconsistent that the LCMS insists that the pastoral ministry is the only form of the ministry established by Christ, and then it has its district presidents leave that ministry in order to serve as overseers of those pastors. It also seems inconsistent that the LCMS does not consider its school teachers to be ministers of the gospel in a doctrinal sense but does regard them as such in a legal sense when dealing with government regulations. The alleged distinction of one form of ministry instituted by Christ and other forms established by the church has no basis in Scripture.

Your Question Can a divorced person serve as an elder in a WELS church? I interpret Titus 1:5,6, which says he must be the husband of only one wife, to mean that he cannot.

In Titus 1 and 1 Timothy 3, the Scriptures set the qualification that an elder (who in the New Testament was more similar to our pastors than to our elders) must be a "one-woman man," who has a good moral reputation in the church and with outsiders. This requirement would make a man who divorced his wife for unscriptural reasons, one who committed adultery or other sexual immorality, or a polygamist ineligible to serve in such an office. The passage does not refer to a man who remarries after the death of his first wife.

A man who was the victim of an unscriptural divorce brought about by the unfaithfulness or desertion of his wife would not necessarily be disqualified by a divorce, but the need to avoid offense might make it difficult or impossible for him to continue to serve in the same congregation immediately following the divorce.

Obtaining an unscriptural divorce disqualifies a person from serving as a pastor or elder. Can a person who has become ineligible through such a sin regain eligibility through repentance? Repentance does not instantly restore eligibility. The person must reestablish a good moral reputation. Whether or not this is possible and how long it might take would depend on a number of factors, including whether the person was a Christian when the offense occurred, whether the person was already in a position of trust when the offense occurred, and the notoriety of the offense.

Your Question If an elder is living with a woman and is not married to her, how does the Wisconsin Synod view this?

I assume that by an elder "living with a woman" you mean in such a way that people are concluding that there is a sexual relationship between them without marriage, and that this is not a case of a brother and sister living in the same house or of people living in a boarding house, etc. If a person is living in a sexual relationship outside of marriage and if he is impenitent and continues in such a relationship, the church must discipline him. Such a person obviously should not serve as an elder, since an elder must be a good Christian example, who has a good reputation in the church and in the community. See 1 Timothy 3:1-12 and Titus 1:6-9 for a listing of the scriptural qualifications for a person serving in such an office.

It is important that individuals or the church not act on the basis of rumors in such situations. Those who observe or hear about such conduct should speak directly to the person involved. If the person is indeed living in a sexual relationship outside of marriage and he refuses to repent, the matter must be reported to the church. If a person persists in sinful conduct, he must ultimately be excommunicated. There must be clear evidence of guilt for a person to be excommunicated. Lack of a good reputation, however, is sufficient reason that a man should not serve as an elder. A man whose conduct is causing offense or raising doubts should not serve as an elder.

4
The Sacraments

God has given the church two rites that share three characteristics: (1) they are given to the New Testament church by divine command; (2) they are for the forgiveness of sins; and (3) they have a visible, earthly element. Only Baptism and the Lord's Supper share these three traits. By tradition we call these two acts sacraments. The name "sacrament" is not divinely mandated, but we cannot make human rites equal to Baptism or the Lord's Supper. Particularly because of the views of other churches on this issue, we receive many questions about the sacraments.

Your
Question **Dear WELS, I am a Christian who is continuing to grow in my walk with the Lord. I have been looking for a church that I can worship in and partake in. My entire family is Catholic and my new faith in Christ is something that I only give God the glory for, I don't deserve it. But my family and friends are dead in their own sins and don't understand this power and understanding that the Holy Spirit has done in my life. I am very interested in the WELS church but as I continue to read and study Scripture and talk with my Christian friends who are not WELS members, they are set in their ways, and it seems we just get in a stalemate about such topics as infant Baptism, rapture, Communion, fellowship. Your Q and A pastors do a good job in answering all these question but sometimes are just sufficient in your answers instead of complete. For example, infant Communion, your answer to this question "Does the Scripture prohibit infants from communing?" It does not directly address the issue, but it just talks about preparation for the Lord's Supper. We have no evidence infants are capable of this preparation. Could you have gone further in answering this and showing biblical proof for your answer, or is it you don't know the answer so you are just silent? So WELS has no scriptural evidence that infants are capable of this preparation on**

Communion but children can have faith. So if you ask an infant (from *Christian Worship: Occasional Services*) "Do you reject the devil along with all his lies and empty promises?" this infant is not going to answer yes; it can't even speak. But by Scripture we don't know if they can understand. We just go by Scripture that says infants can have faith. Fair enough. But aren't the parents acting as witnesses for this child. WELS says, Well, how do we know if that child can or cannot answer that question, Scripture doesn't tell us so we baptize our children because of Mark 10:13-16, Matthew 28:19,20, etc., but don't allow infants to take part in Communion. To me as I read WELS statement, you are saying that infants can have faith because Scripture says so but can't understand the true understanding that Christ is in the "bread" and "wine" and therefore can't partake in Communion until they can speak their confession. The WELS understands that Communion and Baptism are sacraments but infants can only take part in one of them and only when they can confess their knowledge of Christ's true presence in Communion can they take part in it. Isn't this allowing infant Baptism because "all nations" (Matthew 28:19) includes infants but not allowing infants to take part in Communion a problem? WELS says they both are a sacrament but infants can only take part in one of these sacraments. Please answer this question to the fullest possible way and please don't tell me, here read this book and it will tell you about it. I want to thank you for listening and I hope you can answer this question. I have this question on my mind and until I get my beliefs in order and grow and understand these beliefs, I cannot be a member of WELS. God bless you and please pray that God gives me wisdom and understanding in topics like this.

Many of the questions that are addressed to our Web page have been answered in books of hundreds of pages and even then the answers could not be considered complete. We can't offer complete answers or anything close to that on this site (or in this book). The answers on this site are the kinds that a pastor would offer to questions that arise in a Bible class. For more complete answers, a person must study lengthy books or study in a class or an entire course on the subject and, most of all, regularly read the Scripture from cover to cover. There is no shortcut or way around this. We regularly give references to further resources, because it is impossible for this site (or this book) to serve as a substitute for in-depth Bible classes and personal study.

In the case of your question, this is not a problem since you have already given the complete answer in your question.

Why do we baptize babies? Scripture says we are to baptize all nations, Baptism is for sinners, and Baptism is for those who can believe. Children, even infants, meet all three qualifications. Scripture very clearly says that they are guilty of sin and they can believe. It says nothing about a need for them to examine themselves. There is no valid objection to their being baptized.

Scripture says the Lord's Supper is for those who recognize the Lord's body and blood in the Sacrament and who can examine themselves. There is no evidence in our experience and no statement in Scripture that infants can do either, so we don't commune them until they are able to examine themselves. There is no other statement about this in Scripture, either negative or positive, so there is nothing more that can be said to make the answer more complete.

Since there is nothing in Scripture that specifies the age at which a child can do these things, we do not dogmatically set an age for first communion but have agreed on a common practice.

Baptism

Your Question **Your former Q&A on baptism and immersion were good, but I felt I needed a little more explanation. I understand and believe that we were not commanded to immerse vs sprinkle or pour and therefore it is permissible to do any of those ways. While on a visit to family members in the Bible Belt (Southern Baptists thru and thru) they asked about other things regarding other Lutherans and the "Catholic" affiliation. I replied to their questions and additionally stated that basically the WELS Lutherans believe in the inerrant word of God—if it is in the Bible, we believe it; if it's not, we don't. To which they replied, "The Bible says that Jesus came UP OUT OF the water" after his baptism and every other baptism, so if we believe in the inerrant word of God, how come we don't believe in immersion? The reply of what was commanded vs not commanded did not satisfy them. Do you have any other biblically based suggestions? Does the Greek really say "UP OUT OF" and can that only mean "after immersion"? I understand that the focus is on the water with the word, but I cannot get their focus off of "UP OUT OF" the water. In other words, how could I have been a better witness?**

Mark 1:10 says the Spirit came on Jesus "as Jesus was coming up out of [from, Greek *ek*] the water." Matthew 3:16 says "as Jesus was baptized, he went up out of [away from, Greek *apo*] the water." Acts 8:38,39 uses the same expression as Mark 1 when it says that both Philip, who was doing the baptizing, and the eunuch, who was being baptized, went down into the water and came up out from the water. Unless someone claims that Philip immersed himself, it is clear that the expression refers to entering and leaving the river or pool, not to the method of Baptism, since both parties went down into the water and came out of it. As Jesus was climbing out of the stream, the Spirit came upon him.

You were correct in stressing that even if Jesus was immersed (for which there is no evidence one way or the other), it is not commanded that we immerse. The Greek word for *baptism* is not restricted to immersion.

You gave a clear testimony. One does not have to be able to answer every question to explain what they believe. If there is something you do not know or cannot answer, you can always search the Scriptures further, as you are doing.

Your Question **In the Large Catechism why does Luther describe Baptism as submersion in the water when we believe that sprinkling constitutes a valid baptism? (*Book of Concord*, Tappert, p. 444, *Triglotta*, p. 749)**

Luther expressed the opinion that baptizing by immersion would provide a better symbol of "drowning the Old Man" and of a new man coming forth to a new life than would baptizing by pouring or sprinkling water, but he also stated that immersion was not necessary for a valid baptism (see Plass, *What Luther Says*, p. 58). Luther often referred to baptism by pouring, and his Order of Baptism prepared in 1523 specified baptism by pouring.

The Lutheran church chose not to follow Luther's preference for immersion, and he himself seems to have become less committed to the idea later in his life. It is likely that two factors prevented the Lutheran church from adopting baptism by immersion. The force of tradition favored the retention of baptism by pouring, and the demands of some sects that baptism *must* be by immersion prompted the Lutherans to retain baptism by pouring as a testimony against this false demand.

At any rate, there is abundant evidence that Luther never believed Baptism must be done by immersion in order to be valid. Luther's views on immersion are discussed at length in Krauth, *The Conservative Lutheran Reformation and Its Theology*, pp. 519-544.

Please speak about the current practice of reaffirmation of a baptism. We were taught that one baptism is sufficient. Why the second application of water and the Word?

Because Baptism is the sacrament of rebirth, it is done only once. If a person has been validly baptized, there should be no second application of the water of Baptism. Because Baptism is God's promise to us, not our promise to God, the church should not do anything that gives the impression that any subsequent action of ours can make a baptism more valid than it already is.

If a child has been baptized at the hospital, no further rite is necessary. If the family and congregation choose to have a prayer in the service, asking God's continued blessing on the child and recognizing that the child has been received as a member of the congregation, and if they wish to state publicly their commitment to teaching the child the faith, there is nothing wrong with this. To call this "reaffirmation of baptism" is not desirable, however, because it can easily give the impression that the baptism was a promise we made that we are now repeating. Any ceremony performed in the Sunday service to recognize a baptism performed outside of church should focus attention primarily on what God did in the baptism, not on the actions of sponsors or witnesses. Our new baptismal rite is designed to emphasize the action of God in Baptism. Any secondary ceremonies should be designed to do the same.

If a person is baptized a second time because it is doubtful that their first baptism was a real trinitarian baptism, this is not a reaffirmation but a first baptism, since the previous baptism was not valid.

Why has the renunciation of the devil and all his works been eliminated from the baptismal rite in *Christian Worship* (p. 12)? I believe that renunciation of the devil acknowledges the great change God works in us through Baptism, and thus it is a good preparation for the administration of Baptism (if time permits).

The baptismal rite in *Christian Worship* was written primarily for use within the regular liturgical service of the congregation. One reason that some elements from the old rite were omitted was to keep the order brief. The service book that supplements *Christian Worship* has fuller baptismal rites for special baptismal services.

In the baptism of infants, the custom of addressing questions to the infant's sponsors *before* the baptism was confusing to some. People often thought this required the infant to make a promise to God before the baptism. In the new order, no questions are addressed to the infant. Instead, the emphasis is properly placed on the promise God is giving to the infant in Baptism. Deliverance from the devil is specifically mentioned as a benefit God gives in Baptism (p. 13). The new order focuses our attention on God's promise and power, rather than on a confession made in the name of the child by sponsors. Some questions are addressed to adults who have come to be baptized since they are able to answer for themselves on the basis of the instruction they have received in God's Word. In the case of infants, however, the new rite properly emphasizes that they are brought to God bringing nothing, so that they may be recipients of his grace.

Your Question Is there any hope of salvation for a child who has not been baptized?

Scripture does not answer this question directly. Our answer must be limited to pondering four points that Scripture does make.

All children are by nature sinful and in need of salvation. "Surely I was sinful at birth, sinful from the time my mother conceived me" (Psalm 51:5). "Like the rest, we were by nature objects of wrath" (Ephesians 2:3). We cannot assume that unborn children are innocent and, therefore, automatically saved.

We are told of no other way that God works saving faith in people other than through the means of grace, the gospel in Word and sacraments. We should never deprive children of Baptism, "the washing of rebirth and renewal by the Holy Spirit" (Titus 3:5).

We know of one extraordinary case in which the Holy Spirit worked in a child before his birth—the case of John the Baptist (Luke 1:41-44).

We are told again and again that God is a compassionate God, whose judgments are fair. "The LORD is compassionate and gracious, slow to anger, abounding in love. . . . He does not treat us as our sins deserve or repay us according to our iniquities. For as high as the heavens are above the earth, so great is his love for those who fear him" (Psalm 103:8-11).

Putting it all together, we see that we can in no way minimize the seriousness of depriving an unborn child of its opportunity to be baptized through parental neglect or abortion. The only hope we can hold out in such cases is the mercy of God and the hope that although God has limited us to Baptism as a means of working faith in children, he has not limited himself. Luther wrote, "God can, to be sure, save without baptism, as we believe that the little children who at times because of an oversight of the parents or some other chance did not receive baptism are not damned on that account. However, in the church we are to teach and judge according to the ordained order of God, namely, that without the rite of baptism no one can be saved." (A summary of Luther's thoughts on this matter can be found in Plass, *What Luther Says*, pp. 49,50.)

Often, in the comfort that he gave in connection with the death of an unbaptized child, Luther pointed to the prayers of faithful parents who had entrusted their child to God as one basis of his hope for the child. A child may also hear the Word even before birth as John did. We do not understand what is going on in an infant's mind.

Finally, when we have said everything we can on the basis of Scripture to offer both warning and hope, we must become silent and confess as Paul does in Romans 11:33-36, "Oh, the depth of the riches of the wisdom and knowledge of God! How unsearchable his judgments, and his paths beyond tracing out! 'Who has known the mind of the Lord? Or who has been his counselor?' . . . For from him and through him and to him are all things. To him be the glory forever! Amen."

Your Question Is there any hope of salvation for a child who has been killed through abortion?

See the points made in the previous answer. Here I will comment only on a few factors applicable especially to the case of abortion.

Often, in the comfort that he gave in connection with the death of an unbaptized child, Luther pointed to the prayers of faithful parents who had entrusted their child to God as one basis of his hope for the child. In cases of abortion, very often there will have been no such prayers. To those who are contemplating abortion and to society in general, we must speak the strongest possible warnings of God's law against the horrible sin of placing an obstacle between a child and the Savior (Matthew 18:5,6). Those contemplating abortion should realize that they are not only depriving the child of life on this earth, but are also depriving it of its opportunity to be baptized and to hear the gospel. This multiplies the dreadfulness of this sin.

To those who grieve because of the deaths of such children, such as perhaps the grandparents, we can offer the hope of the grace and mercy of God, as Luther did in the statements referred to above.

To those who grieve because they have committed this sin of abortion, we can offer the gospel assurance that this sin too was paid for by Christ and will be forgiven for those who repent. This in no way minimizes the seriousness of the sin. It emphasizes the greatness of Christ's merit and his mercy.

Finally, we say again, we must become silent and confess as Paul does in Romans 11:33-36, "Oh, the depth of the riches of the wisdom and knowledge of God! How unsearchable his judgments, and his paths beyond tracing out! 'Who has known the mind of the Lord? Or who has been his counselor?' . . . For from him and through him and to him are all things. To him be the glory forever! Amen."

Your
Question **I have always understood if you are not baptized, you are not saved. My husband was raised Baptist but was never baptized. Does this mean he is not in heaven?**

It is strange that your husband was never baptized if he was an active Baptist. Baptists baptize, but they wait till a later age.

Jesus says, "Whoever believes and is baptized will be saved" (Mark 16:16). This emphasizes the importance of Baptism as a means of grace through which God creates faith. We should never neglect or despise it or deprive our children of it.

Jesus does not say, "Whoever is not baptized will be damned." He says, "Whoever does not believe will be condemned." God can create saving faith in persons through Baptism or through his Word. If God has created saving faith in an unbaptized person through his Word, the person will be saved even if unbaptized. We should, however, remind them not to neglect God's command concerning Baptism.

Your Question **What is the connection between Baptism and salvation? My pastor says you must be baptized to be saved. This contradicts the Bible—that you are saved by grace not by anything you do.**

Baptism is not absolutely necessary for salvation. A person can be saved by faith without being baptized, if faith has been created in them by the Word. No one, however, should despise or neglect Baptism. Baptism is "necessary" in the sense that we should obey God's command so that we receive the benefits of Baptism. No one should say, "I have faith. I don't need to be baptized."

Scripture very directly says that we are saved by Baptism: "This water [of the Flood] symbolizes baptism that now saves you" (1 Peter 3:21). This in no way contradicts the truth that salvation is by grace alone, because Baptism is not something we do. It is something that God does to us. It is not our promise to God, but his promise to us.

Your Question **In a previous answer you said that Baptism is not something we do. It is something that God does to us. It is not our promise to God, but his promise to us. Therefore, do you think it is possible for one to baptize oneself? Thank you for your help with this question.**

Scripture does not explicitly address the issue, but since Baptism is something we receive, we teach that a person should not baptize himself. He should be baptized by another Christian. We have no example of anyone baptizing himself, not even Jesus.

Your Question **Is Baptism a replacement of the circumcision of the Old Testament? If so, how was an infant girl brought to faith during Old Testament times?**

Colossians 2:11,12 draws a parallel between circumcision and Baptism. We also know that circumcision was a seal of faith and an entry into a covenant relationship with God, just as Baptism is (Romans 4:11). Beyond this, Scripture does not answer the question of whether circumcision and Baptism are parallel in all respects. Christ's command to baptize is not connected to circumcision with the same directness that the institution of the Lord's Supper is connected to the Passover.

As a preceding question indicates, a person who has faith can be saved without Baptism. God created saving faith in the children of Israel, male and female, through his promises of the Savior. We can also assume that the daily sacrifices for sin, which were offered each day in the temple for the sins of the nation, applied to the children as well as to the adults.

We know that we are no longer required to practice circumcision, the Passover, or the sacrifices. We are to use Baptism and the Lord's Supper. That is really all we need to know.

Your Question **In Acts 10:44-48 Peter is amazed that the Gentiles have received the Holy Spirit. He then says nothing prevents them from being baptized. Why did he baptize them if they had already received the Spirit?**

The giving of the special gifts of the Holy Spirit was a sign that the Gentiles were accepted by God and should be included in the church. Some of the Jewish Christians did not want to accept the Gentiles unless they were circumcised. This sign from God showed them that they were wrong. At other times the special gift of the Holy Spirit followed Baptism, as it did in Acts 8 when the gospel came to the Samaritans. The "gift of the Holy Spirit" here does not refer the gift of faith, which comes through Baptism or the Word, but to the special gifts such as speaking in tongues, which were present in the New Testament church.

Your Question **In Matthew 3:11 John says that he baptizes with water, but Jesus will baptize with the Holy Spirit and with fire. What is the difference between baptism with water and with fire?**

John's main point is that he was the forerunner of the New Testament era. Christ would initiate it in its fullness. John's baptism was a real means of grace, but it still pointed ahead to Christ's work. The New Testament era was fully inaugurated at Pentecost when Jesus baptized his disciples with the Holy Spirit and with power. After that, Jesus' disciples went throughout the world, baptizing in the name of the Father, Son, and Holy Spirit. The main emphasis here is not the difference of the nature of the two baptisms, but the difference of the mission and authority of the two messengers.

116

Your
Question **Many passages speak of repenting and being baptized. How can infants repent and be baptized if they don't know they need a Savior?**

Why do we believe infants can have faith, since they don't seem to have the powers of reason? Very simply, because Scripture speaks of the faith of infants and little children and even holds it up as an example to us (Luke 18:15-17; Psalm 8:2).

Since Baptism is a washing of rebirth and renewal (Titus 3:5), it works as a means of grace, which begins faith in an infant who does not yet have it. Adults can respond to the Word, so we instruct them before we baptize them. For them, Baptism is a seal of the faith they already have. Compare Romans 4:11.

Your
Question **Can an unconscious person be baptized, since Baptism works as a means of grace for babies, seemingly without their consent or awareness? I am thinking of a case in which an unbaptized teenager who was attending church and instruction class fell into a coma as a result of an accident. His parents asked that he be baptized before he died.**

We normally do not baptize adults without a confession of faith on their part. We would not baptize a comatose person who had despised the ministry of the Word. In this case, the young man's regular church attendance and participation in membership class is evidence of faith. This is especially the case if Baptism had already been discussed in the class and the individual was planning to be baptized.

Baptism does indeed work as a means of grace, which depends only on the power of God's Word, not on any power in the recipient. We do not have any assurance, however, from Scripture concerning the baptism of an unconscious adult, but neither do we have a clear statement that Baptism has no power in such cases. For this reason, I would not refuse Baptism in such a case if it was requested for someone who had previously accepted the ministry of the Word.

If I performed such a baptism, it would be with the hope the person was still hearing me, just as we read and pray with those who appear to be comatose. We know such people sometimes hear. If the parents asked me to baptize their son in such a case, I would tell them that it was not our normal practice and that we could base our hope for their son on his willing hearing of God's Word. However, if they very much wanted the baptism, I would not refuse it.

There are reasonable arguments against such a baptism, but there does not appear to be a clear command against it either. Roman Catholicism with its belief that a sacrament works simply because it is performed by a priest has no problem with such baptisms and performs them frequently.

Since this is a doubtful matter, I wouldn't pass judgment on a pastor whether he did or did not baptize a person in such a case. In my funeral sermon following such a case, I would emphasize the person's willing hearing of the Word before the accident.

Your
Question I have concerns and questions about the baptizing of infants whose parents are not members of any church. A number of such baptisms have occurred in my WELS church. Members have questioned the pastor about why he performs these baptisms. The pastor says that he baptizes these infants because the Bible directs us to baptize. I agree that the infants should be baptized. However, I have concerns about the parents. The pastor said he asks the parents if they would like to become members of the church and that a number of them said that they want their child to be baptized but are not interested in attending church. Why would parents want to baptize their child, but not attend church? It appears that perhaps the parents do not have an understanding of the true nature of Baptism.

The reason parents might act this way might be one of many—traditionalism, family pressure, a presentation of the baby to their friends. Whatever it may be, at least it presents a spiritual opportunity for the child.

We would not deprive children of Baptism because of the negligence or indifference of their parents. It is necessary to stress to the parents that Baptism must be followed with instruction. If the parents are not willing to take responsibility for this, the congregation will. I would tell the parents that we intend to invite the child to Sunday school and confirmation class. A member of the congregation, such as the child's Sunday school teacher or neighbor or a relative, could serve as a sponsor for the child who assumes responsibility for the child's spiritual welfare. I would not ask the parents to make a promise that they have no intention of keeping but would instruct them concerning their duty as parents. Our willingness to care for the child does not excuse their negligence or their indifference to their own spiritual needs, but we will do what we can for the child and continue to reach out to the parents.

The Lord's Supper
What It Is

Your Question Is the celebration of the Lord's Supper just that— a CELEBRATION—as when it is celebrated at an Easter sunrise service, or is it to be viewed more as a penitential sacrament? I've always thought of it in a more serious, reverential tone, but am sensing a shift in approach. Or was my upbringing one-sided?

The most important message of the Lord's Supper to those who receive it is the same as the chief message of every service: "Your sins are forgiven because Christ died for you." Since the Lord's Supper is a proclamation of the gospel, joy is the predominate response that it calls forth in those who receive it. Many of the Lutheran Communion hymns reflect this joyful tone by speaking of the Lord's Supper as a feast or banquet.

There are two reasons, however, why a reverent tone is nevertheless in place during a Communion service. The proclamation of forgiveness presupposes true sorrow and repentance for our sins. Several Communion hymns emphasize this in their opening stanzas (see *The Lutheran Hymnal* [TLH] 315:2-4 and CW 310). Such hymns often shift to a more joyful tone in their closing stanzas. Such hymns provide us with a useful pattern for the Communion liturgy as a whole. A serious reflection on our sins is not so much a part of the celebration of the Lord's Supper per se but is preliminary to it. We begin with a more solemn, penitential tone during the confession of sins and other elements of the service that prepare us for the reception of the Lord's Supper. In the Lord's Supper itself, the joy of forgiveness predominates.

Still, a reverent, serious demeanor is in place throughout the celebration of the Lord's Supper. This is true because in the Lord's Supper we receive not only the "bare word," but the very body and blood of Christ, which was given and shed for us on the cross. Many Communion hymns speak of the awe, wonder, and reverence this mystery should create in us. (TLH 304:1 is a very strong example of this: "An awe-full mystery is here To challenge faith and waken fear.") The scriptural warning against failing to recognize the presence of Christ's body and so receiving this Supper to our condemnation also points us in the direction of a reverent, respectful attitude and demeanor during the celebration of the Lord's Supper. Casual and frivolous attitudes and actions are out of place.

The balance between these aspects of the celebration of the Lord's Supper is expressed well in the Maundy Thursday hymn "The Death of Jesus Christ, Our Lord" (TLH 163, CW 135).

1 The death of Jesus Christ, our Lord,
 We celebrate with one accord;
 It is our comfort in distress,
 Our heart's sweet joy and happiness.

4 His Word proclaims and we believe
 That in this supper we receive
 His very body, as he said,
 His very blood for sinners shed.

8 They who his Word do not believe
 This food unworthily receive,
 Salvation here will never find—
 May we this warning keep in mind! (CW 135:1,4,8)

Your Question **Why does the pastor speak of forgiveness of sins in the Lord's Supper if we already have forgiveness in the gospel and in confession and absolution? Does the Lord's Supper give us extra, more powerful forgiveness?**

The host of a well-known children's program used to sing, "There are many ways to say 'I love you.' There are many ways to say 'I care.'" The love of a husband and wife, which they feel all the time, can be expressed in many different ways—by saying, "I love you," by wedding vows, by a ring, by a hug or kiss, by a gift, and by helpful acts. We like to be reminded of the love that is there all the time by all of these different expressions of that love.

In the same way, God expresses his forgiving love to us in many ways. He already said it all at our baptisms when he made us members of his family and promised us forgiveness through Christ. But he constantly reassures us of that same love in the reading or hearing of the gospel, in private or public confession and absolution, and in the Lord's Supper.

For a person who has faith in Christ, God's grace is not a commodity that he distributes to us a bit at a time only whenever we ask for it. For a Christian, receiving forgiveness of sins is not like taking a shower once a week and getting rid of a week's accumulation of dirt. It is like standing out in a gentle rain that is constantly washing us clean. For those who have faith, God's forgiving grace is an attitude he has toward us all of the time. It is a condition in which we stand (Romans 5:1,2).

Because of our need for assurance, God declares this forgiveness to us in many ways. The forgiveness we receive through the confession of sins at the beginning of the service, through the gospel message found in the readings and sermon, and through the Lord's Supper is essentially the same. What is special about the Lord's Supper is the unique way we are assured of that forgiveness—each one of us individually receives the very body and blood of Christ, given and shed to obtain our forgiveness. What more powerful declaration of forgiveness could there possibly be?

God has many ways to say, "I love you; I forgive you." For our assurance and peace of mind, he wants us to use them all. The Lord's Supper has a special place among them.

Your Question

Hello, I was Lutheran when I was a teenager, but have fallen away and am attending a Catholic church now. One thing I never understood about WELS and LCMS is why you require one hundred percent agreement on all matters of doctrine before members of different churches can commune together or even pray together. I could understand requiring a general agreement on Christ being the Savior and the doctrine of the Trinity and the presence of Christ in the Eucharist, but requiring agreement on ALL points of doctrine does not make sense. Roman Catholics, Lutherans, Episcopalians, and Reformed all believe in the "Real Presence" in the Eucharist but define that term in different ways. Why is it not correct to say that the Bible says the bread we break is a *koinonia* of the body of Christ and the cup we share is a *koinonia* of the blood of Christ and the different doctrinal formulations churches use to explain that are different theories and we can all just agree to disagree about which formulation is correct?

What people mean by a statement depends upon how they define their terms. If *koinonia* and "real presence" mean different things to different people, they will have a very different understanding of the Lord's Supper. Why is it essential that people have the same understanding of the Lord's Supper if they are to attend the Lord's Supper together? The first reason is that Scripture warns us that those who use the Lord's Supper in an improper, unworthy way receive judgment rather than blessing through their misuse of the Sacrament.

The Roman Catholic church believes that the communicants receive Christ's true body and blood, but they believe that the mass is a sacrifice or "re-presentation" of Christ's sacrifice. In the mass the work of paying for sin is still being done. Masses can even benefit the dead. This teaching denies the once-and-for-all nature of Christ's sacrifice. It makes our forgiveness of sins an incomplete thing, which still needs to be supplemented by further acts of ours. The Catholic concept that the priest receives the power to change the bread and wine into Christ's body and blood through his ordination also introduces a false concept of the ministry into the church.

The Reformed believe that Christ is "really present" to believers during the Sacrament, but they do not believe that his body and blood are really received along with the bread and wine by all who receive the elements. Thus they are in danger of the very thing Paul warns against in 1 Corinthians 11—eating and drinking to their own judgment because they do not recognize the presence of Christ's body and blood.

The view you advocate in your question is similar to the view of the Episcopal church, which accepts a wide range of doctrines of the Lord's Supper. Your view would be rejected by all Catholics who are true to their church's teaching. The position of the Catholic church is that acceptance of all of the church's teaching is necessary. The previous two paragraphs have already shown what is wrong with the Episcopal practice of allowing Lutheran, Catholic, and Reformed views of the Lord's Supper to stand side by side—this practice exposes communicants to the danger of receiving the Sacrament to their own judgment.

The Lord's Supper provides an excellent example of why it is necessary to agree in all doctrines. Every departure from the doctrine of Scripture exposes people to spiritual danger, whether to a greater or lesser degree. This is certainly true in the doctrine of the Lord's Supper.

Your Question In Holy Communion, what does the term, "in, with, and under" mean? I know Lutherans have been labeled as calling their Communion, "consubstantiation." I know this is wrong. Also, is it proper to call a Lutheran Communion a "Eucharist"?

The formula "in, with, and under" is a way of confessing our belief in the real presence of Christ's body and blood in the Lord's Supper, but at the same time confessing that we cannot explain the miracle of how they are there. We believe it because Christ has told us it is there.

"In" confesses that the body and blood are not simply received spiritually by faith, but they are united with the bread and wine in sacramental union.

"With" confesses that the bread and wine are still there. They have not been changed by transubstantiation.

"Under" says that we see, smell, and taste only the bread and wine. The body and blood are, so to speak, hidden behind the bread and wine.

Consubstantiation could be understood correctly since it means Christ's body and blood are *with* the *substance* of the bread and wine, but we do not use the term because opponents of the Lutheran view use it to imply that the union of the body and blood and bread and wine is a physical mixture like raisin bread or a mixed drink.

Eucharist is from a Greek word that refers to the blessing of thanksgiving that consecrates the Lord's Supper, so there is nothing inherently wrong with the name. We do not usually use it as the main name for the Lord's Supper because it focuses on our thanksgiving rather than on Christ's body and blood as the term *Communion* does. The most important element of the Lord's Supper is not what we do, but what God gives us.

Your Question Calvin in his definition of a sacrament writes that "it is an external sign, by which the Lord seals on our consciences his promises of goodwill toward us, in order to sustain the weakness of our faith, and we in turn testify our piety towards him, both before himself, and before angels as well as men. . . . We conclude, therefore, that the sacraments are truly termed evidences of divine grace, and, as it were, seals of the goodwill which he entertains towards us" (*Institutes* II, XIV, 1,9). Does the WELS disagree with this definition?

Calvin's definitions of the sacraments often do not sound too bad unless one is aware of the fuller explanations that lie behind them. They often sound quite Lutheran until one sees his full comments or qualifications. Phrases like "evidences of divine grace" and "seals of goodwill" are intended to say less than the Lutheran term "means of grace." Also, the role of the sacraments as a testimony of our piety is secondary to their role as a testimony to us of God's grace. Calvin at times seems to make the two functions nearly equal. We could understand what Calvin says in this statement as correct statements about the sacraments. It is other points that Calvin does not assert (such as the reception of Christ's body by the unworthy) or that he explicitly denies which reveal the difference between the Lutheran and Calvinist views of the sacraments.

Your
Question **My friend goes to an ELCA church. He told me that they believe that the bread and wine only represent Christ's body and blood. Also he said that for the ones who wish to not drink from the chalice they offer the bread only for them. Is this what ELCA really teaches about Communion?**

The ELCA has a paper subscription to the Lutheran Confessions, so they officially believe that with the bread and wine we receive Christ's true body and blood. But they also officially endorse joint Communion with Reformed groups that do not believe in the real presence of Christ's body and blood. No one who believed seriously in the real presence of Christ's body and blood in the Sacrament could endorse or engage in such a practice.

Your friend's confusion is understandable. Already many years ago an LCA (now ELCA) member told me that it was very narrow-minded of me not to let him attend Communion in my church since he believed that the bread and wine represent Christ's body and blood the way all Lutherans do. LCA congregations in the area were practicing union communions with the Reformed. Sometimes people's actions speak louder than their words. The ELCA's words say that they believe in the real presence. Their actions often say otherwise. It is understandable if some of their members are confused.

Perhaps the confusion is in some cases deliberate. I saw an ELCA bulletin which announced that they believed Christ is really present when we celebrate the Lord's Supper. Is this a confession of the

Lutheran belief? Some unsuspecting person might think so when he hears the words "really present." But notice that there is no mention of Christ's body and blood being present. The Reformed too believe Christ is really present when we celebrate the Sacrament, but they believe that it is a spiritual presence only and only for the faithful. This bulletin statement is at best confusing or inadequate, at worst deceptive.

The Officiants

Your Question **Who is permitted to serve Holy Communion when the pastor is not present? I have observed teachers or elders serving the pastor or vicars serving the congregation.**

In discussing this, we will distinguish between assisting the pastor with the distribution and administering the Sacrament in the pastor's absence. It is quite common in our congregations for elders or male teachers to assist the pastor in the distribution to the members or to give Communion to the pastor, if they are properly instructed and called by the congregation to do so.

Vicars and seminarians who have received sufficient training may administer the Sacrament in the absence of the supervising pastor, if the congregation has approved of this practice.

Although complete seminary training and ordination are not an absolute prerequisite for administering the Sacrament (to be "rightly called" is a requirement), under normal circumstances it should not be necessary to ask a layman to administer Communion in the absence of the pastor. If the pastor's absence is extended, the congregation should be served by a vacancy pastor. If the pastor's absence is brief, a "reading service" in which the pastor is responsible for the contents can be held during his absence. Except in cases of extreme necessity, preaching and the administering of the sacraments should be conducted only by men who have been both thoroughly trained and properly called. Another reason why delegating the administration of the Lord's Supper to someone other than the pastor is not advisable is that the responsibility for admitting someone to Communion or denying him Communion is not a responsibility lightly delegated.

This subject is discussed in more detail in Volume 3 of *Our Great Heritage*, a set of doctrinal essays available from Northwestern

Publishing House, which is recommended for laypeople who want to undertake a more thorough study of Christian doctrine.

Your Question **Is it appropriate for the principal to serve Holy Communion when the pastor is not present? If elders or the principal conduct services while the pastor is gone, isn't this downgrading the Lord's Supper to a fellowship meal? Is it proper for anyone other than ordained clergy to give absolution?**

Most of the points in this question are addressed in the answer to the preceding question. A couple of new points are addressed in what follows.

The reality of the Sacrament does not depend on the character of the officiant, but on whether Christ's institution has been followed. Celebration of the Sacrament by a layperson would not eliminate the real presence of Christ's body and blood or downgrade the Sacrament to a fellowship meal. The issue here is one of order and propriety. The reality of the Sacrament is not in question.

Any Christian may hear the confession of another Christian and assure the repentant of forgiveness (James 5:16; Matthew 18:18-20). The reality of absolution does not depend on ordination. But to give public absolution *in the name of the congregation,* a person must be rightly called.

Your Question **Would sacraments performed by a woman pastor or priest be valid?**

Yes, the validity (that is, the reality) of a sacrament does not depend on the character of the officiant but on Christ's institution. If Christ's institution is followed, it is a real sacrament even if the officiant is a hypocrite or an unbeliever. The propriety, or we might say the legality, of the sacrament is another matter. We should not receive Communion from a woman pastor, but it is just as important that we should not knowingly receive either preaching or sacraments from any false teacher. Some people in the Lutheran state churches of Europe who are very averse to receiving sacraments from women pastors should be equally concerned about receiving the preaching of false-teaching male pastors in those churches.

Luther deals with this issue in "Concerning the Ministry," written to the Bohemian brothers in 1523 (American Edition, Vol. 40, pp. 3-41). He says:

The second function, to baptize, they themselves [the Catholics] have by usage allowed in cases of necessity even to ordinary women, so that it is hardly regarded any more as a sacramental function. Whether they wish or not we deduce from their own logic that all Christians, and they alone, even women, are priests, without tonsure and episcopal "character." For in baptizing we proffer the life-giving Word of God, which renews souls and redeems from death and sins. To baptize is incomparably greater than to consecrate bread and wine, for it is the greatest office in the church the proclamation of the Word of God. So when women baptize, they exercise the function of priesthood legitimately, and do it not as a private act, but as a part of the public ministry of the church which belongs only to the priesthood. (LW 40, p. 23)

Luther clearly says "ministry of the Word" is done by women. Luther's point is that Rome despised Baptism and made a false distinction when they said anyone could baptize, while at the same time reserving the rule of the Lord's Supper to their priests. We would not call baptisms performed by women public ministry as Luther did, since we use the term *public ministry* only in reference to people who have received a distinct public call. Luther's point in calling such a baptism a public ministry seems to be that the child has entered the church through the baptism performed by the woman. The church accepts this baptism performed by a woman as its own and does not rebaptize the child as it would have to do if there were something missing from the baptism performed by a woman. Luther makes a similar statement about the Lord's Supper.

The third function is to consecrate or to administer the sacred bread and wine. Here those in the order of the shorn [Catholic monks and priests] vaunt themselves and set themselves up as rulers of a power given neither to angels nor the virgin mother. Unmoved by their senselessness we hold that this function, too, like the priesthood, belongs to all, and this we assert, not on our own authority, but that of Christ who at the Last Supper said, "Do this in remembrance of me" (Luke 22:19; 1 Cor. 11:24). This is the word by means of which the shorn papists claim they can make priests and give them the authority to consecrate. But Christ spoke this word to all those then present and to those who in the future would be at the table, to eat this bread and drink this cup. So it follows that what is given here is given to all. Those who oppose this have no foundation on which to stand, except the fathers, the councils, tradition, and that strongest article of their faith, namely, "We are many and thus we hold: therefore it is true." A further witness is the word of Paul in I Cor. 11 :23, "For I received from the Lord what I also delivered to you," etc. Here Paul addresses all the Corinthians, making each of them, as he himself was, consecrators. (LW 40, p. 24)

A woman can baptize and administer the Word of life by which sin is taken away, eternal death abolished, the prince of the world cast out, heaven bestowed; in short by which the divine majesty pours itself forth through all the soul. Meanwhile this miracle-working priest changes the nature of the bread, but by no other or greater word or power, and it has no other effect than that it increases his awe and admiration before his own dignity and power. Is not this to make an elephant out of a fly? What wonder workers! In despising the power of the Word they make marvelous their own power. (LW 40, p. 25)

Luther clearly says the Lord's Supper belongs to the whole church. He did not believe that laypeople should officiate at the Lord's Supper since they had no call to do so. He, however, strongly warns pastors against the popish notion that the privilege of consecrating the Lord's Supper is a right and power that sets them above God's people.

In Europe, Pastor Tom Hardt of Sweden, who had a very high view of both the pastoral ministry and the Lord's Supper, upheld the validity of sacraments of women priests, but, of course, not their propriety or legality.

The Recipients

I don't understand your practice of closed Communion. Is not the Lord's table open to all who believe the same as you do? I have been a lifelong Lutheran and do not see your Communion service any different than what I was used to in other Lutheran bodies I have

attended. I do see the tendency however to turn people away from the church by not allowing them to commune. I have attended a WELS congregation for 5-6 years now, but am still denied to kneel at the altar for Communion. I just don't understand where the Bible states limitation of the Sacrament to believers. I was taught we must examine ourselves before going to the altar. No one is able to do that for us, we must search our own souls and be accountable. Can you help me understand your thinking?

Yes, our Communion is open to members of all churches who have the same beliefs that we do.

To attend Communion together, people need to be believers in Christ, since beneficial reception is impossible without faith in Christ. To attend Communion together, people need to recognize the real presence of Christ's body and blood, since otherwise they will be receiving the sacrament to their condemnation. These points are covered in 1 Corinthians 11:17-32. For this reason, it is clear that non-Christians or Reformed Christians cannot attend the Lord's Supper with us.

One might think that this would permit all Lutherans to attend together, but this can no longer be assumed. The ELCA, for example, now has Communion with Reformed churches who do not believe in the real presence of Christ's body and blood in, with, and under the bread and wine. They no longer believe that denial of the real presence is a barrier to fellowship. As a result, many of their members do not have a proper understanding of the Lord's Supper (see pages 124,125).

Another element of attending Communion is that it is an expression of unity and fellowship between those who attend (1 Corinthians 10:16,17). Christians have always regarded the Lord's Supper as one of the strongest expressions of unity. We cannot express such unity with the ELCA, for example, because of its denial of the inerrancy of Scripture and other basic doctrines of the Bible. There are also doctrinal differences between us and the Missouri Synod. The LCMS too officially believes in closed Communion, so its members on the basis of their own synod's beliefs should not commune with us.

It is not membership per se that is the issue but a person's confession. A person does not have to be a member of our church to commune with us, but has to have the same confession of faith that we do. In other words, a person could be a member of some other church that is in fellowship with us and commune with us. But if, for example, the person is a member of a church that does not believe in the real presence in the sacrament or does not believe in the inspiration of Scripture, he or she would not be in fellowship with us. A person cannot properly be in two contradictory fellowships at the same time. The standards for attending Communion are faith in Christ, self-examination and repentance, recognition of Christ's body and blood in the sacrament, and unity of faith and confession. Under normal circumstances this confession is reflected by a person's church membership. This issue is discussed in quite a few answers in the archive section of our Web site that are about fellowship and the sacraments.

The Elements

Your
Question **Please explain the use of grape juice, rather than wine, for the Lord's Supper for recovering alcoholics, as is done in some WELS churches.**

The motives for doing so are perhaps obvious, namely, to avoid contributing to their problem of alcoholism, to alleviate their fear of not being able to handle even small quantities of alcohol, or to avoid causing unpleasant physical reactions when they are using certain drugs that cause a zero tolerance to alcohol.

How widespread the practice of using only grape juice is in our circles is unknown to me. I believe that many of those who have trouble with alcohol will say that receiving wine in the Lord's Supper does not cause problems for them. The quantity of wine received can be made even smaller by taking a very small amount or by diluting the wine with water. A mixture of wine and water was, in fact, quite common in biblical times and perhaps was what was used when Christ instituted the Sacrament in the upper room. For many of our congregations and for many individuals, this should perhaps be the preferred solution to the problem.

Concerning the legitimacy of using only grape juice, remember that Scripture does not expressly specify "wine" as the earthly element used in Communion, but "the fruit of the vine." Because grape wine was used in Passover meals, the Lutheran practice is to use grape wine (rather than other fruit wines). Since Scripture explicitly says only that Jesus used "bread" and "fruit of the vine" as the elements, we are cautious in making demands above and beyond that. Hebrew, Aramaic, and Greek all have clear, specific words for wine. The Holy Spirit could easily have specified wine and unleavened bread in the biblical text, but he did not. Since Jesus used unleavened bread, we use unleavened bread too—but some churches (including many in the early church) use leavened bread. To my knowledge we have never claimed that their sacrament was invalid because they did not use unleavened bread as Jesus did.

In asking if grape juice qualifies as "fruit of the vine," we may turn to Old Testament passages such as Numbers 6:3 and Judges 13:14. Here all products of the vine are dealt with as a unit, regardless of the percentage of alcohol they contain. For this reason we have been quite cautious in insisting that a certain percentage of alcohol must be present for something to be considered a true "fruit of the vine." Even in English the word *wine* does not always refer to fermented products. My dictionary lists as a third meaning of *wine*: the juice, fermented or unfermented, of other fruits used as a beverage or sauce. You can now buy "wine" with no alcohol in it. It is wine, but it is not intoxicating. Would its use make the Sacrament invalid? In celebrating the Lord's Supper in the fall season soon after the grape harvest, when may Christians begin to use the new "wine" for the Sacrament? What percentage of alcohol is necessary for it to be wine? These are questions about which we cannot be dogmatic. In normal circumstances, I would avoid raising questions by using only what is clearly recognized as grape wine.

It is possible, perhaps inevitable, that some consciences may be troubled by the use of grape juice, just as some people are troubled about the use of wine in this day of widespread alcohol abuse. Rather than key primarily off emotions and preconceived notions of what must or should be used, we should return to the biblical text to observe the vocabulary used by God. Then we ask what qualifies as a legitimate or permissible application of what is said. For the most part we find the use of grape wine ideal, but we acknowledge the possibility of using grape juice within the bounds of Scripture.

I would not make grape juice available as a general option, but would turn to this option only after counseling with the individuals involved to see if a solution that would preserve the unity of the distribution was possible.

Your
Question **Is it possible that Jesus used grape juice for the Last Supper as some temperance advocates contend?**

It is highly unlikely, but not completely impossible, that anything other than fully fermented grape wine was used at the Passover, but this is a historical argument, not a matter stated in the text. There is evidence that in Roman times, natural products were refrigerated for long times with cold water in caves. It does not seem at all probable that this was done for the Passover, but one cannot be dogmatic about it. Fifty days after the Passover, at Pentecost, the apostles were accused of drinking "new wine" or perhaps more accurately "sweet wine" (*gleukos*) (Acts 2:13), but with the implication that it was intoxicating. Why is the product at Pentecost called *gleukos*? This is a rather puzzling use of the term, but it warns us against being too dogmatic in conclusions drawn from our less-than-complete knowledge of the use and meaning of these terms. Most likely *gleukos* makes it clear that the wine though intoxicating had not yet soured. On this problem, see the article on *yyn* (wine) in Botterweck/Ringgren, *Theological Dictionary of the Old Testament*, Vol. 6.

Question **Does the same principle apply to the bread?**

Since Scripture just says "bread," we can accept bread from any grain. In a culture where they don't have bread, we would not want to substitute poi or tapioca or something made from roots or some other plant parts, but any bread is allowable. For the regular use of the congregation we as a rule want to stick with wheat or barley which is what Jesus used, but in a number of our congregations people who cannot tolerate wheat or certain other grains provide the pastor with some other bread that they can use. Since it is just for them, it should not bother anyone else's conscience. It should be on the altar by the other wafers during the consecration.

Practices

Question **An LCMS pastor recently claimed that it is doubtful if there is any real presence if many small glasses are used to distribute the wine because the Bible mentions only one cup. Yet he insists we**

should use many wafers even though Jesus broke one loaf. How do you evaluate this?

The contradiction between his two principles seems to indicate a practice based more on tradition than on scriptural principle or example.

We do not make one cup and one loaf essential to the reality of the sacrament even though they are mentioned in the institution. We do not insist that the bread must be broken even though Scripture mentions this. When distributing to hundreds of communicants, we do not have to repeat Jesus' method of distribution. (In fact, we do not know exactly what it was in all details—did he go to each communicant or pass the elements?) We do not recline around tables as they did at the first supper. We do not insist on standing or kneeling.

I believe we should use unleavened bread and fully fermented grape wine in the Sacrament so that we do not introduce doubt, but I cannot prove that this is Christ's command from the words of institution. I prefer the common cup and wafers even though the use of wafers is clearly not Christ's practice. Call this traditionalism, if you wish. I also prefer that the pastor distributes the elements directly to each communicant though I cannot prove this is the way Christ distributed the elements. I prefer kneeling to standing. I am not fond of walking by a pastor who is distributing the elements in so-called continuous distribution. I prefer receiving the Sacrament by "tables." But I cannot be dogmatic about this, nor can I make it an issue of discipline and divisive of fellowship against those who may use a practice I think is less meaningful or unwise.

Your
Question **Is use of a common chalice for the Lord's Supper commanded by Scripture? Even though I have always believed the Lord's Supper to consist of the bread, the wine, and Christ's command to eat and drink in remembrance of him (and not the chalice), I need some help here. Though we are aware of the WELS position on this issue, the president of our congregation and chairman of our board of elders has informed the elders that he considers use of the individual cup contrary to the Word of God. He believes this is not a matter of adiaphoron and has informed us that he can no longer assist the pastor in distribution of the Lord's Supper so long as we distribute both common and individual cups, because he feels the individual cup is wrong. It is especially critical that we**

study carefully and thoroughly the Word of God in order to answer such questions faithfully. Your assistance is greatly appreciated.

You have already answered your own question. In the four accounts of the Lord's Supper, Jesus commands us to take bread and wine and to eat and drink the bread and wine that have been consecrated. He does not tell us we must use one cup or one loaf of bread. When hundreds are being communed at one time, this will not even be possible. One cup would have to be filled many times. One loaf would not extend to all the communicants. In the accounts it is clear that Jesus used a cup and a loaf of bread, which he broke to distribute.

Historically, WELS churches have preferred to use a common cup (or in settings in which many are communing more than one common cup). We have retained a form of unleavened bread in the wafer, but somewhat inconsistently. We have not retained the breaking of one loaf.

The question facing you is this: Do any of the accounts of the institution command us to use one cup for all the communicants no matter how many they may be? We cannot make reports of what Jesus did into commands for us unless the text itself does so. If Jesus' precedent of using one cup is a binding command for us to use one cup only, then it is also a binding command to use only one loaf, which we break, since the statements about the two elements are parallel in the text of 1 Corinthians 10:16,17. It is inconsistent to insist on the one and not the other. We do not have to recline around a table to receive the Lord's Supper as the apostles did. Nor do we attach it to a Passover meal, as Jesus did, or to an agape feast, as the early church did. What we must do is obey Christ's commands.

It is true that there is a special symbolism in the common cup and common loaf as 1 Corinthians 10 indicates. We may have a strong preference to retain the common cup since we desire to retain not only Christ's commands but as much of his practice as we can, but we cannot go beyond the text and insist on making commands of points that are not commands in the text. We also cannot be selective in arbitrarily choosing certain items from the text (like the one cup) but dismissing others (like the one loaf or the breaking).

Your
Question **Why don't we Lutherans have Communion every Sunday like the Catholics do? The Bible says do this often.**

The words "Whenever you eat this bread and drink this cup, you proclaim the Lord's death until he comes" imply that we should celebrate the Lord's Supper often, but they give no indication what they mean by *often*—daily? weekly? monthly? The frequency with which Communion is celebrated in various churches, therefore, is a matter of custom and tradition, but it also reflects to a degree the different beliefs these churches have about the Lord's Supper.

Reformed churches (here used in the wide sense including Calvinists and Zwinglians) do not believe that the Lord's Supper is a true means of grace which gives forgiveness of sins. For them the Supper is more of a sign or seal of grace. They do not believe that all communicants eat and drink Christ's true body and blood along with the bread and wine. Because they view the Lord's Supper as a commemorative meal, many Reformed churches celebrate it relatively infrequently, in some cases, as infrequently as once a year on Maundy Thursday. (This is truer of Zwinglians/Arminians than of Calvinists/Reformed, who hold the Sacrament in higher regard.)

Roman Catholics, on the other hand, view the offering of the Lord's Supper as a sacrifice that presents again Christ's sacrifice for sin. Masses may be said, that is, Communion may be celebrated, even for the benefit of the dead in purgatory. Priests, therefore, may celebrate masses without the presence of a congregation to receive it. For these reasons, the *Catechism of the Catholic Church* says, "The Eucharist is the source and summit of the Christian life." Most Catholic churches, therefore, offer it very frequently, often daily.

Lutherans believe that the Lord's Supper offers forgiveness of sins as a result of the once-and-for-all sacrifice of Christ on the cross, but that the mass cannot benefit the dead, nor should it be celebrated apart from a congregation being present to receive it (private Communion for the sick being an exception). Historically, Lutherans, therefore, generally have celebrated the Lord's Supper more frequently than the Reformed, who regarded it as a commemoration, and less frequently than Catholics, who regarded it as a sacrifice that continues the work of paying for sin.

In the not too distant past, it was the practice of many Lutheran churches in America to celebrate the Lord's Supper once a month or even less. This relatively infrequent celebration was at least in part a reaction (overreaction?) to Catholicism's overemphasis on the

Sacrament at the expense of preaching. Lutheran churches tended to center on preaching as the "source and summit" of Christian worship. In recent years, however, there has been a tendency to move toward more frequent celebration of the Lord's Supper in WELS congregations. Many congregations now have Communion twice a month. A smaller percentage observe it weekly.

It is good that we ask ourselves whether the frequency with which we celebrate the Lord's Supper (and more important, the frequency with which we attend) demonstrates the great value we should place on the Sacrament.

Your
Question In ELFK, the German sister church of WELS, according to the Internet, there is a parish that practices "early Communion." This means that the Lord's Supper is celebrated before the service. How do you commend such a practice? Is this recommendable?

There is no command concerning the relationship of the Lord's Supper to the rest of the service. The early church commonly celebrated the Lord's Supper outside of the public service, after the dismissal of the nonmembers. Some WELS congregations have celebrated the Lord's Supper after the dismissal blessing, though this practice is becoming less common than it was in the past.

Communion before the service is not our practice, but there is no reason to condemn the practice as long as the scriptural principles of proper preparation are observed.

Your
Question What should be done if the pastor runs out of bread and wine during the Lord's Supper?

The Formula of Concord, one of the chief confessions of the Lutheran church, states:

In the administration of the Holy Supper the words of institution are to be publicly spoken or sung before the congregation distinctly and clearly, and should in no way be omitted, . . . in order that the elements of bread and wine may be consecrated or blessed for this holy use, in order that the body and blood of Christ may therewith be administered to us to be eaten and to be drunk. (SD VII, 79)

Neither Scripture nor the Confessions specifically say whether a second consecration is necessary for elements that were not on the altar during the first consecration, but in *The Shepherd Under Christ*, the pastoral theology textbook used at our seminary, pastors-to-be are taught, "Should the supply of either element be exhausted and replenishment be provided, consecrating the new supply will avoid any doubts about the continuing validity of the sacrament" (p. 93). It is wise to consecrate the new supply to avoid doubt or offense on the part of any recipients. Better yet is to provide sufficient bread and wine so that you do not run out. Unused elements can be retained for use at future celebrations of the Sacrament.

Your Question

In response to a question regarding the Catholic Church practice of using only the common cup, the following comment is given: "The risk from the common cup is small if handled correctly. There is a small degree of risk also in having the bread passed to you and in being next to the other communicant."

My question: Is it really proper to speak of there being any "risk" at all from Communion (common or individual cup) when a communicant receives the body and blood of Christ worthily, trusting in this gift of forgiveness alone for salvation? Scripturally, it seems to me that the only personal risk (both spiritual and physical) from taking Communion is when it is received unworthily, and a person does not recognize the body and blood of Christ present, distributed, and received in the blessed Sacrament. This is the reason, as I understand it, Lutherans have historically (with good scriptural and loving reason) practiced closed Communion, so that the true blessing and risk of the Sacrament could be known by all, as well as a testimony to the unity of faith. Would you agree with this analysis?

There is always some risk of contracting illness from being in close physical contact with other people—whether communing with them, talking with them, caring for them, etc. These are risks we can try to guard against, but they are risks we must undertake to live a normal life in the world. There is no assurance in Scripture that there is a supernatural, miraculous protection during the Lord's Supper, so in pastoral theology there were always instructions to take care in distribution to the sick, especially during a time when plagues often swept through populations. An article on this problem from the

17th century in the Summer 2004 issue of the *Wisconsin Lutheran Quarterly* begins:

> What should be done in the villages in time of plague, in what manner should the Holy Supper be given to the infected person, so that the whole church is not infected by fear of the pastor?

Response:

> Pastors ought to take care of their own sheep without fear, for this is the way of the pastors' call, and they can be safe under the protection of divine wings. But for the sake of the people, the pastor ought to proceed cautiously, so that no one is deterred by an unwholesome fear of the pastor, or even by the sight of the pastor.

Though the risk of such spreading of disease is much less in modern societies, we should take steps to alleviate fears people may have about receiving the Sacrament, whether the fears are real or exaggerated.

Your Question Do members of WELS churches always have to sign up on a sheet before taking Communion?

The Lutheran church had the custom that those who were planning to attend the Lord's Supper should "announce" their intention to attend to the pastor so he could be faithful to his responsibility to give the Lord's Supper only to those who were properly prepared to attend. This "announcement" was made to the pastor in person. In the past this was sometimes done in the setting of a confessional service. The announcement in written form is a remnant of this custom. It does not serve all the purposes of the custom of announcement, but it does help the pastor know who is attending Communion so that he can seek out those who may be beginning to drift away. Each congregation can determine its own practice in this area.

Your Question In all the WELS churches I've visited, instead of a table there appears to be (don't get me wrong) a mantle (it looks almost like a fireplace mantle) built into the wall at the back (or the front, depending on which way you are looking) of the church. I presume this is an altar, but is there a reason why you don't use a table?

The Lutheran churches of Germany and Scandinavia retained the traditions of church architecture they had inherited from the medieval church, and this included the altar. The churches built by the immigrants in the United States retained this style. Many newer churches or remodeled churches have a freestanding altar or an altar and a table. Again, this is a matter of custom. There is no rule on this matter.

Your
Question **Why does the pastor have his back to the congregation (is that to face the altar)? It seems like a throwback to medieval Catholicism. In most liturgical churches I've visited, the pastor stands behind the table, facing the congregation.**

The traditional practice is that when the pastor is speaking to God in behalf of the congregation (prayer), he faces the altar, which symbolizes God's presence. When he is speaking to the congregation in the name of God, he faces the congregation. When the pastor speaks the words of institution of the Lord's Supper, he is speaking them as words of consecration setting aside the elements for the Sacrament. The traditional practice was facing the altar and the elements during these words. With a freestanding altar or table the pastor can speak the words over the elements while at the same time facing the congregation. The essential thing is that the words are spoken to consecrate the elements and that they are heard by the congregation. The direction the pastor faces is not essential. In churches that have an altar against the rear wall, the pastor can address the words of institution to the congregation and at the same time point to the elements as he consecrates each one. In this way both aspects of the words of institution, as consecration of the elements and as instruction to the congregation, are confessed.

Your
Question **I notice that Roman Catholic priests bow down to the host. Is this what the Confessions condemn as "adoration"? The WELS believes in the Real Presence. With Christology in mind, why don't WELS believers bow down to their Savior when present in the sacrament?**

The Confessions criticism of the adoration applies primarily to the veneration of the host, outside of the celebration of the Sacrament, as in the Corpus Christi procession. Outside the celebration we have no assurance of the continued presence of the body and blood. Jesus said, "Take and eat." He did not say, "Keep and bow to" or "Keep and carry in a procession." Whether one bows when receiving Communion as a confession of the real presence is an adiaphoron, which is neither commanded nor forbidden. Luther commented on this in the American Edition, Volume 36, pp. 294-297. Excerpts follow:

> We say now that one should not condemn people or accuse them of heresy if they do not adore the sacrament, for there is no command to that effect and it is not for that purpose that Christ is present, just as we read that the apostles did not adore the sacrament since they were sitting and eating at table [Matt. 26:20,26]. On the other hand, one should not condemn and accuse of heresy people who do adore the sacrament. For although Christ has not commanded it, neither has he forbidden it, but often accepted it [this is a reference to people bowing to him while he was on earth]. Free, free it must be, according as one is disposed in his heart and has opportunity. Therefore both parties are to be blamed when they take a stand on either of these two sides and quarrel over this matter and condemn one another, and both of them miss the middle way. The first group would like to compel people not to adore the sacrament, as if Christ were not there at all; and the other group would like to compel people to adore it, as if Christ's state of glory were in the sacrament as it is in heaven.

> With this kind of quarreling they both get off the track, so that they emphasize the sacrament and neglect the words. The sacrament then becomes a mere work and faith perishes. For while they busy themselves trying to decide how they may properly honor Christ and do him abundant service, they never do get around to considering what he does for them in the sacrament and why he is there and what they are supposed to receive from him, just as if he were there solely for the sake of their worship and service. We have it backwards when in the sacrament we think only of the works that we ourselves might do and accomplish for the sacrament, and pay no attention to the works that the sacrament is supposed to do and accomplish for us.

> And so I repeat what I have said above, that a person should note carefully these two things in the sacrament: first, the Word; and second, the bread and wine. The words teach you to give thought and attention to why Christ is present; they will cause you to forget your work and to wait only upon his. For a sacrament is a

matter of faith, because in it only the works of God proceed and are effected through his Word! Therefore, those who consider the sacrament to be thus in the Word will forget both worship and adoration. That is what the apostles did at the Supper [Matt. 26:26] and yet without any doubt they were most acceptable and did him the proper honor. They acted just as one does when he hears the gospel, the Word of God to which the highest honor is nonetheless due because God is nearer in it than Christ is in the bread and wine. Yet no one thinks of bowing before the gospel; instead everyone sits still, and in listening gives no thought whatever to the kind of honor he will do to the Word.

Bread and wine, or the body and blood of Christ, regarded without the words, will teach you to give thought and attention to your own works. They will drive you away from pondering God's work and the reason why he is present, so that you will be quite anxious to do a lot for him, and will not let anything be done for you. Thus the sacrament becomes purely a matter of works. But if you first exercise faith rightly, at the most important point, namely, with respect to the words, then the adoration of the sacrament will afterwards follow beautifully in its own place; and if it did not follow, that would be no sin. But where faith, the most important thing, is not right and is not exercised with respect to the Word, there one cannot teach anybody properly to worship, even if he were to write the world full of books.

Now, therefore, let me describe in order four groups of people. The first are those whose entire interest is in the words of this sacrament, so that they feed their faith; they receive the bread and wine with the body and blood of Christ as a sure sign of that Word and of faith. These are the most secure and the best. They probably seldom descend so low as to bother themselves about worshiping and adoring, for they pay attention to the work God does to them and forget about the works they do for the sacrament.

The second group are those who exercise the right sort of faith, and then descend to their own works and worship Christ spiritually in the sacrament. That is, they bow inwardly with their hearts and confess him as their Lord, who does all things within them; and they prove their inward worship by outwardly bowing, bending, and kneeling with the body.

The third group are those who worship him inwardly only. The fourth group are those who worship him outwardly only. These last are completely worthless, and I have already said enough about them. Nevertheless, you can see that adoration of this sacrament is a dangerous procedure if the Word and faith are not inculcated; so much so that I really think it would be better to follow the example of the apostles and not worship, than to follow our custom and worship. Not that adoration is wrong, but simply because there is less danger in not adoring than in adoring; because human nature tends so easily to emphasize its own works and to neglect God's work, and the sacrament will not admit of that. But what more should I say? For this sacrament and for every work of God there must be Christians. Where there are no Christians, it will be done wrong, please God, whether they adore or not.

Luther's preference was that there not be adoration of the Sacrament, but he did not condemn it if it was done with the proper motive. Luther's comments are quoted at some length here since they are a model of how we should approach such questions of sacramental practice. Many of the recent divisive conflicts over the Supper could have been avoided if Luther's example had been kept in mind and followed.

Your Question

In a response to one of your earlier letters, your answer indicates that Scripture does not tell us at what point Christ's body and blood are present in the Sacrament of the Altar. Doesn't Scripture indicate that when Christ instituted the Lord's Supper, he said, "This IS my body"? Would it not be, according to a clear reading of Scripture, safe to assume that when a pastor distributes the elements, he is also distributing the body and blood of Christ? If this is not the case, it seems Christ would have said, "This will be my body . . . blood," and so to be honest, Lutheran pastors would have to say something similar during the distribution. I am a member of the LCMS, but would I be considered a heretic in the WELS if I believed that the Words of Institution effected the Real Presence in the Sacrament? I am not trying to stir up controversy, just trying to clarify the position of your synod.

Jesus said, "This is my body" during the distribution (he gave it to them, saying . . .). Our pastors follow Jesus' example during the distribution when they say, "Take eat. This is the true body. . . ."

The WELS doctrinal statement *This We Believe* says:

We believe that all who join in the Sacrament of the Lord's Supper receive the true body and blood of Christ in, with, and under the bread and wine (1 Corinthians 10:16). This is true because, when the Lord instituted this sacrament, he said, "This is my body. This is my blood of the covenant, which is poured out for many for the forgiveness of sins" (Matthew 26:26,28). We believe that Christ's words of institution cause the real presence—not any human action.

We reject any attempt to set the precise moment within the celebration of the Lord's Supper when the body and blood of Christ become present. We therefore reject the view that one must believe that Christ's body and blood are present as soon as the words of consecration have been spoken and the view that one must believe that Christ's body and blood become present only at the moment of eating and drinking.

Since the 17th century most Lutheran theologians, including virtually all of the theologians of the Synodical Conference, believed that Christ's body and blood are present only when the communicants receive the bread and wine. I am not aware that any of them ever made this a dogmatic issue. It was an opinion. More recently some theologians have insisted that Christians must believe that the body and blood are present as soon as the pastor speaks the consecration and that it is divisive of fellowship if they do not. We reject this opinion, because Scripture makes no such specification. All we need to know, as the Confessions say, is that what is distributed and received is Christ's body and blood. People can hold different opinions about the moment at which the body and blood become present, but these are opinions not dogmas of Scripture.

5
Church Fellowship

When people think of the Wisconsin Synod, the first doctrine that comes to mind is often the doctrine of church fellowship or some aspect of it, such as closed Communion or our position against lodges and scouting. Although we do not regard fellowship as the most important doctrine (that spot belongs to justification by faith), fellowship is an important doctrine for preserving all other doctrines of Scripture. Because this doctrine is not widely taught or practiced in the Christian church today and because it often touches people's daily life very directly, we tend to receive quite a lot of questions about this point. Here we cannot repeat all the scriptural principles and the historical circumstances of our debate with the Missouri Synod about this issue, but we will have to limit ourselves to a selection of the practical questions that commonly come up.

The Bible teaches that we must avoid false teachers. That means that we cannot carry out joint religious activities together with people who impenitently adhere to any false doctrine. This biblical concept of church fellowship as taught in Wisconsin Synod has sometimes been called the "unit concept" of church fellowship. This is an appropriate name, since church fellowship must be dealt with as a unit in two different respects. First, when the doctrines of Scripture are being discussed as a basis for the practice of fellowship, they must be dealt with as a unit. Since all the teachings of Scripture have the same divine authority, and we have no right to add anything to them or to subtract anything from them, the practice of church fellowship must be based on agreement in *all* of the doctrines of Scripture. Second, the various activities that may express church fellowship must be dealt with as a unit. Since various ways of expressing church fellowship (such as joint mission work, celebration of the Lord's Supper, exchange of pulpits, transfers of membership, and joint prayer) are merely different ways of expressing the same fellowship of faith, all expressions of church fellowship require the same degree of doctrinal agreement, namely, agreement in all of the doctrines of Scripture. These principles are discussed in more detail in the book *Church Fellowship: Working Together for the Truth* (People's Bible Teachings series, Northwestern Publishing House, 1996).

Principles

Your Question A gentleman of the WELS has told some other family members that because they are not Lutheran, they are not saved/will not go to heaven. Is this an official doctrine? And please document from your writings.

We believe that everyone who has faith in Christ as his or her Savior from sin is a member of the holy Christian church and will be saved. If churches mix error with the true teachings of Scripture, that error is a danger to saving faith. If the departure from the faith is too great, that error may kill faith. We warn against the seriousness of any departure from God's Word, but whether or not people are saved is dependent on whether or not they have faith in Christ as the Savior from sin, not on their denominational affiliation. We have never taught that only WELS members or only Lutherans are saved. We do teach that only those who are trusting in Christ as their Savior and not on their own works will be saved.

You can find this in our doctrinal statement *This We Believe*, which is posted on our WELS Web site, especially in the section on the church.

Your Question I have seen several Q & A regarding fellowship, and I have seen the passages used to explain the WELS position. However, the passages themselves don't appear to be used in complete context. For example, Matthew 7:15-20 has been used to warn us to "watch out for false prophets." While we would not agree with many positions of other Protestant denominations, our use of this section of Scripture is troubling. Verses 18,19 say that a "good tree cannot bear bad fruit, and a bad tree cannot bear good fruit. Every tree that does not bear good fruit is cut down and thrown into the fire." Therefore, if we are to avoid fellowship of any kind with members of other denominations that do not agree with Scripture 100 percent, we are equating them with the false prophets described in Matthew 7. This seemingly goes against the core gospel passage of John 3:16 that states whoever believes shall not perish, and is a very troubling position to hold. The second passage used is Romans 16:17 where we are to "watch out for those who cause divisions and put obstacles in your way that are contrary to the teaching you have learned. Keep away from them." That passage seems in line with our fellowship doctrine until one reads verse 18, where it describes those we should stay away from. "For such people are not serving our Lord Christ, but their own appetites. By smooth talk and flattery they deceive the minds of naive people." And verse 19 says, "but I want you to be wise about what is good, and innocent about what is evil." Anytime we deviate from the Word of God, it is in fact evil and considered sin. However, to use Romans 16:17 we are describing "other Christians" (hereafter assumed to be Christians not in agreement with God's Word 100 percent) as "not serving our Lord Christ," but rather "their own appetites"—that they set out to deceive people "by smooth talk and flattery." That the work they do is evil (v. 19). Thankfully many people are brought to faith in Jesus through the work of "other Christians," yet are we saying in the use of this passage for fellowship doctrine that they are not serving Jesus? Are we saying that they are only serving themselves? Are these the "bad trees" again described in Matthew 7 in danger of being thrown into the fire? Our use of this passage is serious indeed as it indicts them as those not doing the kingdom work, but rather work that is evil. Two possibilities come to mind in our use of these verses and I am willing to consider another alternative. First, we may be stating that, yes, we base our doctrine of fellowship on these verses and, no, we are not saying that "other Christians" are "bad trees," "not serving the Lord Christ," will be "eternally condemned," and in fact their work is "wicked." (This explanation is less problematic, but seems to disregard the context of these passages, however.) Or second, we are saying that we base our position of fellowship on these verses and "other Christians" are indeed "bad trees," "serving their own appetites," may be "eternally condemned," and "do not have God." I know that consistently the responses in the Q & A have been that we don't believe that those who believe in Jesus as their Savior will be condemned, but our use of these verses seem to be telling another story. Can you comment on the context of these verses as this is an important issue for many of our members in our churches? Thank you.

It is clear both in Matthew 7 and in Romans 16 that the false teachers whom we are to avoid are within the visible Christian church. It is Scripture that applies the condemnation of these passages to "other Christians." If you have any disagreement with this application, it is with Scripture not with WELS.

Consideration of two passages will help you understand why this application is proper. In Matthew 16 when Peter tried to discourage Jesus from going to Jerusalem to complete his God-given mission, Jesus said, "Get behind me, Satan." Peter's words and actions in this case were satanic—a rerun of the temptations Satan himself threw at Jesus. Jesus says that Peter's opposition to God's will was satanic, however well-meaning Peter's words may have been. How Jesus' words must have stung! In the same way, every false teaching is fruit of a bad tree, every false teaching is serving one's own appetite, every false teaching is not from God. These are the warnings of God's law, which we cannot minimize. Every false teaching is a grave threat to faith and salvation. Every false teaching is sin worthy of damnation.

But the sin of false teaching too can be forgiven if it is a sin of weakness or ignorance. This brings us to the second passage—1 Corinthians 3:11-15. Here Paul speaks of teachers who built on a poor foundation, which damaged their work and decreased their reward, yet they themselves are saved from the fire. The solution to your dilemma is found in distinguishing law and gospel. The group of passages you cite is the verdict of the law on false teaching. The passage in 1 Corinthians 3 is the verdict of the gospel concerning the sins of the weak.

The solution to your dilemma is also found in distinguishing the responsibility God has given to us from that which he retains for himself. If you read Matthew 7, you will see two kinds of judging. One is judging the teaching of the teachers and keeping away from false teachers. That is our responsibility. Judging the person's salvation on the basis of whether they retain faith in their hearts is God's responsibility—he will judge whether their false teaching has destroyed their faith or is a sin of weakness that is forgiven. Our duty is to identify and avoid false teaching. The other judgment of the heart we leave to God.

Your
Question In Bible Information Class we have not covered every doctrine or the whole text of the Bible. If I need to be in agreement with every doctrine to be a member, how can I join the church? It's

puzzling to me how one could assure unity of doctrine in just one month or year or several years of dialogue.

A thorough Bible information class or books like *Basic Doctrines of the Bible* or *This We Believe* cover the whole range of Bible doctrines. Also if the pastor knows your religious background, he should have a pretty good idea of the issues that need to be discussed with you. He can anticipate many of the things that could become questions later. Reaching and maintaining unity is an ongoing thing. As new questions come up, we answer them together by going to Scripture. This process is described in Ephesians 4:11-15:

[Christ] gave some to be apostles, some to be prophets, some to be evangelists, and some to be pastors and teachers, to prepare God's people for works of service, so that the body of Christ may be built up until we all reach unity in the faith and in the knowledge of the Son of God and become mature, attaining to the whole measure of the fullness of Christ. Then we will no longer be infants, tossed back and forth by the waves, and blown here and there by every wind of teaching and by the cunning and craftiness of men in their deceitful scheming. Instead, speaking the truth in love, we will in all things grow up into him who is the Head, that is, Christ.

Being in agreement in doctrine does not mean that we have to have the same understanding of every passage. Questions about the meaning of a specific passage are called *exegetical* questions. For example, 2 Peter 1:4 refers to us "participating in the divine nature." Some interpreters think this refers to us being renewed in God's image, that is, in righteousness. Others think it refers to God's living in us (the mystic union). Since both of these doctrines are true, since they are taught elsewhere in Scripture, we do not have to have the same interpretation of every passage. In the case of hard passages like Ezekiel 40–48, we need to agree that it does not refer to an earthly millennial kingdom but to Christ's kingdom, which is built up by the gospel. This kingdom begins in the church now and reaches its fulfillment in the new heavens and the new earth. We do not have to agree on what is symbolized by each detail of this section or of some of the parables.

For unity of faith it is not necessary that every individual know and understand fully every teaching or every passage of the Bible—what is necessary is that they not reject any teachings that have been pointed out to them. Holding a false belief does not in itself immediately break fellowship. Persisting in that belief in spite of admonition and correction from Scripture does make it necessary to break fellowship. When people do end their fellowship with us, it is rarely because of some teaching of ours that they did not know about but because they changed their belief about some teaching that they knew already in catechism class, such as infant Baptism, for example.

Your
Question It seems to me that the WELS is far too narrow in its definition of what constitutes an "open question." Issues such as transubstantiation, infant Baptism, the end times, etc., have all been hotly debated by brilliant theologians, and no consensus has been found. How is it that the WELS can claim that they and they alone are correct in their interpretation of Scripture? To make my point I bring up one example. Without having actually seen the end times, how can the WELS be 100 percent sure that the doctrine of the antichrist being the papacy is correct? I understand that these doctrines have been formed through careful and prayerful scriptural research, but they have admittedly been formed by sinful humans who make mistakes. How can the WELS claim that its humans have not erred, and that other humans in other denominations have? I believe that Scripture has but one true interpretation, but to say that WELS has it all right seems rather arrogant, doesn't it?

Our definition of "open question" is "any question that Scripture has not answered." Can you suggest any other possible standard? If the standard is "any doctrine on which some Christians disagree," there is no doctrine of Scripture that is not an open question. The Catholic church rejects justification by faith alone. Baptists reject infant Baptism. Most Reformed churches reject the real presence of Christ's body and blood in the Lord's Supper. Some Lutherans reject the inerrancy of Scripture. Should all these now be open questions? Who has the authority to decide to make some teachings of the Bible open questions?

The Lutheran answer to your question is the answer Luther gave at Worms when virtually the whole church stood against him. His conscience was captive to the Word of God, and it is neither safe nor right to sin against conscience. Unless someone convinces us from Scripture that our position is wrong, it is not safe or right to abandon it. To think that we have the right or ability to decide which doctrines of Scripture we will leave as open questions is arrogance. The only time we can change doctrine is when we become convinced from Scripture that our position is wrong. WELS has, in fact, done this—for example in changing its early rather lax practice on fellowship.

Your Question

I challenge you to answer this question with a direct answer, since the WELS and other conservative Lutherans seem to believe that something is black or white, right or wrong, and one cannot ride the fence. I go to an ELS college and no one here, including several theologically trained pastors, seem to like this question very much, and it is quite a simple one: Do the WELS/ELS believe that they are THE correct religion, and that the only sure way to enter heaven is to abide by, and believe, teach, and confess all of their doctrines? It seems to me that no matter which way one answers, one runs into a paradox with the WELS/ELS belief system. If you answer yes, then you will have to admit, publicly, that you believe that we other Lutherans (I myself am a member of the ELCA) and the other Christian denominations are not Christians after all and that we are damned to spend an eternity in hell. If you answer no, then the WELS/ELS doctrine on fellowship seems absurd, since the purpose of that doctrine is, as one pastor put it, "to demonstrate that we believe these doctrines that separate us ARE important, and that fellowship with others suggests that they are not." This would then mean that the WELS/ELS could just as easily say "yes we believe that you people are Christians as much as we are, and that you're going to heaven when you die, but we still don't want to have anything to do with you." So, which is it, yes or no?

"No," I suppose, would be the best one-word answer.

But since questions to which people demand a "yes or no" answer are almost never valid questions and since such questions are almost never asked with a proper attitude, we will give more of an answer than you requested.

Saving faith is trust in Christ as our substitute who gave the full payment for our sins. Saving faith is trust in the gospel promise and nothing more. That is why we can't say that only WELS or ELS Lutherans or even that only Lutherans will be saved.

But the faith that God wants is acceptance of his whole Word and everything it says. We cannot condone the rejection of any part of it. The rejection of any part of it is poison to faith. Not every dose of poison is fatal, but we cannot knowingly take or give anyone any dose of poison.

151

The reason your question is invalid as a yes-or-no question is that it is not one question but two. The first question is what is necessary for salvation. The answer to that question is trust in Christ as our substitute. Sometimes that trust can survive in spite of false teachings that are poison to the soul, but that does not mean we should accept any dose of poison no matter how small.

The second question is what is necessary for God-pleasing church fellowship. The scriptural answer to that question is agreement in all of the doctrines of Scripture. We cannot continue in fellowship with those who continue to reject doctrines of Scripture in spite of admonition.

The reason we cannot have fellowship with the ELCA is that the ELCA rejects the inerrancy of Scripture. It has entered into agreements with Reformed churches that compromise the belief in the real presence of Christ's body and blood in, with, and under the bread and wine of the Lord's Supper. It has accepted an agreement with the Catholic church that compromises the central teaching of the Bible, justification by grace alone through faith alone. Its official magazine has said that the teaching that Jesus paid for our sins as our substitute is just one of the theories that people have used to explain Jesus' death (*The Lutheran*, March 30, 1988, p. 46). All these teachings are poison to the soul. By your membership in the ELCA, you condone these teachings, unless you are taking a clear public stand against them.

Scripture commands us to keep away from such teachings and from those who hold on to them in spite of admonition. Such separation is necessary to give the strongest possible warning against such teachings.

We do not believe that everything is black and white, but many things are. That salvation is by faith not by works is black and white. That the Bible is God's errorless Word, not an error-filled human message, is black and white. If people do not recognize any of these issues as black and white, either-or issues, it is not likely that they will see anything as black and white.

Your.
Question **God's Word is holy and without error, as written in the original Greek and Hebrew texts. Everything written about God's Word is man's work and is flawed by original sin. From man's writing come theology and religion, and God has confounded writing and language (Genesis 11:7) so that we cannot really understand one another. Lutherans call the papacy the antichrist and Catholics condemn those**

who believe in justification by faith alone to eternal damnation. We break fellowship with other Lutherans based on reams of writings of man, and try to hide God's love from them. Shouldn't we be aware that all man-made Christian churches are flawed to some extent by man's sin, that we should repent of our sin and try to be more loving of all members of the invisible holy Christian church?

There are two deadly fallacies in your comments.

The first fallacy is that the differences that have separated us from other churches are just different human opinions. It is God's errorless Word that says that we are saved by faith not works. When the Catholic church says we are saved by faith and works together, this is directly contradictory to God's Word; and this belief, therefore, must be rejected as deadly to faith. The Bible says it is true in its entirety. The ECLA says it is not. These are not just two different, equally valid opinions. We must reject one and hold the other. To say that every human is sinful does not mean that every theological statement made by humans is false. The statement that we are saved by grace alone through faith alone, not by works, is made by sinful people, but the statement is completely true because it rests on Scripture.

The second fallacy is that it is unloving to speak against error or that it can be loving to overlook or be silent about faith-destroying error. Your advice is equivalent to saying, "If your neighbor is sleeping in a burning house, don't yell at him or disturb his sleep." It is never love to be silent about errors that jeopardize people's souls. Love always requires that we warn against error, even by separating from those who hold the error.

Your statement about "trying to hide God's love from them" ignores the history of what actually happened in the church. The reason the Lutheran church is separate from the Catholic church is not that Luther tried to hide God's love from them. He worked very hard to show God's saving love to them, but he was excommunicated and condemned to death for his efforts. The Lutherans tried for years to reach peace with the Catholic church, but the only response was persecution of the Protestants. We are not in fellowship with the ELCA because they knowingly and persistently reject our belief in the inerrancy of the Bible. Do you think I would be allowed to teach biblical inerrancy in an ELCA seminary? The end of our fellowship with LCMS came after 25 years of strenuous efforts to restore the unity of the Synodical Conference. In none of these cases can the end of fellowship be said to have come about because we were hiding love.

When error arises, the first thing to do is to speak to the brother or sister about it. Fellowship comes to an end only when such efforts have been rejected. Luther was ready to be corrected by Scripture, and we are too, but this does not mean we can go along with teachings that clearly reject Scripture.

Your
Question I was just scanning through your Web page and couldn't help but notice the attention you and several other Lutheran groups pay to detail. It all seems a bit like the Pharisees' attention to law. I do not mean to be rude, but are you not being Pharisaic? I can't imagine Jesus doing the theological hairsplitting that I see WELS doing.

Jesus never criticized the Pharisees for attention to detail. In fact, he had said, "Not the smallest letter, not the least stroke of a pen, will by any means disappear from the Law until everything is accomplished. Anyone who breaks one of the least of these commandments and teaches others to do the same will be called least in the kingdom of heaven, but whoever practices and teaches these commands will be called great in the kingdom of heaven. For I tell you that unless your righteousness surpasses that of the Pharisees and the teachers of the law, you will certainly not enter the kingdom of heaven" (Matthew 5:18-20). The Pharisees' problem was not that they were too scrupulous, but that they were not scrupulous enough. They majored in the fine points of the Law and ignored the big points. Jesus told his followers, "The teachers of the law and the Pharisees sit in Moses' seat. So you must obey them and do everything they tell you. But do not do what they do, for they do not practice what they preach" (Matthew 23:2,3). Jesus told the Pharisees, "Woe to you, teachers of the law and Pharisees, you hypocrites! You give a tenth of your spices—mint, dill and cummin. But you have neglected the more important matters of the law—justice, mercy and faithfulness. You should have practiced the latter, without neglecting the former" (Matthew 23:23). Jesus gives no support whatsoever to your idea that details of God's Word are unimportant.

The greatest error of your question is summarized by the words "I can't imagine." You cannot base your beliefs on what you can or can't imagine but on what Jesus says.

Since it appears that we have some disagreements with some of the sayings and writings of Martin Luther (i.e., writings about Mary, the significance of James, etc.) and it is also clear that we are to have complete doctrinal agreement for there to be fellowship, would we in the WELS be in fellowship with Martin Luther if he were with us today? I would also appreciate clarification on why we would or would not be in fellowship.

If Luther were here today holding on to and defending the beliefs that he held in 1511, we would not be in fellowship with him, but neither would the Luther of 1525. Luther did not come to clarity of doctrine instantly but gradually. Those who ultimately joined him in the Lutheran church did not all come to agreement with him with identical speed. Some came quickly to clear understanding; others took longer. Some, like Zwingli, could be recognized as brothers for a while but did not remain so. If we had been around in the 1520s, the likely question would have been how quickly would we have caught up with Luther in recognizing the errors of Rome, not whether he could keep up with us. We stand on his shoulders, and a lot of church history has flowed by since his day, so in some respects we may see issues that he never had to deal with. We cannot expect him to have wrestled with questions that were not being asked in his day.

There are, however, no doctrinal differences between us and the mature Luther, so there would be no barrier to fellowship. For example, you mentioned Luther's negative comments about James. But Luther came to see that there was really no contradiction between Paul and James, and he never removed James from his Bible. On some other occasions, he expressed views that we cannot agree with, such as his advice to Phillip of Hesse concerning polygamy, but these are not doctrinal positions of the Lutheran church, and they were not such even in Luther's lifetime. No Lutheran theologian ever accepted everything Luther said as a standard for doctrine.

The fact that someone holds a doctrinal view which disagrees with Scripture does not instantly dissolve fellowship. It is persisting in such a position contrary to Scripture, in spite of admonition, which destroys fellowship. It is not at all unusual to find that a member of a congregation in our church fellowship holds a view that does not agree with the Bible. This becomes divisive if they reject admonition, but if they accept instruction and correction, it does not.

Fellowship—WELS and the LCMS

Your
Question What, specifically, are the "doctrinal differences" that separate the LCMS and the WELS? I am interested if the WELS views the split from the LCMS in the same light as the LCMS. Could you please comment on this LCMS answer I found on the LCMS Web site, regarding the differences between the two?

From the LCMS perspective, the three main theological differences between the LCMS and the WELS are the following:

1. **The biblical understanding of fellowship. The WELS holds to what is called the "unit concept" of fellowship, which places virtually all joint expressions of the Christian faith on the same level. In an official statement made in 1960 the WELS states, "Church fellowship should therefore be treated as a unit concept, covering every joint expression, manifestation, and demonstration of a common faith" (Doctrinal Statements of the Wisconsin Evangelical Lutheran Synod, 1970, pp. 51-52). The LCMS, however, has historically not understood or practiced church fellowship in this way. Our Synod, for example, has made a distinction between altar and pulpit fellowship (for which full doctrinal agreement is required) and other manifestations of Christian fellowship, such as prayer fellowship (which do not necessarily require full doctrinal agreement). Disagreements on this issue led the Wisconsin to break fellowship with the LCMS in 1961.**

Comment: This is essentially correct. For example, WELS believes that it was wrong for leaders of the LCMS to pray together with theologians of the ALC who publicly defended false doctrine from the 1930s to the 1950s and that it is wrong to pray with such leaders of the ELCA who persistently defend false doctrine or to join in ecumenical interfaith prayer services like the Yankee Stadium prayer service. The LCMS defends these actions. We would disagree with the statement that this was the historical practice of the LCMS before the 1930s. We believe our view is the same as Walther's and Pieper's and that the view of the LCMS and WELS was the same in the early decades of the 20th century. The LCMS has also gone beyond its own principles of church fellowship by entering church fellowship with Lutheran World Federation churches.

2. **The doctrine of the ministry. With respect to the doctrine of the ministry, since the days of C. F. W. Walther [the LCMS] has held that the office of the public ministry (the pastoral office) according to the**

Scriptures is the one divinely established office in the church, while the church possesses the freedom to create other offices, by human institution, from time to time to assist in the carrying out of the functions of the pastoral ministry. The WELS' Theses on Church and Ministry, however, expressly deny that the pastoral ministry is specifically instituted by the Lord in contrast to other forms of public ministry (see Doctrinal Statements, pp. 9-11; cf. the Commission on Theology and Church Relations' 1981 report on The Ministry: Office, Procedures, and Nomenclature).

Comment: WELS does maintain that the pastoral ministry is instituted by Christ but not to the exclusion of other forms of ministry. Christ has left the church much freedom in establishing other forms of ministry such as seminary professor, teacher, etc. Those who serve in such forms of ministry are also serving in the ministry established by Christ. We do not agree that the current official LCMS position is the position of Walther, as one sees if one looks at all his statements in their context. In addition to the current LCMS statement, which is summarized above, the LCMS has also published works that agree with the WELS position. See the section on the ministry for further discussion.

3. **The role of women in the church. While both the LCMS and the WELS strongly oppose the ordination of women to the pastoral office on Scriptural grounds, the LCMS has concluded that the Scriptures do not forbid woman suffrage. The WELS opposes woman suffrage as contrary to the Scriptures.**

Comment: The WELS opposes women voting in assemblies that have governing authority over the church, such as voters assemblies and synod conventions and governing boards. The heart of the issue is exercise of authority as stated in 1 Timothy 2:12. This is a larger issue than simply voting.

The three problems pointed to by the LCMS answer correctly indicate three key issues between the LCMS and WELS: fellowship, ministry, and the roles of men and women. Because of their brief scope, they do not give a full explanation of the situation. They also do not mention another very critical problem, lack of church discipline. The greatest problem with the LCMS right now is that it is a house divided. Some LCMS congregations and pastors would be very similar to the WELS; others would be as liberal as some ELCA congregations. Some are almost "high church" in their liturgy, some have abandoned the liturgy, some are charismatic. Open Communion seems to be widely endorsed. A person could encounter almost anything, depending on the congregation. But wherever one is a member, he would be part of a church torn by these conflicts. This is a key issue that needs to be addressed by the LCMS before there could be progress on discussing the three key issues cited above.

Your Question

Where does Scripture declare that agreement in all doctrine is necessary for fellowship? (I can understand agreement on the essentials, but what about secondary issues?) Do we need to agree with the LCMS on all doctrine for fellowship?

There is nothing in the Scriptures to suggest that the unity of faith which is required as the basis for the outward expression of church fellowship is limited to agreement only in the doctrine of justification or a few fundamental doctrines. It is true that many of the doctrinal disputes referred to in the New Testament involved fundamental doctrines. When he wrote Galatians, Paul was battling a denial of the doctrine of justification by grace. In his epistles John appears to be battling a heresy that denied Jesus' humanity. But many other types of doctrinal error are specifically referred to in the New Testament, including denial of the resurrection of the body (2 Timothy 2:18), teaching Christians that they could disregard God's commandments since the forgiveness of sins was free (Revelation 2 and 3; Jude 3-10; 2 Peter 2:1-4,13-20), forbidding marriage and prohibiting certain foods (1 Timothy 4:3), and quarrels about genealogies and the law (Titus 3:9). This list is comprehensive enough to demonstrate that the apostles' concern for doctrinal purity was not limited to a few key doctrines.

Agreement in adiaphora (things that God has neither commanded nor forbidden) and ceremonies is not necessary for fellowship (Romans 14). Christians do not have to be agreed on liturgical forms or worship styles or in their system of church government to practice fellowship together. It would not be right to deny fellowship to someone who had the same teaching that we have, but uses different words to express it.

Although agreement in adiaphora, ceremonies, and wording is not necessary for fellowship, complete agreement in doctrine is necessary. The New Testament admonitions to doctrinal unity and its warnings against false doctrine are all-inclusive, general statements, which in no way imply that some scriptural doctrines can safely be omitted or that some false teachings can safely be tolerated.

The LCMS agrees with WELS that unity in all doctrine is necessary for church fellowship.

Your
Question I belong to a "mixed" extended family; some of us are WELS, and some of us are LCMS. I am one of us in the WELS camp. I look at my LCMS relatives and see strong confessional Lutherans. Certainly, there are some differences, such as women voting, female principals in schools, Boy Scout participation, and the like. And there are other differences evident in that my LCMS relations agree there is not a strongly enforced synodical "line" that LCMS congregations are expected to follow. (They see this as being a strength and a weakness all at once.) But as I said, when I look at my LCMS relatives I see Lutherans who base their faith in Scripture and hold to the Lutheran confessions. There is so much made of the differences separating WELS and LCMS and precious little said about that which connects us. What are the connections, the points of agreement between WELS and LCMS?

A doctor who is trying to diagnose and help a patient cannot focus on what is the same between all his patients. The doctor must focus on what is different—what has gone wrong in the health of one of the patients. It is the changes in the health of the patient that need attention, not the continued healthy functions. This is true because if the health problems are ignored, they will soon jeopardize the other functions of the body as well.

In the old Synodical Conference, WELS and the LCMS were united in the doctrines of the Scripture and the Confessions. Then the LCMS began to turn in a different direction. You have not mentioned the most serious and threatening differences. We can be glad for the good Lutheran doctrine that remains in the LCMS, but when health is deteriorating, the patient needs to focus on what is going wrong and how to correct the condition.

Membership

Your
Question Under what circumstances is a person excommunicated? Are members disciplined by taking away their Communion privileges?

Congregations must excommunicate members who have committed a sin and who have refused to repent even after their fellow Christians have warned them according to the steps described in Matthew 18:15-18. An excommunicated person cannot attend the Lord's Supper or exercise any of the other rights of membership in the congregation.

Members can be excommunicated only if their action is clearly against God's law, if it is proven that they are guilty of this sin, and if they have refused the warnings to repent. Scripture says that an impenitent person has no forgiveness of sins. A valid excommunication, therefore, does not simply exclude an individual from membership in the congregation. A valid excommunication declares that the offender has excluded himself from eternal life, since no impenitent person has forgiveness of sins and no unforgiven person can enter heaven.

The congregation excommunicates a person in the hope that this drastic step will lead the sinner to come to his senses and repent. The excommunicated person then will be welcomed back to the congregation with open arms. Excommunication, therefore, is an act of love for sinners, which is aimed at saving them from the eternal consequences of impenitence.

If a pastor knows that a person is impenitent, but the case has not yet proceeded to the point of excommunication by the congregation, he should warn the person not to come to Communion, since Communion offers forgiveness only to the repentant. Those who come without repentance bring harm upon themselves by their misuse of the Sacrament. Exclusion from the Lord's Supper has the same evangelical purpose as excommunication, namely, to win the sinner to repentance. The pastor can take such action only if the guilt and impenitence of the person are clearly established, but the congregation has not yet had an opportunity to act on the case.

Your Question

I was raised in the WELS and attended a WELS school through the 8th grade. We have children of our own now who will be starting school soon and I would like them to receive the Christian education I received. I am aware that my place as a woman in the church is not considered to be equal to that of my husband. I have listened to the justifications and Scriptures used to justify the position of the church, but I really do not agree. I have always reconciled my membership in the church with my nonbelief in this particular doctrine

by classifying the position that women in the church can't vote or do any activity that might exercise some "authority over men" as one being my faith and the other being a policy of the church. I guess I looked at it as being an administrative procedure that I disagreed with, but that I did not disagree with the religious teachings of the church. We recently moved and it was our intention to join the local WELS church. However, in a discussion with a family member who is currently a member of that congregation, I was told that I must accept this doctrine in order to become a member of the church. Is this the view of the church? Are women who don't accept this doctrine doomed to hell in the eyes of the church? Why?

Justifying faith, that is, faith that receives forgiveness of sins and salvation is trust in Christ as the one who paid for our sins. The object of saving faith is God's grace, nothing else. But this does not give us a license to omit or reject any teaching of the Bible. To knowingly reject any teaching of the Bible destroys faith and salvation, because it is a form of impenitence. If a person does not accept some teaching of the Bible because he or she does not know about it or because the person does not see it in the Bible, this does not always destroy faith, but it is a danger to faith because it departs from God's Word. We cannot always judge whether or not an error in doctrine has destroyed an individual's faith. This is for God to judge. We can, however, never condone any departure from Scripture.

After long and intense study of Scripture, we do not believe that our practices concerning the roles of men and women in the governing bodies of church are simply church administrative rules, but that they are reflections of biblical teaching. Men and women are spiritual equals before God, but he has not given them identical roles in marriage or in the church. We are not free to depart from those roles. Our practices are an attempt to apply the principles of Scripture consistently.

A person who is wrestling to come to a biblical understanding of some doctrine and patiently studying it on the basis of Scripture is very welcome in our church, but if a person after careful and thorough study is convinced that our doctrine in unbiblical and publicly rejects it and intends to work against it, they would not be true to their own conscience to belong to our church. Also you would be exposing your children to teaching that you believe to be wrong.

I would urge you to carefully study through the whole Bible study *Man and Woman in God's World* and to try to pinpoint the aspects of our teaching and practice that you believe are unbiblical and to discuss them with a sympathetic pastor. Do not jump too quickly to questions of application but dwell on the biblical principles and the spirit that lies behind them. God meant them for our good, not our harm.

Your Question

What do we do about attending church if we are in an area where there are no WELS churches? Do we participate? If so, how much? Especially in light of the fact that we know false teaching exists in the churches in that area; i.e., LCMS. What is a good rule for our people to follow? God's Word specifically says to separate from them. But for people who do not study God's Word regularly and cannot live without a church building and/or service on Sunday, what do they do? Outward confession of faith with others in a church or synod states belief in God's Word. But to turn around and set it aside when in remote areas because we cannot live without a church seems to be contrary to what God's Word teaches. Can you give me some guidance?

If God's Word does not give us a basis for making exceptions to his command to keep away from false teachers, we cannot take it upon ourselves to justify or excuse such exceptions. We cannot tell people that it is okay to go to false teachers if there are no good ones close by. This is all the more true if the person claims that he or she is weak and has not studied the Bible much, because then they have less ability to evaluate and reject the false teachings.

If people move to an area where there are no orthodox Lutheran churches and decide under those circumstances to join a church which harbors false teaching as "the lesser evil," that is a decision for which they will be accountable to God. We cannot give them a license or excuse for the decision. They must ask themselves, "Are other churches really too far away for me to travel to?" "Can we begin a mission church here?" "If I can't provide for the spiritual needs of my family here, should I really be moving here even for a promotion or some other benefit?" Answers that call on us to make sacrifices for our faith may not satisfy people, but the question we must ask is not "Does it satisfy people?" but "Is it what God wants?" Can we justify placing other considerations ahead of our spiritual welfare?

People have often made great sacrifices to be in a place where they could practice their faith. For example, the faithful people in the

Northern Kingdom of Israel had to become refugees to Judah to escape Jereboam's false religion. At the time of the Reformation, many Protestants became exiles because of their faith. The founders of the Missouri Synod left their homes and positions in Germany to find freedom in a new world.

Your Question

You mentioned in a previous answer that if a person makes the decision to join a church other than WELS that God would hold that person accountable. I'm wondering what you mean by that. In what way would God hold him accountable?

The issue is not that a person attends a church other than WELS but that a person who has known the full truth of God's Word leaves that behind and begins to support false teaching by membership in a heterodox church. For example, what are the implications if a Lutheran who has known the gospel of salvation by grace alone through faith alone turns to the Catholic doctrine of salvation by faith and works?

We are responsible and accountable to God for the teachings we accept and support. A person who supports a false teacher is guilty of being a partner in the sin of false teaching (2 John 10,11). When persons are confirmed in the Lutheran church, they make the declaration that they believe the teachings they learned were the true teachings of the Bible. If they abandon that belief, they will have to give account to God for their action. If they have become guilty of leaving the truth, they bring judgment upon themselves. Read Galatians, especially 1:1-9 and 5:1-12.

The degree of danger to their faith depends on the seriousness of the errors they have accepted, their motivation, and their understanding of the situation. It is not the change of church membership per se that is the problem, but the desertion from biblical doctrine. The same judgment would rest upon a person who was a member of one of our churches, but who had adopted false beliefs. If we knew about this change, we would have to deal with that person through church discipline. In the same way, if someone is leaving our fellowship to accept false doctrine, we have a duty to warn them of the consequences of that sin.

The issue is not whether a person is loyal to WELS teaching. It is whether the person is following God's Word.

Practices in Regard to Church Services

Question I have usually heard our Communion practice referred to as "closed Communion." More recently I have heard "close Communion." Which is right?

In the past, confessional Lutherans regularly used the term "closed Communion" to express the scriptural truth that we should welcome to the Lord's Supper only those Christians who are properly instructed, who recognize the real presence of Christ's body and blood in the Sacrament, who are repentant, and who are united with us in doctrine. The Sacrament is closed to all others to guard them against eating and drinking judgment on themselves (1 Corinthians 11:27-31). Just as a road must be closed when a bridge is washed out to protect travelers from harm, Communion must be closed to those who are not prepared to receive it beneficially.

More recently some people have preferred the term "close Communion," which emphasizes the positive truth that the Lord's Supper expresses a close fellowship between all of those who attend the Sacrament together.

The two terms, thus, complement each other. To be truly "close," Communion must be "closed" to those who are not truly one with us in faith. Although "closed" is the more traditional term, "close" can be used as an alternate term, as long as there is no intention to hide or conceal the fact that Communion is also "closed." The two terms simply are two sides of the same coin. You can't have one without the other.

Question What is our stand on conducting a funeral if the pastor knows that the person who died wasn't a WELS member or even a Christian? Should we do this because it is an opportunity to preach the gospel to the living?

Our regular practice is that WELS pastors should conduct a Christian funeral only for people whose Christian confession is known to us, since a funeral will not be a comfort unless it includes a recognition of the deceased's Christian faith. This means we will normally conduct a funeral only for a person who was a member of our fellowship. However, exceptional circumstances may arise. It may happen that a WELS pastor was ministering to a nonmember during his or her last illness. In response to the pastor's presentation of the gospel, that individual confessed faith in Christ but had no chance to "set his house in order" as far as church membership. On the basis of the person's confession of faith, the pastor who had served him could conduct the funeral. But to avoid confusion or offense, he would explain the circumstances to his council and/or congregation.

If the pastor has no evidence of Christian faith on the part of the deceased, what can he say that will be both honest and a comfort? If he warns the mourners not to follow the deceased's example of spiritual neglect, it will be honest, but not a comfort. If he provides gospel comfort where there was no evidence of faith, it will be a comfort, but it will not be honest.

Because the death of a loved one is a very emotional situation, it is important that pastors and congregations regularly remind their members of our funeral practices and of the reasons for them so that people do not first learn about them in the stressful situation of trying to arrange a funeral for a loved one. Pastors should also make every effort to evangelize the unchurched relatives of their members while they are still alive, when speaking the gospel to them can still do some good. Their friends and relatives should do the same.

Your Question **Explain why lifelong WELS members can't have Christian friends or relatives who are not members of our church sing at their funeral or wedding. Who are we to judge who or who is not a member of God's church?**

First of all, when a situation of church fellowship must be resolved, it makes no difference whether the person involved is a lifelong member of WELS or not a member of any church at all. The biblical principles of church fellowship are the same regardless of who the people are that are involved in a specific situation. The principles are biblical principles that apply equally to everyone.

The biblical principles of church fellowship teach us that we are not to worship or pray with individuals who adhere to false teachings (Romans 16:17; 2 John 10-11; Titus 3:10). If we worship together with people who hold to false teachings, we fail to give clear testimony against the doctrinal differences that separate them from us. It is, therefore, our practice that a leading role in our worship services may be entrusted only to fellow Christians who are in doctrinal agreement with us and with our church.

Christian weddings and funerals are not private, personal ceremonies held to honor the wedding couple or the deceased, but worship services of the church directed to the glory of God and based on the truths of his Word. Therefore, those who take a public role in leading in worship during a wedding or funeral in one of our congregations must meet the same biblical standards of doctrinal unity with us which apply to any other worship service.

We cannot judge who is or who is not a member of the invisible church of all believers, since such membership depends solely on the presence or absence of faith in Christ. This faith can be detected with certainty only by God. Only God can judge who will enter heaven. We are, however, commanded by God to judge a person's doctrine by comparing it with Scripture. In situations that concern the public practice of joint worship, we must use the public confession made by the individual's church membership as the basis for determining whether or not we may join in church fellowship with that individual. This means that if a person is a member of a church which adheres to false doctrine, we may not invite them to take a leading role in our services without compromising our testimony to the truth.

Family ties cannot set aside this rule. When there is a conflict between ties to family and friends and obedience to God's Word, God's Word must always take priority (Matthew 10:32-39). This is hard for us to accept and practice, but God clearly says he will not take second place in our lives. Obedience to his Word must come before every human loyalty we have. Who are we to ignore what God says about avoiding false fellowships?

Your
Question Can a person who belongs to a church not in fellowship with the WELS play the organ at a church wedding before the bride comes in, but while the wedding party is walking in? After they are in, a WELS person plays. After the bridal group is out, the other person plays again.

As noted above, church weddings are worship services of the church, so the same principles of church fellowship that apply to regular services apply to weddings. Only people who are in doctrinal agreement with the church should lead in these services.

In the situation you describe, it seems that an attempt is being made to adhere to our principles of fellowship, at least according to the letter. The idea is that since the nonmember is not playing *during* the service, but only *before* and *after* it, no principles of fellowship are being violated. Although your letter does not make all the details of the situation clear, the practice you describe seems dubious for the following reasons. Is it really valid to pretend that the music before and after the service is not part of the worship? In your letter you said that this music must be approved by the pastor. It is, therefore, recognized that this music is associated with the service. A further problem is that the solution you describe can easily give the impression that the congregation is more concerned about upholding the letter of an arbitrary law than it is about fulfilling the evangelical purpose of our practice.

The pastor needs to discuss with the parties involved their reason for wanting the musician in question to play at the wedding. Do they want this person to participate because they are dissatisfied with the quality of the church's musicians? If so, the pastor should try to show them that their wedding service will be a better testimony to their faith if they use the talents God has provided within our fellowship than if they feel the need to bring in someone from outside. If the reason for including nonmembers is not musical quality, but personal friendship, a second factor comes into play. Is there an unwillingness to give a clear and honest testimony to friends and relatives concerning the doctrinal differences that divide us? Is it really love for friends and family to allow them to hold the impression that the doctrinal differences are not that important and that practicing the biblical principles of church fellowship is a burden we seek to evade?

Careful instruction concerning the biblical principles of church fellowship for all the members of the congregation before individuals become involved in emotional occasions like weddings and funerals can reduce the development of compromising situations like that which you describe, but it must be granted that our principles and practices of fellowship will remain offensive to many people, just as many parts of God's Word are.

Your letter does not specify whether you think this congregation's practice is too lax or too strict. Regardless of which is the case, you should talk to the pastor and leaders of the congregation about your concerns. Be careful to listen fully to their explanations so that you are sure you have correctly understood the situation and their reason for the course they have adopted. Patient discussion, based on the principles of Scripture, is the best way to reach agreement on a sound, evangelical practice.

Your
Question **Our eldest son is engaged to a Southern Baptist. As tradition is, my wife and I are fairly sure they will be married in her church. Could you give a brief idea what WELS parents are biblically allowed to do at other churches without showing religious unity? My wife is sure she will be asked to light the mother's candle at the wedding ceremony in June. And she would like to be able to do this. Would she in this way be participating in the wedding worship service? Or is there a difference and one can participate in the ceremonial part as long as they do not participate in the religious part? Could you also state other things apart from worship that those who are trying to follow Jesus and his teachings may be allowed to join in? This may or may not include pall bearing at funeral services, etc. Does NPH have any books to help explain what may be done in these uncomfortable circumstances? If not, I hope they would come out with one fairly soon.**

We do have books that discuss examples of application of the principles of church fellowship (for example, *Church Fellowship: Working Together for the Truth*). In such books we try to avoid two dangers: (1) giving only principles with no practical help in applying them; (2) giving so many examples that people would regard them as a set of rules that settles every situation and relieves people of any responsibility for making decisions. The general principle is that we cannot participate in worship where there is lack of agreement, but we can participate in ways that do not involve participation in the worship. For example, nonmembers can serve as witnesses/attendants in weddings or as pallbearers at funerals in our churches. They could not conduct part of the worship. The same would be true of our participation at other churches. Serving as attendants, witnesses, and pallbearers would not necessarily involve participation in the worship. It would seem that customs like "giving away the bride" or lighting a mother's candle would usually have the same meaning. There might be cases in which another church insisted that such participation was part of the worship. In that case, you could not participate without giving a false testimony to agreement where none existed. What is important is that you and your son and his wife understand what message is being conveyed by your participation. The most important factor in deciding how to discuss this with your son and daughter-in-law was missing from your question. What are your son's religious beliefs, and what are your son and daughter-in-law and their family going to do about church membership after they are married? This is really a much more critical question than who lights the candle. Will your daughter-in-law remain Baptist? Will your grandchildren be baptized? Would lighting the unity candle give the impression of a spiritual unity between the spouses that really does not exist?

With your knowledge of the situation, you must decide how to best approach this topic. Your main concern here is not to follow the letter of the law but to give the best testimony you can to your son and daughter-in-law about the importance of them basing their marriage on a common faith grounded in Scripture.

Your
Question   **I have been asked to take part in a Catholic wedding. As I am considering becoming a staff minister, the fact that Catholic doctrine considers a wedding ceremony to be a sacrament bothers me. What do you think of this, and what do I say to my friend if I turn down his offer?**

It depends on what you mean by "take part." If you are simply present as a witness of what is happening, whether as an attendant or as a member of the audience, you do not have to refuse. You should not, however, participate in the worship in any way.

We should worship only with those with whom we are in agreement in doctrine. A person may be present at services of heterodox churches for reasons other than worship, for example, to attend the wedding or funeral of a relative or friend or to observe the worship of that church body in order to obtain correct information about it. But in such cases the observer should not participate in the worship, rites, or prayers of the heterodox group.

First Corinthians 8:10 ("If anyone with a weak conscience sees you . . . eating in an idol's temple, won't he be emboldened to eat what has been sacrificed to idols?") may simply be a rhetorical question referring to something that should never happen, but it may refer to a real situation in which a Christian was invited by friends or family to attend a festive meal in one of the rooms at a heathen temple, which served a function similar to our rented banquet halls. There would not necessarily be anything wrong with such attendance, as long as it did not lead weak Christians to sin against their consciences by eating meat sacrificed to idols. But 1 Corinthians 10:14-21 states very specifically that Christians are not to participate in any meals which are rites honoring an idol.

When we find ourselves in circumstances similar to this, we should do whatever is necessary to give a clear testimony. We should not join in the prayers of heterodox churches. We normally would not fold our hands or bow our heads as if praying. We would not kneel or cross ourselves during prayers to Mary or the saints. We could not participate in Communion if it is offered to visitors to the service. Normally a person would stand or sit with the congregation, but not join in gestures of prayer. A person would do whatever would convey polite nonparticipation.

You should also consider how you can give a clear testimony of your faith to your friend at an appropriate time and place.

Your Question **My boyfriend is a WELS member, and I am an American Baptist. I have been attending a WELS church and Bible study with him for six months now. We have talked about a future together, however, neither he nor his pastor have been able to give me a clear answer to this question: Will WELS fully approve of our marriage if I do not become a confirmed WELS member? Therefore am I required to become one before a WELS pastor will marry us? What is the process of becoming WELS? If I choose to remain Baptist, will WELS approve of having both a WELS pastor and a Baptist pastor perform the ceremony together? And finally, is the wedding ceremony defined in the hymnal allowed to be altered and in what ways?**

Your marriage would be a valid marriage regardless of whether it was conducted in either church or in a civil ceremony. In any case it would be recognized as a valid binding marriage since marriage is an earthly contract that is not limited to believers who share a common faith. For this reason, both parties do not have to be members of a WELS congregation for the marriage to be performed in one of our churches, but both parties must consent to the biblical principles of marriage (lifelong union, etc.). This should be established by discussion with the pastor. It is very important, however, that you and your future husband discuss the issue of the church membership each of you will hold after marriage before your marriage, especially in respect to what effect differing church membership would have on your children.

The wedding ceremony cannot be altered in any way that would contradict the biblical principles of marriage and the relationship of husband and wife. The couple can be allowed to give input into the choice of music, readings, etc. The degree of such flexibility is determined by the congregation's policy, not by any synodical rule. Since marriage services conducted in our congregations are a worship service of the church, they are conducted only by our pastors, not by or with clergy of other faiths.

Our congregations offer a series of Bible studies, often called a Bible information course, which present the beliefs of our church on the basis of the Bible. After completing this class, the person is free to decide whether or not he or she wishes to join the church. Beginning such a class does not obligate you to join the congregation. But if you make such a decision, you should do it freely because you have studied the beliefs of the church, believe they are biblical, and sincerely wish to be an active member of the congregation.

You should join our church only because you believe such membership agrees with the Bible and will serve your spiritual welfare. The way to find out if this is right for you would be to take a class (it would be good for you and your fiancé to do it together) and then make a decision on the basis of comparing what you have learned with the Bible.

Your
Question **Please explain why WELS pastors kindly refuse invitations to lead assemblies in prayer at public high school graduations. Why don't pastors of other denominations also refuse?**

Scripture teaches that people should not join in worship and prayer unless they are agreed in doctrine. They should not participate in any religious activity that gives equal status to truth and error. At public religious ceremonies all denominations and even non-Christian religions are given equal status. I was once asked to conduct a high school baccalaureate service together with a liberal Lutheran pastor, who had driven many of my members from his congregation by his false teaching.

What impression would it have given to the members of both congregations and to people in the community, if we would have conducted such a service together? In the minds of many it would have confirmed the common view that it really does not matter what you believe; all religions are basically the same and can cooperate.

Such a false impression may be given even when the adherents of opposing views do not participate in the same service, but take turns in successive services. Love requires us to give a clear testimony against religious indifference that treats truth and falsehood as equals.

Pastors of many denominations do not believe that agreement in doctrine is necessary for joint prayer and worship, so they see no problem in worshiping with people who hold unscriptural positions. Others may feel that they can participate as a testimony to their own view, without giving the impression that they are granting equal recognition to error, but such a distinction will seldom be clear to the general public.

Your
Question The other day I was watching a favorite cable access Bible-teaching program, hosted by a local AFLC pastor. I usually agree with well over 95 percent of what the pastor teaches, including his perspective on social and cultural issues. On the most recent program, however, he touched on the issue of worship, and he commented on Jesus' declaration in John 4 that we are to worship God "in spirit and in truth." This soon led to a comment, "I'm a conservative Lutheran, but there are some Lutherans who are so narrow, that if you're not their kind of Lutheran, they won't pray with you!" "Ouch," I thought, "that's us!" (in the WELS). However, I was not offended by the pastor's remark because I, too, have had great difficulty with this idea that WELS members cannot have prayer fellowship even with other genuine Christians, especially Lutherans of different synods. What if a distraught woman approached you, weeping and crying, and told you she just found out her husband had left her for another woman, and she asks you to pray with her? Suppose you know this woman is a member at an LCMS church—or even an ELCA church. "Whoa! No prayer with you, sorry, not until you become a WELS member!" Would that be our reaction? Would "prayer fellowship" ever be acceptable?

Praying with relatives or friends who are Christians but belong to a church that holds to some false teachings is addressed by the following statement of the WELS Conference of Presidents. Note that what it says is quite different from your impression of what our practice is.

Circumstances Vary, Principles Don't

Those who advocate joint prayer between representatives of Lutheran synods that are not doctrinally one will not be able to obtain clear credentials for their practice. But does this rule out every joint prayer with members of a heterodox synod? Before answering that question, we must remind ourselves that on all occasions where Christians associate with one another, whether in public or in private, whether as synodical representatives or as individuals, the same scriptural principles apply.

What these principles are, this tract has set forth, namely, that it is always the will of God for his believers (a) to manifest in worship and in prayer the fellowship of faith that unites them (Ac 2:42; Eph 5:18-20) until and unless (b) confession of the truth and rejection of error require them to separate (2 Jn 10). These are not legalistic rules but evangelical principles. They are to be applied in the spirit of our Savior, who would not break a bruised reed nor quench a smoking flax. In both these principles, that of fellowship and that of separation, there is inherent the spirit of love and true concern for the spiritual welfare of others. In any given instance, we must do whatever the glory of our Savior and the true edification of the other person may require. This may direct us to join in prayer with others or to refuse to pray with them.

Now we know that there are devout children of God in all synods who unfortunately are not yet informed regarding the matters in controversy and are not aware of their involvement in error through membership in a heterodox synod. I may have an ALC grandmother who has always manifested a simple, childlike faith in her Lord and Savior but who nevertheless is unaware of the intersynodical differences and their implications. When I visit her in the privacy of her home, it might be a grave mistake were I to assert the principle of separation by refusing to pray with her under such circumstances.

What would the Lord have me do? Should I trouble her simple faith with these matters, which are apparently beyond her grasp?

Or is it not my plain duty to support and build up her faith by praying with her or otherwise expressing my own faith?

If, however, my cousin is not only aware of the synodical differences but defends his church's errors, I cannot pray with him—not even in the privacy of his home. In order to make clear to him that the error he defends destroys the unity of our faith, I must refuse to join with him in prayer. In cases of this kind, it matters not how close the other person may be to me as a relative or friend; here the word of Jesus applies: "He that loves father or mother more than me is not worthy of me" (Mt 10:37).

There may be more occasions where prayer together with other Lutheran Christians or even with Christians of other denominations is indicated—in the hospital, for example, at the scene of an accident, or on the battlefield. When peril and imminent death reduce a Christian's confession to no more than a gasping, "Lord Jesus, help me," we pray with that soul in his desperate need, even if he is not a member of our church body. When we stand in the presence of God, one in the awareness of our guilt and one in our complete trust in his saving love, we can unite in prayer as we could have united with the thief on the cross in his simple plea, "Lord, remember me." Let us only be careful that we do not even then compromise the truth nor sanction error.

Finally, we dare not forget that there are those Christians who may be caught in an error, not willfully, but because their understanding of Scripture is insufficient. They are willing to bow to Scripture, but as yet, through human weakness, do not see clearly how the truth of Scripture necessarily rules out their error. What does God say to us concerning such weak Christians? He tells us, "Him that is weak in the faith receive ye, but not to doubtful disputations" (Ro 14:1). Receive, he says; receive such a weak brother and tenderly help him to overcome his weakness. "Receiving" such a weak Christian means that praying with him may well be in place and God-pleasing, and we trust that God will help him to grow in knowledge and strength. Certainly, this could not be done publicly without offense. And if such a person were to defend the error, even privately, then prayer with him would again be a denial of the Lord.

If we let these two principles guide us, that we manifest our Christian fellowship until confession of the truth and rejection of error require us to separate, then these concrete examples will not represent a policy of exceptions, but will constitute a truly biblical and evangelical practice.

Getting back to the thoughts of the AFLC pastor: he quoted Jesus' words that we should worship in spirit and *in truth*. True worship in the Spirit is based on agreement in the truth. If the AFLC is offended that we are not in fellowship with them, the first step to fixing the solution is simple. To seek agreement with us on what is the truth of Scripture. To my knowledge they have never sought such agreement.

Your
Question **I am a member of a WELS church in Florida. A Baptist congregation has contacted us to use our building as a temporary worship facility. They plan on building a mission outreach church in our area. They want to worship in our building twice a week. What do you think of this? What should our stance be? Does this violate synod fellowship guidelines? Wouldn't this appear we are in association with them, much as ELCA is now professing with several other denominations? If you think this is ok, what should we be watching out for or guarding against, to keep from looking like brothers?**

We can enter commercial arrangements with other people without being in fellowship with them. We can buy churches from them or sell churches to them. We can also rent to them or from them. If this is simply a commercial arrangement for a fair price, no fellowship is involved. This can be made clear to all parties. There may, however, be valid concerns about the impression this will give to your members, to the other church, or to the community. If members believe that this will give the impression that you are aiding the mission of a heterodox church (especially if they are given a below market rent that is indirect aid to their mission), you should avoid entering into such an arrangement. Even if the danger of this is not very great, the congregation may conclude that they prefer not to enter into such commercial dealings.

If a neighboring church suffers a disaster like a fire or storm damage to their sanctuary, it may be clear that by helping them out, even letting them borrow your church, you are simply being good neighbors, not endorsing or condoning their views. The circumstance you describe, however, might well be understood as helping in the establishment of a heterodox church for money.

If the situation is as you describe, I would not want to be involved in such a relationship of aiding in the establishment of a heterodox church, even if it could be argued that it was not fellowship.

Your Question What is the WELS position on a congregation hosting a CPR course or a blood drive as a means of community outreach? At what point is a congregation's position in the neighborhood compromised so that it is looked upon primarily as a social gathering place or community center? How about participation in community clothing drives, food drives, angel trees and the like? Is evangelism in the community becoming "by any means necessary"? I appreciate your time and comments.

There is no reason why WELS congregations should not be good citizens of their neighborhood by allowing the blood bank or a polling place, for example, to set up at their church. This is not really outreach, except indirectly and in the widest sense of the word—promoting good relations with the neighbors as a form of pre-evangelism. The purpose is not to evangelize people coming to give blood, but to provide a service to your community. It is simply one way of doing good to all people. It is legitimate as an end in itself. The same is true of charitable projects like a food pantry.

Whether we should participate in community drives would depend on the nature of the drives and the groups organizing them. If they are ecumenical religious projects, we cannot participate. If they are genuine community projects, there is no reason why we as members of the community cannot participate. If such things are so frequent that they are crowding out the programs of the church, then the church's priorities have become confused.

Your Question Although Scripture tells us, and you have pointed it out often in this forum, that we not be in fellowship with those who don't hold to Scripture in its entirety, it is also said that there should not be divisions in the church. My question is what are we (WELS) doing to help the visible church be more like the invisible? Shouldn't we be tireless in rebuking other church bodies for their false doctrine in the hopes that they may change? I know that they probably never will, but it seems like we should never give up testifying to the truth. Am I wrong on this matter? If so, why? And, if not, would you please give me some recent examples of WELS

communication with heterodox church bodies? Thank you, I look forward to your response.

You can personally rebuke only those people who are willing to meet with you. We have a Commission on Inter-church Relations that is willing to meet with anyone who wants to discuss doctrinal issues with us, but there are few takers interested in trying to reach doctrinal agreement on the basis of Scripture. What they are looking for is "agreement to disagree." We have had doctrinal talks with Lutheran churches like the CLC in the United States and the STLK in Finland. We have had contacts with the LCMS whenever they were interested in a frank discussion of the things that separate us. Occasionally, another church will challenge or respond to what we have printed, and we will answer their questions or complaints. But since there is almost no one interested in formal talks, our testimony has to be confined largely to publication and personal contacts.

We participate in free conferences with individuals and groups from other Lutheran churches and will explain our position to anyone who asks. We have made presentations on the issues dividing Lutheranism in both official and unofficial forums. We respond to individuals in other church bodies who ask for our advice in dealing with the false doctrine in their synod. A significant portion of the correspondence to our synod's Web site comes from non-WELS members. Students and pastors from outside our circles make use of our publications and online resources. We have placed books in the libraries of other church bodies so that their students will have accurate information about WELS. Both *Forward in Christ* and the *Wisconsin Lutheran Quarterly* address interchurch issues in almost every issue, but it takes two parties to carry on a conversation.

Your
Question **What is the proper reply when someone states, "I don't understand what the problem is (between Christians, Jews, and Moslems). They/we all pray to the same God, anyway"?**

Both Jews and Muslims make it very clear that they reject the belief that Jesus is God. In fact, in Islam believing in the deity of Jesus is the worst sin. If you are praying to the God of Islam and Judaism, you are praying to a god that does not include Jesus and his saving work. If you pray to the God of Islam and Judaism, you are not praying to the God of the Bible, who says that no one can have the Father without the Son.

There is an issue that I wish to have clarified so I can proceed with a good conscience. It is this: How far do I go in encouraging and not encouraging Christians who are not in fellowship with us? Some questions related are: Do I encourage them to attend their church? Do I encourage them to attend their church's Bible classes? I know I should encourage them to study their Bibles, but how do I encourage without seeming like I support their church or (the flipside) that I am trying to steal sheep? I also heard one of our pastors say that he encouraged a couple that was married or engaged (one went to a WELS church, the other to Catholic) to both attend the same church whether it was WELS or Catholic. That struck me funny because TO ME it seemed to make the statement that it really does not matter which church you attend as long as it is a Christian church. I am very confused on how encouraging or discouraging I should be. Thank you.

We should never encourage anyone to do something that is wrong or to believe something that is false. It is not right, for example, to encourage someone to join the Catholic church as a way of gaining family unity. As we have opportunity to talk to people about religion, we should explain the true teachings of Scripture so that they will come to recognize which teachings of their church are true and which are false. We should not be reluctant to discuss the specific reasons why we cannot agree with the teachings of their church, for example, showing Baptists why we cannot condone their rejection of infant Baptism. Our focus should be on giving a clear testimony to the truth of Scripture, above all the teaching of justification by grace alone through faith alone. If this testimony leads people to seek a fellowship in which the full truth of the Word is taught, this is not "sheep stealing." Rescuing sheep from wolves or false shepherds is not sheep stealing. We are not seeking to build ourselves up but to help people enjoy the freedom that comes from continuing in the Word.

Education

May a WELS Lutheran teach at a Missouri Synod day school?

Our members are sometimes employed by churches, religious schools, or institutions affiliated with a church. Many such jobs, such as janitorial or secretarial work and food service jobs, usually involve no religious fellowship. Our churches and schools sometimes employ nonmembers in such positions. Civil rights laws requiring nondiscrimination in hiring may also come into play in some of these cases. Other jobs, such as teaching or musical leadership, may involve a worker in the religious ministry of the church or may require participation in worship. Accepting such a job would then involve a compromise of fellowship principles. Other cases may be unclear, such as some teaching of specific secular classes or coaching positions. In such cases a person should examine each situation on its own merits or demerits. How does the employer define the job? What are the requirements of the job? Ambiguous situations are sometimes a matter of judgment. Two Christians in very similar circumstances may come to different conclusions. In such situations we should be cautious about judging the decisions made by others.

Though some Missouri Synod schools seem to regard teachers of some secular subjects as hired teachers not as called ministers, in most cases it might be difficult to avoid the religious fellowship of teaching God's Word and joining in worship unless one was hired to teach purely secular classes. In any case, one should not join in the worship of this church. If a person has a job that requires him or her to escort people to services, as for example is common in a care facility, this does not necessarily involve religious fellowship. One is present simply to carry out one's duty of giving care. If the job is basically to give day care to the children, one may be able to avoid entanglement in fellowship, but it may be difficult in most cases. One would have to decide this by discussing the terms of employment with the employer.

In most cases, it would be difficult to avoid practice of fellowship unless one was simply hired to teach certain classes. If the school is truly a Christian school, it would be very difficult to teach without being involved in the religious life of the school and church.

Your
Question When given the options of (1) attending a public school where required curriculum forces humanism, evolution, and anti-Christian morality (safe sex, abortion) upon the students or (2) attending a Christian school which is not in fellowship with the WELS where Scriptural principles on fellowship are sacrificed, what would be the God-pleasing choice?

This is admittedly a very difficult situation. It is, however, not possible to answer the question as it is written since it implies that one of the options must be God-pleasing or at least less "God-displeasing." This is not necessarily so. It may well be that neither option is God-pleasing.

In a sinful world it is possible that we can be cornered in a situation in which the only choices we have are both evil. This may happen, for example, if we have promised to do something which would be wrong, and then are faced with the choice of doing wrong or breaking our word. We should recognize that such dilemmas are the result of our sin or the sins of others, and we should seek forgiveness.

However, most of the time when we feel we must "choose between two evils," it is likely that we have created the dilemma by limiting the options too narrowly. Are there really only two choices? In the situation you describe another option may be home schooling. In the letter that accompanied your question, you state that this is not an option in your case, but you did not state why it was not. On the high school level, our synod prep schools or area high schools are another available option. Throughout history Christians have moved and even migrated to other lands to escape religious conditions that were dangerous to them and to their children. All of these options may have been ruled out as too extreme, but in dilemmas like the one you describe we must honestly ask ourselves, "Has God really left us with no other options, or have we ruled out good options that God has provided for us but that would call for sacrifices we are unwilling to make?" Before we convince ourselves that we are locked into a choice between two evils, we must be sure we are not ignoring other options that would be morally right but would require sacrifice on our part.

But, for the sake of discussion, let us suppose that the only two options are the ones you have listed. What then? We must distinguish between situations that may confront us with temptation or danger to our faith and situations that require us to sin. God may well require us to face temptation and defeat it. He does not require us to sin. Let us look at the two options you presented from this perspective.

I don't know of any public school where the required curriculum "forces humanism, evolution, and anti-Christian morality (safe sex, abortion) upon the students." The curriculum may force them to be exposed to teachers and materials that advocate such views, but the students and their parents do not have to accept or practice these views.

Being exposed to such views may be a danger, but it is not in itself a sin. It may, in fact, be an opportunity to testify against such views.

Parents should be sure they know what the school is actually teaching and not rely on rumors. They should then oppose the teaching of anti-Christian values. They may explore opportunities for their children to opt out of certain classes. If the classes actually do require the children to do things that are sinful, they must, of course, refuse to participate.

In a non-Lutheran school the children may also be endangered by exposure to teaching that is unbiblical. Such subtle false doctrine may be more dangerous to faith than the more crass and obvious errors of some public schools. I assume that children attending a private religious school have waived any right to oppose or contradict the teachings of that school. If the school, as a condition of attendance, requires children to participate in worship that violates the biblical principles of fellowship, this does not merely expose the children to danger. It also requires them to sin. This a parent cannot accept or allow.

Limited to the choices you describe in your question, I would use the public school, but would carefully seek accurate information about what was being taught, speak against those teachings that were unscriptural, seek relief from them where possible, and teach my children the truth that opposes those teachings.

Difficult situations such as the one you describe sometimes are a matter of judgment. Two sets of Christian parents in very similar environments may come to different conclusions. We should be slow to judge the decisions made by others. When confronted with such a dilemma, we should become fully informed, discuss our situation with a few trusted Christian friends, and make the best decision we can, trusting the Lord's promise, "God . . . will not let you be tempted beyond what you can bear. . . . He will also provide a way out so that you can stand up under it" (1 Corinthians 10:13).

Your
Question I have a question about a recent WELS/NET response to a question about whether a WELS member should send her children to an LCMS school. My question lies in this particular passage from the response: "If the school, as a condition of attendance, requires children to participate in worship that violates the biblical principles of fellowship, this does not merely expose the children to danger. It

also requires them to sin. This a parent cannot accept or allow." Obviously, the LCMS and the WELS are not in fellowship; but, this passage seems to say that to allow a child to worship in an LCMS service is to cause the child to sin. For instance, Romans 16:17 (as I understand it) certainly warns against contact with false teaching (with the implication that it can LEAD to sin), but it does not say that contact with false teaching IS sin. Where does the Bible say that to worship (and by worship I mean prayers and hymns and everything up to—but not including—Communion) with those outside one's synod's fellowship is a sin?

God commands us not to practice fellowship with those who hold to false teachings in many passages of the Bible including the one you cite. These passages are listed and reviewed in various questions in the archive section on fellowship. The definition of sin is lawlessness, that is, breaking any command of God. Certainly God wants us to avoid false teachers so that we will not be contaminated by their teaching. But this is only one of several reasons for avoiding them. Even if we escape being contaminated by their teaching and committing the sin of holding false doctrine, the sin is not merely in exposing ourselves to their teaching, it is the very act of associating with the false teacher in his deeds, because we are giving credibility to his work. Among the passages that state the principle of "guilt by association" with false teachers are 2 John 10,11: "If anyone comes to you and does not bring this teaching, do not take him into your house or welcome him. Anyone who welcomes him shares in his wicked work"; and 1 Timothy 5:22: "Do not be hasty in the laying on of hands, and do not share in the sins of others. Keep yourself pure."

"Contact with false teaching" in the sense of hearing someone proclaim it is not sin in itself. There may be legitimate reasons to do so, such as to oppose his teaching. Joining in with him in any way, however, is in itself sin because it gives the impression of assent to his teaching. It does not matter whether this "joining in" consists of giving him money or help, wishing him well, or participating in his worship. Your question suggests that you see a difference between praying with him and attending the Lord's Supper with him. There is no scriptural basis for such a distinction. There are not different levels of fellowship with different rules and principles.

Your
Question Recently a questioner asked you which is better, a state school or a Christian school not in fellowship with WELS. It is my contention that the operative question is this—what is education and who is responsible for it? A careful overview of Scripture clearly commands parents, not the state, to carry out these duties. Christian liberty allows us to either hire a tutor, Christian day school, or educate our children at home. With God's help any parent can see to it that their children receive a Christian education.

Scripture repeatedly assigns responsibility for a child's spiritual and moral training to the parents (Ephesians 6:4; Deuteronomy 6:4-9). Scripture does not directly address the question of whether a government may take a role in secular education. Scripture nowhere states that the government has a duty in education in the same way that it has a duty to punish evil and reward good. It does not forbid the state to have such a role, nor does it forbid Christians to use a non-Christian school or non-Christian teachers in some phase of the education of their children.

Your letter lists three permissible options for parents, but it does not mention use of a school supported by the state. Since Scripture does not forbid the use of public schools on the elementary, high school, or college level, this too is in the realm of Christian liberty, except in cases where there is some other scriptural principle that forbids participation.

Organizations

Your
Question I have heard that the Boy Scouts have changed and we no longer have to be against scouting. When did this happen?

The Boy Scouts are among the most respected organizations in this country, and the skills, activities, and companionship they offer could benefit any child. Yet, for more than 60 years, the Wisconsin Synod has warned its members that their children should not participate in the Scouting program.

Our basic objection to scouting was that the required promise and law contain religious elements which imply that the Scout can do his duty to God regardless of what religion he belongs to. This contradicts the clear statements of Scripture that no one can perform works pleasing to God without faith in Christ.

Over the years the wording of the Scout law and its explanation has become more vague and less offensive, but the religious principles have been maintained. All members of the Scouts must accept the Scout oath and law, but they may interpret it in their own way. For example, an atheist boy who refused to promise to do his duty to God was denied membership, but when he took the oath with the understanding that "god" was not a personal being, he was permitted to join. This is certainly a very offensive interpretation of the concept of "duty to God."

Recognition of the religious basis of Scouting is not limited to the WELS. Advocates of strong separation of church and state have objected to the promotion of Scouting in public schools because of its religious requirements and perceived anti-gay policy.

Because the religious requirements of Scouting remain unchanged, our WELS congregations cannot make use of the Scouting organizations. We have a better option in the Lutheran Pioneers, which provide many of the same benefits as Scouting, without the objectionable religious requirements.

The religious principles of Scouting remain unchanged, but there has been one notable development. The increased vagueness of the Scouting literature and the fact that some local scout troops may make little use of the religious features make it more difficult for pastors and teachers to convincingly demonstrate from the *Scout Handbook* the false religious principles that underlie Scouting. This makes it more difficult to convince parents that their children should not belong to the Scouts.

Those who would like to make a more thorough study of the current situation are referred to the study prepared by our synod's Committee for Information on Organizations, which is available from your district president.

Your Question Are the Girl Scouts still a religious organization with religious standards for membership?

The following from recent Girl Scout handbooks address this issue. After stating that the Scout Promise and Scout Law remain the foundation of the Scouting program, the 1995 *Guide for Cadette and Senior Girl Scout Leaders* states:

> When a girl becomes a Girl Scout, she makes the Girl Scout Promise and Law as part of her membership requirement. The Girl Scout Promise reflects the spiritual foundation of the movement. Because Girl Scouting encourages respect for the spiritual beliefs of others, girls may substitute a word representing their own faith for "God" in the Girl Scout Promise. This word should be one that most closely expresses their personal spiritual beliefs. The Girl Scout Promise in its written form will be printed with the word "God" in it.
>
> For most girls in your troop/group, there will be no change in the way they make the Girl Scout Promise. If the word "God" is not the most relevant word for a girl and there is any question of which word is most appropriate, you can work with her, her family, and religious leaders to find a substitute word to say. You will not find a list of appropriate substitutions from which to choose. The way a girl fulfills her beliefs is an individual matter and is not defined by Girl Scouting. You are not expected to judge the suitability of the word she has chosen. If you have questions or concerns, contact your Girl Scout council office for assistance.

The Girl Scouts retain a religious requirement for membership but allow it to be made to any god or to a substitute for God. Yet an adult ceremony for Scouting says, "We, the members of the Girl Scouts of the United States of America, united by a belief in God and acceptance of the Girl Scout Promise and Law, do dedicate ourselves to the purpose of inspiring girls with the highest ideals of character, conduct, patriotism and service." It stresses that a Girl Scout's Own is not a religious ceremony or service, but an inspirational occasion where Girl Scouts of every faith and creed can participate. Its content will depend on the design of the girls and their leaders. Scouting's religious awards are designed by the individual religions, so they can include recognition for projects on devotion to Mary and for religions that reject the Trinity.

We cannot say that such a group is "united by a belief in God." How can we reconcile participation in such a group with the First Commandment?

Your
Question Our church constitution specifies that members may not belong to organizations like lodges. May a person belong to a service organization like a veterans group, AARP, or trade unions that may begin meetings with prayers?

Christians should not belong to any organization in which their membership would imply acceptance of beliefs and practices contrary to the Bible. Before joining any group, Christians should analyze the beliefs and practices of the group to see if they conflict with Scripture.

Some groups, like the Masonic Lodge, have unscriptural beliefs and rites as part of their very reason for existing. Christians should never belong to such a group.

Some groups, including even the United States Congress and many state legislatures, may have objectionable practices as an incidental part of their meetings, such as beginning the business meeting with unionistic prayers. If a Lutheran Christian is a member of such a group, he or she should express their disagreement with these practices and should not participate in such prayers. They may participate in the nonreligious activities of the group.

Your
Question I am a member of the WELS with a daughter off at college. She wants to join a sorority and I was wondering what our synod's view was on sororities. She has provided me with some literature about this sorority and in the few brief pages I could find nothing that sounded like it would be against our belief. Any advice you might have would be appreciated.

Before joining any organization, a Christian should ask what are its principles, its goals, and its practices. If a sorority or fraternity has religious principles contrary to Scripture, as organizations like most lodges and the Scouts do, a Lutheran should not join. If there are no such features, there are a number of other questions to be considered. What kind of activities does the group sponsor? Are its parties or other events ones that Christians should be attending? Are its goals self-centered or do they include service to others? Does the group promote study and achievement or "good times"? What are its attitudes toward nonmembers? Does it view itself as a separated elite or as a group that gathers to support and encourage one another and to help others? What are its motives for its activities, self-pride or service? In weighing such questions, a Christian should be able to decide if membership in this group is compatible with their Christian values and goals.

Question I enjoy reading *Family Voice,* the magazine of Concerned Women for America, and make information from it available to my kids and other young people. (My pastor-husband will not touch this material with a ten-foot pole.) I have to give a minimum donation to get the subscription, but I do not join in any of the group's prayer activities or sign their post-card petitions. How should your average Christian view organizations such as CWA?

The stated purpose of Concerned Women for America is to preserve, protect, and promote traditional and Judeo-Christian values through education, legal defense, legislative programs, humanitarian aid, and related activities which represent the concerns of men and women who believe in these values. Except for an Easter hymn and a list of prayer requests, all the articles in a recent issue of *Family Voice* are aimed at political action to influence government policy on such issues as taxation, abortion, education, homosexuals in the military, and so on. Since the CWA is registered as a tax-exempt organization, it has a separately incorporated affiliate to carry out its lobbying and electioneering efforts, since such activities are forbidden to tax-exempt organizations.

Christians, of course, should not belong to any organization that requires them to accept principles or teachings contrary to the Bible. Nor should they join in prayer and worship with groups or individuals who hold teachings contrary to the Bible. They should not offer financial support to such organizations. The Masonic Lodge and similar lodges would be examples of such organizations.

The task of drawing clear lines may become more difficult when the organization in question is not a religious organization and has no religious requirements, but it does have some religious activities or motivations attached to it. In such cases a number of considerations may help Christians decide to what degree, if any, they may be involved.

For the sake of obtaining information, Christians can always buy books or subscribe to periodicals even from groups whose philosophy they reject and which they would not join. For example, our synodical libraries subscribe to many periodicals published by groups our students could not join. The subscription price paid is for goods received. A somewhat similar situation may exist at times with such groups as the YMCA. The foundations of this organization are Christian and full membership involves religious activity. But the organization recognizes a different level of "membership" at which the participants simply become users of the athletic facilities in exchange for a certain payment.

As citizens WELS members may participate in political action groups that try to influence legislation and government policies to bring them into closer agreement with the moral principles set forth in the Bible. For example, members of WELS Lutherans for Life (now Christian Life Resources) might also be members of a nonreligious right-to-life group in which they join with people of other faiths or of no faith at all in efforts to influence government policy. In the WELS group, changing people's hearts through God's law and gospel would be their goal and method. In the secular group, changing people's minds through education and changing their conduct through civil law would be the goals.

A problem arises when such organizations begin to blur the line between religious groups and nonsectarian political action groups by introducing prayer or other religious activities into their program. (The same problem can arise in groups as different as the local garden club or the US Congress.) If such activities are seen as an essential activity of the group and are prominent in its program, you should not join such a group or participate in its activities. If the objectionable activity is incidental to the purpose and program of the group (such as prayer at the opening of the convention of a political party or Congress), Christians should refrain from participating in that activity and should express their objections to the practice. They may participate in the regular, secular functions of the group.

An additional problem with many political action groups that are under heavy Reformed or Catholic influence is that they often confuse the responsibility of the church and its members (changing people's conduct by first changing their hearts with the gospel) with the responsibility of the state and its citizens (changing people's conduct by enforcing beneficial laws). Many of these groups include efforts to change society by lobbying and legislation within the mission of the church as such. Christians should be clear on the distinction between what they do as Christians (preaching the Sixth Commandment to lead to repentance) and what they do as citizens (seeking laws against various forms of sexual immorality as a protection to individuals and society).

How do these principles apply to CWA? Receiving the publications of such groups does not in and of itself involve any fellowship problems. If the CWA would stick to its stated purpose of serving as an educational and political action group, membership would not be wrong either. I was not able to obtain firsthand information about the meetings and activities of CWA, but the names of the group's leaders and some of the contents of the magazine suggest that the line between joint religious activity and political action is not always kept clear. If this is the case, you shouldn't join as a regular member. If such actions are not part of the regular activity of the group, but intrude occasionally into the activities of the group, don't participate in them and object to them.

In short, don't join any organization without inquiring about its beliefs and practices. If either its beliefs or practices conflict with the Bible, don't join. If incidental violations of biblical principles arise, object to them and do not participate in them. If subsequent to joining, you find that membership is involving you in beliefs or practices contrary to Scripture, or if activities involved in membership trouble your conscience, quit.

Your Question

A friend of mine has asked me to bowl with him in an Elks league. He is not a member of the Elks and, obviously, neither am I. Would I be violating any of our beliefs if I choose to bowl with him? Thanks for your help.

There is not necessarily any fellowship involved in being in a sports league. Many of our schools are in leagues with schools of other denominations and congregations may be in church leagues with churches from outside our synod. If this is an open league in which anyone can participate without any affiliation with the Elks, there is not a problem unless participation in the league would be misunderstood or create offense among members of your church or community. You should inquire to see if there are any strings attached to participation or if participation could be confusing to people.

6
Last Things (Eschatology)

The word *eschatology* is based on a Greek word that means "the study of the last things." Eschatology treats the points of Christian doctrine that deal with death, judgment, the end of the world, and eternity.

Death and the Time Between Death and Resurrection

Your Question **Every age thinks that the end is near. I have often wondered if the imminence of the Last Day has to do more with the day of our deaths, which we cannot know, versus only the final Day of Judgment since at our death our fate is sealed.**

When people die, they immediately go to heaven or hell (Luke 16:22; 1 Peter 3:19,20). Already at the time of their deaths, people are assigned by God to heaven or hell without any investigation or trial since he knows the heart of every individual. In several places the Bible speaks of conscious reactions of souls in hell or heaven. The rich man is afraid that his brothers will join him in hell (Luke 16:27,28). Jesus descended to hell to proclaim his victory to the spirits of those who had died in the flood (1 Peter 3:19,20). Jesus promised the repentant thief that he would be with him in paradise "today" (Luke 23:43). The souls of the martyrs live and rule with Christ in heaven (Revelation 20:4) and pray for his justice to come upon the earth (Revelation 6:10). In this sense, "our fate is sealed" on the day we die.

The Bible, nevertheless, teaches us to look forward to the day of resurrection and judgment. Our goal is not to die and to have our souls go to heaven. Our goal is to have our souls and bodies joined together again as God created them to be. Our goal is not just to escape the injustice of life on earth through death, but to have injustice on earth come to an end. As was noted above, even the saints in heaven pray for judgment day.

The passages that refer to the nearness of Christ's coming (such as James 5:7-9; 1 Peter 4:7; Revelation 1:3; 22:10,12) do not seem to be pointing so much to the day of our deaths as to the day of Christ's appearing. If nearly two thousand years have passed, how could this event be said to be "near" already in the days of the apostles? Certainly, one factor is that God's way of looking at time is not the same as ours (2 Peter 3:8,9). But a more important factor from our perspective is that the Bible treats everything since Christ's first coming as "the last days" (Acts 2:17; Hebrews 1:2). To put it another way, we could say "Christ's return is near" means "everything is ready for Christ's return." All of God's plans for salvation have been completed except for the one event that remains, Christ's return. The clearest expression of this is in Hebrews 9:26-28. In saying Christ's return is near, God is not measuring days on a calendar but completeness of the preparations. Everything is ready. God's banquet is ready. He needs no more time to get ready. But in patience he is giving the people of the world time to get ready.

Yes, for all practical purposes, the day we die is the Last Day for us. But the Bible teaches us to eagerly await the Last Day for this earth when Christ's assignment as Savior is completed and God is all in all (1 Corinthians 15:24-28). That day is near.

Your
Question **When Lazarus died, Jesus said, "Lazarus has fallen asleep." Between death and resurrection is the soul conscious or is it asleep?**

As noted above, as soon as people die, their souls go directly to heaven or to hell.

When the Bible speaks of death as "sleep," the reference is primarily to the body. Sometimes death is called "sleep" in a negative sense: the dead can no longer participate in any earthly activities (Psalm 76:5). The main point of comparison, however, is positive: just as we awake each morning from sleep, our bodies will awake from the grave on the morning of resurrection. "Multitudes who sleep in the dust of the earth will awake: some to everlasting life, others to shame and everlasting contempt" (Daniel 12:2).

Luther and other orthodox writers sometimes spoke of a rest or sleep for the soul after death. Their aim was to stress that those who have departed in faith now enjoy rest from the toil of this life. The point of comparison was *rest*, not *unconsciousness*. It is better, however, not to refer to sleep of the soul. Today false teachers who deny the continued existence of the soul after death use the term "soul sleep" to describe the temporary dissolving of the soul, which they believe will be re-created on the Last Day. Since "soul sleep" is used to mean "soul death," it is best to avoid the term altogether.

Your
Question   **I have been having discussions with a coworker regarding the soul being reunited with the body on judgment day. She is a believer in the "rapture" and says that flesh will not inherit heaven. She thinks I'm a little foolish for believing that my body will go to heaven. She can certainly quote the Bible and cannot believe that I think my body will some day be in heaven, only your soul goes there. Can you tell me how to respond to this?**

Your coworker must be confused about something her church believes unless she belongs to a very unusual group. People who believe in the rapture of believers as a separate event that is prior to judgment day do believe in the resurrection of the body. They, in fact, believe in more than one resurrection of the body—that is, different resurrections for different people at different stages of the end times. The main passage that allegedly teaches the rapture, 1 Thessalonians 4 (actually it is talking about the first event of judgment day), very clearly mentions the resurrection of the body.

The resurrection of the body is very clearly taught in 1 Corinthians 15. Your friend's idea seems to be a misunderstanding of 1 Corinthians 15:50—"flesh and blood cannot inherit the kingdom of God." It is very clear in the context that this is not denying that we will have our bodies in heaven, but that our bodies must be changed to glorious bodies before they can enter heaven. This must happen even for those who are alive at Christ's return, who never pass through death.

Only between death and resurrection is the soul in heaven without the body.

Your
Question Is there any biblical support for the idea that departed Christians become angels who can look down from heaven and observe our daily activities?

In heaven we will be similar to the angels in two respects: we will not die and we will not marry and reproduce (Luke 20:35,36). But we will not be angels. After the resurrection we will have bodies and souls. The angels are and will remain pure spirits. There is nothing in Scripture that suggests that the saints in heaven have any knowledge of specific events taking place on earth. Isaiah 63:16 suggests that they do not: "But you are our Father, though Abraham does not know us or Israel acknowledge us; you, O LORD, are our Father." We are to look to God as the one who watches over us, not to departed saints.

Passages that seem to imply knowledge that people in heaven have about events on earth speak only of a general knowledge of the way life is on earth, not about a knowledge of specific events that occurred on earth after the saints' departure from earthly life (Luke 16:27,28; Revelation 6:10).

There is no need for the saints in heaven to watch over our lives on earth since the Lord sends his angels to watch over us and he himself knows every hair on our heads. Would we want our loved ones in heaven to be burdened with the affairs and concerns of life on earth?

Signs of the End and the End Times
Millennialism

Your
Question I hear all of these end times terms such as Zionism, Millennialism Pre- and Post-, 1,000 year reign, seven year reign, rapture, Left Behind, etc. Could you better define the Lutheran doctrinal teaching on eschatology in a concise way to explain to someone who believes in the end times the way that the majority of evangelicals do?

We believe that there is just one return of Christ for which we are waiting. On that one day, in a time of trouble for the church, when the faith of many has grown cold, Christ will appear in glory in the heavens. The dead will rise, and all believers will be gathered to meet him as he comes. The judgment will follow. Believers will enjoy eternal life in the new heavens and the new earth. Unbelievers will be sentenced to hell.

The most common contemporary form of millennialism believes that Christ will come to rapture believers out of the world, after this the Jews and those who remain will come into great tribulation and conflict with the Antichrist, judgment will follow this seven-year period, then will come the millennium, then a renewed attack by Satan, finally another coming of Christ and judgment, followed by eternity. Various aspects of millennialism are discussed in subsequent questions.

Your Question

Dear WELS, I became a Christian six months ago and have been studying the Word ever since, but many questions have been coming up. My first question is about Revelation 3:10, the hour of trial. What is this hour of trial? The devil or antichrist creating counterfeit miracles or what? What trial are they talking about? Many people believe this to be the tribulation which the true believers of Christ will be raptured right before. But through many passages of the Bible, it talks only of one other return, not two. And second, these people bring up 1 Thessalonians 4:13-18—the coming of the Lord in the air, not touching the earth. But in Zechariah 14:4, it says, "On that day his feet will stand on the Mount of Olives. . . ." And in Acts 1:11, "This same Jesus, who has been taken from you into heaven, will come back in the same way you have seen him go into heaven." When Jesus rose and went to talk to his disciples, he was in physical form but in the air, he never touched earth. So my question is, do 1 Thessalonians 4:13-18 and Zechariah 14:4 talk about the same day or two separate things? First the dead in Christ, then all who are alive, and then once that happens, Jesus will come back to earth and reign with all his believers. Are these two verses from the Bible put together evidence that Christ will first take his believers and then come to reign and destroy evil? Thank you for listening.

Revelation 3:10 refers to all the trials that come on believers between Christ's first and second comings. It does not refer to removing believers from the world by a rapture but to keeping them safe through all the danger they face. This is very clear when you compare this passage with Jesus' prayer in John 17:15. Jesus' prayer is not that God take us out of the world, but that he keep us safe from the evil.

You have correctly stated that we are to expect only one return of Christ. Not all of the passages that discuss the Last Day discuss every event of that day. Some of the passages refer only to some of the events of that day, depending on the question they are addressing. First Thessalonians 4 is a good example of this.

The views you describe are basically the views of pretribulation, premillennialism. This theory separates Christ's gathering of believers, which they call the rapture, from the coming of Christ to set up his millennial kingdom by a seven-year period, during which conflict between the Jews and the antichrist leads to great tribulation for the Jewish people. There is no basis in Scripture for any of this.

The unique idea of this theory is the claim of a *rapture* of believers separated in time from Christ's visible return. As used in this context, the word *rapture* means "seize and take up." It refers to the words "caught up" in 1 Thessalonians 4:15-17:

> According to the Lord's own word, we tell you that we who are still alive, who are left till the coming of the Lord, will certainly not precede those who have fallen asleep. For the Lord himself will come down from heaven, with a loud command, with the voice of the archangel and with the trumpet call of God, and the dead in Christ will rise first. After that, we who are still alive and are left will be *caught up* together with them in the clouds to meet the Lord in the air. And so we will be with the Lord forever.

Those who use the word *rapture* to refer to this event usually teach that believers will be carried away from the world before the great tribulation comes on the earth in the last days. Then after this tribulation, Christ will come to the earth to begin his millennial kingdom, which will last a thousand years. At the end of the millennium, Christ will come again.

Scripture, however, teaches only one return of Christ, not three. The gathering together of believers to meet Christ takes place on the day of the last judgment. It is not a separate event. Here Paul says that the first event that has to take place on the Last Day is that the dead believers must rise so that they and the believers who are still alive when Christ comes can all be gathered to meet Christ together as he comes to judge all people. This will be similar to the joyful crowds on Palm Sunday that ran out to meet Jesus. The unbelievers are not gathered to meet Christ. They want to hide from his judgment. They will not be able to do this, however, since all people will have to appear before his judgment. Unbelievers too will be gathered to judgment, but not as part of the happy welcoming crowd.

In the text above, "the dead in Christ will rise first" does not refer to a resurrection of believers that precedes a second resurrection for unbelievers a thousand years later. "First" is contrasted with what occurs in the next sentence. The dead in Christ will rise first so that after that, we who are still alive and are left will be caught up together with them to meet Christ. Together they will welcome him to the earth and Christ will complete the judgment. First Thessalonians 4 describes only the first events of the Last Day because that was all that was necessary to answer the Thessalonians question: "What will happen to our loved ones who have departed?" Zechariah 14 and other passages refer to subsequent events on the Last Day.

Scripture does not teach a special period of seven years of tribulation at the end of time. It teaches that the whole New Testament era will be a time of tribulation for the church with an intense period of tribulation at the end. The three and one-half years described repeatedly in Revelation ("time, times and half a time"; 42 months) is a figurative expression for the whole New Testament era. This is especially apparent in Revelation 12, where the three and one-half years begins with Christ's ascension and ends with his return. The millennium in Revelation 20 is not a thousand-year rule of Christ on this earth after believers have been raptured away from the world. It is the whole time of the New Testament era.

Your
Question I'm hoping you can help me with some questions I have about Israel. I can't seem to find any reference material that is not written from the dispensational/millennial viewpoint. If you could point me to something written primarily with this topic in mind and is scriptural, I'd really appreciate it. Regarding the Land of Israel, Genesis 17:8 says, "The whole land of Canaan, where you are now an alien, I will give as an everlasting possession to you and your descendants." The boundaries of the land are identified in Genesis 15:18-21 and Exodus 23:31. I'm not certain, but I don't think the Israelites ever occupied all of that land. Was the promise of the land somehow conditional? If not, should we look for Israel to get the land in the future? Hebrews 8:13 ("By calling this covenant 'new,' he has made the first one obsolete") would seem to suggest not. However, I'm bothered by the phrase "everlasting possession." Regarding the

people of Israel, I know that there is only one way to heaven and that's to believe in Jesus Christ as your Savior, whether Jew or Gentile. Does Scripture indicate that in the last days, God will pour out his Spirit and cause a large number (not all, possibly a remnant) of unbelieving Jews to believe in Jesus Christ as their Savior? Is the growth in the number of Messianic Jews today perhaps some evidence of this? To me the following Scripture passages seem to lend some credence to this idea. Romans 11 overall, but particularly verses 11, 25, and 26. Verse 11: "Salvation has come to the Gentiles to make Israel envious." Also verses 25 and 26: ". . . Israel has experienced a hardening in part until the full number of the Gentiles has come in. And so all Israel will be saved . . ." Luke 21:24: "They will fall by the sword and will be taken as prisoners to all the nations. Jerusalem will be trampled on by the Gentiles until the times of the Gentiles are fulfilled."

The word *Israel* can, of course, sometimes refer to the nation of Israel, but Scripture makes it clear that the promises belong to the Israel of faith, not to the physical Israel. Among the passages that teach this are Romans 9:6-8; Galatians 4:24-31 (especially 28); Galatians 6:16; John 8:39,44; Revelation 3:9; and Philippians 3:2,3. No one who is not a believer in Christ is an heir of any of the promises. That the restoration of David's kingdom is the result of the worldwide preaching of the gospel is clear from a comparison of Amos 9:11,12 with its fulfillment in Acts 15 by the mission work of Paul.

The way that "all Israel" is saved in Romans 9–11 is through the salvation of Jews who remain as natural branches attached to Christ and the salvation of the wild Gentile branches who are grafted in. Certainly large numbers of Jews may be converted to Christ by the preaching of the gospel, but we are not to look for a mass conversion of the nation as a condition for Christ's return.

Israel briefly dominated the area to the Euphrates in the time of David. The outward fulfillment of the promises of the land and the kingship depended on obedience. The warning of exile was already contained in Moses' warning at the end of Deuteronomy. The line of David that ruled the state of Judah ended and the people went into exile as a result of persistent idolatry, but the deeper significance of the prophecy is fulfilled in the rule of Christ and in the new heavens and new earth, the Jerusalem above.

We don't have a book just on this subject, but commentaries on the above passages and on Revelation will treat the issue.

Your
Question **We are having a discussion at work, there is this woman
and she heard today on the news that there was a suicide bombing in
Megiddo and she is saying that this is where the final battle will take
place before the end. She gave me a Bible passage of Revelation 16:16
that this Megiddo is mentioned. Does this particular Scripture say that
this is true? In our Bible study of Revelation, we were told there is no
geographical location known as Armageddon, which she is referring
to happening in this place called Megiddo. I do not want to speak
before I know what I am talking about. We belong to the Wisconsin
Synod. Thank you.**

Megiddo was an ancient city located near a key mountain pass in
Israel. It now lies in ruins. It is believed that the word *Armageddon*
derives from the Hebrew words that mean "mountain of Megiddo."
Because of its strategic location, many battles have been fought there.
The mountain of Megiddo (Mount Carmel) is also the place where
Elijah had his showdown with the priests of Baal.

Revelation, like the rest of Scripture, often speaks of the end time
attacks against the church. The great battles in Revelation are not
military actions against the political nation of Israel but against God's
church, his new Jerusalem. This imagery of battle is a symbolic way of
describing all attacks against God's people. Because Megiddo was a
very famous battlefield, John used it as a name for the last great battle
against God's people, just as he used Babylon as a name for the great
enemy of the New Testament church, the Antichrist.

Your
Question **I am puzzled about how we as Lutherans argue that the
Antichrist is a person in a specific office that exists throughout history
(the papacy), rather than a single end time individual. The text does
not speak of "the men of lawlessness," but rather "the man" and "the
lawless one," rather than "the lawless many."**

**Although I agree that the pope is certainly antichristian in character,
and the signs and wonders and even the name *antichristos* fits his
description, the only stumbling block here for me is the fact that we
speak of the Antichrist as an office.**

**This causes me to ask two questions: 1. What is found in the context
that shows us that the antichrist is not one person but a line of people
in a specific office? 2. Are there any other instances of an office spoken
of in this fashion in Scripture?**

The answer to your second question is "yes." It is normal in biblical language for an institution or office that is a succession of individuals to be named by a singular name of the office holder, that is, "king" may refer to a succession of kings holding the same office.

Unfortunately the NIV does not always make this clear. In Daniel 7:17 the NIV calls the Babylonian, Persian, Greek, and Roman Empires four "kingdoms." The Aramaic actually refers to four "kings." The NIV does not convey the wrong idea, since these same four empires were called kingdoms in Daniel 2. But a more literal translation would be better since the NIV obscures the biblical idiom.

In Daniel 11 each one of a succession of Seleucid and Ptolemaic kings is called the king of the North or the king of the South. We can do the same thing in English. I can say the pope claims jurisdiction over the whole church, or I can say the papacy claims jurisdiction over the whole church with no difference of meaning. I can say the president of the United States has constitutional authority to do x, y, and z, and it is understood that I am referring both to the office and to all its incumbents. On the other hand, if I say the president of the United States is coming to town tomorrow, it is understood that the reference is to the current incumbent. In exactly the same way I can say the pope is the Antichrist or the papacy is the Antichrist.

In response to your first question, it can be added that in 2 Thessalonians 2 the force of the man of sin is already at work in Paul's day but is being restrained from coming out into the open. The force that is holding him back is called both a person (probably the Roman emperor) and a thing (the Roman empire). The man of sin is not destroyed until Christ's return. It must therefore be an institution, not one end time person.

Also in the book of Revelation, the visions cover the whole New Testament era, not just one event or person. This is especially clear in chapter 12, which goes from Christ's ascension until his return.

Your Question Is the Roman Catholic Church the great whore mentioned in Revelation 17:5,6?

Throughout Scripture the prostitute is the false church, whether Old Testament Israel (as in Ezekiel 16) or the New Testament false church in Revelation. In Revelation 17 the false church is connected with the city of Rome. The other traits also fit the Roman church. See the previously answered questions concerning the Antichrist. The Roman papacy is the Antichrist. There are many other antichrists. The false church in Revelation 13 likely includes also these other antichrists.

Your Question Which numbers are used symbolically in Revelation? What do they mean? Why/How does one know what they exactly mean?

Since the whole book of Revelation describes real events, but by means of symbols, all of the numbers in Revelation have symbolical value. In a few cases the numbers also refer to real things—for example, the seven churches in Asia Minor referred to in chapters 1 and 2 were seven real churches. However, they were not the only churches in Asia Minor. They seem to have been chosen to represent the whole church.

The other numbers we have to interpret by letting Scripture interpret Scripture. The Bible says God is only three persons, not nine, so we cannot interpret the seven spirits in chapter 1 as seven persons of the Trinity, but as figures representing the one Spirit with all his gifts. Chapter 12 makes it clear that the "time, times and half a time"—three and a half years or 42 months—cover the time from Christ's ascension to his return, so we can interpret it in the same way in its various occurrences throughout the book.

Your Question What is the Mark of the Beast as described in Revelation? I have read many things about this mark. What is the WELS view on the mark? Could it be a literal mark on a person's hand or forehead, or could it be like the Seventh Day Adventists' view of Sunday worship? Just curious on the WELS viewpoint. Thanks!

First we have to identify the beast. Actually there are two beasts in Revelation 13. The first beast uses the force of government persecution to oppress the church; the second uses false teaching. Both elements, of course, have figured prominently in the history of the papacy. Some Lutheran commentators have seen the first beast as typical of the way the papacy operated before the Reformation, and the second as typical of the way that it has operated since the Reformation. This is true, but in Revelation 13 the image is probably wider than just the papacy. It warns against all use of government power and false teaching to oppress God's people.

Many attempts have been made to identify the number 666 with the name of an individual by giving a numerical value to each letter of a name and adding them up to see if they total 666. Since the numbers in Revelation have symbolic value, it seems best to understand this number in the same way. Since 7 is the number of God's completed word, the number 666 means something like "triple failure." It often seems as if Satan and his henchmen will destroy the church, but they always fall short.

Receiving the mark of the beast means making whatever accommodations are necessary to be allowed to prosper in his kingdom. In the Roman Empire, it meant getting the little certificate that stated that one had burned incense to the emperor. In Communist lands it might mean initiation into the Communist youth organization rather than confirmation in the church in order to get into the university. In Western countries it might mean having to accept evolution to get a science degree. Any faith-denying compromise to get along with the world and with the false church would be receiving the mark of the beast.

Your
Question **Explain the 1,000-year reign of Christ.**

Every Lutheran commentary on Revelation 20 speaks about this reign in detail. One of the best discussions is in Siegbert Becker's commentary *Revelation: The Distant Triumph Song*, pp. 303-315. To gain the best understanding of the context, one should read his comments on all of Revelation 20. The main points are the following.

The passage says nothing about a thousand-year reign of Christ on earth as millennialists falsely claim. The passage describes the souls of those who have died for Christ as reigning with him in heaven after their death and before judgment day. The first resurrection is when our souls come alive through faith in Christ. Through faith we live and reign with Christ. This life continues even when the body has been killed. We speak of this reign every time we speak of the life of souls in heaven. One of the clearest descriptions of this reign is in Ephesians 2:4-6: "God, who is rich in mercy, made us alive with Christ even when we were dead in transgressions—it is by grace you have been saved. And God raised us up with Christ and seated us with him in the heavenly realms in Christ Jesus." In the context of Revelation and from the larger context of Scripture, it is clear that the thousand years here refers to the whole time between Christ's first and second coming. Through this whole time, the souls of believers live and reign with Christ. This is a truth we speak about very often. This reign is what we are looking forward to, not a millennial kingdom on this earth.

Your
Question **My heart is concerned. Overall, my main concern is regarding the teachings of the End Times theology of Grace Lutheran and Lutherans in general as compared to those of millennialists. After last night, hearing a preacher (Jack Van Impe Ministries, Troy, Michigan) say that his life is devoted to rooting out Amillennialism because it is a blasphemous, dangerous, and the most wicked theology of lots of churches today, is cause for concern for me. The next step is for me to suspend my Lutheran beliefs in what I have been taught by End Times theology because I hear so much about it in contrary terms by others all around me. I am not there yet, but I am very close. Obviously, both doctrines aren't correct. You say that you are correct (regarding your End Times theology) for various reasons and you can back up your assertions through Scripture. But the Millennialists also have Scripture to back up their assertions made about the tribulation, rapture, and 1,000 year reign of Christ. Can both come from the Holy Spirit? I don't think so. One is wrong! Thank you for your time and consideration into this matter.**

There is, of course, no short and easy answer to this concern. It requires a thorough study of prophecy on the basis of the principle "Scripture interprets Scripture." Millennialists claim that they are interpreting Scripture literally and that we are departing from the literal meaning. We say that we are to interpret Scripture according to its own interpretation. If Revelation itself says that some things in Revelation are symbols of real things rather than a literal description of these things (as it does in chapter 1), we are to accept what Scripture says. If James in Acts 15 says that Amos' prophecy about the building of David's kingdom is fulfilled by New Testament preaching, we are to believe him.

A place to start addressing your concern is with a study of Revelation as it is explained by the whole of Scripture. Three books that will help you do this are the Revelation commentaries of Siegbert Becker, Luther Poellot, and Wayne Mueller and the Revelation Bible study by John Brug, which are available from Northwestern Publishing House (these are listed in order from the most in-depth to the most simple). All of these follow the principle of directing you to other passages so you can apply the principle "Scripture interprets Scripture." Many aspects of this doctrine, such as tribulation and rapture, are discussed under other questions in this section of this book and in the online archive.

The key point is to let Scripture interpret Scripture, not to let someone impose an interpretation on Scripture based on imagination and speculation. When we interpret according to this principle, it is clear that Revelation 20 does not teach an earthly millennium. The first part of Revelation 20 describes three main events: the binding of Satan, the rule of the saints with Christ, and the loosing of Satan.

The definition of the binding of Satan is that he cannot deceive the nations anymore. Nations that were slaves to him can come to Christ. This happened as a result of the first coming of Christ. Among the passages that show this are John 12:32; Luke 10:18; 1 Peter 3:18,19; Colossians 2:15; and 1 John 3:8. Revelation 12 also makes it clear that the time of Satan's binding begins from when the divine child returns to heaven (Jesus' ascension) until when he returns. This section is saying the same thing as the great commission: "All authority in heaven and on earth has been given to me. Therefore go and make disciples of all nations" (Matthew 28:18,19).

The loosing of Satan is that he again deceives the nations, and nations that had been free of his rule go back to serving him. This has already happened in many of the Christian countries of Europe and is occurring in a lesser degree in the United States. This "short season" of apostasy before Christ's return is spoken of throughout the New Testament.

Since the "millennium" occurs between Christ's first and second coming, it is identical with the New Testament era. It is not a literal thousand-year period after the history of the church has been completed. The rule with Christ described here is the rule of the souls of those who were beheaded for their faith, who are now gathered around the throne of Christ. Everywhere throughout Revelation, the throne of Christ is in heaven, not on earth. This same reality is described in the fifth seal in Revelation 6, where we see souls kept safe in heaven. The first resurrection is the passing from spiritual death to life that takes place when we are born again by being brought to faith in Christ. This life continues in heaven even when the body is dead in the grave. The second resurrection is the resurrection of the body, which everyone experiences on the Last Day, but to two different results—salvation or damnation.

There will be only one return of Christ at the end of history, not two or more as millennialists teach.

Judgment

Your
Question **When does God judge us? Are we judged already in this life? Are we judged when we die and again at judgment day?**

Disciplinary suffering that God places upon a Christian in this life may be called a *judgment* (1 Corinthians 11:29-32). The purpose of such discipline, however, is to correct us, not to punish us. Some of the Corinthians experienced such judgment because of their misuse of the Lord's Supper.

An unbeliever who has hardened his heart or committed the sin against the Holy Spirit may be finally rejected by God already while he is still alive (1 John 5:16). This appears to have been the case with King Saul (1 Samuel 16:1; 28:6) and Judas (John 13:27).

As soon as people die, they go directly to heaven or hell (Luke 16:22,23; 1 Peter 3:19,20; Luke 23:43). God, who knows all, does not need an investigation to determine where they belong. The Bible speaks of no formal appearance before God's judgment at the time of death.

We will, however, appear before God's public judgment when we rise from the grave on the Last Day (Matthew 25:31-46). The purpose of this judgment is not for God to determine who belongs in heaven or hell, but to demonstrate the justice of the judgment God already made when he sent people either to heaven or to hell.

Judgment day, therefore, is not like an earthly trial in which God needs to determine people's guilt or innocence. Judgment day is more like the day of sentencing in our earthly system of justice. On the day of sentencing, the judge pronounces sentence on the guilty criminals who have been held in prison while they were waiting to be sentenced. The judge presents the reasons that justify his sentence. Judgment day will be similar to such a day of sentencing. On judgment day God is not determining guilt or innocence, but he is showing the justice of his sentences to heaven or to hell. Judgment day will display the justice of God's judgments to all.

Hell

Your Question **What does the WELS believe about hell? Is it a place of fire and brimstone where unbelievers literally "burn" for eternity? The Bible calls it a "lake of fire" but also "the darkness where there is weeping and gnashing of teeth." Recently the pastor of my WELS congregation said that "darkness" and "fire" don't go together so it's not really a place with fire. I was brought up (in a WELS) church believing that it was. Now I'm confused.**

It is clear that the fire of hell is supernatural. It does not burn up those who are in it. It is also clear that the main point of comparison between the fire of hell and fire on earth is pain. The main point of comparison between the darkness of hell and darkness on earth is gloom and sadness. Since both the fire and darkness of hell are supernatural, maintained by the power of God, there is no reason why fire and darkness are incompatible.

Whether or not *literal* is the best word to describe the fire of hell may be debatable, but without a doubt *real* is an appropriate word. Whether or not the chemistry and physics of fire in hell is the same as fire on earth, the reality is the same—the experience of suffering is the same. The gloom of hell is also the same experience as darkness on earth. Though our Lutheran theologians sometimes hedged on whether *literal* or *physical* were the best words to describe the fire of hell since that fire is supernatural, the reality of it is not to be questioned. *Real but supernatural* seems to be the best combination of terms.

Your Question **What is *sheol*? I have heard that it was a place where all the Old Testament dead were, and that Jesus rescued Old Testament believers from there after his resurrection.**

Sheol is a Hebrew word that means "the place or condition of death." It can refer to the grave, to the condition of all the dead, and occasionally to the place where unbelievers go, that is hell. Hades, Gehenna, Tartarus, the Abyss, prison, and the lake of fire are other biblical names for hell. These are not different places but different names for the same place, just as heaven, paradise, and Abraham's side are names for one place, heaven.

Because *sheol* sometimes means "the grave" or "the condition of death," it can be said that everyone goes to Sheol. On this basis, negative critics teach that the Old Testament people believed that all the dead, believers and unbelievers alike, went to a kind of shadowy underworld and that belief in heaven and hell only developed later. This we reject. Though heaven and hell are not described in the Old Testament in the same detail as in the New, the people then understood that there were different destinations waiting for believers and unbelievers.

Many Catholic writers teach that before Jesus' resurrection Old Testament believers were kept in the limbo of the fathers, a part of Sheol. According to this view, Jesus' descent to hell was really a journey to Sheol to get these people and take them to heaven. There is no basis for this belief in the Bible. When Old Testament believers died, they went immediately to the presence of God. They were not kept in a temporary storage place.

Your Question **My father spoke to a Wisconsin Synod pastor yesterday who told him there are levels of hell. I've never heard that. Are you teaching purgatory?**

No, we are not. All places in hell are permanent, not temporary like those in Catholic purgatory. Some places in hell are worse than others. The Bible does not explain exactly what the degrees of punishment in hell will consist of, but it does say that those who have greater knowledge are more guilty than those who had less knowledge and that those who are more guilty will receive greater punishment.

Perhaps the best starting place is Luke 12, since both points are mentioned. Luke 12:47,48: "That servant who knows his master's will and does not get ready or does not do what his master wants will be beaten with many blows. But the one who does not know and does things deserving punishment will be beaten with few blows. From everyone who has been given much, much will be demanded; and from the one who has been entrusted with much, much more will be asked."

To the Jews, who had the benefit of Christ's preaching to them in person, he said: "I tell you, it will be more bearable for Tyre and Sidon on the day of judgment than for you" (Matthew 11:22). To Pilate he said, "The one who handed me over to you is guilty of a greater sin" (John 19:11).

Romans 1:18 through 2:28 compares the Gentiles who were guilty of suppressing the natural knowledge of God and his law and the Jews who disobeyed the revealed will of God. You may want to read this whole section. Paul concludes that both are guilty, but all will be judged by the standard of what they had. "God does not show favoritism. All who sin apart from the law will also perish apart from the law, and all who sin under the law will be judged by the law" (Romans 2:11,12). Paul says clearly that all are without excuse (Romans 1:20). All are guilty, but those who have greater knowledge have greater guilt. Scripture gives us this warning so that the knowledge we have does not become a curse to us rather than a blessing. This does not encourage anyone to have a casual attitude toward unbelief because there are no good places in hell, only worser and worstest.

Your **Question** **The pastor I'm studying with has been a big help in answering my questions, but I thought I'd ask some questions on this Web site as well.**

Regarding hell: According to Ecclesiastes 9:5,10 and Psalm 146:4, the dead do not experience pain and are not conscious . . . so how can they be tormented for eternity in hell? Wouldn't they need to have consciousness in order to feel torment? Since the above verses are from the Old Testament and seem to indicate there is no consciousness after death, why does the New Testament seem to say otherwise?

These passages deal with the fact that once we leave the earth we have no further contact with life on this earth. Even of his Christians, Jesus says, "As long as it is day, we must do the work of him who sent me. Night is coming, when no one can work" (John 9:4).

Your **Question** **Jeremiah 7:31 refers to how some people built places in order to burn their sons and daughters in the fire. The Scriptures say that God said this practice was, "a thing I had not commanded and that had not come up into my heart." So the question is: If it never came into God's heart, then how could he use such a thing on a larger scale? Also, is it just to punish people for eternity for sins committed during one short lifetime?**

The difference between child sacrifice and hell is the difference between punishing the innocent and punishing the guilty. The punishment for a crime is not determined by how long it takes to commit the crime but by the degree of the offense. Murder takes only a minute to commit but is punished by life in prison or death. A sin against the infinite, holy God incurs infinite guilt. That is why only Christ can pay for sin. Those who reject his payment can never pay the debt themselves.

Heaven

Your Question **Regarding heaven: Do the Scriptures at Acts 2:34 and Matthew 11:11 indicate that neither David nor John the Baptist went to heaven? If not, then what do these verses mean?**

Acts 2:34 deals only with the fact that David's body died and was buried and remains in the grave. Jesus, on the other hand, rose and ascended to heaven. The point is that Psalm 110 cannot be about David but must be about Jesus. It is not dealing with the question of what happens to the soul after death.

Matthew 11:11 has nothing at all to do with this subject. It just compares John with past prophets.

Your Question **Also, doesn't John 3:13 say, "No one has ever gone into heaven except the one who came from heaven—the Son of Man"? So according to the above Scriptures, what happened to Old Testament believers?**

John 3:13 is not dealing with the issue of the life of the soul after death. It is dealing with the question of how we know what it is like in heaven. No one has gone up there and returned to tell us about it, but Jesus has come down from heaven to tell us about it.

Your Question **Revelation 20:6, 1 Corinthians 6:2, and Revelation 5:10 all seem to indicate that believers in heaven will have a specific task: priests of God, judging the world, ruling as kings over the earth, etc. If this is so, then who exactly are Christians in heaven supposed to be "ruling" over as kings?**

They will all have the status of kings, but some will have greater authority (as the parable says ten cities, five, or one, or the apostles on 12 thrones, judging Israel).

I am a member of the LCMS, and my pastor believes there is a difference between paradise and heaven. He teaches that paradise is prior to judgment day and heaven is after judgment day. I have never, ever heard this before. I was taught that they are synonymous. Do you have any idea where this might have come from? Is this heresy? Thank you so much for your help in this matter.

The name *paradise* is not common in Scripture, but it is quite clear that it is appropriate to use it both for the present heaven (Luke 23:43) and our eternal home (Revelation 2:7 compared with Revelation 21 and 22).

Our eternal home can be called the new heavens and the new earth. We would not call the present home of the saved the *new* heavens and the *new* earth. Those who are in heaven now are there as souls only. After the resurrection they will be there body and soul. This is the only significant difference.

I heard that in heaven no one knows anybody else the way we know each other here on earth. If that were true, then it would mean that after we die we will not be reunited with family in heaven. Is this true? Why would God want us to have close family lives here on earth if we will never know these people again in heaven?

In 1 Thessalonians 4:13-18, we read about meeting our loved ones at Christ's return. In some other accounts, there are recognizable people in heaven, such as Abraham in Luke 16. Elijah and Moses were recognizable when they appeared at Christ's transfiguration (Matthew 17). All of this, plus that fact that we will be raised with the same bodies we had in this life, strongly implies that in heaven we will be known as the same people we are in this life. We have no information, however, about the "how" of any of this. Will we live together in a special closeness with those we were closest to in this life? We have no detailed information about this.

We know there will not be marriage in heaven (Matthew 22:23). We will not have the same husband-wife or parent-child relationships we have here.

**I know it is not by any works of our own that we get to
heaven. From what I understand, there are different "degrees" of glory
in heaven, depending on how you conducted yourself on earth. Is this
correct? That appears to say works do matter?**

The Bible speaks of differences of rewards in heaven. See
1 Corinthians 3:10-15; Matthew 25:14-29; Matthew 19:28-30; and
others. We should not, however, serve God with a work-for-wages
spirit (Matthew 20:1-16). The Bible makes it clear that these rewards
are due to God's grace, not to our deserving them. They do, however,
encourage us to be diligent in serving with the gifts the Lord gives us.

The rewards may be differences of responsibility or honor, but
there are no degrees of happiness in heaven since everyone will be
perfectly happy.

7
Other Churches and Religions

Other Lutherans

The differences between WELS and other Lutherans will not be dealt with comprehensively here because they are dealt with in the book *WELS and Other Lutherans* (Northwestern Publishing House, 1995, 2009).

Your Question **Have the significant differences that caused the break in fellowship between the WELS and LCMS in 1961 been rectified? If not, what current efforts are under way to mediate these differences?**

The differences in the doctrine of fellowship that led to the end of WELS-LCMS fellowship have not been resolved. In fact, the gap has grown wider. WELS still maintains that there must be agreement in all doctrine for any expression of church fellowship, including all joint worship and prayer. The LCMS maintains that agreement in all doctrine is necessary for pulpit and altar fellowship but not for joint prayer and other types of worship.

There have been and are quiet consultations between the presidents of the two synods, but there are no ongoing, formal discussions of the doctrine of fellowship. WELS is willing to participate in discussions that have the goals of addressing these differences on the basis of Scripture, but the WELS Commission on Inter-church Relations has not received any indication that the LCMS desires such substantial talks in recent years. Under President Bohlmann this was treated as an issue that the LCMS regarded as settled. Under former president Barry, it appeared that the efforts of the leadership of the LCMS were directed toward establishing greater harmony of fellowship practices within the LCMS concerning such matters as closed Communion. This appeared to be appropriate as a focus of attention at that time.

Things took a decided turn for the worse with the LCMS approval of the participation of one of its district presidents in a prayer service involving non-Lutheran and even non-Christian clergy. District President Benke was at first suspended by one of the LCMS vice presidents for his participation, but this suspension was overruled. Though it appears that the suspension was scriptural and valid, it seems to me that Benke's action was not a violation of the Missouri Synod's often-stated position on prayer fellowship. For 50 years the LCMS has been stating clearly and publicly that joint prayer with those with whom we are not in doctrinal agreement is not necessarily church fellowship. LCMS guidelines permit joint worship and celebration with liberal Lutherans as long as there is not a sermon by vested clergy and there is no Lord's Supper. It appears that President Benke's actions fall within these guidelines. The only special circumstance at the Yankee Stadium service that caught people's attention was that non-Christians participated in the service, though it does not seem that they necessarily actually joined in the Christian prayers. I doubt that most Muslims would do so, even if invited. I have, however, observed an LCMS professor lead a joint devotional service with ELCA theologians, which included joint prayers, hymns, readings, and a sermonette. When I and others objected to this service at an academic meeting of people not in fellowship, the service was defended as not involving church fellowship. What Benke did seems to be within LCMS policy concerning joint prayer. This whole situation has created great dissension in the LCMS. This inner turmoil needs to be resolved before any significant discussions with WELS would be possible. What happens next will be a critical event in the history of the LCMS, perhaps more critical than the Seminex crisis.

Other doctrines that would need to be discussed if such talks were ever to become feasible are church and ministry, the role of women in the church, and the role of the confessions in establishing doctrine.

Your
Question I was writing in hope that you could help clarify a question for me. I am, Lord willing, coming to be joining a WELS congregation in the near future. When I was getting ready to come over to the

WELS, I did much reading and research on the differences and was able to get a solid grounding on women in ministry and fellowship but have not been able to get a strong grounding on the doctrine of the ministry. In looking more into the question of Scripture, I have come across a few verses that are pointed out in the LCMS as pointing to the establishment of the pastoral ministry (Titus 1:5; Acts 14:23; 20:28; 2 Timothy 2:2; 1 Peter 4:10,11; and Hebrews 13:17). If possible can you please explain why these are not pointing to the establishment of the pastoral ministry and are only pointing to a human invention instituted for keeping good order? Thank you and God bless.

WELS believes that the pastoral ministry has been instituted by God and is not simply a human invention for good order. The passages cited above do show that the pastoral ministry is an institution of God. What we disagree with in the so-called Missouri Synod view of ministry ("so-called" because not everyone in the LCMS agrees with it) is that the pastoral office is the *only* form of ministry instituted by God, to the exclusion of other forms of ministry as being simply auxiliary human offices. God has not prescribed the forms of ministry of the Word. A church may have one pastor who does everything including teaching school, as was often the case in pioneer days. It may have several pastors who share all the duties or several pastors who divide the duties among them. It may establish various divisions of duties among pastor and teachers or deacons or evangelists. It may have district and synod presidents and seminary professors. All of these people would be serving in the ministry instituted by God. God has not prescribed these specific forms, but in giving the ministry of the Word to the church, he has given the church the right to create a wide variety of forms within that ministry. All of these forms are subdivisions within the ministry of the Word. They are divine in that they are authorized by God. They are human in the specific form or arrangement they may take in different circumstances.

Your
Question **I am a member of an ELCA church. I would like to know how you can publicly say that the ELCA denies the virgin birth of Christ and that the ELCA also denies that the only way to heaven is through faith in our Lord Jesus Christ? This simply is not true. I believe and my church believes both of these things.**

The doctrinal statements of the ELCA in its constituting documents state that the ELCA belief and practice is in agreement with Scripture and the Lutheran Confessions. But we believe that a church body's teaching is determined not only by what its constitution says but by what its seminaries teach, by what its publishing houses and periodicals print, and by the public teaching which it tolerates and leaves undisciplined. My belief that the accepted public teaching of the ELCA departs from Scripture in almost every doctrine is based on regular reading of ELCA periodicals and the publications of Augsburg Fortress, a study of ELCA preaching, contacts with ELCA theologians in SBL (Society of Biblical Literature) and other forums, and serving a congregation that was made up of a high percentage of people who had left the (E)LCA for doctrinal reasons. Further evidence of the ELCA departure from Lutheran doctrine is provided by the statements of "convergence" with Roman Catholicism on justification and with several Reformed churches on the Lord's Supper. Casual intrusion of different doctrines into a church body does not immediately become its publicly accepted teaching, but a church becomes responsible for all teaching which it tolerates, especially that which it publishes, and that which it leaves undisciplined.

We do not say that everyone in the ELCA supports all these departures from Lutheran biblical teaching, but we see that the diversity of theology which is allowed and even encouraged in the ELCA permits denial of scriptural inerrancy and denials of the miracles in Scripture, denial of the virgin birth, and denial of salvation through Christ alone to become acceptable public teaching in the ELCA. This is documented on pages 78-170 of the book *WELS and Other Lutherans* (Second Edition), which is available from Northwestern Publishing House. In this volume, evidence is presented from official ELCA documents, periodicals, and textbooks.

The most critical difference between WELS and the ELCA is the difference on our view of Scripture. The most harmful result of this difference is the ELCA's willingness to make compromise agreements on the doctrine of justification with Roman Catholicism. If these were the only differences separating WELS and the ELCA, this would be a huge difference, a tragic division of Lutheranism.

However, the differences that divide us are by no means limited to these points but appear in virtually every doctrine of Scripture. When I have been on panels with ELCA theologians contrasting the views of WELS and the ELCA, they have disagreed drastically with my views, but they have never questioned my assessment of the degree of difference between us. In fact, they have usually regarded my views as so many light-years away from the position of the ELCA that there was little point even paying any attention to them. As a result, they focused their attention on comparing the ELCA and the LCMS. Would a theologian who agreed with the doctrinal position of WELS be allowed to teach in an ELCA seminary? No, the gap would simply be too huge. I have never left a meeting with ELCA theologians without a painful awareness of the width of that gap.

There was a time when some of the predecessor bodies of the ELCA and WELS were in fellowship. Then there was a time when they were separated by intra-Lutheran debates about lodges, pulpit and altar fellowship, election, and so on. Sad to say, those days are gone. It would be extremely difficult for representatives of the ELCA and WELS to have meaningful theological discussions because we have such radically different views of the nature of Scripture. I wish this were not true, but an objective comparison of the public teaching of the two churches does not allow any other conclusion. This causes us great sadness, but the evidence of this sad reality is plain. Our paths have diverged so greatly that even our basic approach to theology and to doctrinal unity is very different.

Your
Question **Is there a doctrinal difference between WELS and the CLC?**

Over the years there has been considerable debate about whether there is a difference of doctrine between the WELS and the Church of the Lutheran Confession (CLC), or whether there is disagreement about the application of the doctrine of church fellowship to the termination of fellowship with the Missouri Synod. Those who felt that there was a difference of doctrine usually identified that difference as a failure on the part of the CLC to allow for admonition before termination of fellowship with an erring church or as a willingness on the part of WELS to remain in fellowship with an erring church body even after it had been identified as persisting in its error. For this reason, the 1987–1990 talks between representatives of WELS, the ELS, and the CLC focused on the role of admonition in termination of fellowship with an erring church body.

During the 1987–1990 talks, representatives of WELS, the ELS, and the CLC agreed with the following principles:

Admonition continues until the erring individual or group either repents of its error and turns away from it or until it shows itself to be persistent in its error by adhering to it in its public doctrine and practice, by demanding recognition for it, or by making propaganda for and trying to persuade others of it.

All groups agreed on the necessity of admonition before the termination of fellowship. All of them also accepted the following statements on the limited duration of the admonition:

The imperative *ekklinate* calls for a clean break of fellowship with those who persistently adhere to error. When it has been ascertained that a person or church body is causing divisions and offenses . . . by teaching contrary to Holy Scriptures, the directive to avoid is as binding as any word addressed to us by our Savior in his holy Word. Pleading a debt of love dare not serve as an excuse for putting off a break of fellowship with those who have shown themselves to be not weak brethren but persistent errorists. . . . We reject the view that the decision to continue or discontinue admonition and proceed to "avoid" is to be made on the basis of a subjective human judgment or conjecture about the possible outcome of the admonition. . . . We reject the view that permits the use of human judgment to prolong fellowship with persistent errorists as contrary to Scripture.

In response to the CLC request for a preamble to deal with past statements of the respective synods and individuals within them, the WELS representatives suggested a preamble that included these words:

This Joint Statement, therefore, when accepted by our three church bodies, supersedes any and every previous statement that might be or might appear to be in conflict with this document. Any and all such conflicting or possibly conflicting statements are herewith disavowed.

On the basis of this agreement that recognized both the need for admonition and the need for immediate termination of fellowship with persistent errorists, the WELS Commission on Inter-church Relations concluded that there was no difference of doctrine between WELS and the CLC. When our commission asked the CLC representatives for the basis of their assertion that there is a doctrinal difference between the CLC and WELS, they did not provide a simple direct answer but merely provided copies of old documents.

Since the CLC broke off the negotiations with WELS in 1990, the question, What is the doctrinal difference? has kept popping up both in the CLC and WELS. WELS representatives have maintained that if the CLC really accepts the principles their representatives agreed to in the 1990 statement, there is no disagreement in doctrine but questions about whether the doctrine was properly applied.

In response to the continuing questions, the CLC has provided several documents in an attempt to provide a basis for the claim that such a doctrinal difference exists. In response to a request from a CLC congregation in Albuquerque, New Mexico, that the CLC state what the doctrinal difference is, the CLC 1994 convention adopted the following statements:

> Whereas, the WELS, having already "marked" the LC-MS in 1955 as a causer of divisions and offenses nevertheless at its 1959 convention adopted the following principle on the Termination of Church Fellowship: "Termination of church fellowship is called for when you have reached the conviction that admonition is of no further avail and that the erring brother or church body demands recognition of its error," and

> Whereas, the CLC holds to the scriptural principle set forth in its official publication, "Concerning Church Fellowship," which says: "We further believe and teach that suspension of an established fellowship is to take place when it has been ascertained that a person or group is causing divisions and offenses through a false position in doctrine or practice" therefore, be it

> Resolved, that we let the doctrinal contrast between these two official statements from the respective church bodies stand as our answer to the memorial of Holy Spirit congregation of Albuquerque, NM. (For the full resolution see CLC Proceedings, pp. 66,67.)

It is as though the WELS-ELS-CLC meeting had never taken place. The WELS position is misrepresented by the detachment of a single sentence from its context, and the CLC statement does not even mention admonition of the errorist, which was the focal point of the 1987–1990 discussions.

The 1994 convention statement is rather vague, but the misunderstanding of the WELS position is more flagrant in a 1994 essay that refers to the same quotation of the WELS position cited above. It paraphrases the WELS position in this way: "It is wrong to avoid in this way only when we come to some sort of subjective judgment that admonition will never be heeded (as the WELS and ELS falsely teach)." That this is a caricature of the WELS position should be apparent to anyone who has read the Joint Statement of the WELS-ELS-CLC meetings or past WELS statements in their entirety.

A 1994 conference essay by a CLC pastor summarized the WELS-ELS position as "mark, admonish, and avoid." We would have no problem with this as long as "mark" is properly understood as "watch out for," a point that was agreed upon in the 1990 statement. The CLC position is summarized as "mark and avoid" with no mention of admonition. The essay goes on to state that one basis for the assertion that WELS has a different doctrinal position than the CLC is that WELS has never officially adopted the Joint Statement. But this is because the CLC broke off talks before the preamble they had requested could be agreed upon. When the CLC refused further discussions, there was no reason to present the statement to the WELS convention for adoption. We would want to make the Joint Statement the starting point for any future negotiations.

It is sad that the talks which began so promisingly failed to produce concrete steps toward removing the division between WELS and the CLC. It is doubly sad that CLC spokesmen ignored the Joint Statement and based allegations of a doctrinal difference between WELS and the CLC on a misunderstanding of the WELS position, which WELS representatives could not accept as a valid summary of its view. Readers who want to reach their own conclusion should read the WELS *Reports and Memorials*, 1993, pp. 232-241; and the CLC *Journal of Theology*, 1994, pp. 31-34.

Though the question continues to appear at regular intervals on the WELS Web site and in CLC sources, the last decade has not brought about any significant progress or clarification of the situation.

Your
Question **I have heard the Covenant Church described as "renegade Lutherans." Are they really an offshoot of the Lutheran church?**

The Evangelical Covenant Church of America is the name adopted in 1957 by the Swedish Evangelical Mission Covenant of America, which had been founded in the late 19th century by Swedish immigrants. The official state church in their homeland, Sweden, is Lutheran. Already in Sweden, people who were dissatisfied by what they perceived to be a lack of spiritual vitality in the Lutheran state church had formed mission societies that were influenced by German Pietism and Methodism. When some of these people moved to America, they formed the Swedish Lutheran Mission Synod, which later merged into the Swedish Mission Covenant. It is in that sense, I suppose, that some have labeled them "renegade Lutherans."

Although they may have been provoked in part by the shortcomings of the Lutheran state church, it must be noted that they also departed from biblical teaching at a number of points. They value a conversion experience and consecrated living more than doctrinal clarity. Though they use the Apostles' Creed, they do not have a clearly defined doctrine position and they allow a certain amount of doctrinal diversity. They practice infant Baptism but allow other views. They have placed a strong emphasis on mission work.

Roman Catholicism

Because the large number of Catholics in the world and in the United States leads to frequent contacts between Catholics and Lutherans and because of memories of the separation of the Lutheran church from the Roman church during the Reformation, questions about Catholicism are very common on our Web site.

Your
Question **My niece is coming to stay with me and she is Lutheran. Her Catholic school told her she had to receive first Communion in a Lutheran church. I am Methodist. What is the difference between the two religions? While she is with me, I want her to grow in her religion. I am trying to help her know more. What is the difference between Catholic and Lutheran? Thank you very much for helping me.**

The general practice of the Catholic church is to give Communion only to Catholics. The historic position of the Lutheran church has been that only Lutherans commune at Lutheran altars. Not all Lutherans follow this practice today, but our church, the Wisconsin

Evangelical Lutheran Synod, does. Thus we agree with the advice given to your niece—that Lutherans commune in Lutheran churches, Catholics in Catholic churches. This is discussed at more length in the section of this book about church fellowship.

The most important differences between the Catholic church and the Lutheran church can be boiled down to two points. (1) How do we obtain forgiveness of sins? Lutherans say by God's grace alone, through faith alone. Catholics say through faith and works together. (2) What is the authority over the church? Lutherans say it is the Bible alone. Catholics say it is the Bible and the tradition of the church as proclaimed by the authorities of the church, with the pope as the supreme and final authority.

The Catholic church teaching is "not by faith alone" and "not by Scripture alone." The biblical Lutheran belief is "by faith alone" and "by Scripture alone."

Your
Question My Catholic friend says the Bible never uses the words "saved by faith alone" or "the Bible is the only authority." She maintains you are saved by faith and works and that the tradition of the church is equal to the authority of Scripture. Is this a case of semantics or blatant false teaching on their part?

When Lutherans say we are saved by faith alone, we mean we are saved by faith and not by works. We are not excluding God's grace, Christ's merit, or the means of grace as causes of our salvation. We are excluding works. This is exactly what Scripture does say very explicitly in numerous passages. For example, Romans 3:28: "We maintain that a man is justified *by faith apart from observing the law*"; and Ephesians 2:8,9: "It is *by grace* you have been saved, through faith—and this not from yourselves, it is the gift of God—*not by works*, so that no one can boast." Scripture very explicitly excludes works as a cause of our salvation.

The Catholic church does not exclude faith from salvation, but it teaches salvation by faith and works together. Even in speaking of faith, however, it is using a different definition than the biblical definition. The faith that Rome speaks of is not the faith called for by Scripture, namely, trust in the merits of Christ alone for forgiveness of sins. The faith Rome calls for is assent to all the teachings of the church and willing obedience to God.

The Catholic church also teaches salvation by grace, but it is using a different definition of *grace*. In the Bible, saving grace is the loving attitude of God by which he freely forgives our sins. In Roman Catholicism saving grace is an ability God puts into us which will enable us to do the good works that complete our salvation. To support their definition of *grace*, Catholics often apply passages that talk about God's gracious gifts which enable us to grow in sanctification (Christian living) as if they applied to justification (forgiveness of sins). When we are trying to answer the question, How are we justified? we must look only at those passages that speak of the grace by which we are justified, that is, forgiven. All of these speak of justification as a verdict of God that excludes our works. A few examples are Romans 3:23-26; 4:16; 11:16; Galatians 3:18; 5:4; and Ephesians 2:8-10. The question here is whether the Bible allows our works to play any role in obtaining our forgiveness of sins. The clear answer is no. The problem with the Catholic view is that they take passages which say God gives us gifts of grace to enable us to do good works and then they claim these good works are part of the cause of our forgiveness. Scripture clearly says such works are the result of forgiveness, not the cause. We do good works not to gain justification but to show our love and gratitude to God because we have been justified.

Lutherans say that the person who stands under the grace of God in faith has complete justification. The imputation or declaration of righteousness to us is complete now. Catholics say justification is a gradual process that is completed by what we do. Lutherans teach that if we have saving faith in Christ, we can be confident we will enter heaven when we die. Catholics teach that we may (probably will) have to complete payment for some of the temporal penalty of our sins in purgatory. The Catholic doctrines of purgatory, indulgences, and the merits of the saints are consequences of an unscriptural view of justification.

Rome does play some word games here by trying to redefine such words as *grace* and *faith* or by claiming that the only works Paul is excluding are works of the Old Testament law not works of the New Testament church, but this is not a matter of dispute about words. It is a blatant denial of Scripture by Rome.

Scripture also says very plainly that no human authority can be set alongside Scripture, for example, Matthew 23:9,10 says, "Do not call anyone on earth 'father,' for you have one Father, and he is in heaven. Nor are you to be called 'teacher,' for you have one Teacher, the Christ." No human, not even the pope, can claim to be a father and teacher alongside Christ. We can teach nothing except what Christ has taught in his Word. In spite of this, the Catholic church denies "by Scripture alone." It teaches that we must accept the traditions and authority of the church (that is, the pope and bishops) alongside (in reality, above) the authority of Scripture. This is directly contrary to Scripture and marks the pope as the Antichrist.

Your Question

Saving faith is trust that Christ paid for all of our sins. The Catholic Church teaches that we have to pay for our sins, at least in part, either by good works or suffering in purgatory. Do Catholics have saving faith?

The *Catechism of the Catholic Church* makes it very clear that Roman Catholicism still teaches that we must provide part of the payment for our sins and that some of this payment is rendered in purgatory (par. 1031). Such a teaching is destructive of saving faith, because any mixing of our own works with God's grace destroys grace, which is a totally free gift (Galatians 5:3,4; Romans 11:6).

But the gospel is still present in the Catholic church alongside the church's false teachings. People still hear the Scripture readings and read their Bibles. These Scriptures testify to Christ. They proclaim that salvation is by grace alone, through faith alone. Through these teachings of the Bible, saving faith can be created and preserved in spite of the false teachings of Rome.

For this reason, we believe Catholics may have saving faith in spite of the false teachings of their church. Nevertheless, we should warn them against those false teachings, which are a serious threat to their faith. Former Catholics testify that it is extremely difficult to find the gospel in the Catholic church as is shown in the following statement:

> As a former Catholic turned Lutheran and a regular reader of your fascinating Q&A, I am intrigued by the repeated statements in your section on Catholicism that despite all the error in the Roman Church, the gospel is still taught there. I understand the gospel to be the message that the death of Jesus totally suffices to save us from our sins. Whereas the Catholic message, unambiguously, is

that the death of Jesus makes it merely possible for us to save ourselves with works. Not only are the sufficiency of God's grace and Christ's atonement not actively taught in the Catholic church, but loudly condemned as heresy not only by official theologians but by every Catholic with a smidgen of religious education. Next to this, the fact that they use the name of Jesus Christ, tell the story of his death and resurrection, maintain a technically correct doctrine of the Trinity, etc., seems like so much window dressing. To me, "the gospel" is much more than the historical story of Christ's death and resurrection, but also includes a proper understanding of its meaning. Mormons and Jehovah's Witnesses also say that Christ died and rose, but we don't say they have the Gospel. I wonder what definition of "the gospel" you are using that allows you to say that people who deny the sufficiency of Christ's atonement have the Gospel? Furthermore, you shouldn't make the mistake of thinking that the average Catholic is ignorant of this difference between Catholicism and evangelical Christianity or that they don't take it seriously. That idea uncannily parallels the Catholic doctrine of "anonymous Christians." A lot of evangelicals try to win Catholics over, and a lot of everyday, unlettered Catholics successfully resist them, precisely out of loyalty to the doctrine of works. There are Christians in Catholicism but that is a miracle of God, not attributable to anything that is going on in Catholic preaching and teaching. You shouldn't discount the testimony of many people like me who say we never heard the gospel in the Catholic church. I was no casual, "cultural" Catholic, but a serious student of their theology, with a degree from one of their most conservative institutions. Trust me . . . if they were preaching "the gospel" to any degree, however slight, I would have been one of the few to hear it. And I didn't. So . . . when you say things like the gospel is still found in the Catholic church despite all their errors, what do you really mean?

It is very difficult to dismiss or minimize such powerful testimony. Nevertheless, we should remember that in the darkest days of the Catholic church, Martin Luther found the gospel there—in the Bible itself. Where the Scriptures are still read, the Spirit can still work through them. Beyond that, we agree with everything in the previous testimony. Some years ago I took an instruction course in the Catholic church. One of the questions I was asked on the test was "How do we receive forgiveness of sins?" I chose the answer "by faith alone." I was very clearly told by the priest who corrected the test that the right answer was "by faith and by works." A blessing taught in the course said, "May the merits of our Lord Jesus Christ, the merits of Mary and the saints, and the good that you do and the evil that you suffer profit you unto remission of sins." In working with Catholic children in VBS, I experienced that they were taught to change the most beautiful biblical stories of grace (such as the thief on the cross) into stories of salvation by works. Nevertheless, when priests preach the text, grace can show through. When I was researching a Bible class on Catholicism today, I wrote that I had never found a Catholic sermon where salvation by grace alone through faith alone was taught. The next week I was listening to a Catholic sermon on the sinful woman in Luke 7. The priest was preaching a fine sermon on salvation by faith alone. I thought I was going to have to modify my statement about Catholic sermons. Suddenly, in the last paragraph, he realized that the sermon he was preaching from the text was contrary to the teaching of the Catholic church. He interjected the comment, "From this text we would think we were saved by faith alone not works, but we know that there is more to it than that." As soon as he let go of the text, he was back in the chains of the Catholic church. We hope the parishioners will remember what he preached from the text more than they remember his retraction. Luther felt that this was the case for some of the monks in the monasteries. When death approached, they went back to the text. That is the only hope they have. There may be Catholic sermons that preach salvation by faith alone—not by works, but I still have never heard one. We should not overestimate the presence of the gospel in the Catholic church.

Your Question In one of your posted answers, you stated that the Catholic religion teaches that they are the only true religion by which to be saved. My mother, who is Catholic (I converted to WELS), believes that anyone who follows their own religion (Jews, Buddhists, Hindus included) devoutly will be saved. Is my mother "adding" to her religion or is this what they are teaching her? I have pointed out to her that the Bible tells us in John 14:6 "I am the way and the truth and the life. No one comes to the Father except through me." God bless you and your work.

What your mother believes is what the Catholic church believes. Though it is contradictory, they teach both that one cannot be saved without being a member of the Catholic church, while at the same time that the heathen can be saved. They reconcile these contradictory teachings by claiming that the heathen who live good lives are "anonymous Christians," that is, they are Christians without realizing it. This exposes the erroneous view of the Roman Catholic church about the nature of the Christian faith. If they believe that works without faith in Christ can make a person a "Christian," then the essence of Christianity is works. In this one doctrine, they include the two opposite errors—claiming that the Catholic church is the one saving church and claiming that the heathen can be saved without faith in Christ.

These two contradictory doctrines are clearly set forth in the recent Catholic document *Dominus Iesus* (2000), which reasserted that the Roman Catholic church is the one true church and that adherence to this church is necessary for salvation: "There exists a single Church of Christ, which subsists in the Catholic Church, governed by the Successor of Peter and by the Bishops in communion with him." The Roman church regards dialogue with other churches and religions as part of its evangelizing mission to lead them to acceptance of the full truth, which Rome alone possesses.

According to this Catholic teaching, most Lutheran churches are not real churches since they have not preserved the valid episcopate of pope, bishops, and priests and, therefore, do not have a real Lord's Supper. However, they state that those who are baptized in these ecclesial communities are, by Baptism, incorporated in Christ and thus are in a certain communion, albeit imperfect, with the true church. A member of another church or religious organization is really a member of the Catholic church through Baptism, which by right belongs to the Catholic church. According to this way of defining things, one does not need to be "enrolled in a Catholic parish" to be a "member" of the Catholic church or to be saved "through the Catholic church." It must come as quite a slap in the face to Lutheran churches like the ELCA that have entered ecumenical agreements with Rome to be reminded of the fact that they do not even rate the name "church" with Rome.

The declaration quickly establishes that Rome's teachings incorporate "the worst of both worlds," since on the one hand, it denies the full validity of other churches, on the other, it nevertheless holds open the possibility of salvation for the heathen by works.

A fuller description of the document *Dominus Iesus* is found in the *Wisconsin Lutheran Quarterly* (Summer 2001), pages 131-134.

Your
Question I seem to recall hearing that several years ago the Catholic church "lifted" its 16th-century excommunication of Martin Luther, as a step in the so-called "ecumenical movement." While I would regard such a proclamation as being simply an expression of "political correctness" in a world obsessed with that path, I have to wonder if such a move wouldn't technically be an overt recognition that Luther, and the Reformation, was in fact correct? By lifting Luther's excommunication, wouldn't the Catholic church in essence be admitting to the errors Luther pointed out?

There have been Catholic groups that have requested the lifting of Luther's excommunication. In looking at many Web sites, I can find no evidence this has ever been done. On some Catholic sites, there was a statement that this has not been done and that reports of such a revocation of Luther's excommunication are unfounded rumors. This appears to me to be correct, since when Lutherans and Catholics signed a joint statement on justification, Catholic spokesmen clearly said that the removal of the condemnations of Lutheran doctrine applied only to the Lutheran doctrine as found in the joint statement (which is really not the Lutheran doctrine at all). The removal of condemnation does not apply to the Lutheran doctrine as taught in the Lutheran Confessions. All the public statements of the Catholic church at that time made it very clear they were yielding nothing. It was the Lutherans that did all the surrendering.

Your
Question I have trouble with your teaching that the pope is the Antichrist. I always thought that the Antichrist would be evil and lead people away from Christianity. The pope is very religious and far from evil and doesn't do anything to lead people away from Christianity. If the pope is the antichrist then wouldn't that make Peter the apostle an antichrist, since the papacy goes back to its founding when Jesus said to Peter "Peter you are a rock and upon this rock I build my church" (Matthew 16:18)? It's hard enough to believe that one of Jesus' disciples, Judas, would turn on him and hand him over, but to believe that Jesus' most beloved disciple, Peter, would be an antichrist. What are your comments?

First of all, there is no historical or biblical evidence that Peter was the first bishop of Rome or that Jesus made him a pope over the other apostles. Even if he had been, the popes of Rome do not follow Peter's doctrine and cannot claim to be his successors. Peter was not an antichrist. The pope is.

The Lutheran Confessions cite two main reasons for labeling the pope as the Antichrist. (1) He takes to himself a right that belongs only to God, the right to make laws for the church. If he says it is a sin to eat meat on Friday, it is. If he says it is okay, then it is not a sin anymore. He forbids priests to marry, contrary to the will of God. He refuses innocent victims of divorce the right to remarry, a right Scripture grants them. In these and many other instances he acts as a usurper of a right that belongs only to Christ. (2) He curses the most basic doctrine of the Bible, justification by faith alone. In the decrees of the Council of Trent, he curses anyone who holds this doctrine, and he teaches salvation by faith and works. What could be more anti-Christian than that?

A church is free to choose someone to be its leader, but this is not what the pope claims. He claims that he is by divine right the head of the whole church on earth and that all Christians must submit to his authority, not just Roman Catholics. He says that churches that do not submit to him and to the bishops are not real churches. Our Lutheran church, for example, is not a real, legitimate church according to his standards. He on his own authority can make rules binding on the whole church. He can make these rules without Scripture and without the approval of a church council. It is this claiming of divine authority and his teaching that salvation is not by faith alone which make him the Antichrist.

The fact that the pope is religious and in the church does not disqualify him from being the Antichrist. It is, in fact, one of the prerequisites, since the Antichrist is a religious deceiver within the church. He is not only an opponent of Christ but a usurper of Christ's position.

Other Teachings and Practices

Your
Question I recently read a book review of *God-Sent: A History of the Accredited Apparitions of Mary,* by Roy Abraham Varghese. The book

promotes Mariolatry, and from the review it is possible to discern some of the beliefs Roman Catholics have which elevate Mary. Can you clarify the following statements in the review about who it is Roman Catholics think Mary is and where the Lutheran church disagrees and why?

> Ever since her apparition to the Apostle John as the woman clothed in the sun in the Book of Revelation, Mary has been the God-sent one, calling both young and old to be witnesses to her Son, as she did, as His first witness. Especially important in understanding Mary as a continuing witness for Christ is Revelation 12:17: "Then the dragon was enraged with the woman and went away to make war on the rest of her children, that is, all who obey God's commandments and bear witness for Jesus."

> There was a time, up until the Reformation, when all Christians were devoted to Mary and venerated her image. Church councils dating back to Ephesus in 431 taught that Mary is "Theotokos," Mother of God, and well before that Scripture and Tradition recognized her as such. The author makes a strong appeal to Protestants: Why do you accept only some early Church doctrines, such as the Trinity, but not this one?

> God chose Mary to be the Mother of His incarnate Son, the new Adam, and Mary's obedience to God's will established her as the New Eve. The author also recalls another of Mary's ancient titles, the New Ark of the Covenant. Her "overshadowing" by the Holy Spirit at the Annunciation prepares a tabernacle for the Son of God. This action by God prompts Mary's response, in which she says that because of what God has done for her, "all generations will call me blessed." One aspect of her blessedness is that she continues to appear to all generations until Christ comes again.

> Mary is not only the first witness to Christ but the mother of all who witness to Christ. And like any mother, she comes to the aid of her children in need. Thus there should be nothing surprising about her apparitions to her children down through the ages!

The woman in Revelation 12 is not Mary. She is the church, the spiritual Israel. She remains in the wilderness, that is, in the world, for the whole time till Christ's return. She is attacked by Satan until Christ returns to rescue her on the Last Day. Mary is not in the picture in Revelation 12. Here Christ is portrayed as the child born to the church as he is in Isaiah 9:6.

That Mary is the mother of the child who is true God is reason to worship Jesus, not reason to worship Mary. We have no objection to honoring Mary for her example of faith, but there is no scriptural basis for praying to her, nor is there any need for such prayers. We can pray directly to God through Christ. We do not need Mary as a mediator since there is one mediator between God and man, the man Christ Jesus.

The reason we reject the apparitions of Mary as deceptions is that they direct people to pray to Mary rather than directly to God. They, therefore, cannot be from God.

Your
Question **Thank you for having this Q & A site available. I would like a bit more information on the Catholic Church's position on the Immaculate Conception; especially how they determined that Mary was "without sin" when she conceived Jesus.**

The idea that Mary was preserved sinless from the time of her conception apparently was developed after the fact, in order to justify the fact that Mary was being venerated as a co-participant with Christ in the work of salvation. There does not seem to be any evidence that this doctrine was determined by any objective study or specific Bible passages, but it had become necessary to justify the practice of virtual worship of Mary that had developed. For this reason an argument supporting veneration of Mary arose on the basis of reason and "probability." The line of reasoning was "Jesus was conceived without sin. Jesus was conceived by Mary. So it is probable that Mary was born without sin too." An apocryphal story in the so-called Protevangel of James is cited as a basis for the belief in a supernatural nativity of Mary. Martin Chemnitz discussed the development of this doctrine in Volume 1 of *Examination of the Council of Trent*, pages 379, 380.

Your
Question **I had a friend tell me he was going to perform a rosary for me. I do not know enough about the Catholic religion to judge whether I should be happy for that or not. I know his intentions are good, but the whole rosary-type prayer seems a little strange to me. What is involved with a rosary?**

A rosary is a set of prayers that consists of repetitions of the Lord's Prayer, each of which is followed by a tenfold repetition of the Hail Mary. A full rosary is 15 repetitions of this cycle. Usually only five repetitions of this cycle are done at one time. Rosary beads are intended to help with keeping count of the prayers. Other prayers may also be included in addition to the basic cycles. The prayer is supposed to be accompanied by meditation on the lives of Christ and Mary. The central point of the rosary is prayer to Mary to help us now and at the time of our death.

Your
Question I have a friend who is Roman Catholic, yet he seems open to scriptural Christianity. While he sees it pointless to pray to many saints when he can instead pray directly to God, he does pray the "Hail Mary." I want to correct him on this, but I want to do so firmly yet with gentleness, not to cause offense, other than the "offense" of the gospel. I would think our first objection to the Ave Maria (Hail Mary) "prayer" is that it is directed to Mary and not to God. Scripture nowhere tells us to pray to another human being. How could such a "prayer" be seen as simply intercession and not some form of worship reserved for God alone? Do Catholics believe they are merely "honoring" Mary as we might honor a living saint (a fellow Christian), thankful for how God has used him/her in furthering his kingdom? Or is Mary worshiped (Mariolatry) as though she were some kind of lesser god? Is Roman Catholicism even consistent on this teaching throughout the world? For clarity, could you please print the Hail Mary "prayer" phrase by phrase, and intersperse between the phrases your commentary as to which parts are scriptural and which phrases we reject for having no foundation in God's Holy Word? I would find this a helpful tool for future talks with my friend, and I'm sure this would be a resource which could benefit many of your readers (those with a Catholic background, or even just for those with friends who are Catholic).

Hail Mary, full of grace, the Lord is with thee. Blessed art thou among women and blessed is the fruit of thy womb, Jesus. Holy Mary, Mother of God, pray for us sinners, now and at the hour of our death. Amen.

The problem with this prayer is not so much the phrases themselves (much of the prayer comes from the greeting to Mary in Luke 1) but with the interpretation given to the words and the use made of them.

Full of grace—the point in Scripture is that Mary is a recipient of grace, the privilege of being the mother of Jesus. The implication in the Hail Mary is that Mary is a source of grace for us. This is wrong—she is a recipient of grace, not a dispenser of grace.

Holy Mary—the Catholic church teaches that Mary is without sin. This is false. Mary is holy only in the way that all Christians are holy saints—by forgiveness of sins through faith in Christ. She herself testifies to her need for forgiveness, calling God "my Savior" (Luke 1:47).

Mother of God—in itself this phrase is correct, since the child born to Mary was true God, but the implication is that Mary is so exalted that we serve her also as Mother of the Church.

Pray for us sinners—nothing in Scripture indicates that we can or should pray to Mary. There is no evidence the saints in heaven can hear our prayers. Nothing in Scripture indicates that we need to pray to Mary. We can take our prayers directly to the Father through our faith in Christ. Jesus taught us to pray to his Father and "Our Father," not to his mother or our mother. Prayer is to be directed only to God. We can ask any Christian on earth to pray for us, but there is no support for the idea that there is a special class of saints in heaven who have greater access to God.

The only things Mary can do for our benefit she has already done—by God's grace she gave birth to the Savior and she has left us an example of humble faith. She has no other role in our salvation.

The Catholic church likes to claim it distinguishes between worship, which is given to God, and veneration, which is given to the saints, but this is just a distinction in words that is not reflected in reality. Praying to Mary is wrong by whatever name you call it.

Your
Question **The Roman Catholic church is talking about naming Mother Teresa and Pope John Paul II saints. As believers in Jesus Christ and what he did for us sinners, wouldn't they already be saints? What reason does the Catholic church give for doing this? What biblical support do they use?**

Catholics do not believe that believers necessarily go to heaven when they die. They may be in purgatory to pay the remaining temporal debt for their sins. Catholics further believe that we can pray to God through Mary and other saints as our intercessors. For us to pray to or through such a person, it is necessary to know that the person is actually in heaven and is hearing and answering prayers (or they might prefer to say is interceding for us). How can we know this about anyone? If people want someone like Mother Teresa to be a saint, they begin praying to her (or seeking her intercession). When people come forward and testify that they have received a miraculous healing through praying to Mother Teresa or John Paul and when the testimony has been examined and endorsed by the church, Mother Teresa and John Paul can be declared saints, that is, they can be placed on the recommended list of saints to whom one can pray. There is no scriptural basis for this.

Christians, of course, can and should pray for one another, even while they are on earth. But passages that state this cannot be used to prove that we need to pray through saints in heaven or that they can hear our requests from earth.

Your Question Bach, Beethoven, and Mozart all composed masses: Mass in B minor (Bach), Missa Solemnis (Beethoven), and Mass in C minor (Mozart). These masses are well known and well loved. Were they masses with a Catholic priest in attendance? Were they meant to be masses to be conducted in a Catholic church? I'm very hazy on this type of music and would like some information on it.

When we use the term *mass* in theology, we are usually referring to the Catholic belief that by the consecration of the Lord's Supper, the priest is offering a sacrifice for sin. Lutherans must reject "the mass" in this sense. But when the term *mass* is used in reference to music, it simply refers to music composed for the main parts of the liturgy. Luther's German liturgy was still called the German mass. Whether the "mass" was written specifically to be used in a Lutheran service or a Catholic service would depend on the faith of the composer or of the person who commissioned the composition. Some "masses," like those of Bach, were written by Lutherans for Lutherans. Since many parts of the Catholic and Lutheran liturgies are the same, some of the music of a "mass" might fit in a service of either church. Orchestras most frequently perform the best masses simply as musical compositions apart from any service.

Our Attitude Toward Catholics

Your Question I was very disturbed after reading an insert I found in my WELS church bulletin on Sunday. The statement was written by a former Catholic as she shares how her son led her to the Lutheran

church. I think the only way to explain my question is to quote from her passage: "I took this opportunity to invite my neighbor to attend church with us on Christmas. My neighbor snickered, 'I'll be going with my mother to the Church of Perpetual Agony.' Smiling, I replied, 'I was raised Catholic too.' With this simple remark, I can often find common ground with unbelievers to begin building a relationship." What is the underlying meaning here, that Catholics are unbelievers? My fiancé is a God-fearing Catholic with a very strong faith. He attended this church service with me and was as disturbed as I was to read this passage. My fiancé and I felt the underlying message was that God is not found in the Catholic church.

The first thing to note is that the part of the article you highlighted does not reflect a WELS attitude toward Catholicism. It is a Catholic attitude toward Catholicism that I have often heard expressed in these exact words or similar words. What would lead two Catholics to refer knowingly to the Catholic church as the Church of Perpetual Agony? This common saying gives evidence to spiritual pain that we who have been raised with the freedom of the gospel that the Lutheran church proclaims can hardly begin to imagine.

The author's experience speaks for itself, but her experience is something that I have encountered again and again when dealing with Catholics and former Catholics during my ministry. What is it that leads Catholics to refer knowingly to their church as the Church of Perpetual Agony? From experience in classes and counseling with Catholics over the years, I would suggest it is experiences like the following:

- It is coming home from Grandma's funeral and not knowing if she is in heaven with Jesus or in purgatory, suffering the final penalty for her sins. It is going to the priest to have a mass said on the tenth anniversary of your brother's death and asking, "How long before Joe gets out of purgatory?" and being told, "We can't be sure."

- It is the pain of a woman, betrayed and forsaken by an adulterous husband, who will be denied the Sacrament if she divorces and marries again.

- It is the pain of a woman who has been a faithful wife and mother and who finds that her husband has left her for a younger woman and is seeking an annulment of their marriage through the procedures allowed by the church so that he can receive the Sacrament.

- It is the pain of a young man who wants to serve God in the priesthood but also has the natural desire for marriage, but who is told the rule of the church won't let him marry.
- It is the dilemma of a young couple that is conscience stricken by the church's rules about family planning, which are not based on Scripture but on church decree.
- It is the puzzlement about how it could have been a sin to eat meat on Friday before and how the decree of the church can now make it not a sin anymore. If eating meat on Friday in Lent is a sin, how can the church say eating corned beef on St. Patrick's Day on a Friday in Lent is permitted?

The Lutheran church follows the teaching of the Bible that Jesus paid completely for all of our sins and by believing in him we can be confident that we will be with him in heaven from the hour of our death. Neither Mary, the saints, nor I have anything to do with obtaining remission of sins for me.

The Catholic church, however, teaches that Jesus' sacrifice for us did not complete all the penalty for our sin. As long as any least bit of our forgiveness depends on us, we will never be able to be sure when we have done enough. Our consciences can never be at rest in life or in the hour of death. We can't be sure if Mom and Dad are in purgatory or heaven. That is agony.

It is very common for Catholics who come to understand the biblical teaching that we are saved by grace alone and by faith alone to feel that they have had a great burden lifted off their shoulders. When they find that many of the rules of the church which have burdened them are not God's will but are man-made rules, they find joy in their newfound freedom in Christ.

We can hope that because the Word of the gospel and the sacraments are still present in the Catholic church, Catholics can be saved by them, but we know that great barriers are in the way of the gospel there. We are very sad that the man-made rules of the Catholic church burden people's consciences and that its mixing of faith and works as a source of forgiveness deprives people of the joy and peace they should have in complete forgiveness. We speak against these teachings of the Catholic church, because in our love for Catholics, we want them to find the freedom and peace we have found in Christ alone.

Your
Question **I am a WELS member and have a nonpracticing Catholic mother in-law. This is a question I received from her: "Since Jesus Christ, the Son of God, started the Catholic Church and the Lutherans broke away from the Church, how do you believe in that church? I ask this with a sincere heart and the curiosity of wanting to know how this is explained to you from your church's point of view."**

Christ did not found the Roman Catholic church. He founded the Christian church. The doctrines of the papacy, purgatory, the assumption of Mary, the forbidding of marriage to the priests, and many others held by the Roman church are not taught in the Bible by Christ or the apostles. These doctrines were added later in opposition to the Bible. They are not truly catholic, that is, universal and true. Luther did not break away from the Catholic church. He tried to reform the church by urging it to get rid of the nonbiblical doctrines it had added to the teachings of the Bible, especially the teaching that salvation is by faith and works, rather than by faith alone. For this effort he was excommunicated from the church. The Lutheran church is not a new church. It is the catholic (universal and true) church without the nonbiblical teachings added by Rome. Lutheranism retained the true things of the catholic church: the creeds, the Lord's Prayer, the Sacraments of Baptism and the Lord's Supper, the rite of confirmation, much of the liturgy, and much more.

A person leaving the Roman church to join the Lutheran church does not leave his or her catholic heritage behind. They keep what is best and true in that heritage.

Catholic doctrine and practice and how we should reach out to Catholics are discussed more fully in the Bible study *Catholicism Today* available from Northwestern Publishing House.

Protestants

Your
Question **In a recent article in the *Northwestern Lutheran,* the author said that he avoids the preaching of evangelists like Billy Graham, because of his false teaching. But doesn't he preach Christ crucified? What then is false teaching?**

False teaching is any teaching that departs from God's Word. Some false teachings are a greater danger to faith than others, but no false teachings can be safely ignored.

Among the most dangerous false teachings that are common among television evangelists are a denial of the power of infant Baptism, failure to recognize the real presence of Christ's body and blood in the Lord's Supper, and the idea that we can contribute something to our own conversion by making a decision for Christ. Many TV evangelists also teach that we should look for a millennial kingdom of Christ on this earth. All of these errors are a danger to faith.

Your
Question I have a friend who is mildly interested in a Methodist church in North Carolina. He was a Lutheran when he lived in Minnesota. He's concerned about the differences between the Methodist beliefs and ours. Can you outline them for me?

The most serious problem with Methodist churches today is that many of them are extremely liberal and do not hold even to the basic teachings of Methodism. The United Methodist Church is one of the most liberal Protestant churches in America both in its doctrine and in its moral positions.

But what about a traditional Methodist church that remains faithful to the Methodist doctrine and practices? Though Methodists emphasize the gospel of salvation through faith in Christ, there are serious doctrinal problems with Methodism. Methodists are part of the branch of Protestantism known as Arminianism. This branch believes that people can cooperate in bringing themselves to faith, that is, we have some spiritual ability remaining in us to make a decision for Christ. Methodists placed a greater emphasis on Christian living and on Christian experience than on doctrine. John Wesley, the founder of Methodism, believed that if one followed strict *methods* of sanctification, one could become free of sin already in this life (hence the name Methodism). This emphasis on "entire sanctification" or "perfectionism" and on subjective feeling led to the "spin off" of the holiness churches and Pentecostal churches from Methodism by those who wanted to carry these principles a step farther. Methodism also downplays the sacraments as real means of grace and sees them as symbols. These are a few of the areas of greatest difference between Lutheranism and Methodism.

For further information, see *A Lutheran Looks at Methodists & Holiness Churches* (Northwestern Publishing House, 2011).

Your **Question** I am a Baptist dating a Lutheran. I learned about the differences between our denominations on your page. Am I correct in stating that the only differences between our faiths are "once saved, always saved" and Baptism/Lord's Supper as symbolic acts? Also, I was wondering two things: (1.) Do Lutherans believe in predestination? (2.) If I cannot do anything to earn eternal life (by faith through grace), then how can I do something to lose it once God gives it to me?

The points you mention are key differences between Baptists and Lutherans, but there are others.

Most, or at least many, Baptists hold views of the rapture, tribulation, and a millennial kingdom that are very different from what Lutherans believe is the scriptural view. We believe that there will be only one return of Christ to set up his eternal kingdom in the new heavens and new earth. The rapture is the gathering together of believers in the one Last Day. Different accounts of the Last Day focus on different events or different aspects, but there is only one judgment day. There are a number of discussions about this in the eschatology section of this book.

Most Baptists believe we can cooperate in our conversion, making a decision for Christ. Lutherans believe we cooperate with the Holy Spirit only *after* our conversion. He is completely responsible for the change that takes place in our conversion.

We believe in election to salvation as taught in Ephesians 1. The Bible clearly says that there is no predestination to damnation, but that God wants all people to be saved.

We believe a person can fall from faith because the Bible says we can (Hebrews 10:26-31; 1 Corinthians 10:12). We don't base this conclusion on reason. But in this case, the principle is the same as a common principle of daily life: if I give you a gift of money, you have not done anything to earn it; but if you foolishly throw it away, you lose the benefit of the gift. Faith and forgiveness are a pure gift, but the person who throws them away loses the blessing that was his or hers.

Question **A member who had visited the Web site of the Evangelical Free Church of America asked me about the differences between that church and WELS. What information can you give me about this?**

The EFCA's statement of faith confesses many points of biblical doctrine, but the site also reveals a number of significant differences between WELS and the EFCA. Among the areas in which the EFCA departs from biblical teaching are the following:

- The EFCA denies that the sacraments are real means of grace. The doctrinal statement of the EFCA says that water baptism and the Lord's Supper are ordinances to be observed by the church during the present age. They are, however, not to be regarded as means of salvation.

- The EFCA confuses the invisible and visible church. "The true Church is composed of all such persons who through saving faith in Jesus Christ have been regenerated by the Holy Spirit and are united together in the Body of Christ of which He is the Head. That only those who are, thus, members of the true Church shall be eligible for membership in the local church." One cannot use membership of the invisible church as a basis for membership in the visible church since no one except God can judge who has faith. Our fellowship with a person on earth can be based only on his or her confession of the whole truth of God's Word.

- From the EFCA's confused view on the preceding point follows a false view of church fellowship that overlooks differences of doctrine. "The Distinctives of the Evangelical Free Church of America" say that the Evangelical Free Church of America is inclusive not exclusive. A person is not excluded from membership because he or she does not agree on every fine point of doctrine. Within the Evangelical Free Church, there is allowance for legitimate differences of understanding in some areas of doctrine. These statements emphasize quality of life over doctrine.

- The EFCA accepts millennialism.

- The EFCA strongly emphasizes congregational freedom and autonomy. This is not wrong in itself, but as endorsed by the EFCA, it seems to allow for differences of doctrine among EFCA congregations.

Could you please explain the beliefs of the Assemblies of God church and how they differ from the Lutheran church? Also, if possible could you provide me with some information about some of the beliefs of the Alliance churches?

The name Assemblies of God is used by several different churches. The General Council of the Assemblies of God is one of the largest Pentecostal bodies in America. Its local churches are encouraged to use the name "Assembly of God," so it is likely that you are referring to this group. It is a typical Pentecostal church, which emphasizes speaking in tongues and Christ's premillennial coming.

The Christian and Missionary Alliance is an Arminian, perfectionist church, which emphasizes the church's missionary obligation. Its beliefs are similar to those of other revivalist churches. It is also premillennial. A brief doctrine statement can be found on its home page.

For further information, see *A Lutheran Looks at the Assemblies of God* (Northwestern Publishing House, 2008).

Can you tell me more about the New Life Community Church that is an affiliate of a Reformed Church in America? They accept three confessional statements of beliefs, Heidelberg Catechism, Belgic Confession, and The Canons of Dort. I read the Heidelberg Catechism, and I agree with mostly all of their points. Can you tell me a little more about their history and are they a good church?

Reformed churches are those that follow the heritage of John Calvin. Besides churches that have the name Reformed in their title, the main Reformed churches are Presbyterian.

If this congregation follows its confessions, it is a Calvinistic church, which teaches predestination to damnation and has a view of the sacraments that tries to find a middle spot between the Lutheran view and the purely symbolical view of Zwingli that the sacraments are not true means of grace, in the Lutheran sense, but mere signs of grace. Reformed churches that maintain their traditional doctrine have a strong doctrine of Scripture, of original sin, and of grace. They do not, however, believe that Christ died for all people (limited atonement). Though there are strong points of Reformed doctrine, there are important differences between their position and the Lutheran position.

The Reformed Church of America in recent years seems to be hedging somewhat on some of its traditional doctrinal positions toward what some would call a "moderate" position on such issues as ordination of women and methods of Scripture study. Some congregations and individuals seem to hold more traditional doctrinal positions than others.

Your
Question **What exactly does "charismatic" mean when applied to a church? Why is it frowned upon among Lutherans?**

The original meaning of *charismatic* was simply "gifts of grace." It could refer to any spiritual gifts. The term, however, has now become associated with an emphasis on such gifts as speaking in tongues and faith healing. Pentecostals would say that these gifts are desirable or even necessary for all Christians. The New Testament does not teach us to expect the continuation of these special gifts that were given during the apostolic era. Today's charismatic speaking in tongues does not seem to be the same as that in the New Testament, which was speaking in real languages in all the instances about which we have definite information. The real point of our disagreement with the charismatic churches is that their doctrine is not in agreement with the Bible and that the emphasis on charismatic gifts is often used to minimize the importance of doctrine.

Our way of evaluating messengers who claim to speak in tongues or do miracles is quite simple: God tells us to look at their teaching. If it is not in agreement with the Bible, it must be rejected. Unbiblical teaching cannot be validated by claims of miracles or special gifts. See Deuteronomy 13:1-3.

In much reading about charismatic gifts, I have never been able to find a contemporary case of speaking in tongues which could be verified by independent researchers as real, unlearned human languages. All the research projects I have seen which were done independently by analyzing recordings of tongues have reported that the contemporary unlearned tongues are not real languages.

We cannot rule out the possibility of unlearned knowledge of real languages that comes from the devil to sow confusion in the church. Fraud is another possibility. Unexplained healings may be due to the power of prayer, but they may also be fraudulent, psychosomatic, or demonic. See 2 Thessalonians 2.

Fortunately, we do not have to be able to sort out these happenings by our subjective judgment. All we have to do is subject the teaching of the healer or speaker to the light of Scripture. If the teaching does not agree with Scripture, it is not to be accepted. If it does agree with Scripture, it is not new. We already knew it. It adds nothing to God's Word.

Your Question

I am sending my son (13) to a Lutheran school. His teacher read a book after my son did a report on it. The book by Tim LaHaye and Jerry Jenkins is titled *Left Behind.* She did not want him to read any more of the series because she felt it was teaching "false doctrine." I have found this very disturbing since its main message is this, "Nothing is more important than making a decision NOW where you stand with Jesus Christ. Don't wait until it is too late. Read the gospel of John from the Bible and consider your life in light of God's love." Does this series of books go against the doctrine of the Lutheran church? It is one of the best selling books in Christian bookstores across the nation (over 1.5 million sold).

This series of novels gives a fictional portrayal of life on earth after the rapture for those "left behind." The Bible does not teach a rapture that is a separate event from Christ's coming to judge the world. The "rapture" is the gathering of believers to meet Christ on the day of his return. (See section on end-time prophecies). This series of books conveys a very distorted view of biblical prophecy. Even their blurbs convey the impression that we can make a decision for Christ, rather than stressing that this change of heart is produced in us by the Holy Spirit. These are probably the main reasons the teacher did not want these books to be used as part of a class assignment. Her advice was good.

Your Question

What are the beliefs of the Quaker religion?

It is difficult to list the beliefs of the Quaker religion since they give greater priority to following a common lifestyle and style of worship than to doctrinal statements. For them, religious experience is more important than creeds. The basic principle of Quakerism is that God communicates with people through the "Inner Light," a form of direct revelation, apart from the written Word and sacraments. Historically, Quakers were very negative toward pastors, church buildings, liturgy, and the sacraments. In the typical Quaker meeting, members sat around waiting for someone to receive a revelation from God. Quakers were strong advocates of social reform, were pacifists who opposed all war, and opposed oaths.

More recently, Quakers have been influenced by evangelical Protestantism. Many of their services differ little from evangelical Protestant worship, and their theology ranges from fundamentalist to liberal. Today it is difficult to say what the Quakers' position is, even on such basic issues as the Trinity, the Bible, and the sacraments, because there is no unanimity. Nevertheless, the basic premise remains the same: the "Inner Light" is sufficient to lead people to salvation, even without knowledge of the historical facts recorded about Christ in the Bible. This belief separates them sharply from Lutherans, who emphasize the importance of the Word and sacraments. Lutherans are also separated from Quakers by our insistence that the historic acts of redemption accomplished by Christ take priority over and are the basis for our personal religious experience.

Cults

Your
Question "Anyone who believes that Christ is his Savior who made complete payment for his sins will be saved regardless of what church he belongs to, but the false teachings which many churches place alongside the gospel of Christ are a danger to faith, and we are commanded to avoid them." How should one rephrase this above statement when talking to a Mormon friend who believes Jesus died for him, but thinks he has to pay Christ back for his kindness three-fold by his works? I guess what I am asking is this: Is it not important for saving faith for people to realize Jesus is the one and only true God and also their only Savior? Or does simply just knowing Jesus died for them save? Are some Mormon wards changing and becoming Christian? Or have they just learned the language of Christians?

The statement you quote at the beginning of your question applies to Christian churches that have preserved the essence of the gospel among them but have some errors in doctrines which are not essential to salvation. It does not apply to cults like the Mormons, which are not Christian churches because they do not retain the fundamental doctrines of the person and work of Christ.

Mormons often retain Christian terminology but the terms are not used in a Christian sense. Some Mormons may be exposed to and give consideration to the Christian gospel as it is presented in the Christian churches around them, so an individual Mormon might be able to have a saving faith through hearing the correct preaching of the gospel from a source outside the Mormon religion. But I know of no evidence that any Mormon "congregations" are becoming Christian in their message.

Your Question Do we accept the baptism of the Mormons since they baptize and use the trinitarian name? Does a Mormon who joins the Lutheran church need to be rebaptized?

Though Mormons use the trinitarian name, their teachings are a repudiation of the biblical doctrine of the Trinity. They do not uphold the true deity of Christ nor the personality of the Holy Spirit. They also allow people to become "gods." A true Baptism requires more than the use of the words "Father, Son, and Spirit." It must be based on a confession of the triune God as revealed in the Bible. (Baptism does not, however, depend on the sincerity of the personal faith of the baptizer.)

Since the Mormons do not believe in the Trinity, their baptism is not Christian baptism. For this reason Mormons who join the Lutheran church should be baptized, since they have never really been baptized.

The same would be true of converts from other non-trinitarian sects that have some form of baptism. Christian churches that substitute some other formula for the words given by Scripture cast doubt on the validity of the baptism they perform.

Your Question I grew up Lutheran in Wisconsin for 22 years of my life. When doing a paper on the Church of Jesus Christ of Latter Day Saints for a paper in college, I changed. I was stunned at how rudely I was treated and how disrespectful Lutherans, who say they are Christians, treat "Mormons." Why is this? Also, where does the Lutheran church get their authority to form a church? In the Bible, God always called a prophet and gave them authority directly. Why aren't "Mormons" considered Christians when that term is referred to anyone that believes in Christ? I fully believe in Christ and he is my only source of salvation!

It is good that you believe in Jesus Christ as the only source of your salvation, but if you believe that Jesus is truly the eternal Son of God, equal to the Father in every way, and that our entire salvation is entirely due to Christ's death on the cross, you are not in agreement with the teachings of the Mormon religion. In fact, if you believe this, you are not a Mormon.

Mormonism teaches that the atonement Christ achieved for us was achieved primarily not by his death on the cross but primarily by his suffering in Gethsemane. It limits the salvation Christ achieved for us to a general salvation, which is freedom from Adam's guilt and the right to a resurrection. The salvation Christ won for us does not include individual salvation or exaltation to godhood. This conditional salvation must be won by us by full obedience to celestial law. Mormonism emphatically condemns the belief that our entire salvation has been won by Christ's death on the cross. Mormonism, therefore, is not Christian in the biblical sense of the term. Mormonism itself recognizes this when it condemns traditional churches as apostate. Mormonism has declared itself in opposition to the teaching of all orthodox, traditional Christian churches on many doctrines.

If Lutheran friends have warned you very strongly against the unbiblical teachings of Mormonism, they meant it in a loving way. This is not rudeness but an expression of loving concern for you, since the teachings of Mormonism are a rejection of historic, biblical teaching and a rejection of God's plan of salvation. Many books have been written that contrast the teachings of biblical Christianity and Mormonism. Among them is *Speaking the Truth in Love to Mormons*, by Mark Cares, available from Northwestern Publishing House. We encourage you to study it or a similar book very carefully. You are traveling on the wrong road to salvation—a dead-end road.

Your
Question I have been watching a lot of TV on a station of the Seventh Day Adventists. They seem very biblical, and I have learned a lot of scriptural facts from them (they know the Bible better than the WELS does!) but emphasize two things I think very strange: worshiping on Saturday is mandatory (it is the true Sabbath day) and people must be vegetarian (the station has a variety of shows, one that I found most amusing was cooking with tofu!). For vegetarianism they cite Daniel 1 because he ate vegetables and water for 2 weeks instead of the king's diet of rich foods. Also they say that

this was the diet in the Garden of Eden (God commanded them to eat from any tree in the Garden except the Tree of the Knowledge of Good and Evil). I can see this from two perspectives (the issue of vegetarianism): First, is it possible that they would have a point, since man fell into sin and then God gave them all creatures? (Abel sacrificed a lamb, God made the official command to Noah after the flood.) Therefore the vegetarian diet is the "diet before sin"? But the negative point is that the diet is mandated by them, where in Old Testament law they eat meat, and in most of the Bible people eat some sort of animal product (Jesus ate fish!) so why do the SDA's advocate true veganism? Sorry if this question is loaded. Please expound on this and their insistence on following the Saturday Sabbath day. I agree that a vegetarian diet is good if all nutrients are obtained and don't eat much meat myself, but what should this have to do with obtaining salvation (I agree we should regard our bodies as the temple of the Lord and take care of ourselves)?

In regard to the sabbatarian views of the Seventh-day Adventists and similar groups, there are two separate issues: on what day should we worship and how should we observe that day?

It is true that God commanded Israel to worship on the seventh day and to observe that day as a day of rest from all regular labor. It is true that we have no right to change any of God's commandments. But it is also true that God has the right to limit the application of commands he gives to certain people and to certain times. Not all of his commands apply to all people. The command to observe the seventh day as a day of rest was such a limited command. It applied only to Israel and only for the duration of the Old Testament.

The New Testament specifically tells us that we have been freed from the Sabbath command. Paul told the Colossians, "He forgave us all our sins, having canceled the written code, with its regulations, that was against us and that stood opposed to us; he took it away, nailing it to the cross. . . . Therefore do not let anyone judge you by what you eat or drink, or with regard to a religious festival, a New Moon celebration or a Sabbath day. These are a shadow of the things that were to come; the reality, however, is found in Christ" (Colossians 2:13-17). Since Christ has completed the payment for sin and has abolished the ceremonial law, which stood as a barrier between the Jews and the Gentiles, we should not let anyone judge us on the basis of whether or not we observe a day of Sabbath rest. We also must refrain from judging others on this basis. "One man considers one day more sacred than another; another man considers every day alike. Each one should be fully convinced in his own mind. He who regards one day as special, does so to the Lord. . . . You, then, why do you judge your brother? Or why do you look down on your brother? For we will all stand before God's judgment seat" (Romans 14:5,6,10). There is no longer a commanded day of Sabbath rest, not even Sunday.

In the Christian church, Sunday is not a day of physical rest in the Old Testament sense but a day for worship in which we obey Christ's command, "Let us not give up meeting together, as some are in the habit of doing, but let us encourage one another—and all the more as you see the Day approaching" (Hebrews 10:25). The first Christians in Jerusalem met daily, not weekly. "Every day they continued to meet together in the temple courts. They broke bread in their homes and ate together with glad and sincere hearts" (Acts 2:46). Within 20 years of Jesus' death, Sunday had apparently become the main meeting day of the church. Paul commanded, "On the first day of every week, each one of you should set aside a sum of money in keeping with his income, saving it up, so that when I come no collections will have to be made" (1 Corinthians 16:2). Revelation 1:10 also seems to refer to Sunday as the Lord's Day. The earliest church fathers also refer to Sunday as the Christian day of worship. It appears that Sunday was chosen because the first day of the week was the day of Jesus' resurrection. We therefore have both the permission of the Lord and the example of the New Testament church in using Sunday as our primary day of worship.

You have already answered the question about vegetarianism. Although meat was not used before the fall, when there was no sin, God specifically authorized the use of meat after the flood. He commanded animal sacrifices. The Old Testament Passover involved eating the lamb, and Jesus himself observed the Passover. Anyone who maintains that vegetarianism is a command of God can do so only by ignoring the Bible. It should be clear to you that anyone who demands acceptance of the two doctrines you have asked about really does not know anything about the Bible at all, contrary to what you said in your question. It takes more than simply quoting some Bible passages out of context to make a person's theology biblical.

The two issues you raise are not the worst problem with Adventism. They are just symptoms of a much more serious disease. Adventism is a system of legalistic work-righteousness, which does not truly teach justification by faith. Although some Adventists have tried to teach the biblical view of justification, they have not succeeded in winning the denomination. Since Adventists do not see Christ in Scripture, we have to say they really do not know Scripture at all, no matter how much they quote it. They are like the Jewish legalists of Paul's day who read the Scripture with a veil over their eyes.

Your
Question The LCMS Q&A section on their Web site recently issued a warning concerning the practice of yoga and meditation. They warned that yoga ultimately leads to involvement with the false gods of Hinduism. I was wondering if you saw a similar danger in the practice of a form of meditation called "zazen," associated with Zen Buddhism? I use this form of meditation briefly before training in the Japanese martial arts. I have never felt I was praying to the Buddha, I am a confessional Lutheran. I simply use this technique as a form to promote relaxation, correct breathing, and to clear the mind before training.

Most forms of oriental meditation and many forms of oriental exercise and martial arts in their original form are connected with oriental religions. Most of the zazen sites I looked at on the Internet connect the practice with perfecting the Buddhist way. Perhaps one can divorce some of the physical relaxation techniques used in zazen from Buddhism, but I don't think that what is left could be regarded as zazen anymore. It seems that zazen is intended to be more than a physical relaxation technique.

While working on this section of the book, I ran across an article on Christian yoga. Hindus reject this concept, claiming that true yoga is inseparable from its Hindu roots.

8
Creeds and Confessions

Your Question Why would a confessional body need to make doctrinal statements about fellowship today if avoiding errorists was already an apostolic practice? The documents from the ELS, WELS, and Missouri Synods from the last century teach that fellowship must be based on like beliefs. This is similar to the apostolic fathers who pretty much avoided breakaway groups. Five hundred years ago the Lutheran Confessions included an epitome and solid declaration of the Formula of Concord. They listed the faults that were never to be accepted. Pretty much strict adherence to doctrine is the underlying theme. Are there unique fellowship principles that need to be re-explained over the centuries to reflect the same truth?

Your question is the same as asking why Christians needed the Nicene and Athanasian Creeds when they already had the Apostles' Creed. It was because heretics like Arius, Nestorius, and Eutyches had found new ways of attacking scriptural truth and a new vocabulary for doing so. Why were the Lutheran Confessions needed if everything they say was already in Scripture? It was because Rome had twisted the words of Scripture in attempts to justify their false teachings. In every age the church must make a clear confession concerning the doctrines that are being attacked in their time.

The reason WELS had to make a new statement on fellowship in the 1960s was because the LCMS was no longer practicing what had been the common practice of the Synodical Conference and it was claiming that its view was the old view of the Synodical Conference. It also claimed a distinction between joint prayer and church fellowship, which appears to be an innovation in the church. It created "levels of fellowship." Valid confessions do not make new doctrine, but they defend the biblical doctrines that are under attack at any given time and expose the devices of the false teachers. The need to make clear confessional statements will never end until Christ returns. Satan focuses his attack one time on this doctrine, another time on that.

Your Question

I understand that since we cannot look into the heart, we must base our fellowship on people's confessions. Hence, if people's confession does not agree with my confession of faith, I am instructed to not engage in fellowship with them. Please correct me if this is wrong. If this is correct, then how can we communicate with Christians that have reacted to close-minded dogmatism by rejecting the need of a confession, as so many nondenominational churches have done?

Your question incorporates the faulty premise that acceptance of confessions is closed-minded dogmatism and that rejection of all confessions is not. The confessions of the church like the Nicene Creed were not closed-minded dogmatism. They were carefully worked out by the church in response to false teaching that went against Scripture. Orthodox confessions are testimonies to what Scripture teaches. Rejection of such confessions is based either on rejection of the scriptural teachings they confess or on a rejection of the clarity of Scripture on such matters as salvation through faith alone or the real presence of Christ's body and blood in the Lord's Supper. A rejection of confessions is a confession, a confession that one is unwilling to confess a scriptural answer to controversies that have arisen in the church.

If people have an aversion to confessions, we can begin by discussing their beliefs on the basis of Scripture alone. That is really the best starting point for any doctrinal talks.

Your Question

Who wrote the Apostles' Creed?

No one knows. *Studies in the Lutheran Confessions* by William Allbeck states, "The Creed originated in the obscurities of ancient church history. The most careful research has failed to discover the exact story." It apparently originated as a baptismal confession. It seems to have existed in variant forms. The creed as we have it apparently was adopted by the church in Rome from a form developed in France.

There is no clear evidence to support the tradition that it was written by the apostles, but it does teach apostolic doctrine.

Your
Question Why do we have the Athanasian Creed in our hymnal? (CW, pp. 132,133) It seems to teach salvation by works when it says, "Those who have done good will enter eternal life." It says nothing about justification by faith.

The official confessions of the Lutheran church include three creeds written before the Reformation, the so-called ecumenical creeds, the Apostles', Nicene, and Athanasian Creeds. The Apostles' Creed was developed by the early church as a brief summary of the faith, to be used in connection with Baptism. The Nicene and Athanasian Creeds were written to combat the false teachings of the Arians, who taught that Jesus Christ was not eternal God, equal to the Father. These two creeds respectively are named after Nicaea, the city in Turkey where an important council against the Arians met, and after Athanasius, who was the hero of the battle against Arianism.

Creeds usually cover primarily the doctrines that were being attacked at the time when the creeds were written. The Athanasian Creed therefore focuses almost entirely on the Trinity and the deity of Christ. It is a thorough summary of the main points of these doctrines, but does not cover other important doctrines.

The Lutheran church retained these creeds to defend itself against the false charges of the Catholics that the Lutherans were a new religion that did not uphold the historic Christian faith in the Trinity. The three ecumenical creeds confessed what the Lutherans held in common with the Catholic church.

None of the ecumenical creeds, however, presents an adequate treatment of the doctrine of justification by faith, which separated the Lutherans from Rome. For this reason the official confessions of the Lutheran church include six Lutheran confessions that treat this subject more fully: Luther's Small and Large Catechisms, the Augsburg Confession and the Apology to the Augsburg Confession, Luther's Smalcald Articles, and the Formula of Concord.

Although the ecumenical creeds are incomplete, nothing in them is incorrect. The words that seem to be evidence of work-righteousness can be understood correctly in the way in which Paul uses them in Romans 2:6-8. In this context "doing good" includes faith in Christ as its foundation and the works that flow from faith. Such good works are not a cause of forgiveness but a result of saving faith. Jesus also will point to our works as an evidence of justifying faith on judgment day (Matthew 25). Although the words can be understood correctly, it must be granted that the Athanasian Creed does not present a clear statement on the doctrine of justification. That is why we need other confessions.

Because it is quite technical in its vocabulary, the Athanasian Creed is seldom used in church. But with explanation, it is useful for a careful study of the doctrine of the Trinity. It is sometimes used for this purpose on Trinity Sunday. This is the main reason it is included in the hymnal.

Your Question

First question: Why did *Christian Worship* change the opening words of the Nicene Creed to "We believe"? Since none of us can confess faith for someone else, we should say, "I believe" as the old hymnal did.

Second question: I am dismayed that the synod would find the words "We believe" acceptable in the new version of the Nicene Creed. If our service were restricted to believers only (as it was in the early church), the words "we believe" might be appropriate. But when guests of other faiths are present, this wording makes us express fellowship with those who don't share our faith. I was taught this is "unionism."

Christian Worship did not change the opening words of the Nicene Creed to "We believe." In *Christian Worship* the opening words of the Nicene Creed were restored to "We believe," simply because this was the original wording of the creed. This wording is also used in both hymn versions of the creed in our hymnal, including the one written by Martin Luther (CW 270,271).

Christians have never been reluctant to confess their faith together. Jesus taught us to pray, "*Our* Father, who art in heaven." Paul told the Corinthians, "It is written: 'I believed; therefore I have spoken.' With that same spirit of faith we also believe and therefore speak, because we know that the one who raised the Lord Jesus from the dead will also raise us with Jesus and present us with you in his presence" (2 Corinthians 4:13,14). Peter confessed the faith of the apostles, "We believe and know that you are the Holy One of God" (John 6:69). The beauty of his confession was not lessened by the presence of the hypocrite Judas (John 6:70).

We can jointly confess our faith with all the other members of the congregation without worrying about whether some hypocrite is present. Weeding out the hypocrites is God's job, not ours.

But what about the concern of the second question? Does using the new version of the Nicene Creed (which is, however, actually the oldest version) place us into a situation of doctrinal compromise?

First of all, whether we use the word *I* or *we* in the creed makes no difference in determining whether or not the recitation of the creed is unionistic. It would be no less unionistic to recite the "I believe" of the Apostles' Creed together with adherents of false teaching than it would be to say the "We believe" of the Nicene Creed with them. The joint confession of faith would be the offense, not the wording of the creed.

In other words, it would be wrong to recite either version of the creed in a worship setting that allowed equal rights to truth and error. Our services are not such a setting. No rights or recognition are given to error there. Visitors of other faiths who are present are not providing their own input to the service; they are receiving our doctrine. Visitors of other faiths who are present to witness an event such as a baptism can, and often do, refrain from participating in the service.

If we were to say that nonmembers should not be present during the creed, they could not be present during the hymns or any prayers of the service either, since there is no essential difference between these and the creeds. Even in the early church, nonmembers were not excluded from the service, but only from the celebration of the Lord's Supper.

Your
Question *Christian Worship* changed the translation of the Nicene Creed from "who for us men and our salvation" to "for us and our salvation." Was this in keeping with the Greek as the original language? Was "for us men" redundant or was the Creed stating which part of creation was being redeemed? Was this for the sake of politically correct, gender-free language?

The most literal translation of the Greek would be "for us people." The Greek word refers to human beings regardless of their gender. In older translations this word was translated "men" in the generic sense of "human beings."

The hymnal committee felt that the translations "people," "humans," and "human beings" sounded awkward and that the use of "men" in the generic sense is no longer a universally recognized usage. The committee felt that it was not necessary to retain the noun since it would be clear to readers that Christ came to pay for the sins of people, not for animals, angels, or some other part of creation. The decision to omit the word from the translation was, thus, due partly to the feeling that it was redundant and partly to the feeling that the word *men* would create unnecessary offense for those who no longer recognize the generic sense of the word. There is nothing wrong with striving for inclusive language where Scripture intends to be inclusive (see 2 Corinthians 6:18).

It is, of course, debatable whether the word is truly redundant or whether it was an attempt by those who wrote the creed to emphasize the fact that it was human beings that Christ came to save, not angels (Hebrew 2:14-17). The omission was a judgment call on the part of the committee with which one may disagree.

Your
Question I have been a WELS member all my life and have always taken pride in our traditional conservative practices. Some time ago, I noticed the change in the Nicene Creed. It bothered me to see the words "became fully man" changed to "became fully human." I do not know why this change was made because it seems to be, in a very subtle way, downplaying our Lord's nature as 100 percent man and 100 percent God. Please tell me that this change was not to satisfy feministic views of the true nature of Christ. I have really been bothered by this because I hear in the news all the time about how churches all over the world have changed hymns and Scripture to gender-neutral words.

First of all, it should be noted that this change was not made by the WELS or our hymnal committee, but by the International Consultation on English Texts (ICET), which prepared the translations of the creeds that are the currently accepted standard among English-speaking Christians. It has been our practice to use Bible translations that are the widely used English standards, such as the King James and NIV, so that people would not have the impression that our doctrine was based on our own private translations. In our former hymnal the translations of the creeds were, for the most part, the English translations that were in common use at the time the hymnal was published. The same is largely true of the texts in *Christian Worship*. The hymnal committee made only minimal changes to the ICET texts, for example, retaining "holy Christian Church" rather than the more literal translation of "holy catholic Church" that was preferred by the ICET. A detailed analysis of these translations and the rationale for them was published in the Summer 1989 issue of the *Wisconsin Lutheran Quarterly*.

Concerning the specific point you asked about: the original Greek text of the creed contains an unusual verb that could be literally translated as "he became in-humaned." This verb is based on the Greek word *anthropos*, which usually refers to mankind or man in the generic sense, including male and female. Jesus came to be the Savior for the whole human race, male and female. The emphasis is on Jesus' possession of a complete human nature. "Became fully human" is about as close as one can come to a literal translation of the Greek that does not sound wooden. It also exactly expresses the main point that the creed was attempting to make—rejecting the view of false teachers such as the Apollonarians, who taught that Jesus was not fully human because he did not have a complete human soul, since the higher part of his soul was replaced by the divine nature. The hymnal committee thus saw no need to reject this part of the new translation, since it actually seems to express the intention of the original creed as clearly or more clearly than the old translation.

Your
Question **Both the Nicene and Apostles' Creeds say, "On the third day he rose again." Why this emphasis on "again"? What does this mean?**

In all three of the ecumenical creeds, the Latin and Greek texts simply have the verb "he rose." There is no adverb meaning "again," but the prefix of the verb sometimes has the connotation "again." This is probably the reason for the traditional English translation "rose again," which was used in *The Lutheran Hymnal* and was retained in *Christian Worship*. The hymnal committee received some criticism of the retention of the word on the grounds that it gave the impression of one or more previous resurrections. The word, however, was simply intended as a proclamation that Jesus, who once was dead, is now alive again. The committee thought that the English expression sounded natural and that there was no need to depart from the traditional translation. The inclusion was a judgment call on the part of the committee.

Recently on a radio service I heard a pastor use these words in the Apostles' Creed "I believe in the holy catholic church." The service was not WELS, but was Lutheran. Someone told me "catholic" was the original word in the creed, but Luther changed it to the "holy Christian church." What would you say about using "holy catholic church" in the creed?

The term *catholic* originated as a Greek word meaning "universal" or "complete." It referred to the whole church as it existed throughout the world, in contrast to local congregations. It also carried the connotation of orthodoxy, referring to the church that kept complete the true doctrine which the apostles had spread throughout the world.

Since the true evangelical Lutheran church teaches the apostolic doctrine of Scripture, we could call ourselves a catholic church. Since *catholic* sometimes also refers to the traditions and the way of worship developed in the Western church, the Lutheran church could properly be called catholic, since it has preserved the best of this heritage.

Nevertheless, there are two good reasons for not using the term *catholic* in our translation of the creed. The real meaning of the term *catholic* has been obscured in people's minds because of the way in which the papal Roman church has usurped the name and claimed that the name belongs to it alone. Although the papal church exists throughout the world, we would deny it the right to the name *catholic* since it does not continue in the apostles' doctrine. Although it might be possible to educate people to the difference between the real meaning of *catholic* and the Roman church's use of it, the word would probably remain confusing to many and thus is best not used.

A more important reason for refraining from using the word *catholic* in the creed is that the term is understood by many as referring primarily to the visible church. But the creed is not talking about any visible organization, denomination, or style of worship. It is talking about the invisible church, the communion of saints. Everyone everywhere in the world who has been brought to saving faith by the gospel is a member of this one church. In contemporary English, as in Luther's German, the phrase "holy Christian church" expresses this truth more clearly than the term *catholic*. For these reasons we retain the term "the holy Christian Church" as used by Luther's German creed. In the Latin version of the Lutheran Confessions, the word *catholic* is retained.

Your Question **I am puzzled about the translation of the Apostles' Creed. Some translations say, "Jesus sits at the right hand of God," but our hymnal says, "He is seated at the right hand of God." Who seats whom?**

God the Father seated Christ at his right hand, that is, the Father exalted Jesus to a position of power after Jesus had completed his work of redeeming us (Psalm 110:1; Philippians 2:9-11). In our current translation of the creed, however, the verb "is seated" is not a passive verb, which emphasizes the action of God the Father in exalting Christ to his right hand. It is a stative verb, which describes a state or condition in which Christ remains. Because God the Father seated Christ at his right hand, Jesus is seated and will remain seated at God's right hand, that is, he will continue to rule with his Father until he returns on judgment day.

Your Question **What would be your response to someone who tells you that teaching Dr. Martin Luther's Catechism is not necessary?**

It is not absolutely necessary to study the catechism, since one can learn the essentials of the faith directly from the Bible, but the chief parts of the catechism are mostly key passages of the Bible followed by Luther's brief explanations of the passage. It also contains the Apostles' Creed, the most universal creed. Unless one is convinced he has better summaries than those written by Luther, why would he neglect to use Luther's, which have stood the test of centuries?

9
Christians and Government

Your
Question The real reason churches remain silent on politics is the fear of losing their tax-exempt status (this could be seen as greed). We are to follow the laws made by our government leaders, as long as they don't go against God's Word. Laws making abortion, same-sex marriage, etc., legal are against God's Word. It's time we put our greed aside and start endorsing candidates who publicly state they are against these social moral issues, which, by the way, are not complex, but just plain wrong. Separation of church and state was intended for the protection of the church from the state not to protect the state from the church. Most religious leaders today fear offending someone in their congregation and losing their tax-exempt status (both are greed) and have bought into ignoring society's problems by remaining silent. I'm worried God doesn't see this as a positive position.

You present no question here, just misleading statements and implied accusations that are at best half-truths. First of all, churches are not remaining silent on politics. All kinds of churches—liberal, Evangelical, Fundamentalist, Roman Catholic—are making all kinds of political statements and forming political action groups that carry the name "Christian." Candidates regularly appear at churches and synagogues.

Your claim that separation of church and state was intended for the protection of the church from the state, not to protect the state from the church, may have been true for some of the founding fathers, but it was not true for others such as Thomas Jefferson, who was just as concerned about protecting the government from an established church as vice versa. It is also presumptuous for you to make sweeping generalizations about the motives of nearly all church leaders.

The implied accusation of your statement is that WELS churches do not become involved enough in political campaigns because they fear political involvement will mean financial loss. But the reason for this restraint is not government restrictions on politicking by tax-exempt organizations but biblical principles that would apply whether or not there were any such laws.

God has given the church and the state different roles and different tools.

We will, therefore, begin by briefly reviewing the purpose and the means of government on the basis of Romans 13:1-7 and 1 Peter 2:13-17. God has established government so that people may live in some degree of peace in a sin-filled world. The government's responsibility is to preserve the greatest possible peace and order in the world by punishing evildoers, rewarding those who do good, and protecting the rights of the law-abiding. To accomplish this, governments may make laws based on reason and enforce them on the disobedient even to the extent of imposing the death penalty when necessary and appropriate. Every state is based on force.

The mission and tools of the church are quite different. God has established the church so that people may live with him in peace forever. The church's responsibility is to preach the gospel and to administer the sacraments through which saving faith is created and nourished. The church does not wage its battles with the sword of the state, but with the sword of the Spirit, the Word of God (Matthew 28:19,20; John 18:36,37; also 2 Corinthians 10:4-6; Ephesians 6:10-18). The church is not responsible for disciplining those outside the church (1 Corinthians 5:12).

Since God has assigned to both the church and the state their own distinct purposes and distinct tools, these should not become mixed or confused. Neither church nor state should try to do the work of the other. Neither should ask the other to do its work. Neither should seek to accomplish its ends by using the tools of the other. Observing these distinctions of purposes and tools is what we mean by the "separation of church and state." Such separation of church and state is a valid deduction from the distinct missions and tools God has assigned to church and state.

Since there are some areas in life in which both the state and the church have a valid interest—such as marriage, sexual morality, education, and so on—their interests and activities may sometimes overlap. Perhaps it might, therefore, be clearer if we would speak of "avoiding a confusion of the roles of church and state," rather than of a "separation of church and state." It is not possible to demand a total separation of all activities of church and state. One area in which we regularly accept a certain overlap of interests is in the public establishment of a marriage. In the marriage of a Christian couple, the church is interested in helping the couple begin their marriage on the basis of God's Word and in seeking his blessing upon them in prayer. The state is interested in a witnessed, written confirmation of the legal contract, which has serious implications regarding property rights and inheritance. We allow both of these purposes to be fulfilled on the basis of a single ceremony.

The Lutheran Confessions clearly set forth these scriptural principles of the separation of church and state, especially in Article 28 of the Augsburg Confession. "The power of the church and the civil power must not be confounded. The power of the church has its own commission to teach the Gospel and administer the Sacraments. Let it not break into the office of another. . . . Let it not prescribe laws to civil rulers concerning the form of the commonwealth" (*Triglotta*, p. 85).

The church needs to preach the whole law of God to every person, so that law may serve as a mirror of sin and a curb of sin to all people. The law can serve as a rule for true morality only to those who have been reborn in Christ. It is not the duty of the church to make non-Christians behave as if they were Christians. The mission of the church is to make people God's children in faith. Such citizens will, of course, have an effect on the society in which they live. Active citizenship is encouraged in the Lutheran Confessions, but the roles of church and state are not confused. Christians are to understand the difference of the roles in the two realms.

Christians may properly work for good laws and good government, but they are doing this as citizens, not as a direct part of the work of the church.

Your Question

Can WELS Christian schools make use of aid from the government in the form of vouchers?

The general scriptural principles of church and state are summarized in the preceding answer. The legal separation of church and state is not based on Scripture but on the US Constitution. The Bible does, however, teach that God has assigned different tools and different duties to church and state. Each should stick to its own duty without interfering with the other.

There is no explicit discussion of the separation of church and state in Scripture. In the Old Testament theocracy there was, of course, no sharp separation of church and state, of civil and moral law, or of religious offenses and civil punishment. The leaders of the post-exilic Jewish state were willing to accept financial aid even from the heathen Persian government for the construction of the temple and for the sponsorship of religious services (Ezra 6:8-10; 7:13-26). They apparently regarded it as a kind of reparations for past damages.

In the New Testament era, the only significant threat to the separation of church and state was the oppression of the church by both the Jewish and Roman states. It is therefore not surprising that there is little explicit discussion of the topic of government aid to churches in the New Testament. The passages that are most often adduced as proof passages for a doctrine of the separation of church and state address the issue only indirectly. For example, in Jesus' remark "Give to Caesar what is Caesar's, and to God what is God's" (Matthew 22:21), he simply states that the political realm and the spiritual realm are distinct kingdoms and that we have responsibilities toward both. The specific responsibility he is addressing is paying taxes. He gives no directions for keeping the activities of the two kingdoms separate. However, since Tiberius claimed the title "Pontifex Maximus" (high priest) on the back of his denarius, Jesus' remark, "Give to God what is God's," may contain a subtle rebuke of Tiberius' pretensions in spiritual matters that was more obvious to Jesus' contemporaries than to us.

In his statement, "Man, who made me a judge or an arbitrator between you?" (Luke 12:14), Jesus simply states that he had not come to be an authority in legal disputes, but as the messenger of the gospel. Again he offers no specific guidelines on the separation of church and state.

The doctrine of the separation of church and state is established not so much by direct statements of Scripture but by a comparison of the work and the tools that God has assigned to church and state as noted in the preceding answer. Since God has assigned to both the church and the state their own distinct purposes and distinct tools, these should not become mixed or confused. Neither church nor state should try to do the work of the other. Neither should ask the other to do its work. Neither should seek to accomplish its ends by using the tools of the other. Observing these distinctions of purposes and tools is what we mean by the "separation of church and state."

How do these principles apply to Christian schools receiving voucher payments?

In dealing with issues of church and state and Christian education, we have to distinguish between three questions: (1) Is this activity scriptural? This, of course, is determined by the Bible. (2) Is this activity legal? This is determined by the courts. (3) Is this cooperation with the state wise or might this entangle our school in government controls? Finally, this judgment rests with the responsible governing body of the school. Such judgments are not made by the synod except for synodical schools.

The most controversial issue involving the constitutional clause against government establishment of religion is the question of government aid to religious schools, whether directly to the school or funneled through parents. Previous court cases have established that public funds may not be used to make payments to religious schools even for secular subjects, nor may "auxiliary services" be provided on religious premises. According to legal precedents, indirect aid to religious schools is permissible only if it meets at least three tests: (1) it has a secular purpose, (2) its primary effect neither advances nor enhances religion, and (3) it avoids excessive entanglement of church and state. Some justices have suggested that such aid must pass a fourth test: it does not create political divisiveness. The Supreme Court will allow indirect and insubstantial aid, but not aid that is direct or substantial.

Overall, the Supreme Court appears to have erected a substantial barrier to aiding religious schools. The exception is church-affiliated colleges and universities, since they are considered to be providers of a more general education. For example, government funds can be used for buildings at church-affiliated colleges if they are not used for religious purposes.

This battle is now being fought again over school choice and various voucher systems. Because plans vary from state to state, a comprehensive treatment is not possible. Of special interest is the struggle in Wisconsin. In 1989 the legislature approved a limited voucher program whereby public funds could be used to pay for tuition at nonsectarian private schools. In 1995 the program was expanded to include religious schools. In January 1997, after the state supreme court deadlocked on the issue, a state circuit court ruled the voucher plan unconstitutional since it forces taxpayers to support religious institutions. The judge quoted from the schools' own statements of purpose, which clearly state their religious aims. In June 1998, however, the state supreme court upheld the constitutionality of the plan on the grounds that it has a secular purpose, did not have the primary purpose of advancing religion, and avoided excessive entanglement. It is the last point that is especially debatable. Some of our schools have concluded that there are enough entanglements and strings attached that they should not participate. Others are very actively involved in the program (*Wisconsin Lutheran Quarterly* [Winter 1999], pp. 66-68; *Northwestern Lutheran* [October 1998], p. 20). Voucher battles are going on in at least a dozen states, and it will probably be some time before the last word is heard.

To summarize: (1) The Bible does not forbid the government to help Christian education. (2) The courts have the last say on what is constitutional. (3) Because the government almost never gives money without controls attached, we should be alert to the potential danger of such programs. Dangers include dependence on government funds that can be withdrawn at any time, government controls and regulations attached to the aid, and effects on Christian stewardship. The final judgment on whether to participate in aid programs that the courts have ruled to be legal rests with the congregation in the case of Lutheran elementary schools or with the responsible board for high schools, colleges, and noncongregational elementary schools.

Groups involved with such schools that receive government aid have issued their own statements and guidelines about their participation.

Your Question I have a question concerning politics. Where I live there is a political party called "Christian Democrats." They were started in the 1960s by some Christians who wanted a "Christian" alternative to the secular parties. Their main agenda is an ideology based on "Christian ethics." They are against homosexuality, abortion, euthanasia, etc. Earlier they also wanted to have more Christian education in schools, alternative education concerning creation (creationism and not only

evolutionism). Today they might not be as (positively) radical as they used to be.

I have heard some Christians say we are free to vote for any political party in our Christian freedom, except maybe "Christian Democrats" because of the name of the party and because Christian faith has nothing to do with politics.

I would say the name "Christian" is not a real problem, since they nowhere claim to represent Christian faith. They claim to be a party that is an alternative to the modern secular materialistic ideology though, and they claim to cling to the "Christian tradition" of our culture. It bothers me that some Christians in fellowship with me keep saying we cannot vote for them because of the name "Christian" and because state and church must be separated. Some say Christians cannot claim the right to have the "natural law" (expressed in this ideology). I agree its very important not to mingle church and state, but I don't find any problem with this name as long as they don't claim to be "Christian" (as representing our faith) and as long as they don't force our faith upon anyone. I also believe Christians can vote for any other party they prefer, according to their conscience. My only objection is to limit the Christian freedom, when it seems to be based on a faulty view of this party's intentions. For me it is still an adiaphoron, even if I would prefer that they changed their name to something else. Do you have any input on this matter? Would you say it is wrong to promote a party that uses the name "Christ-" or "Christian"? I am in fellowship with the WELS.

Christians will seldom find a political party or candidate that they can agree with 100 percent when they evaluate the candidate's or party's positions on the basis of Scripture. Quite often one candidate may contradict the Bible at one point, the other candidate at another. The voters' options are therefore to vote for the candidate whom they believe will best serve the overall needs of society or not to vote for any of the candidates. The simple fact that a party has the word *Christian* in its name would not disqualify it from receiving the same consideration as any other party on the basis of the standards mentioned above. When all things are considered, such a party might, in fact, be the party that best reflects a Christian voter's views on the types of laws needed by society. As noted above, there is the danger that such parties incorporate a Reformed/Catholic view of the mission of the church, but you would be voting for the party not as a way to advance the mission of the church but because it is the best way to promote civic righteousness.

**What does WELS think about state churches as they are
found for instance in Europe? Even the Lutheran church after the
Reformation was not a "free church." Was Luther too inconsistent
there and "questions of power" overshadowed the truth? Why was
Luther first against infant Baptism and later changed his mind?
Often he is accused of having done this to establish the state church.**

In the strict sense, "state church" refers only to a church controlled
by the state, usually with the head of state also serving as the legal head
of the church. Some of the national or territorial Lutheran churches of
Europe are not state churches in the strict sense, but they do receive
favored support from the state. Here we are not discussing all contact
or co-operation between the state and a church or churches. That issue
is discussed in other questions. Here we are discussing only state
control of the church.

You give no evidence to support the claim that Luther switched to
infant Baptism to help a state church. I know of no evidence for this.
The fact is that Luther opposed a state church. Luther's views were
remarkably clear and consistent, considering the attitudes and
conditions of his day.

> After the abolition of the Law the secular emperors, kings, and
> princes were entrusted with the sword of iron, and the oral sword
> was assigned to the apostles and us preachers. This distinction
> must remain intact; and let all who can lend a hand to that end.
> But if the princes continue to jumble the two, as they are now
> doing, then may God in his mercy shorten our lives that we may
> not witness the ensuing disaster. For in such circumstances the
> Christian religion must go to wrack and ruin. This is what
> happened in the papacy when the bishops became secular princes.
> And if the secular lords now become popes and bishops and insist
> on sermons that defer to their wishes, then let the wretched devil
> preach to them, for he preaches too. But let us pray God that
> neither the spiritual nor the secular realm abuses its office that way.
> ("Commentary on John 2," LW 22, p. 228)

But Luther lacked opportunity to put his views into practice. "I do not
yet have available the persons necessary to accomplish it [the actual
separation of church and state and implementation of proper
congregational life] nor do I see many who strongly urge it" ("German
Mass," LW 53, p. 64).

The Lutheran Confessions also clearly set forth the scriptural principles of the separation of church and state, especially in Article 28 of the Augsburg Confession. "The power of the church and the civil power must not be confounded. The power of the church has its own commission to teach the Gospel and administer the Sacraments. Let it not break into the office of another. . . . Let it not prescribe laws to civil rulers concerning the form of the commonwealth" (*Triglotta*, p. 85).

The Reformed and the Catholic churches both entangled church and state. Roman Catholics claimed that the state was subject to the church. The Reformed generally saw the state as the partner of the church in enforcing God's law, including the first table (Calvin, *Institutes*, V II 780). This was really not far removed from the Catholic position, which made the pope the head of all secular rulers, since in both cases the punitive power of the state was used to enforce the laws of the church.

Unfortunately, the clear Lutheran position was never really put into practice, and the Lutheran dogmaticians who followed Luther learned to live with a state-church mentality. If Luther's views would have been put into practice, a separation of church and state similar to that which existed in 19th-century America might have resulted. Practical difficulties and a deterioration of the Lutheran position prevented this from ever happening.

In spite of the good start made by Luther, the greatest achievement in the separation of church and state would take place not on Lutheran soil in Europe but elsewhere. At the time of the American Revolution, the convergence of such factors as the prevalence of separatist denominations (most notably the Baptists), the personalizing of religion in the Great Awakening, and the aversion to any state church on the part of the deists among the leaders of the revolution brought about the constitutional separation of church and state that we enjoy today. When Lutherans fleeing the state churches of Europe, especially the Prussian Union, came to America, they found an environment in which they could put Luther's scriptural understanding into practice.

Your
Question   As Christians, we are to support our government and elected leaders. Also as Christians, we refuse, with God's power, to submit to evil and laws contrary to God's law. In war, people die, property is destroyed, and the wealth of nations is depleted. Can you

point out Scripture that could help me decide if the present war we are involved in is moral or immoral?

The traditional Christian criteria of a just war (or perhaps better, a justified war) are not drawn directly from a list in Scripture but are based on scriptural principles. They are a war (1) waged by a legal authority, (2) for a just cause, such as self-defense or protecting the innocent, (3) as a last resort, (4) with a reasonable probability of success, (5) with proportionate means, and (6) with regard for the innocent.

Luther's tract "Can Soldiers Too Be Saved?" (1526) remains the classic treatment of the subject of war and conscientious objection from a Christian point of view. He also deals with the subject in "Temporal Authority" and "War Against the Turk."

Luther bases his conclusion that Christians can serve in just wars on Romans 13 and 1 Peter 2, on John the Baptist's directions to soldiers in Luke 3, and on the wars conducted by Old Testament saints. Other appropriate references are to the believing centurions in the New Testament church and to Psalm 144, "Praise be to the Lord, my Rock, who trains my hands for war, my fingers for battle."

Luther recognized both the evil of war and its necessity in a sinful world.

> When I think of a soldier fulfilling his office by punishing the wicked, killing the wicked, and creating so much misery, it seems an un-Christian work completely contrary to Christian love. But when I think of how it protects the good and keeps and preserves wife and child, house and farm, property, honor and peace, then I see how precious and godly this work is, and I observe that it amputates a leg or a hand, so that the whole body may not perish. . . . What men write about war saying that it is a great plague is all true. But they should consider also how great the plague is that war prevents. ("Can Soldiers Too . . . ?" LW 46, p. 96)

Luther recognized that wars could be selfish and unjust and advised Christians to refuse to participate in wars they knew to be unjust. It is not just for a ruler to enter a war of rebellion or to start a war of aggression against the innocent. A just war is a war of self-defense in which the enemy has rejected offers of peace. If a citizen is uncertain whether a war is just, he should obey his ruler and leave the ruler's judgment to God.

I am writing a paper for history class. My topic is whether atomic warfare can be justified. I was wondering what the Bible said about warfare especially in respect to genocide, which accompanies an atomic bomb. I would appreciate a response as soon as possible.

Your school library should have books on the morality of war, both from within the just war tradition and from the pacifist tradition. Two recent books are *War and Christian Ethics*, by Arthur Holmes, and *When God Says War Is Right*, by Darrell Cole. The Lutheran Confessions also deal with the issue (see the preceding questions).

Nuclear weapons have been used only once in warfare—to end World War II. My father was among the American Marines preparing for the invasion of Japan after the horrors of the kamikaze attacks at Okinawa, the last island to be conquered on the way to the Japanese homeland. It was expected that a million American lives would be lost in the invasion of Japan. Historians can second-guess President Truman's decision, but at the time it seemed the nuclear attacks also saved more than two million Japanese lives, which could have been lost in a suicidal resistance to the invasion. Was dropping the bomb genocide or the saving of lives on all sides?

Nuclear weapons would have to be considered within the criteria for just war just as any other weapons would be. The question of excessive vengeful force can be applied to conventional bombing as well—as for example in the Allied bombings at Dresden, Germany. Nuclear weapons, horrible as they are, contributed to only a small percentage of the casualties deliberately inflicted on civilians by both sides during the war. During the Cold War, did nuclear weapons prolong Communism's reign of terror or did they check its advance?

Now that the nuclear genie is out of the bottle, so to speak, it is clear there is no going back to pre-nuclear days.

It is time for our synod to speak in unequivocal terms about the Bosnian situation, publicly for all the world to see and hear. I am sure you are aware of the facts—the "ethnic cleansing," the use of rape by the Serbs as a policy of war. Would there be this deafening silence if WELS Lutherans were raped and slaughtered? The Bosnian Muslims are also God's creation. Surely we Christians cannot stand idly by while the horror continues.

Your question involves more than the Bosnian situation (referring to the bitter warfare and atrocities between Serbs, Croatians, and Bosnian Muslims in the 1990s). The larger question is "How does the church oppose injustice?"

The mission God has given to the church is to preach his law, which condemns all sin, and to proclaim his gospel, which changes the hearts of sinners so that they love God and their fellow human beings.

As part of their preaching of God's law, his spokesmen impartially denounce specific sins of both the mighty and the lowly. They make it clear that God hates tyrants and oppressors (Psalm 58:1-6; Isaiah 13–34; Ezekiel 12–32).

Christians should oppose oppressors with prayer, as David did in the Psalms and as the saints do in heaven (Revelation 6:10). Too often today even Christians seem to think that the only two options we have when facing evil are resorting to violence or "doing nothing." Let us not neglect the third option, the powerful weapon God has given us in prayer.

As preachers of God's law we certainly can and should condemn the atrocities you cite in your letter. Many difficult practical questions arise, however, if we try to implement your suggestion that our synod convention should issue a resolution condemning the Bosnian Serbs.

To whom do we address it? To the Serbs? They have shown that they have no regard for the opinion of the united nations of the world. Will a resolution of a small church they never heard of impress them? Is the resolution addressed to public opinion in our country and abroad? The world does not lack information about what is happening in Bosnia. The problem is that it does not care enough to do anything about it.

If we address our resolution to our own government or the UN, what do we ask them to do? Bomb the Serbian's military positions? their industries? their civilians? How much violence is appropriate to end the violence?

If we denounce the Serbians, who are at the moment the most successful aggressors, do we denounce the Croatians and Muslims, who have also driven people from their homes when they had the chance? In the Middle East, do we denounce Israel, which is occupying the Palestinian land captured in a defensive war, or the

Arabs, who are killing as many of their own people as the Israelis? Do we denounce Saddam Hussein or US forces for causing so many Iraqi casualties? In South Africa, do we denounce the apartheid government or the black factions who are killing more of their fellow Africans than the white government? Do we denounce Somali "warlords" or UN troops who have shot demonstrating women and children? And what about Mozambique, Angola, Liberia, Cambodia, Sri Lanka, Armenia, and the other countless corners of the world where people are slaughtering one another? What of abortionists, pornographers, and street gangs? There are not enough pages in the synod's convention reports to contain the names of all the oppressors and tyrants in this world who need to be denounced.

The world is filled with horrifying, heartbreaking hatred and violence, which TV and other media bring into our homes daily. We grieve for the victims and feel a desperate desire to help them. But church resolutions are not an effective way to help them.

The church's assignment is to change people's conduct by changing their hearts through the gospel. Its mission is not to pressure the government into changing people's behavior with bombs and guns. Our method is preaching and proclaiming, not lobbying. As a church let us carry out our duty of confronting every sinner we can reach with God's Word. Our priority should be the sins of our hearers, not absent enemies. We have an interesting example of such preaching in Amos 1 and 2. Amos does indeed denounce the atrocities of all the nations around Israel, but he does it as a prelude to his real emphasis, confronting the sins of his own hearers in Israel and Judah.

As members of the church, we can also pray against evildoers. We also should do everything we can to provide aid and relief to victims and refugees.

As citizens of our country, we have the right to ask our government to pursue policies that will protect innocent victims throughout the world. But even here we should remember that this is often easier said than done. As I am writing this article, the well-intentioned humanitarian intervention in Somalia is starting to produce more casualties, including civilians, but the country's underlying problems do not seem to be any nearer to a solution. Four decades of peace efforts have not brought peace to the Middle East.

As church members we should make spiritual efforts to oppose evil by preaching and by prayer. As citizens and neighbors we may make political and military efforts. But we should not lose sight of the fact that the only way we can finally remove war and atrocities from the world is to pray, "Come, Lord Jesus" (Revelation 22:20).

Would our reaction be any different if the victims were fellow Lutherans? When Jesus, the apostles, and the early Christians were persecuted, they used their legal rights, but they did not call on others to defend them with violence. At the time of the Reformation when the Catholic church and Catholic rulers were using force to suppress the Reformation, Luther was very reluctant to call for military force to protect him from persecution. He accepted the legal argument that Protestant princes and rulers had the duty to confront Catholic force with force, but he stated that as a Christian he was ready to suffer persecution rather than call for violent help (Plass, *What Luther Says*, p. 600). If we were to be in the same circumstances he was, we should pray for the same strength and courage he showed.

God has placed two servants into the world with the duty of opposing evil on his behalf. One is the church, which is to oppose evil with the Word and prayer. The second is the government, which is to oppose force with force. God's purpose is best served when each of his servants opposes evil with the tools he has assigned to it. Neither of God's servants is to take up the tools or the duties of the other.

As a church we are to use the tools God has given us to carry out the duty he has given us: changing sinful, hateful hearts with the power of the Word. That is more than enough of an assignment to occupy us full-time until Christ returns. For this reason WELS has wisely refrained from trying to influence government actions with its resolutions, in order to concentrate on its duty: changing hearts with the gospel.

Your Question A recent column in the *Northwestern Lutheran* about abortion referred to the Bible's prohibition of "murder of any human being." Does this relate to the death penalty? What is the WELS stance on the death penalty?

The Bible authorizes capital punishment in both the Old and New Testaments (Genesis 9:6; Exodus 21:12-14; Romans 13:4). The Old

Testament civil law made a distinction between premeditated murder and negligent homicide. The death penalty applied to the former, not the latter. The death penalty and all other penalties for crime should be applied impartially without bias due to wealth, class, or race.

It is clear that the Fifth Commandment, which is given as moral law in Exodus 20, does not prohibit the death penalty, which was given as part of Israel's civil law in Exodus 21.

Your
Question Recently on the Q & A page there was a question about medical treatments which are being developed from research using fetal tissue obtained from abortions. The answer said that we cannot support research which uses fetal tissue. I agree with this, but can you say a little more about the morality of using treatments that were originally developed using fetal tissue? If we use such treatments after the fact, are we accomplices to the abortion?

This is an extremely complicated question because of a number of factors. It would take a book to discuss them, but I will try to summarize the main issues.

There are two main types of treatment involved. In one type, tissue taken from an aborted baby is actually transplanted into the patient to try to stimulate or replace a bodily process that has begun to fail. For example, brain tissue taken from aborted babies is transplanted into Parkinson's patients to increase the supply of the neurotransmitter dopamine in the patient's brain. In the second type of treatment, fetal tissue was (or is being) used in the development of an immunization or treatment, but the patient does not receive the fetal tissue directly, only the product that was developed with the use of fetal tissue. The treatment may now be being produced without the continued use of fetal tissue.

One basic problem in analyzing specific cases is the difficulty of obtaining reliable information. There are claims and counterclaims concerning almost every individual case.

Among the immunizations allegedly produced through the use of fetal tissue are some immunizations for chicken pox, rubella, and polio. Reliable information about exactly which vaccines have been developed by use of fetal tissue may sometimes be hard to obtain, since drug companies are not very eager to publicize the fact. It seems clear and undisputed that some very common vaccines were developed using fetal tissue and that people have been using them without any awareness of their origin.

There are also many disputes about the medical necessity and value of treatments based on direct use of fetal tissue or on lines of stem cells produced from them.

It is disputed whether research could be done just as well using tissues of babies that had miscarried naturally. Some doctors say there would be a risk that the tissue carried some defect that was the cause of the miscarriage. Others say this need not be the case since miscarriage is often the result of a problem in the mother's body rather than a problem with the child. Others report that researchers prefer tissue from aborted babies because it is more convenient and reliable to go to an abortion clinic than to rely on miscarriages, which are by their very nature unscheduled.

There are many published articles that raise serious doubts about how effective the transplants of fetal tissue really are. There are other ways to develop treatments, which would not require the use of fetal tissue. For example, reports that brain cells may in fact be able to reproduce raise hope for other approaches to treating diseases that affect the brain, which would not require fetal tissue. If research in stem cell development can be done without using fertilized eggs or unused embryos from IVF procedures, it may lead to new methods for organ regeneration without the use of fetal tissue.

These are a few of the scientific and medical questions or issues of fact that are disputed as part of this debate. We now turn briefly to the main moral issues.

Some ethicists maintain that one can never benefit from a deliberate abortion without in some sense being an accomplice in it. Others have stated that while refusal of a vaccine or tissue transplant might serve as a moral testimony against abortion, the final judgment about "after-the-fact" use of such treatments must be left to the patients or to their parents if they are minors. Some claim that receiving tissue from a fetus is no different than receiving a transplant from a person who was killed by a drunk driver. It is claimed that salvaging a good outcome from an evil event does not make one party to the event. The weakness of this analogy is that the abortionist and the woman who obtains an abortion are more comparable to the drunken driver of the car who caused the person's death than they are to the victim who signed an organ donor card or the grieving family that allows a transplant from their loved one's body. We would not ask the murderer for consent to use his victim's body, nor would we arrange to meet him at the time of his planned crime to obtain parts from his victim. Even less would we ask him to harvest those parts for us and to deliver them to us. The research institute that cooperates with an abortion clinic to obtain fetal material for transplants is much different than the hospital that saves organs from an accident victim. There must be cooperation between the clinic and those obtaining material for fresh transplants. If the clinic seeks the mother's consent for the use of fetal tissue, she becomes a partner of sorts in the whole operation (such consent may not always be sought). There is a cooperative relationship involved throughout the process even if the clinic delivers the bodies to another facility for processing. The procedures for abortions are allegedly altered to obtain better tissue for transplant or experimentation, even though this may increase danger and cost to the mother. There is financial and psychological benefit to the abortionist from being involved with providing fetal tissue. All of these factors weigh against comparing the use of fetal tissue to the use of transplants from murder or accident victims.

Another aspect of the argument is the so-called slippery slope danger. Will the acceptability of harvesting organs from dead, aborted fetuses lead to "live abortions" to obtain better parts or even to experimentation on still living or about-to-be-aborted babies? There are many published reports that such experimentation is already occurring. There are also conflicting reports about the role of the suction removal of the baby's brain in "partial birth abortions" in obtaining material for brain transplants. Many fear that the end of the process is creation of embryos specifically for research or harvest of "spare parts" and tissues. The more cures created and the more respectability fetal research gains, the greater the need for increased "fetal harvest."

Another fear is the so-called redemption factor. The idea that the abortion of her baby can provide a medical benefit or transplant for someone else may make the abortion seem less selfish to the mother and help her overcome a reluctance to obtain an abortion. After all, something good can come of it. This hope gives a redeeming social value to a horrible act. The person who accepts a transplant from a murder victim is giving comfort to the innocent survivors not to the perpetrators. The use of benefits from fetal tissue, on the other hand, may be giving comfort to those who were party to the abortion.

These are just a few of the factors that must be investigated and evaluated in determining the morality of using treatments developed or carried out by the use of fetal tissue. Sometimes a person will not know whether a treatment was developed by use of fetal tissue. Paul told the Corinthians that they did not have to research every piece of meat they bought in the market to find out if it had come from a heathen temple, but to avoid using it if their action would seem to condone the idolatry behind the sacrifice (1 Corinthians 8 and 10). The principles discussed in those chapters may help us wrestle with this question. We clearly do not want to do anything that will in any way encourage or condone abortion. Whether after-the-fact use of vaccines that may have been developed with the use of fetal tissue involves such a condoning is an issue which each person will have to decide in his or her own conscience on the basis of the best information available. Using vaccines produced from fetal tissue research could in some circumstances suggest endorsement of fetal tissue experimentation from aborted children, but in other circumstances it might not carry such significance. In evaluating the propriety of using such medical treatments we must consider not only on the motive of the user but also on the impression left from using them.

We might also ask how effective a protest against abortion it is to refuse to give our children protection against a potentially dangerous disease because of the vaccine's supposed or even actual development from an aborted fetus many years ago in secret. The public might take greater notice of our children being deprived of protection than of the alleged origin of the vaccine. Writing letters to the editor in defense of the unborn, campaigning and voting for politicians that defend life, and developing a lifestyle of good repute might make a much clearer and more positive statement against abortion. There might, on the other hand, be circumstances in which refusing the vaccine might be a very strong testimony against abortion.

We may also recognize a difference between using an immunization developed from fetal tissue many years ago under cover of darkness and benefiting from transplants and experiments that are taking place today in broad daylight. Perhaps we should focus our attention on stopping what is going on today rather than focusing on what was done in the past in the dark. Individuals will have to evaluate the evidence that specific treatments are based on fetal tissue research and conscientiously determine how to protest most effectively against such practices.

There is voluminous material on this issue from all points of view on the Internet under such searches as "fetal research" or "fetal tissue research." Materials are also available from pro-life groups such as WELS Christian Life Resources.

Your
Question Jesus said, "Do not resist an evil person" (Matthew 5:39). Are Christians allowed to use self-defense?

In the Sermon on the Mount, Jesus makes this statement to warn us against using the valid legal principle of "an eye for an eye" as the measuring stick for our personal conduct.

The government, as God's servant, is to exact proportionate punishment (revenge) for every offense, but in our personal dealings with people, we are to be forgiving, not vengeful. We are not to insist jealously on our rights or to retaliate for injustice.

But Christians may use legal remedies to protect themselves against injustice, as Paul did in Acts 16, 24, and 25. Our Lutheran confession, the Apology to the Augsburg Confession, says, "The gospel forbids private redress. . . . Public redress, which is made through the magistrate, is not advised against, but is commanded and is a work of God (Romans 13:1)" (*Triglotta*, p. 341).

But in cases where the police are not available, may Christians use force to protect their lives or the lives of others? The Old Testament law allowed self-defense (Exodus 22:2,3). We do not have specific examples of this in the New Testament, but Jesus, who told Peter not to use his sword to defend him from arrest in Gethsemane, told the apostles to buy swords before they went on their dangerous missionary journeys (Luke 22:36). When asked if Christians were permitted to use violence to defend against criminals, Luther replied, "Yes, indeed. In that event [if I was attacked by robbers], I should be the authority and wield the sword because no one else would be near to protect me. I should strike as many dead as I could and thereupon receive the Sacrament and should consider myself to have done a good work. But if I were attacked as a preacher for the sake of the Gospel, I should fold my hands and say, 'Well, my Christ, here I am. I have preached you. If my time has come, I commit myself into your hands. And thus I should die'" (Plass, *What Luther Says*, p. 243).

In using the legal tools God has given them to resist evil, Christians should be careful that they are seeking the glory of God, the defense of the gospel, and the good of their neighbors, not personal revenge.

Your Question **Luther wrote about the two kingdoms: God's and man's realms. The Lutheran church believes in letting the state do its job and that Christians are to obey unless laws violate God's teachings (Acts 5:29). That said, is WELS against racial separation if it's rooted not in blind supremacy, but in honest desire to preserve the unique cultural traits of race/ethnicity? Separation avoids hierarchical injustices of segregation/apartheid. A small town in South Africa called Orania seeks to do just this: keep nonwhites out in order to avoid racial influence on their white Afrikaner culture.**

The thinking behind the situation you describe is hard to understand. If a culture is so weak and means so little to its members that the only way the culture can preserve itself is to prevent its members from coming into contact with another race, what is it about the culture that is worth preserving? If a culture thinks it will be contaminated and destroyed by mere contact with any people of another race, what is the difference between that view and "blind supremacy"? How is enforced separation different from segregation/apartheid? They do not seem to be two different views but one. How can excluding some people and accepting others purely on the grounds of race without any regard to their character be justified? Race is not a valid reason to pass judgment on any individual.

The Bible teaches that there is only one race, that descended from Adam. All are sinners and all are redeemed by Christ.

Your Question **I saw an article in the Sunday *Milwaukee Journal-Sentinel* written by an ELCA pastor where he apologized to the Jews for Martin Luther being anti-Semitic. At first I was disturbed that he would accuse Martin Luther of such a thing, but he included a quotation from Martin Luther in a political letter to the German ruler advising him on how to deal with the Jews in Germany. The remarks sounded anti-Semitic. Now I was rather shocked and confused. What was Martin Luther's attitude toward the Jews? Was Martin Luther anti-Semitic? Many other**

WELS members are confused by this article. A good and accurate response to these accusations by the _Northwestern Lutheran_ would be appreciated.

The Lutheran apology for Luther was echoing an earlier apology by the Catholic archbishop of Milwaukee for the role of the Catholic church in persecution and mistreatment of Jews. Should Lutherans be apologizing for Luther?

Later in his life Luther wrote some very strong denunciations of the Jews, which we cannot condone. But to evaluate them fairly, we have to understand them in the context of his lifetime and of all of his writings. The claim popularized by certain historians, such as William Shirer in _The Rise and Fall of the Third Reich,_ that Luther's views were similar to those of the Nazis entirely ignores the historical context of his comments.

Early in his career Luther wrote in defense of the Jews, and he held hopes that when the persecutions and false teachings loaded upon them by the Roman Catholic church were taken away, Jews would turn to Christ. He wrote, "The fury of some Christians (if they are to be called Christians) is damnable. They imagine that they are doing God a service when they persecute the Jews most hatefully. . . . Whereas according to this psalm [Psalm 14] and Paul (Rom. 9:1), a man ought to be most heartily sorry for them and continually pray for them. . . . By the example of this great cruelty they are, as it were, repelling Jews from Christianity, whereas they ought to attract them by all manner of gentleness, patience, pleading, and care" (Plass, _What Luther Says,_ p. 683).

When his hope was disappointed and the Jews continued to reject Christ and to speak against him, sometimes in blasphemous terms, Luther wrote some very harsh judgments against the Jews because of their unbelief (as did such Jewish prophets as Isaiah and Jeremiah). Luther's harshest remarks are in a tract written a few years before his death: "Against the Jews and Their Lies." His opposition against the Jews was not racist as Hitler's was, but was based on God's judgment against rejection of his Word.

Luther did not believe that Jews had the right to propagandize against Christianity in Christian territory. In Luther's time, religious rights were territorial. Lutherans did not have rights in Catholic lands or vice versa. Luther therefore advocated that those Jews who remained opposed to Christianity be forcibly expelled from Germany and be given their own territory in Palestine. He also proposed that what wealth they had gained by lending money at interest, which he regarded as an immoral practice for Jews or Christians, should be confiscated for the support of the needy among them. In Luther's time, usury and blasphemy were sometimes crimes punishable by law.

Even in the preface to his harsh comments, Luther says, "We must indeed with prayer and the fear of God before our eyes exercise a keen compassion towards them and seek to save some of them from the flames. Avenge ourselves we dare not."

Luther's language in this writing was very harsh, but in this he was a child of his time. The attacks against him by Roman Catholic writers were even sharper. We cannot defend the tone and many of the specifics of Luther's denunciation of the Jews, but it is unfair for historians to misrepresent them by detaching them from their context and times. For a more detailed discussion of this topic, see Neelak Tjernagel, *Martin Luther and the Jewish People*, and John Warwick Montgomery, *In Defense of Martin Luther*, both published by Northwestern Publishing House.

What about apologizing for Luther? We neither condone his sins nor defend his errors (nor would he want us to), but it is presumptuous to think that we have the right to repent or apologize for the sins of a hero of faith who is no longer living. The current fad of apologizing for the past sins of someone else smacks of self-righteousness. If we want to apologize for sins, we have more than enough of our own to keep us busy.

As far as our attitude toward Jews goes, we must beware of the common errors in two directions. On the one hand, we must strongly speak against anything that promotes prejudice or persecution. On the other hand, we must not neglect to preach the gospel to them in order to bring them to Christ. Jesus Christ, born of Israel, is the Savior for Israel. If we are making a list of things to apologize for, our own slackness in preaching the gospel to them should be at the top.

The Christian attitude toward Israel is expressed in Romans 9–11, the reflections of Paul the Jew. His prayer is ours: "Brothers, my heart's desire and prayer to God for the Israelites is that they may be saved" (Romans 10:1). This was Luther's prayer too.

With the recent terrorist attack on 9-11, there has been a surge in patriotism within the country. Many are wearing flag lapel pins, sweatshirts, and other displays of pride in their country. You cannot go anywhere without seeing posters, stickers, or other banners with which to display, "Proud to be American." A question comes up, though. If pride is sinful, is it a sin to be proud of your nationality/ country/heritage?

There can be a right kind of pride, but maybe a better word would be *thankful* to be an American. National pride becomes wrong when it becomes pride in our achievements more than gratitude for God's blessings. Read Deuteronomy 8, especially verses 17 and 18. National pride becomes wrong when it focuses on the sins of other nations and is blind to our own sins. During the Civil War Abraham Lincoln did not speak proudly of the North as innocent and the South as guilty but recognized that neither side could claim to be undeserving of the chastening from God. National or ethnic pride becomes blind when it sees only the good in its own culture and feels superior to everything in other cultures.

We can and should be supportive of our nation in this time of crisis, cherishing the freedoms it has given us, especially the freedom of religion. We should not, however, be blind to the areas in which we need repentance. Jerry Falwell and Pat Robertson were not wrong when they pointed to such sins as abortion, sexual immorality, rejection of the biblical roles for men and women as sins that make our nation deserving of judgment. Their answer would have been more accurate, however, if they had laid equal stress on such sins as racism, materialism, religious pride, and self-righteousness. Luke 13:1-5 presents the proper perspective when reflecting on disaster.

I am a WELS member and listen to a local Protestant Evangelical radio station. I deny the majority of their teachings and listen to it more to strengthen my strong Lutheran beliefs against their Arminian teachings. I get frustrated when I hear that they are trying to boycott everything in secular society. They boycott Disney for being pro homosexual, they boycott movies that are rated R, they boycott Kodak for being a pro homosexual, they boycott Target stores for supporting abortion, they boycott Harry Potter movies and books for their mysticism, the Lord of the Rings books and movies, and on and on. What I mean by boycott is to never buy an item associated with

this item or company and tell others to not buy anything associated with them as well. In addition going out in front of stores, etc., and holding up signs to get their point across. I understand that there are some immoral things wrong with everything in society, granted we live in a sinful world. But, what is the Lutheran view on boycotting and how do we approach those who want to boycott everything in society that is non-Christian including secular music by only listening to their Christian contemporary music? I would personally say that I don't believe in boycotting. How do we say no to boycotting it without them [evangelicals] thinking, "If you were a real Christian you would boycott this too"? What is the theological basis for this?

Many Evangelicals are confused about the mission of the church. The mission of the church is to change people's hearts by the preaching of the gospel so that they have forgiveness of sins through saving faith in Christ. This will change people's behavior, since faith and thankfulness for forgiveness will motivate people to live in a God-pleasing behavior. It is not the mission of the church to make non-Christians act as if they were Christians by enforcing laws against them. The church aims to lead non-Christians to do the right thing for the right reason—faith in Christ motivated by the gospel. It is not the church's assignment to enforce outward reform of society by law.

Christian citizens may support laws that promote values that will benefit society, such as laws against abortion, against pornography, and so on, but this is not part of the work of the church as the church. Christians, naturally, also should refrain from buying things that are immoral. They may choose not to buy from companies that support immoral causes (they should, however, be very careful that they are not acting on the basis of misinformation). They may protest against the sale of certain products, publications, or broadcasts. But it is clear in the Bible that we may do business with the world (1 Corinthians 5:9-12). It is not the business of the church to discipline those outside the church.

Your
Question I just read a recent question regarding scouting. While you answered the specific question of scouting, there were some other questions raised that interested me. Does stating "one nation, under God" fit into the same category as acknowledging the existence of a creedless god as the scouts do? What about the inscription "In God We Trust" on currency? Finally, is it wrong for a Christian who is interested in getting politically active to take an oath of office which includes

both an oath to country and to "God"? What is the biblical evidence for our stance?

The Bible does not directly address the role of oaths to God in an officially secular society, since such a society did not exist in biblical times. We obviously can never swear in the name of a false god.

In the context of American civic religion, the statements "One Nation Under God" and "In God We Trust" can refer only to the generic anonymous god who also appears in the teachings of scouting and the lodge. If taken as religious statements or confession, these statements promote a false concept of God, which we have to warn against. Their purpose, however, is to assert that the laws and actions of a nation are subordinate to the laws of God and that a nation has no right to ignore the laws of God or to supersede them. As a statement of principle in the Pledge of Allegiance, "under God" is a correct statement of the principle that governs nations, but it is not an accurate statement of the reality in our country today. In discussing the statement with others, we have to make clear in what sense it is true and in what sense it is false. We should not use the pledge in contexts where it would give the impression of agreement with a false view of God.

If we take oaths that include the name of God in legal settings, we can make it clear that we are swearing in the name of our God, the true God, not of any other. In fact, the law usually allows substitution of an affirmation for an oath. There should not be a situation in American civic or political life that requires us to make a pledge or oath that involves a false god.

Your
Question **Explain why our pastors are not active in their communities—attending community programs, having a service at nursing homes, prayers at public functions, etc. The public sees the pastor at funerals and weddings. Our pastor is not known outside the church. The synod has community problems.**

Your question is difficult to answer because it makes some assumptions that are invalid and because it mixes together various kinds of community involvement that must be kept separate.

You draw some general conclusions about the participation of WELS pastors in community affairs, apparently from what you perceive to be a lack of participation by your own pastor. There is a great deal of difference in the opportunities our pastors may have for community involvement. A pastor whose children must attend a public school will have more occasion and opportunity to be involved in the affairs of the public schools than a pastor who has to attend functions at both a Lutheran elementary school and an area high school and maybe a synod school as well. A pastor in a small town may have opportunity to help with a volunteer fire department or ambulance service, which a pastor in a large city will not.

Many of our pastors have services at local nursing homes, but they should not participate in circumstances where there is an ecumenical rotation of preachers who hold all sorts of different beliefs. Such participation would not be serving the community, but confusing it by blurring the necessity of separating true doctrine from false. The same would be true of ecumenical prayers at public events.

A pastor also must be very careful about getting involved in political affairs or on school boards and zoning boards, which often must take unpopular and divisive positions. The pastor needs to be available as a shepherd to people on all sides of such political issues. Too direct an involvement by the pastor in such political affairs may alienate people who are prospects for his ministry of preaching the law and gospel.

The best thing a pastor can do for the community in which he lives is to be available as a faithful preacher and teacher of law and gospel. Weddings and funerals are two of the most common occasions when people from outside the church may have the opportunity to see him in such a role. The best way for a pastor to come into contact with more unchurched people who are in need of such counseling is through the contacts members of the church have in the community. If the members of the congregation are talking about their faith in their daily lives and are referring friends and relatives to the pastor, he will have more people to visit in the community than he can keep up with. Many of our pastors spend many hours each week visiting and counseling people from outside the church. When I was a young pastor beginning two mission congregations, I often worked long hours, a significant portion of which were spent visiting people from outside the congregation who had been referred to me by members. There simply was not much time for other community involvement. For many of our pastors today, I believe the greatest danger is not too little community involvement but too little time for family.

It is good for a pastor to have involvement and visibility in the community to the degree that his pastoral duties and his abilities and interests permit. It is very important that a pastor be a "people person." He must, however, devote the great majority of his time to the ministry of the Word for which he was trained and called. Many other activities and services both within the congregation and the community can more effectively be carried out by lay members of the congregation, allowing the pastor to devote more time to the ministry of the Word (Acts 6).

If it is true that a congregation has a "community problem," the responsibility for remedying the situation is shared by the pastor but even more so with the lay members of the church, since they are the ones who have the most contacts within the community. If the pastor's days and nights are heavily scheduled with church responsibilities and visiting prospects, it is unreasonable for the congregation to expect extensive community involvement unless they are willing to share with the pastor more of his responsibility for evangelism visits and other congregational duties.

In cases where a pastor is neither very busy with church responsibilities nor very active in outreach or in community contacts (a situation which I believe is relatively rare), those who are concerned about the situation should talk to the pastor about it. In many cases, they may find that his schedule is much fuller than they had thought. If it is true that the pastor is really not very involved in people contacts, members of the congregation can do their part by introducing him to prospects and inviting him to community affairs or to social events to which they have invited people whom they would like him to meet. In cases where the problem remains unresolved, it may be necessary for the pastor and congregation to seek advice and help from a neighboring pastor, the circuit pastor, or a mission counselor.

If you feel your pastor and congregation have a problem in this matter, be sure you actually have an accurate understanding of the situation, be willing to be part of the solution, and be ready to work together with the pastor and others in a patient, kindly way.

10
Sexual Morality, Marriage, and Divorce

Issues Outside Marriage

Your Question **A member of our congregation is living with his girlfriend even though they are not married. When I talked to him about this, he said it is okay because they are married in God's eyes. What should I say to this?**

Ask him where he got the idea that anyone can be "married in God's eyes" without being married in man's eyes. Although God established the institution of marriage for this earthly life, a specific marriage is not a commitment that a man and woman establish with God by faith, nor can it be established by a secret commitment, hidden in their hearts. Marriage is a legal, lifelong commitment between one man and one woman, which must be publicly witnessed to be valid. A dictionary defines *marriage* as a "social institution under which a man and woman establish their decision to live as husband and wife by legal commitments and/or religious ceremonies." Where there are no legal commitments, there is no marriage.

The way in which this legal commitment is established may vary in different societies. Some may require a marriage license to be registered with the state. Some require a civil ceremony. In other societies marriage is a privately arranged legal contract between individuals or families. But in every society the commitment must be public and witnessed.

289

The God-given purposes of marriage are the companionship and lifelong union of one man and one woman, the raising of children, and the prevention of sexual sin. A publicly witnessed, legal marriage protects the property rights of both spouses and of any children that may be born to them, shows respect for the laws and customs of society, and testifies to the lifelong, exclusive character of marriage. In a society that maintains decent moral standards, a public marriage also warns others against becoming involved in a sexual relationship with either spouse. A church wedding seeks God's blessings on the marriage and publicly testifies to the couple's intention to live according to the directions God has established for marriage. If a Christian couple has a genuine, unconditional, lifelong commitment to each other and respects these other needs of society, what valid reason can there be for refusing to establish a legal, witnessed marriage?

One must suspect that in many cases, the refusal to marry is due to the lack of a genuine, unconditional commitment. An escape hatch is being kept open. If a couple is living together as if they are husband and wife without an unconditional, lifelong commitment, the couple is sinning against the standard God has established for marriage. They are unmarried in God's eyes.

If a couple has indeed made an unconditional, lifelong commitment privately to each other, they still have not established a legal marriage, but only the intention to establish one. If they break this promise and separate, they are sinning by being unfaithful to their word, but there has been no marriage. In either case, the "commitment" without a legal document does not excuse or minimize their sin.

Your
Question When discussing the topic of living together before marriage, you have to answer another one: when according to the Bible does a marriage start? With the official act at the government office? The ceremony in the church? None of them seems to be found in the Scriptures. Thus some persons claim that a man and a woman can live together if they live together "responsibly"—then they also could be considered to be married.

Marriage is established by a witnessed, unconditional, mutual commitment of the couple to a lifelong union in marriage. Since marriage is a civil contract, not a spiritual sacrament, for the marriage to be valid and binding, it does not matter whether the public commitment is established by a religious ceremony, a civic ceremony, the signing of a contract, or some other form of witnessed, public consent, as long as the laws and standards of society are respected. The marriage starts at the time specified by the contract or commitment. For example, in biblical times the contract that established the marriage often specified a specific future date for the marriage to begin. Though legally bound to marriage from the time the contract was signed, the spouses did not have the rights of marriage until the agreed upon date.

To be validly married, a couple must have made a witnessed, unconditional commitment to a lifelong union. This is precisely what is missing in most "live-in" arrangements. The live-in arrangement is, in fact, intended to evade such a commitment. No one can be living together "responsibly" without such a witnessed, public commitment.

Your
Question   God's Word clearly condemns sexual intercourse outside of marriage, but what additional guidance does God have for dating relationships? How would God's Word address the issue of boyfriend and girlfriend sleeping together without having sex?

The Bible gives no specific direction about the amount of physical expression of affection that is appropriate for couples during various stages of courtship, nor does it give any rules about dating couples being together without the presence of other people. Perhaps a major reason for this omission is that the culture of the biblical writers placed stricter limitations than our culture does on the freedom of young men and women to be alone together during courtship.

There is one detailed, poetic description of a courtship in the Bible, Song of Songs. This song frequently refers to kisses and embraces between the couple and of their eager anticipation for their marriage, but it is difficult to derive clear guidance from this song because of the poetic nature of the language, the underlying spiritual symbolism of the song, and the difficulty of determining with certainty which verses refer to the time before the couple's marriage and which verses to the time after. The song does, however, clearly indicate that people of biblical times were aware of the dilemma you raise in your question. This song is one of many indications that there was no absolute separation of young men and women during courtship in biblical times, so they faced at least some of the same temptations young couples face today.

In the absence of more specific scriptural directives, couples who are dating will have to take responsibility for conscientiously applying several general principles Scripture gives us:

1. First Thessalonians 4:3-5 says, "It is God's will that you should be sanctified: that you should avoid sexual immorality; that each of you should learn to control his own body [or acquire a wife] in a way that is holy and honorable, not in passionate lust like the heathen, who do not know God."

2. Christians should take care to avoid placing themselves into tempting situations where they unnecessarily expose themselves to the danger of falling into sin.

3. Christians are responsible for other people. We therefore should be very careful not to subject a person we are dating to temptation that may be too strong for him or her.

4. We should be careful that our use of our freedom does not lead other, weaker Christians into sin. For example, if certain practices we follow do not tempt us to sin, but our example encourages a couple we know to do the same thing and this leads them to sin, we have lovelessly sinned against those fellow Christians.

5. We should take care not to offend other Christians by careless actions and attitudes, which may lead them to doubt that we are living a pure, Christian life.

To these scriptural principles we can add some commonsense observations:

1. Couples should honestly discuss the degree of commitment they have to each other. Expressions of physical affection should not be allowed to get ahead of the degree of commitment to marriage the couple has to each other. Sexual intercourse, however, belongs only in marriage, not even in engagement, which is not marriage but a commitment to marriage.

2. Couples should have clearly agreed upon limits that do not place either one of them on the threshold of temptation.

3. In seeking to avoid sin, the goal of Christians is not to get as close to the edge of the cliff as possible without falling over but to allow a healthy margin of safety.

4. Intimate caresses are called *foreplay* because they very naturally prepare both the body and the mind for sexual intercourse. If you

do not want to arrive at that destination, it is dangerous and foolish to set out on a downhill road that leads only in one direction.

5. Christian couples should plan their dating activities in such a way that they frequently include other people. They should plan their activities together in such a way that they are widening their circle of mutual friends, rather than focusing too narrowly on only the two of them.

Your question about sleeping together without sex is best answered by considering the preceding principles. Although it is possible to imagine innocent examples of sleeping side by side without sex (as when Ruth laid down by Boaz at the harvest camp to give him the hint that he should propose marriage to her), it is hard to imagine circumstances in which this should be a normal, regular practice. In the example cited from the book of Ruth, Boaz is concerned that this action might cause offense. Can a couple confidently say (1) our sleeping together will not tempt us to sin; (2) our example will not encourage friends of ours to do the same thing, thereby placing them into a situation that is too tempting for them; and (3) our action will not offend people who may find out about it or lead them to have doubts about the purity of our Christian life or our truthfulness? Unless a couple can be sure that none of these dangers is present, they should avoid such an action, which is filled with a great deal of potential for temptation and offense.

Our sexuality and sexual relations within marriage are a good gift of God. The proper way to guard against the improper use of them outside of marriage is not by covering them with silence or shame but by teaching young people to carry on their dating and courtship in ways that honor sexuality as a good gift of God that is to find its fulfillment in marriage. Couples will benefit more from a conscientious effort to practice the general principles given in Scripture than from a set of rules that try to answer every question for them. If their actions during courtship show respect for God, for his gifts, and for each other, they will be preparing themselves in the best way possible for enjoyment of God's gift in marriage.

Your Question **Should Christ-serving landlords rent an apartment to a couple who indicate that they are living together out of wedlock?**

The Bible does not deal directly with the question of whether a Christian can sell something to someone who might use it in a sinful way.

A Christian would not knowingly sell a gun to someone he knows is going to use it for a crime, and a bartender should not sell liquor to someone who is intoxicated, but a seller is not responsible for the possible misuse a buyer makes of a legitimate product or service. The guilt rests with the buyer who misuses it for a sinful purpose, not with the seller.

An additional practical problem is that the laws of some jurisdictions might forbid a property owner to discriminate against such couples. If we lived in a society that observed at least the natural knowledge of the law, this would not be a problem because living together, adultery, or homosexual practices would not be lawful, much less protected by law. We must, nevertheless, ask ourselves whether this is a case that requires us to break the law because we must obey God rather than man.

How do these principles apply to the question at hand? A financial transaction with a sinner does not make us a supporter of his cause. A Christian could sell bricks and lumber to Muslims building a mosque. A Christian realtor could sell a house to a man who was leaving his wife to marry another woman. We cannot single out the case of a couple living together as a special sin we must try to prevent by refusing to do business with the perpetrators. Our responsibility to the couple is greater than simply turning them away from housing. It is to give a clear and continuing testimony against their sin.

If these are fellow Christians who are living together outside of marriage, it is our responsibility to warn them against this sin and, ultimately, to remove them from the church if they do not repent. Our responsibility to unbelievers is not to force them to act like Christians but to preach the whole law and gospel to them so that they become Christians. Simply turning them away from housing is not likely to prevent their sin. We may have even more opportunity to continue such testimony and invitations if they are living on our property. There may be occasions where refusing such a rental would be a clear testimony, but more often a clear, continuing testimony to the law and the gospel will be more powerful.

The basic question we must ask in such situations is, How can we best give a firm, patient, and loving testimony to the couple?

Your
Question **What is the church's stance on oral sex? Is it premarital sex when done by unmarried teens?**

The Bible does not address the issue directly so there is no formal statement of the church on this issue. Although oral sex is not sexual intercourse in the narrowest legal sense of the term, it is a sexual act and it would fall under the Bible's prohibition of *porneia* (sexual impurity) anytime it is between two people who are not married to each other. If a married person is involved in such an act with someone other than his or her spouse, it would be an act of adultery.

Married couples might also consider that God has clearly designed male and female bodies for genital sexual relations, not for oral and anal sex. They should beware of possibly substituting something else for God's design.

Homosexuality

Your Question The dispute over whether homosexuality is an inborn disposition or a free choice, the national debate over the legalization of same-sex marriages, the conflict that is rising in many denominations over the ordination of practicing homosexuals, and the sharp disagreement about the blessing of same-sex marriages by the church are among the current issues that may lead people to ask, "What is WELS's stance on these issues?"

WELS does not have an official doctrinal statement on these issues, but our public teaching and practice is based on what the Bible teaches concerning homosexuality.

The best place to begin a discussion of the issue is with 1 Corinthians 6:9-11, because this passage emphasizes both the law and the gospel elements of addressing this issue.

Do you not know that the wicked will not inherit the kingdom of God? Do not be deceived: Neither the sexually immoral nor idolaters nor adulterers nor male prostitutes nor homosexual offenders nor thieves nor the greedy nor drunkards nor slanderers nor swindlers will inherit the kingdom of God. And that is what some of you were. But you were washed, you were sanctified, you were justified in the name of the Lord Jesus Christ and by the Spirit of our God.

On the basis of this and other passages of Scripture we must draw the following conclusions about homosexuality:

- Scripture declares that homosexuality is a sin. It is contrary to God's intention in creating man and woman. Sinful resistance to the revealed will of God is a factor in this sin. People may become slaves to this sin (Romans 1:18-31; 1 Corinthians 6:9,10).

- Many factors contribute to individual acts of sin: the sinful nature we are born with, the weaknesses of our bodies, evil influences in our environment, temptations and encouragement from other sinners, and our own sinful choices join together to lead us into sin. All of these factors contribute to homosexual sin. The proportionate role of these various factors may vary from case to case.

- We must warn the impenitent that homosexuality, like all sins, excludes people from eternal life (1 Corinthians 6:9,10).

- We can be happy to assure the repentant who are struggling against this sin that they have complete forgiveness through the blood of Christ. When Christ died for all of the sins of the whole world, he gained forgiveness for homosexual deeds, for homosexual desires, and for the inborn sinful nature, which produces these sins (1 Corinthians 6:11).

- We should sympathize with all who are struggling against this sin, remembering that we too have "pet sins," which may have a strong hold on us. We warn against a selective morality, which harshly condemns homosexuality or other sins we observe in others while treating those sins that are present in our own lives more lightly (Matthew 7:1-5). We should be impartial and unbiased in warning against all sins.

We all look forward to the resurrection of the body. Then all the weaknesses of body and soul that now lead us into sin will disappear forever. Then all of us will be able to serve God perfectly and purely in everything we do.

Note on Homosexuality as Innate or Chosen

Some advocates of legal and religious tolerance of homosexuality claim that homosexuality has a genetic cause. Some reports claim that some homosexual men share a particular pattern in the X sex chromosome that they received from their mothers. Other researchers have claimed the existence of other types of biological similarities between homosexual men. These researchers acknowledge that their discovery cannot account for all homosexuality and may merely be associated with homosexuality rather than being a direct cause of it. Most researchers conclude that the origins of homosexuality are complex and varied and may never be fully understood.

How should we evaluate such claims in the light of the biblical teaching of sin? Is homosexuality a free choice or an inborn tendency?

Like many such either-or questions, this question poses a false dilemma. Every sin is both a choice of the will and the expression of an inborn tendency to sin. Our sinful will is guilty of consent whenever we sin in thought, word, or deed. As a result of our sinful nature, we take pleasure in our sins and defend them. This universal tendency is apparent also in the efforts of gay rights activists to condone their homosexuality and to deny that anything is wrong with it.

Although the consent of our sinful will is present in every sin, it is also true that we are born as slaves of sin. We may also yield to a particular sin so often that we no longer control the sin, but the sin controls us. We may find ourselves yielding to sin even when we don't want to.

Sin infects both one's body and soul. The body, as we have it now, is not the perfect body God created for Adam and Eve. It has been contaminated by the effects of sin. There is no reason to maintain that the specific effects of sin have been identical in each one of us or that we are all equally susceptible to every sin. Our individual degree of susceptibility to some specific sins may be due in part to differences in our bodies. The abuse of alcohol and a hot temper are just two examples of sins that may be affected by the chemistry of our bodies. Few would deny that the pressure to sexual sin is greater at 18 than it is at 8 or at 88 and that a primary reason for this is the changing chemistry of our bodies. It may well be that a person's susceptibility to homosexuality or to certain other sins depends in part on bodily differences.

Even though the weakness of our own bodies may be one factor that leads us to sin, God holds us responsible for all of our sins, even those sins that enslave us and those sins of which we are not aware. We need God's forgiveness even for those sinful desires we resist and do not act upon. These desires too are sin. (Read Romans 7 for a treatment of slavery to sin.)

Your
Question   **I was just reading a questionnaire put out by a well-known televangelist. Readers are asked to check Yes, No, or Maybe to these**

two statements: (1) The effort to eliminate God and morality from the public arena is a serious threat to our nation's future. (2) Homosexual practice must not be elevated to a civil right nor accorded special recognition as a legitimate lifestyle.

How would we answer? If we believe God has no place in public life (military chaplaincy, opening Congress with prayer, etc.) since this involves false fellowship and mixture of church and state, then does it not also follow that a Christian must not oppose homosexual rights, since if he does so he is imposing his religious beliefs on others by law?

First of all, there are a lot of questions that cannot be answered adequately by *Yes, No,* or *Maybe.* In fact, 90 percent of the time when someone demands a yes or no answer from you, it is likely that the question is too complex or the statement is too simplistically worded to be answered yes or no. A "maybe" answer hardly clarifies anything for anyone. None of the questionnaires in this format that I have ever received were designed to obtain my insights into national problems. They were designed to solicit my support, usually my money.

Be that as it may, can the questions be adequately answered if we are allowed more than a yes, no, or maybe? The dilemma that you state in your question is not a real dilemma. It is created by the inadequate wording of the statements and by the questioner's failure to adequately distinguish between a Christian's duty as a Christian and his duty as a citizen who also happens to be a Christian.

"The effort to eliminate God and morality from the public arena is a serious threat to our nation's future." If I must choose, I'll check *Yes* to that one, since efforts to eliminate God and morality from the public arena are very often motivated by humanistic values, which are a threat to the well-being of our nation. The more important question, however, is "How should I as a Christian respond to that threat?" Should I send money to the televangelist's organization so he can lobby the government on behalf of Christianity? I'll answer *No* to that one. I as a Christian have a much better way to oppose godlessness and immorality in society. I will preach God's law, which condemns sin; and I will proclaim his gospel, which offers forgiveness. Nothing I can do as a Christian will do more to ward off serious moral threats to our nation's future than proclaiming God's Word.

"Homosexual practice must not be elevated to a civil right nor accorded special recognition as a legitimate lifestyle." This one is trickier because it entangles my duty as a member of the Christian church with my responsibility as a citizen, eager to be guided by Christian principles in my whole life.

My Christian duty toward homosexuals (and toward the sexually immoral, thieves, swindlers, murderers, slanderers, and drunkards, and any violators of God's will) is clear—to confront the impenitent with God's law, which condemns their sin, and to comfort the penitent with the gospel, which offers forgiveness.

As a good neighbor and citizen, my duty is not to pressure people to accept and practice my religious beliefs, but to promote laws that protect individuals and society from harm. If reason, evidence, and the natural knowledge of God's law, which remains in people even after the fall, all testify that stealing, murder, drug abuse, sexual immorality, abortion, and homosexuality are harmful to individuals or to society, I as a citizen should work for laws that oppose those evils. I do this not to force my religious beliefs on others but, rather, to work together with other people who share a natural knowledge of God's law in order to protect society from evil. The fact that stealing is forbidden by the Seventh Commandment, adultery by the Sixth, and murder by the Fifth does not mean that I as a Christian cannot support laws against stealing and murder. The recognition that these acts are wrong and harmful is not peculiar to Lutheranism or to Christianity. It is based on a natural knowledge of God's law and on experience. This knowledge, therefore, is common to all people, except where sinners have suppressed this knowledge. Read Romans 1:18-32.

As a Christian citizen I should work for laws that will protect society from the harmful consequences of sin. As a citizen I promote such laws on the basis of reason and natural knowledge of the law. If the state tolerates moral evils that violate God's law, I will continue to oppose them on the basis of God's Word.

As a member of the church, my goal is to win people's hearts and guide their lives by God's Word. As a citizen, my goal is to regulate people's conduct so they do not harm themselves or others. Many of the moral principles of God's law are relevant to both goals and may be used in both spheres, but for different purposes. As a member of the church, I use all of God's law as a mirror, a curb, and a rule. As a citizen, I use parts of God's law as a curb against conduct that reason and natural knowledge of the law recognize as harmful to society.

Your
Question Is there a difference between "mutilating" your body by getting your ears pierced and having a sex change? A friend of mine refuses to recognize a difference in God's eyes. I think that because the reasons (I presume) are quite different, there is a difference. How would you answer her?

Having your ears pierced doesn't make you deaf. It does not destroy a God-given function of the body. It is not even disfiguring. People do this in the belief that they will be able to enhance their appearance. But would we say a person should blind herself or cut off her hand because she does not want to work? A sex change is parallel to such a mutilation, not to having your ears pierced. Not only is the motive different in the two situations, but the effect on the body is also drastically different.

A sex change is rejecting a function of the body with which God created someone. If the reason for desiring such a sex change is homosexual desires, the real issue to be dealt with is not "what changes can we make to our bodies" but "what does the Bible teach about sexuality and homosexuality." (We are not here discussing surgery to correct some congenital abnormality.)

Regarding Marriage

Your
Question What is the Wisconsin Synod's view of mixed marriages? Reading some of the other questions, it is obvious that some WELS Lutherans do marry outside of the synod, even with Roman Catholics. Are there Lutheran bodies that frown on such marriages? Are there any that deny matrimonial services for mixed couples?

Since marriage is an institution for this earthly life, marriage does not require a common faith for it to be valid. We generally would perform a marriage for a couple even if only one of them is a member of our church, if the other partner agreed to having the marriage performed in agreement with Scripture. Whether we would advise such marriages is a different question. Since a common faith is a great asset to marriage, counselors might well advise a couple on the difficulties that a lack of a common faith could bring to the marriage, especially where children are concerned.

I am aware of no Lutheran churches that would make a common faith an absolute requirement for a marriage. Some Evangelical churches say that Christians may only marry other Christians.

Your
Question **What does the Bible say about prenuptial agreements? (I don't think it says anything directly, but maybe indirectly.)**

Prenuptial agreements were quite common in Old Testament times. Many examples of such agreements are extant from neighboring cultures to Israel and a number from Jews as well. They usually cover matters of property and inheritance, but sometimes also govern the inheritance rights of children from polygamous marriages or for provision of an heir through a surrogate mother like Hagar.

As you indicated, the Bible says nothing directly about this matter. Naturally, any such agreement that places conditions on the marriage that are contrary to scriptural principles of marriage are not proper or valid. Also if such an agreement were an indication of distrust among the parties or a predisposition to make provision for divorce even before the marriage began, it would be a warning of serious trouble on the horizon.

Your
Question **Where does the synod stand in regards to surrogate motherhood?**

There has never been an official statement on this issue, but we would warn against the dangers of reproductive techniques that involve parties other than the husband and the wife in the reproduction of their child. We see the emotional and moral dangers and problems of surrogacy in the case of Abraham, Sarah, and Hagar. These dangers can be present even when there is no physical, sexual contact between the spouses and the donors.

A good book that discusses this topic in some detail is *Brave New Families: Biblical Ethics and Reproductive Technologies*, by Scott B. Rae from Baker Books.

Your
Question **When two people get married and take the vows, they are making a commitment to each other. What happens when these vows no longer mean anything; when there is no longer any love,**

cherishing, honoring between the two; when counseling and all other attempts to make the marriage a real marriage again have failed? Does this not mean there is no longer a marriage as God intended for marriage to be? That this marriage is not any longer a real marriage? Then shouldn't these people be able to divorce and find others with whom they can have a true marriage? Does God really intend for two people to stay married when all the vows they took at the time of their marriage no longer have any meaning? I would be most interested in your views on this. I have posed the same question to my pastor and am curious to see if your answer will be the same.

First of all, it is not possible for vows that have been freely offered before God to "no longer mean anything." It is possible that people will sinfully break those vows, but the vows can never become meaningless. They stand as a judgment and condemnation on those who break them.

It is possible that one party in the marriage is the guilty party who breaks the vow of marriage and that the other party is a victim of the breaking of the vow. For example, one spouse may break the vow by committing adultery. The other spouse is no longer bound by the marriage vow and may divorce and remarry. The same is true if one party maliciously deserts the marriage.

If both spouses abandon the marriage by mutual consent without any scriptural grounds, both are guilty before God of breaking their vows. The claim that they no longer feel in love or that they feel in love with someone else does not release them from their vows. A vow that a person keeps only when it is to his or her liking and advantage is really no vow at all. Psalm 15 refers to the person whose walk is blameless, "who keeps his vow even when it hurts."

Scripture lists only three things that release a person from the vows of marriage without guilt: death, sexual immorality by the other party, and desertion by the other party. For a discussion of what constitutes desertion, see the WELS Conference of Presidents pamphlet *A Study of Marriage, Divorce, Malicious Desertion, and Remarriage in the Light of God's Word.*

Whether or not this answer agrees with that of your pastor is not the important issue. What is right cannot be determined by majority vote. What is the important question for you is whether the answers you have received are in agreement with what Scripture teaches about the permanence of marriage. If you are wrestling with this issue, you need to study the passages of Scripture that tell us God's will in this matter.

Your
Question I am going to marry a Catholic man this year. I have already contacted my local church, which informed me the WELS church is not open to an interfaith ceremony. Since we have changed our ceremony site, I was wondering if WELS is able to perform an interfaith ceremony outside? If not, would a WELS pastor be able to perform the ceremony alone outside? Thank you for help on this important issue. I look forward to your response.

It is not the place of the ceremony but the nature of the ceremony that is the issue here. WELS pastors can officiate at marriages held somewhere other than a WELS church, in a home or a park, for example, or even in a rented or borrowed church building. They cannot, however, properly participate in religious ceremonies that mix faiths, whether this is at their own church, another church, or a so-called neutral site.

Among the reasons why a joint Lutheran-Catholic ceremony is not proper is that Catholics and Lutherans have different teachings of marriage, not to mention other major differences in doctrine that prohibit such joint officiating by pastor and priest.

The Catholic church regards marriage as a sacrament of the Catholic church. In most ceremonies in a Catholic church, only the Catholic priest could perform the sacramental marriage itself. Non-Catholics would have to be limited to a prayer or a reading or something similar. Lutherans do not believe marriage is a sacrament, but an institution God has established for earthly life. Christians will want to celebrate their marriage by seeking God's blessing, but civil marriage is also a valid, binding marriage.

Catholics believe that even an innocent victim of divorce due to the adultery of his or her spouse cannot remarry. Lutherans believe that although God designed marriage as a lifelong union and divorce is wrong, the innocent victim of a divorce is not forbidden to remarry.

Traditionally, the Catholic church has also insisted that both parties agree that all children be raised as Catholics. A Lutheran cannot in good conscience consent to such a promise, even if only the Catholic partner is asked to make the pledge. Catholics also have different views concerning forms of family planning.

In a more liberal Catholic parish or diocese, some of the traditional Catholic practices may be modified, but all of these religious issues are something that a couple should deal with before marriage, especially the issue of how the family and the children will practice their faith.

Your Question I am a WELS Lutheran married to a Roman Catholic. Because we disagree about theological issues now, neither of us looks forward to having children. (We have none now.) In fact, my husband would like to get sterilized because I can't agree to raise our children Roman Catholic without also teaching them the differences between Catholic and Lutheran. Do we have to be parents simply because we are married? Is it sinful to be married and not want children? In other words, if he does get sterilized, are we sinning against God?

Unfortunately, there is no good solution to your problem. This should have been resolved before you were married. Now you are in a bind.

It is not an acceptable solution to arbitrarily exclude children from your marriage. Children are a blessing from God and are one of the chief purposes of marriage. To deliberately exclude them is to despise a blessing of God. It is also directly contrary to Roman Catholic theology of marriage. Your husband is saying that to avoid the possibility of his children being raised as non-Catholic, he is willing to overthrow what his church says is an essential purpose of marriage.

Sterilization is an even worse solution because it is not easily reversed. What if circumstances change and there is a desire to have children?

For you to consent to raise your children as Catholics, which will expose them to false teachings that threaten their souls, is not an acceptable solution either. You can't deprive them of the gospel.

You can, of course, hope that your husband will recognize that the teaching of salvation by faith alone as held by the Lutheran church is the true teaching of the Bible and will allow his children to receive that teaching, but there is no way to assure this will happen. You can only continue to share the truth with your husband in a quiet way. Read 1 Peter 3. This is really the only good solution open to you.

How did it happen that you failed to resolve this issue before your marriage? Was it simply neglect or has one of you changed his or her position? (You say, "We disagree about theological issues *now*.") Is one party now trying to back out of an agreement previously made? If so, the issue of entering a marriage in a deceptive way, which hinders true consent and might even be grounds for an annulment, becomes a part of the problem.

Another factor you must consider is whether the religious difference is the real reason for the rejection of children or may it be a cover for other motivations. Your husband claims he is trying to uphold his commitment to Catholicism by having no children, but he is directly denying Catholic theology. Something is out of line here.

It was a very serious mistake to fail to resolve this question before your marriage. Now the only good solution open to you is to work and pray that your husband will come to a better understanding of the nature of marriage and of the way to salvation. Also counseling with a marriage counselor or your pastor seems to be necessary.

Your **Question** **My female cousin is getting married in three months and is not planning on taking her husband's name (she will keep her own name, both legally and socially). My aunt and grandmother think that this is wrong, and kind of hint that it is wrong religiously, and that she should take her husband's name. Does our church have an opinion on this?**

Last names are a relatively new thing even in Western culture. How last names are derived and whether they should be the same for husband and wife are determined by culture, not by any rule from the Bible. In some cultures, for example, a married woman may continue to be identified by the name of her father.

If a woman's decision not to take her husband's name is due to a rejection of the biblical principles of the roles of husband and wife as set forth in Ephesians 5, it would be her attitude that was wrong, rather than the retention of her name in and of itself. Whether it would be wrong for a woman to retain her own last name would depend on the culture she lives in and on her reason for her decision.

Your **Question** **I have heard that birth control pills do not prevent conception but really cause early abortions. Is this true?**

The history of "the pill" has been controversial for several reasons. One point of debate has been whether the pill may induce early abortions. Claims and counterclaims make it difficult to give a definitive answer.

Birth control pills work through three main mechanisms: they suppress ovulation; they impede the movement of sperm; and they restrict implantation of the fertilized egg. This last mechanism would in effect be an early abortion.

Part of the disagreement about the effect of birth control pills is due to the fact that there are three main types of pills. The "combination pill" utilizes synthetic forms of the natural hormones estrogen and progesterone. The "mini-pill" uses a synthetic hormone called progestin. The "multi-phastic pill" uses different levels of synthetic hormones.

Some studies claim that the combination pill is very successful at preventing conception and that there is no scientific evidence that it ever causes an early abortion. Others claim that in a small percentage of cases the combination pill may fail to prevent conception and that in these cases this pill may induce abortion. For this reason, they would argue that the pill has to be considered to be an undesirable method of birth control for Christians, even if there is only a slim chance that it would induce abortion.

Some studies suggest that there is a significantly greater risk that use of the mini-pill may result in an early abortion. The multi-phastic pill is relatively new and less information is available.

One aim of newer, low-dose pills is to reduce health risks to the woman. Health risks like nausea and mood swings as well as more serious concerns about cancer, bleeding, and heart attacks have been studied over the years. Although there has not been unanimity in the results and it appears that health risks to the woman have been reduced, there are still concerns any woman needs to consider before adding synthetic hormones to her system.

For more detailed and up-to-date information about this topic and about abortion, contact WELS Christian Life Resources. For a biblical perspective concerning birth control in general see the Northwestern publication *Our Great Heritage*, Vol. 2, pp. 106-124.

Your
Question **A previous answer in this column stated that birth control pills do not always prevent conception, but may sometimes cause an early abortion by preventing implantation of the fertilized egg. Shortly**

after the appearance of this question and answer, the following information was publicized by a government agency and is here provided as a follow-up.

The Food and Drug administration recommends high doses of six birth control pills as safe "morning-after pills." These are ordinary birth control pills containing estrogen and progestin. Used as an "emergency pill" after intercourse, they effect a 75 percent reduction of pregnancy by preventing implantation. Very high doses of mini-pills and IUDs also achieve the same effect.

The Web site at Princeton University, which is being used to promote this use of the pills, claims that they *prevent* pregnancy and do not cause abortion since "science defines the beginning of pregnancy as implantation." This is hardly an honest presentation of the issue. Ironically, this information was publicized the same day a prominent abortion rights advocate admitted that he "lied through his teeth" in his testimony against the ban on partial-birth abortions.

In short, the FDA recommends high doses of birth control pills as a means of preventing implantation. It does not address the issue of how often regular doses, used on an ongoing basis, may have the same effect.

Your
Question **Does the leadership role of a husband change as a long-married couple reach their senior years? What about the helper role of the wife? I acknowledge my role as wife as being the helper and want to be as much help to my husband as I can be, but is not a couple supposed to help each other? My husband has always helped me too, especially when our child was growing up. Both of us have always respected each other's feelings and opinions when it came for a decision to be made and have made decisions jointly. Would that be undermining my husband's leadership? I know the husband is spiritual leader of the family. I have been WELS all my life and he joined my church a few months before we married. He had attended a number of different churches prior to that. He still says churches are all the same. Our child did attend a WELS elementary school, and I was the one who taught her table and bedtime prayers and read the Bible stories to her. I understand the father is the parent who is supposed to do that.**

I also understand the husband is to be leader when it comes to sex. Both of us are older now and no longer have the sex drive as when we were

younger. We sleep in separate bedrooms and find we sleep better sleeping alone. We do sleep together once a week, for the closeness but not for sex. We have been sleeping apart for about two years. We find companionship means more to us than having sex. We have been married nearly 30 years. We were in our 30s when we got married. Now that it is just the two of us in our senior years, what are some of his duties as leader in our marriage? What are some of my duties as wife, apart from helping my husband as much as I can? I attend church regularly. My husband does not attend as often but the services are videotaped and he does usually watch that. Thanks much for your help.

It sounds like you have been very conscientious in trying to be a faithful Christian wife and have done a very good job. Couples are to make decisions as partners, making unselfish decisions, which will be for the good of the family. Your husband should have taken a greater interest in his own spiritual welfare and the spiritual welfare of your child, but it sounds like you filled the need of your daughter in a way that was very proper. This issue is discussed in 1 Peter 3. Your situation is not identical because 1 Peter 3 discusses how the wife should act if the husband is an unbeliever. That is not quite the case in your situation, but the situation is not essentially different if the husband shows less interest than he should in the spiritual welfare of his family and of himself. The wife should set a quiet example and do what is necessary for the good of the child.

The frequency of sex is a decision for the couple to make together by common consent. This is discussed in 1 Corinthians 7. It would be wrong for one spouse to arbitrarily deny sex to the other on an ongoing basis. It sounds as if in your case there is agreement on this issue.

As far as other duties, you have stated a good principle: "Both of us have always respected each other's feelings and opinions when it came for a decision to be made and have made decisions jointly." You do need to continue to be concerned that you speak about the gospel in your home in such a way that you can feel confident that your husband has a clear understanding of the gospel. That is the greatest good you can do for him. Does your pastor talk to him about his church attendance and how does he respond? You want your husband to be prepared for the end of life, which is approaching.

Divorce

Your
Question When one spouse cheats on another, the marriage is considered broken, and divorce is possible. Can't a marriage be broken in other ways too? What if one spouse no longer trusts the other? Jealousy is picking the marriage apart, as one spouse is being falsely accused.

In 1 Corinthians 7, Paul teaches that if an unbeliever deserts a marriage, the believing party is not bound to that marriage. For this reason, "malicious desertion" is often listed as a second grounds for divorce along with adultery. Permanent, voluntary departure from the home is malicious desertion. Persistent actions that make life together in the home impossible can become malicious desertion. Refusal of sexual intercourse, refusal of support, continual threats of violence, or violence against spouse and children can become malicious desertion. The injured party may have to live apart from the abuser while correction and reconciliation are attempted. Patient counseling and pastoral exhortation should be used to effect correction and reconciliation. A person who persistently refuses correction from the Word of God and continues on a destructive course of action proves to be a deserter.

Jealousy is not in and of itself malicious desertion and a grounds for divorce. But persistent unjustified jealousy is poison to a marriage. In such cases the couple should seek counseling in the hope of achieving correction and reconciliation before it becomes too late.

Question In light of Mark 10:11,12 ("Anyone who divorces his wife and marries another woman commits adultery against her. And if she divorces her husband and marries another man, she commits adultery."), why are many WELS pastors officiating at the weddings of divorced persons? If a person divorces shouldn't he or she be resigned to a single life?

In Mark 10 Jesus is making the point that obtaining a legal divorce for the purpose of marrying someone else cannot legitimize the new sexual relationship that arises through that second marriage. Because the offenders sinfully broke a marriage to enter a new marriage, the new union is adultery even though the first marriage was legally dissolved. The fact that the second marriage is legal according to the laws of the state would not make it morally right according to God's law. The church may not give its blessing to such marriages which are entered in violation of the Sixth Commandment.

Under what circumstances then may a divorced person be remarried in the church? The pamphlet mentioned previously, *A Study of Marriage, Divorce, Malicious Desertion, and Remarriage in the Light of God's Word*, deals with this issue also. The following answer is based on this pamphlet, with a few additional observations.

The moral propriety of remarriage after a divorce is not given detailed treatment in Scripture. It is clear that persons who have suffered wrongful divorces, inflicted by their spouses, are free to remarry (1 Corinthians 7:15; Matthew 5:32). Mark 10 must be read in relationship to the parallel passage in Matthew 19:9, which states that where marital unfaithfulness has occurred, the innocent party may get a divorce without incurring guilt.

The question of remarriage by guilty parties who have repented of their sin does not receive explicit treatment in Scripture. Our general practice is that a guilty party may remarry if that person has repented and has sought reconciliation with the spouse whom he or she wronged. The abandoned spouse, however, is not obligated to take the offender back. The abandoned spouse may even have married someone else before the offender repented, making any reconciliation impossible. If the abandoned spouse has died, has remarried, or refuses reconciliation, we would not absolutely deny repentant offenders the right to remarry, since this may subject them to sexual temptation.

In evaluating a request for remarriage from a person who sinfully ended a marriage by adultery or desertion, we look for repentance. Repentance carries with it a desire to stop committing the sin and to restore if possible what sin has ruined. With repentance, therefore, we also expect a genuine desire to restore the broken relationship, if possible. Should reconciliation be truly impossible, there seems to be no absolute prohibition that prevents the repentant person from remarrying. This assumes, however, that, as far as one can observe, the repentance is genuine and the attempt at reconciliation was equally genuine. In other words, there can be no "planned repentance" in anticipation of remarriage, for that is no repentance at all. It is the opinion of many Lutheran theologians that a party guilty of adultery cannot marry a person with whom they had previously committed adultery, even where no reconciliation with their previous spouse is possible. The repentant person must also have the intention of living a godly life in the new marriage bond.

Because there may be many factors about a divorce that are not public knowledge, observers should be cautious about judging a pastor's decision to participate in the marriage of divorced persons. If a specific case is creating questions or offense, the concerned individuals should speak to the pastor about it. In some cases that seem likely to cause offense, it might be wise to try to prevent this by providing an explanation of the case to the congregation or church council.

Your Question I am recently married to a wonderful Christian woman who has helped enrich our lives because we read the Bible and pray together and try and walk with and in God. There is one problem, she is Roman Catholic and she married me in my church because she couldn't marry me in her church because I was divorced over a decade ago, and her priest said since she married me she has committed adultery and now she cannot receive Communion. I talked to the priest and explained that my divorce was due to biblical reasons that I went over many many times with my pastor, but he said he was not interested in that because marriage is a sacrament that needs to be undone through an annulment proceeding. So I have to pay $450.00 to the diocese in my area and go through some process of reliving my pain of my previous divorce. My wife says she doesn't understand why because in the Bible it says there is justification in some cases for divorce. She would like to take Communion with her family who practice Catholicism and I understand that desire. I don't understand why marriage is a sacrament, I know about the wedding in Cana, but I thought Christ never promised salvation through marriage. Am I wrong? I don't understand how Scripture can be dismissed so easily by their church. I am willing to go through this because I love my wife deeply, but recently she has been saying that she doesn't adhere to many practices of Catholicism (i.e., purgatory, etc). I just keep asking her to read the Bible with me and she goes to my church quite often with me and sometime I go to hers which since doing, I notice things being said about sacrifice before Communion and sacrifice of the mass, etc. There is a lot of sacrificing going on there. Are any of these things scriptural? Do we deny Communion to people who commit a sin as viewed by our teaching? I thought

Communion was for the forgiveness of sins. Thanks for reading this long, long question.

Annulment, properly understood, is a declaration that a marriage never existed because no valid consent could be given, for example, if one of the parties was underage or secretly married to someone else. Other grounds for annulment would be consent given while intoxicated or being forced into marriage. Annulment is not a substitute for divorce, which is a legal recognition that one or both parties have broken a validly established marriage.

The Catholic church's position on divorce is unscriptural because it does not distinguish the guilty party from the innocent party in the case of adultery. A Catholic man could wrongfully divorce his wife to marry a younger woman and then buy an annulment of his first marriage and be able to commune. His wrongfully divorced wife, however, would not be able to commune or remarry unless an annulment had been obtained. The way this annulling of marriages is practiced can exonerate the guilty and burden the innocent. It makes a farce of the Catholic church's strong stand against divorce.

The Catholic church maintains that in marriage situations of baptized Christians (not just of Catholics), its authority is greater than that of the civil government. It, therefore, refuses to recognize civil divorces. This is false, since marriage is a contract or covenant for earthly life, not a sacrament of forgiveness.

Also if there are real grounds for annulment, why does the innocent party have to pay for it? Shouldn't the church dispense grace freely, not sell it for a price? (Christians should, of course, support the church with their gifts, but grace and God's gifts should not be sold for a price.)

A person who is repentant of sin should never be denied Communion. It would be proper to deny Communion to someone who is continuing impenitently in sin.

What the Catholic church is asking from you is tyranny on their part. You and your wife will have to decide if you are willing to pay the price of submitting to it. I realize that she may feel pain on being separated from her family in Communion, but this is something the Catholic church is unjustly imposing on her. It is not her fault. If Communion is something she can have only by submitting to the unfair laws of the Catholic church, is it something she really wants?

She has to ask if she really wants the Communion of a church that is tyrannizing her and extorting money from you. Can such Communion really be a benefit to her? Perhaps she will see that becoming able to commune with you as a member of your church where grace is freely offered will be better for her soul than Communion she can obtain only by submitting to the Roman church's rules.

Perhaps the two of you could take an instruction course from your congregation together. This course would not commit her to joining your church, but studying the principles of the Bible together could help you both make an informed decision in this matter.

11
Adiaphora

Adiaphora is a difficult and confusing word. It is derived from a Greek word that means "things that don't make a difference." This is not a very good name, since adiaphora often do make a great deal of difference. Adiaphora may be sin, or they may lead to sin. The misuse of adiaphora may obscure our confession of biblical truth. Perhaps the German name for adiaphora is better than the Greek name. The German name *Mitteldinge* translates into English as "middle things." There are some things God has commanded that we do. There are other things he has commanded that we not do. There are, however, other things that are in the middle between commands and prohibitions—God has not said, "Yes, you must do them"; he has not said, "No, you must not do them." These are the things we call adiaphora.

Though adiaphora are not sin in and of themselves, they become sin (1) if we do them against our own conscience (example: if a person thinks it is a sin to eat meat on Friday, for him it is a sin); (2) if our use of adiaphora leads someone else to sin (example: the way in which I use alcohol leads a weak Christian who is an alcoholic into sin); or (3) if our use of adiaphora fails to give a clear confession of our faith and of God's Word (example: I give in to Baptist demands that we must baptize by immersion).

Questions of adiaphora often cause strife in congregations. For that reason, our understanding of the principles of adiaphora and our attitudes toward them are a very important part of our Christian lives.

We sometimes divide adiaphora into two main groups: matters of worship and matters of daily life.

Recognizing Adiaphora

Your Question How can we distinguish between adiaphora and commands of the Lord in the Bible? For example, Paul tells women to cover their heads in the church, and he tells them not to preach. We seem to regard the first regulation as an adiaphoron and the second as a command, but Paul seems to regard both as commands.

We need to distinguish between three different situations: (1) adiaphora, which are never wrong in and of themselves but which may become wrong if our use of them would harm others; (2) commands in the Bible that apply to certain people but not to all of us; and (3) commands that are binding on all people at all times.

The following tests help us determine whether a statement in the Bible is describing an adiaphoron, a limited command, or a general command that applies to everyone:

1. Does the text say the issue being discussed is an adiaphoron? Romans 14 says eating or refraining from different foods or observing different holidays are adiaphora. The principles governing the use of adiaphora are taught in Romans 14, 1 Corinthians 8, and Galatians 5.

2. Does the context of the passage limit who is addressed? In 1 Timothy 1:3, Paul tells Timothy to stay in Ephesus and to oppose the false teachers present there. It is clear that the command to "stay in Ephesus" is limited to Timothy and does not apply to us.

3. Does another statement of Scripture limit the application of the command? The Third Commandment forbids work on the seventh day of the week. The New Testament tells us that this specific command no longer applies to us (Colossians 2:16).

4. Does the text give a reason for the command? Does the reason for the command apply only to certain people or to all people? In 1 Corinthians 16 Paul tells the Corinthians to set aside money each Sunday so their offering will be ready when he arrives in Corinth so that no gathering of offerings will be necessary after Paul's arrival. The mechanics of this particular collection apply to the Corinthians, not to us, though we may use them as an example if we choose.

How do these principles provide an answer to your specific question? In 1 Corinthians 11, Paul tells the women in Corinth to have a covering on their heads (vv. 5,13,15). He says he is dealing with a "custom" or a "practice" (v. 16). It is a matter of propriety (vv. 13,15). The women in Corinth should not violate this custom for doing so would cause offense. In times and places that did not have this custom, Paul's directions would not be applicable. The meaning of head coverings for both men and women varies with time and place. For example, today for a man to where a hat in church is disrespectful, for him not to wear a hat in a synagogue is disrespectful.

In the same chapter, Paul says man is the head of woman (v. 3). He says that the reason for this is that God created woman from and for man (vv. 8,9). Since this principle is based on an order established by God at creation, it applies to all people in all times.

In 1 Corinthians 14, Paul says women should be silent in the church (v. 34). He says this command is based on the Law (v. 34) and that it is a command of the Lord (v. 37). Furthermore, anybody who ignores this command will be ignored by God (v. 38). In 1 Timothy 2, Paul says women should not have authority over a man (v. 12). As reasons for this command, he gives the order established in creation (v. 13) and the departure from this order in the fall into sin (v. 14). Since these commands are based on an order established by God at creation, it is clear that they apply to all people.

There is a detailed discussion of guidelines for distinguishing between adiaphora and commands in the Spring 1994 issue of the *Wisconsin Lutheran Quarterly*, our WELS theological magazine for pastors. You may be able to borrow a copy from your pastor or from one of our church or school libraries. A version of this article is available from the Wisconsin Lutheran Seminary online essay files under the title "What in Scripture Is Universally Applicable and What Is Historically Conditioned?" by David Kuske.

Adiaphora in Worship

Your Question Since the Third Commandment says "Remember the Sabbath Day" why don't Lutherans worship on the seventh day as God commanded? Didn't Sunday originate as a pagan day for worshiping the sun? Didn't one of the popes change the day we worship from Saturday to Sunday? At least, this is what we have been told.

There are two separate issues here: on what day should we worship and how should we observe that day?

It is true that God commanded Israel to worship on the seventh day and to observe that day as a day of rest from all regular labor. It is true that we have no right to change any of God's commandments. But it is also true that God has the right to limit the application of the commands he gives to certain people and to certain times. Not all of his commands apply to all people. The command to observe the seventh day as a day of rest was such a limited command. It applied only to Israel and only for the duration of the Old Testament. We commonly call such commands ceremonial law.

The New Testament specifically tells us that we have been freed from the Sabbath command. Paul told the Colossians, "He forgave us all our sins, having canceled the written code, with its regulations, that was against us and that stood opposed to us; he took it away, nailing it to the cross. . . . Therefore do not let anyone judge you by what you eat or drink, or with regard to a religious festival, a New Moon celebration or a Sabbath day" (Colossians 2:13-16). Since Christ has completed the payment for sin and has abolished the ceremonial law which stood as a barrier between the Jews and the Gentiles, we should not let anyone judge us on the basis of whether or not we observe a day of Sabbath rest. We also must refrain from judging others on this basis. "One man considers one day more sacred than another; another man considers every day alike. Each one should be fully convinced in his own mind. He who regards one day as special, does so to the Lord. . . . You, then, why do you judge your brother? Or why do you look down on your brother? For we will all stand before God's judgment seat" (Romans 14:5,6,10). There is no longer a commanded day of Sabbath rest, not even Sunday.

In the Christian church, Sunday is not a day of rest in the Old Testament sense, but a day for worship in which we obey Christ's command, "Let us not give up meeting together, as some are in the habit of doing, but let us encourage one another—and all the more as you see the Day approaching" (Hebrews 10:25). The first Christians in Jerusalem met daily, not weekly. "Every day they continued to meet together in the temple courts. They broke bread in their homes and ate together with glad and sincere hearts" (Acts 2:46). Within 20 years of Jesus' death, Sunday had apparently become the main meeting day of the church. Paul commanded, "On the first day of every week, each one of you should set aside a sum of money in keeping with his income, saving it up, so that when I come no collections will have to be made" (1 Corinthians 16:2). Revelation 1:10 also seems to refer to Sunday as the Lord's Day. The earliest church fathers also refer to Sunday as the Christian day of worship. It appears that Sunday was chosen because the first day of the week was the day of Jesus' resurrection. We therefore have both the permission of the Lord and the example of the New Testament church in using Sunday as our primary day of worship.

The argument that Sunday should be disqualified because it was a day of pagan worship bears no weight, since in English all of the days of the week and most of the months are named after pagan gods or goddesses. There simply is no day available that was not used by pagans. We are free to worship God on any day since all the days really belong to him. The early church fathers were aware of the fact that some pagans worshiped the sun on Sunday, but they declared that there could be no better day to rededicate to the true "sun of righteousness." It appears that Constantine, the first Christian emperor, made Sunday a holiday in A.D. 321. At any rate it is clear the pope did not make Sunday the Christian day of worship. This choice was freely made by the first Christians.

In response to the charges of sabbatarians who attack the Lutheran practice of worshiping on Sunday as pagan or Catholic, there are two appropriate responses. First, defend the freedom you have in Christ. Don't let anyone make you a slave to rules that God has not laid upon you. Scripture very clearly says you are not obligated to keep a day of Sabbath rest. Second, use the freedom God has given you. Gladly use every opportunity you have, including Sunday, the day we have chosen for our regular service, to praise the Lord. Gladly hear his Word, and you will experience the true Sabbath rest, the peace of forgiveness through Christ.

Your
Question **It has come to my attention that seminary students are not taught to give the sign of the cross during the consecration of the Communion elements. In the new hymnal the sign of the cross is included in the absolution and benediction, but not the consecration. Is the sign of the cross necessary? Is it inconsistent to keep it in one part of the liturgy and not another?**

The sign of the cross is not a means of grace or a sacramental that brings about a certain blessing. It is a symbolic action, which reminds us of the blessings we have through the death of Jesus on the cross. As such, it is always a matter of free choice, not of divine command. The church is free to use it or omit it.

When we receive absolution or the benediction, or when a person is baptized, the sign of the cross is an appropriate reminder that the blessing which has just been received was won by the death of Christ on the cross.

The sign of the cross has long been used at the time of consecration of the Communion elements. There is nothing wrong with this if it is used with the same symbolic meaning described above. Some Christians, however, have used the sign of the cross superstitiously as if it had magical power. If it is used during the consecration, some observers might get the impression that the sign of the cross is being used to change the bread and wine into Christ's body and blood or that it is being used to indicate the moment Christ's body and blood become present. For this reason, some pastors prefer not to use it at this point. Most pastors use the sign of the cross as the communicants are being dismissed after receiving the Lord's Supper. This seems to be a more appropriate place to use the sign of the cross in the Lord's Supper. At this point it is being placed on the recipients as a reminder that the blessing they have just received was won by the cross of Christ. At this point of the Communion its use is more parallel to that in the absolution, benediction, and Baptism.

Your Question Concerning the new hymnal and liturgy [*Christian Worship,* now not so new]: why do we have to return to Catholicism where the minister chants the psalm or whatever during the Liturgy? That turns me off. I hope I can find a denomination that prays to God directly from the heart and doesn't have to read someone else's prayer from a book.

The singing or chanting of psalms did not originate with Catholicism, but with David, who wrote the psalms to be sung in public worship. If you look at the headings of the psalms in your Bible, you will see that many of them contain musical directions, and many of them were given to the director of music in the temple. These "prayers from a book" are God's own words, given through inspiration of the Holy Spirit. What better songs could we sing in our services than songs from God's own book. Isn't it quite presumptuous of you to conclude that prayers you speak from the heart are better than the prayers David spoke by inspiration of the Holy Spirit or the Lord's Prayer, in which Jesus taught us how to pray?

We do not "have to" sing or chant these songs in any particular style. They can be sung by the pastor, the congregation, the choir, or any combination thereof. Congregations and pastors that prefer to read them can do so. The new hymnal encourages greater use of the psalms than has been common among us in the recent past. For this it deserves to be commended. Congregations have many options in how they choose to use the psalms.

Chanting the psalms is simply returning to their original use as described in Scripture. However, even if the practice had originated in Catholicism, that would not in itself be reason for us to reject it. We should judge such customs on their own merits, just as Luther did at the time of the Reformation.

Your Question Is it proper to clap boisterously and be loud and noisy in the church after a concert or pageant?

Christians in many times and many places have worshiped more boisterously than we commonly do. Sometimes they clap in accompaniment to worship, as is mentioned a few times in Scripture (Psalm 47:1; 98:8; Isaiah 55:12). Such passages, however, are usually poetic descriptions of rivers and trees, not human worshipers, clapping in praise.

Your question, however, does not ask about clapping as part of worship, but which is a response to worship. What does clapping imply in such a context?

In the culture of biblical times, clapping was usually a sign of scorn or of glee at the misfortune of one's enemies (Lamentations 2:15; Nahum 3:13; Ezekiel 25:6)—hardly the message intended in the circumstances you describe in your question. The only place in the Bible where clapping seems to be an expression of approval is 2 Kings 11:12, where a new king is greeted with applause. The Bible, thus, gives us little guidance as to the propriety of clapping in church, since applause did not have the same connotation then that it does for us.

The answer to your question, therefore, is a matter of judgment, determined by the meaning of applause in a given culture and by the nature and purpose of the musical or dramatic performance.

In contemporary American society, applause has three main functions: to welcome a speaker or performer, to approve the contents of a speech, and to express appreciation for the quality of a performance. Certainly approval of the contents of the message is a proper response to any true proclamation of God's Word, whether in word, song, or drama.

But we have traditionally regarded applause as the appropriate response to a *performance* of a work of art, which may be judged by our subjective opinion, not to the *proclamation* of God's Word, which is not subject to our judgment. We don't customarily applaud the condemnation heaped on us by God's law or the absolution that frees us from sin. We don't cheer the creed or give a standing ovation to the Lord's Supper, though we fully approve of their content. It is not our usual practice to interrupt the sermon with applause when we like its content or style, or to boo if we don't like the style of the sermon or what God has to say.

Are the biting condemnations of God's law any different when they are preached by the pastor or sung by a choir? Are a Christmas pageant or a passion play intended to be theatrical performances or dramatic presentations of the gospel lesson? If the music and drama being presented in the church are intended to be preaching rather than performance, it would seem to be most appropriate that we respond to them as we would to any other preaching of the gospel. This is usually quite clear if such presentations occur in a worship service. On other occasions, it is easy to prevent the intrusion of applause through a brief announcement, just as wedding bulletins often ask guests to refrain from flash photography to preserve an atmosphere of worship.

Another consideration, which I am guessing lies behind your question, is that many (or at least some) people who are experiencing the concert or drama as worship and as an occasion for meditation consider applause to be an annoying disruption to the mood and spirit of worship. A glorious anthem takes our minds soaring to a contemplation of heaven, but jarring applause brings us crashing down to earth.

Mingling worship and applause also creates practical difficulties. If worship is treated like performance, do we withhold applause when beautiful truths of the Word are presented in less than elegant style or when the content is eloquently expressed but doesn't appeal to our sinful nature? Is it fitting to applaud a human composition but to respond to the inspired gospel lesson with silence?

We teach pastors that the goal of good preaching is to direct attention and honor to the message, not to the human messenger or his eloquence (or lack of it). Should our goal be any different if the preaching is done in song?

So then, the appropriateness of applause in response to a religious concert is a matter of cultural judgment, but it also depends on how we answer the following questions: What does greater or lesser applause say about our response to God's message? What does applause say to the messengers about our criteria for judging their presentation? Does applause send confusing signals about the relative importance of the substance of the message and its outward form (1 Corinthians 2:1-4)? What does applause do to the worship mood of the congregation?

Your
Question In some congregations just before the service begins the pastor says "Good morning" and tells the congregation the theme for the day. In some churches the congregation responds with a "Good morning." Is there any reason not to do this?

There is no doctrinal reason that preservice announcements cannot include an exchange of greetings. Probably the main reason some congregations include such a greeting is to project an air of warmth and friendship, especially to visitors.

Some worshipers prefer to have such personal greetings exchanged at the door of the church as worshipers enter and leave so that the opening of the service will focus on the invocation of the name of the triune God (*Christian Worship*, p. 15) rather than on human greetings. They point out that our common service already contains an exchange of greetings that is more spiritual than a mere "Good morning." This greeting (The Lord be with you/And also with you) precedes the prayer for the day on page 17 of *Christian Worship*.

Your Question Why don't we use the kiss of peace in our services since the New Testament often encourages it, for example, in Romans 16:16?

The New Testament four times encourages Christians to greet each other "with a holy kiss" and once "with a kiss of love." A kiss was a common form of greeting among people of the ancient Near East, and the New Testament may simply be referring to such greetings. The "holy kiss," however, quickly became a liturgical ceremony. At some point in the service, often just before the Communion, a kiss was exchanged between the worshipers. Reed's *The Lutheran Liturgy* says, "In the early church the men sat on one side of the church and the women on the other, and this familiar oriental greeting, cheek to cheek, was given regularly in the assemblies of the faithful as a mark of fellowship and unity, the men saluting the men and the women the women" (p. 367).

The practice of men and women sitting together in church apparently was a factor in the withering away of the custom of the "holy kiss." Many felt the kiss could no longer remain holy in these circumstances. Some remnants of the "holy kiss" were preserved in the medieval liturgy, as a greeting among the clergy officiating at the mass and in the custom of the worshipers kissing a tablet that was passed through the congregation. Luther preserved the essence of the custom by emphasizing a greeting of peace without the kiss. We still have this in our liturgy, right before the Sacrament. "The peace of the Lord be with you always" (*Christian Worship*, p. 23, and also an exchange of greetings on pages 17 and 21).

Some Lutherans have re-introduced the exchange of peace as a handshake rather than a kiss. Judging from the letters to the editor in Lutheran magazines, this has sometimes been more divisive than unifying. Some people love the custom, and some hate it as intrusive to worship.

The "holy kiss" was an expression of fellowship that was appropriate to the culture and worship setting of the early church. When this form of exchanging peace was no longer culturally appropriate, the church found other ways of expressing unity. We may do the same.

Your Question Jesus gave us a perfect example of service by washing his disciples' feet (John 13:5). Please explain how this applies to us today.

324

You have already answered your own question with the words "example of service." Washing the guests' feet before they reclined for a meal was a very practical and necessary service in the days when people walked along dusty roads in sandals. But because it was a humble job, Jesus' disciples refused to do it. By washing his disciples' feet, Jesus gave an example of how we should serve others.

Some churches have made foot washing into a rite to be performed in church. There would be nothing wrong with this if the ceremony were simply used as an object lesson to remind the members that they should gladly serve others. But the real way to follow Jesus' example is to provide real practical service to others, such as caring for the sick, cleaning up after them, taking out the garbage, and so on. Today some of these services, such as caring for the seriously ill, may be done by health professionals, but all Christians should be willing to serve one another in humble ways as the needs and opportunities arise.

Your Question Some time ago I was discussing Epiphany with some friends. We became curious about the origin of this holiday. In spite of a lot of effort, we have not been able to find any information about its beginnings. Can you tell us how this became a holiday in the church?

The short answer to your question is no. The origins of Epiphany and Christmas are hidden in the shadows of early church history. In the earliest days of the church, there was little emphasis on the celebration of Jesus' birth. The main festival was Jesus' resurrection.

"Epiphany" comes from a Greek word meaning "revelation" or "revealing of glory." It therefore is likely that this holiday originated in the eastern Mediterranean where Greek was the dominant language. By the 2nd century, the church in Alexandria, Egypt, was celebrating January 6 as Epiphany, a festival honoring the miracle of the incarnation (God becoming man). By the 4th century, Epiphany was an important festival throughout the Eastern church. It gradually spread westward to the Latin church.

Christmas began in the West. In the early 200s, the church father Hippolytus maintained that December 25 was the birthday of Jesus, but the first evidence we have for the celebration of Christmas comes from A.D. 336. By the late 300s, Christmas was also being celebrated in the East. A natural result of this development was that the emphasis on Jesus' incarnation was detached from Epiphany and associated with Christmas in both East and West.

We cannot say with certainty whether either December 25 or January 6 is the true birthday of Jesus or whether these dates were chosen to provide substitutes for the heathen midwinter festivals, which celebrated the return of the sun as the days lengthened. As the western Christmas of December 25 became established as the day to celebrate Jesus' birth, the eastern Christmas on January 6 became the end of the 12 days of Christmas in the West. Its celebration became focused on the coming of the wise men, Jesus' baptism, and the beginning of his ministry. These are the emphases of this festival to the present day.

Your
Question **Why do we celebrate a festival called Easter? "Easter" is the name of a pagan spring goddess. If we are going to celebrate the festival, we should call it "Resurrection" or something like that and get rid of this pagan leftover.**

In many European languages the name of the festival of the resurrection is some form of the word *Pesach,* the Hebrew name for Passover. The name Easter apparently originated in the Germanic languages and was carried to England and into the English language by the Anglo-Saxons. The idea that this word derives from the name of a pagan goddess of the spring equinox is a very old one, traced to the Venerable Bede, an 8th-century scholar. Recent scholarship, however, suggests that this notion is wrong.

In the Frankish church, the name of the festival of the resurrection included the Latin word *alba,* "white," because of the white garments that were worn during the festival. When this was translated into German, *alba* was mistaken for the Latin word for "sunrise," which also was *alba.* For this reason *alba* was translated with the old German word for "sunrise," which has come to us in the form "Easter." In many languages, the word for east means "rising." It appears that the English word too has this meaning. Although the evidence is unclear and there are competing theories, it appears that the festival of the resurrection already has the name "Rising" since this seems to be the original meaning of *Easter.*

It is possible that Bede was not entirely wrong and that there was also a goddess named Dawn, since many pagan religions have a god or goddess of the sunrise. It seems highly improbable, however, that the church authorities would have allowed the chief festival of the Christian year to be named after a pagan goddess. They might have been tempted to keep something heathen and call it by a Christian name. They would hardly have taken something Christian and given it a pagan name.

Even if the etymology of the word *Easter* were the same as the name of a pagan goddess, which is doubtful, this would not be a particular reason for alarm. The majority of our day and month names, the names of the planets, and such diverse things as mercury and cereal are all named for pagan deities, and we refer to them all of the time without any concern about their etymology.

There is, however, a larger issue involved here. Much of the anti-Easter sentiment comes from an anti-festival attitude that is promoted by fundamentalist publications, radio, and TV shows. Easter and Christmas are often condemned because they are celebrated at key astronomical points of the year during which the heathen also celebrated seasonal festivals. If anyone is going to find fault with celebrating the festival of the resurrection at the spring equinox, his quarrel is with God, since God is the one who placed it there. In celebrating Easter on the first Sunday after the first full moon of spring, the church is simply acknowledging the fact that God chose the Passover, celebrated at the first full moon of spring, as the time for the death and resurrection of his Son. The Old Testament festivals like Passover and Pentecost, which were commanded by God, were tied to events of the astronomical and agricultural years. The Christian festivals simply followed them.

To pass harsh judgments on fellow Christians on the basis of alleged pagan etymology of festival names or alleged pagan origin of festivals is at best "passing judgment on disputable matters" (Romans 14:1). All too often it passes over into making legalistic judgments on fellow Christians (Romans 14:1-23; 1 Corinthians 8:4-8). It is not too much different than the spirit of the politically correct school board that would not allow Valentine's Day because that would introduce a Christian saint's day into the public school, but did allow "Special Person Day." We do not want to adopt the habits of those who make harsh judgments on the basis of sketchy, uncertain historical evidence and long-forgotten origins.

Question **Why do Jews celebrate the Passover after Easter [as they did in 1997]? If Maundy Thursday was a Passover, Easter should come after Passover. Do they have a different calendar?**

The Jewish religious calendar is a lunisolar calendar, that is, its months are true lunar months based on lunar cycles of approximately 29½ days, but its year is a solar year, on average, of approximately 365 days. Since 12 lunar months are only 354 days, the months would soon drift through the seasons of the year unless adjustments were made. The seasons are kept in line by adding a 13th month to the year in 7 out of 19 years. In ancient times the 13th month was added on the basis of observations of natural phenomena rather than a set pattern. It is this "slack" in the calendar that allows Passover to come after Easter sometimes.

Passover is always celebrated on the 15th of the lunar month of Nisan (with the preparation of the lamb on the afternoon of the 14th). As the midpoint of a lunar month, the Passover is always at a full moon. The early church celebrated Easter on the Sunday after the Passover. (Some Eastern Christians celebrated it the same date of the calendar each year, regardless of the day of the week on which it fell.) The Western church, which always celebrated Easter on Sunday, eventually began to make its own calculation of Easter, independent of the Jewish calendar, according to the rule: Easter is the first Sunday after the first full moon of spring. Because of the drift in the Jewish calendar, the first full moon of spring can occasionally be the full moon before the full moon of Nisan. Under these circumstances Passover will come after Easter.

There has often been disagreement among different Christian churches about the formula used to calculate the date of Easter. For example, the date of Russian Easter, or Orthodox Easter, may be different from the date of Western Easter because the Russian church uses the Julian calendar rather than the Gregorian calendar as the basis for its calculations.

Question **I would like to attend your church but cannot stand the music and worship. I'm forced to go to other churches that I do not agree with their doctrine but enjoy the worship. What is more**

328

important, the worship or the teaching part of the service? I'm 48 years old and I hate the worship format of the typical Lutheran church. I hate to think what younger people feel. Is it because the old people in the church have the money and call the shots that the worship is conducted that way? Is there another church that has the doctrine the same but different worship? I like the way Chuck Smith packages worship.

Doctrine is determined by God's Word. Worship style is determined by human choice. What you have said is that you are placing your preference for worship style ahead of God's Word. In saying this you condemn yourself. No one is forcing you to do this. You are choosing to do this. You will be held responsible for your actions by God.

As far as helping you find a church where you can find both the right doctrine and worship styles that meet your desires or at least your needs, I don't have enough information about your specific situation to answer your question. I don't have enough information to know how much is the fault of the churches you are criticizing and how much is your fault.

Some of our churches have a more contemporary style of worship in some of their services. *Christian Worship* offers quite a variety of hymn styles and liturgical forms, so there should be variety available. Congregations themselves through consultation of the pastor, worship leaders, and members determine the worship style of our congregations. An attempt is made to accommodate the desires of all the members with a certain amount of compromise necessary by everyone on issues that are simply a matter of taste.

Have you on your part made any study of the Lutheran way of worship to understand why we have the forms we do, forms that have been tried and tested over the centuries and in many different cultures? Do you know why set themes for the Sundays and seasons have advantages over just hearing the pastor's favorite topic every week? Is your objection to set form or just to the style of hymns? These are questions you should discuss with the pastor.

Are you looking for a way to show reverence for God and to hear what he has to say to you, or are you looking for entertainment? I found your term "packages worship" to be very interesting. We cannot approach worship choices the same way in which we approach consumer choices such as "Do I prefer McDonald's or Wendy's or Pizza

Hut?" You express yourself more as a shopper looking for customer satisfaction than as a sinner coming before the holy God.

You need to discuss your feelings about worship with someone to try to sort these questions out.

Your
Question   **Is Christian contemporary music wrong? Decision Theology seems to be at the core of most contemporary Christian music that you typically hear on Protestant radio stations. I know some people in the WELS and ELS who refuse to accept this music into our churches. I somewhat agree. I think we resort to following the methods of Protestants in order to go along with the culture if we do that. I know others however who feel it is just fine to have this kind of music in our churches. We even advertise in the bulletins for Christian Contemporary concerts that are coming up. I even see that our Northwestern Publishing House now is selling a couple of different artists on CD on its Web site. These artists would be considered Protestant Evangelicals. Why do we allow this? If we aren't in fellowship with these denominations then why do we allow their music into our churches and into our publishing houses? Especially when the lyrics for the most part to the music is not based on what we believe in the WELS. I sincerely cherish our Lutheran heritage and would hate to see it eventually diminish due to our reluctance to hold strong to our traditions and to our confessions. It seems like there are some WELS churches that still hold strong to our traditions in every way but others have even resorted to adding a contemporary service, and the pastor no longer preaches from the pulpit, but freely roams as he preaches. Also, I have seen a cutting out of some of the liturgy in the service. What comments or concerns do you have about these things?**

Hymns that are theologically unsound have been written in every genre of hymnody throughout the history of the church. The need to sift and sort contemporary hymns is no different than the process that must be applied to the hymns of every generation. Since we use hymns from all ages of the church in our hymnal, we have had to sift through the hymns of all ages—retaining the good and rejecting the bad or mediocre. Some of the hymns in our hymnal have been revised from their original form to eliminate errors or weak statements. Charles Wesley wrote some nine thousand hymns; ten have made it into our hymn book, including such familiar hymns as "Hark! The Herald Angels Sing" and "Oh, for a Thousand Tongues to Sing." Of Charles' hymns, his brother John wrote, "Some bad, some mean, some most excellently good."

We should never use any hymn that is theologically wrong, regardless of whether it is old or new. Contemporary hymns have to be subjected to the same criteria of doctrinal correctness and appropriateness for worship as older hymns. Differences of doctrine cannot be allowed, differences of taste can. If others use hymns in a musical style we do not care for or we consider to be artistically or musically weak, this is a matter of taste not of doctrine. There are many hymns in our hymnal that are fine statements of doctrine but are not top-notch poetry. Some that are quite good poetry may be obscure to the average worshiper. In evaluating the content of hymns, we have to speak not of "this kind of music" but of "this hymn." Is its doctrine correct, its words clear, and its music appropriate to worship? Will it create offense?

I can't comment on specific items included in the NPH catalog or in church bulletins, since you gave no names. In the 2002 catalog, I did not find any items in the category you mentioned. The concerts and recordings you mention may be by WELS members. All items included in the NPH catalog are supposed to be reviewed for doctrinal correctness.

Our concerns should be twofold: (1) that our churches never use doctrinally incorrect music and that they use clear and edifying hymns, (2) that we recognize that God has prescribed no set forms for church music. The Formula of Concord says, "We believe, teach, and confess that the community of God in every locality and every age has authority to change such ceremonies according to circumstances, as it may be most profitable and edifying to the community of God. But in this matter all frivolity and offenses are to be avoided, and particularly the weak in faith are to be spared (1 Corinthians 8:9-13; Romans 14:13ff.)." We need to stress both aspects of this statement.

Your Question As a lifelong WELS member, as are my parents and grandparents before me, I have great concerns as to what direction WELS is headed. I am finding myself distracted from the Word due to all the ceremonial things taking place: ashes, processions, lack of pulpits, etc. I have discussed this at length with other WELS family members and friends, and we all have growing concerns, although to

different degrees. The Lord has commanded us to be fishers of men, but is that at the expense of charter members? If things become offensive to some, hasn't the Lord instructed us to refrain from them? Will the Word become tainted without notice, as these theatrical ideas become more prevalent? My concern is great, and I feel somewhat like a hostage, with nowhere to go. Family members have already left WELS for the CLC. Is that where the Lord is leading me at this time? May the Lord keep the leaders of our synod ever faithful to his Word, and lend an attentive ear in addressing the concerns of its longtime faithful, Christian members.

The first thing to be noted is that all of the things you discuss in your message are adiaphora, not doctrine. The WELS does not, nor should it, dictate to its congregations what they can or cannot do in matters of church architecture or liturgy, which are adiaphora.

I too am a lifelong WELS member and attend many different churches in the course of a year. I have never seen a WELS church without a pulpit or the use of ashes on Ash Wednesday. I do not recall a procession in a regular Sunday service, only on festive occasions. I, therefore, don't know how much you can generalize about these as "WELS" practices.

I don't really care for the practices you mention, but I recognize that all of them are adiaphora, which can be used in a right way or a wrong way. Neither a "high church" nor "low church" style will preserve the correct doctrine. Only obedience to the Word will do that.

We have long used liturgical forms and customs, which many Christians condemn as worldly or theatrical, among them are stained-glass windows, pictures and statues in church, seasonal colors, Christmas trees, and organs. The purpose of these customs is to direct attention to the Word, not to take away from it. There is no doctrinal reason why new customs cannot be created or old ones revived, if they serve the same purpose of edification.

It is important also to be clear about the biblical meaning of *offense*. In its doctrinal meaning, an offense is something that causes people to sin because they have a misinformed conscience. If I encourage someone who believes that it is a sin to play softball on Sunday afternoon to join our game, I would be causing offense. Playing a style of music that is not someone's favorite is not causing offense in the strict sense.

Since WELS does not have any directives concerning any of the things you mention, I have to assume that the congregation to which you are referring freely chose to try or to adopt these practices. Other congregations, perhaps the majority, may choose not to.

When trying new worship practices, worship leaders should be careful that they are not pushing on the congregation things the congregation does not want. They may, of course, encourage the congregation to try new things they believe will be edifying. The majority of the congregation should be careful that they do not hastily adopt things which will be very disturbing to some members. But there is a corresponding duty on the part of those who don't particularly like the new practice not to create "worship wars" by causing strife over things that are adiaphora.

If all of our members insist that their favored customs are the only way to worship, we are in a no-win situation. For everyone who is "offended" because the congregation does something different, there is another one who is "offended" because the congregation never does anything new or different. The congregation should lend an attentive ear to all its members, but it is not possible to have an order of worship in which everyone is going to like everything all of the time. In things that are adiaphora, we have to learn to leave room for a variety of tastes in art and music. The unity of the church is based on unity of doctrine, not on unity of taste. A family can't have everyone's favorite food every meal. Neither can a congregation please everybody's taste in worship all the time. We have to work together to provide a balanced diet in worship customs and formats, which will give consideration to various tastes in outward forms of worship and which will, at the same time, be faithful to the Word in everything.

Your Question

Our congregation permits several members who have a problem with alcohol abuse to receive grape juice rather than wine when they attend the Lord's Supper. One of our members objects vehemently to this since the Lutheran Confessions mention only wine in their references to the Lord's Supper. What is the right thing to do in this situation?

It is quite certain that grape wine was used at the Passover, and the church has, therefore, through the centuries used grape wine as the element for the Lord's Supper. Scripture, however, does not specify "wine," but "fruit of the vine" as the element used. It has, therefore, been the Lutheran practice that no other wine besides grape wine should be used.

We have refused to accept the demands of some Protestant churches that grape juice should be used instead of grape wine because of their claim that all use of alcoholic beverages is wrong. If we would agree to such a legalistic demand, we would be allowing false teachers to add a prohibition of alcoholic beverages to God's law. Scripture warns against the abuse of alcohol, but just as clearly permits it use.

Scripture specifies that Jesus used bread and fruit of the vine as the elements of the Lord's Supper, but it does not insist that we use the exact form he used. Since Jesus used unleavened bread at the Passover, we use communion wafers, a type of unleavened bread, which is similar to, but not identical with the Passover bread. Some Christian churches have used regular leavened bread, and this has not been regarded as raising doubts about the Sacrament.

In the Old Testament laws that regulated the use of wine, such as the law of the Nazarite in Numbers 6:3, all the products of the grape are dealt with as a unit, regardless of the percentage of alcohol they contained. We should not, therefore, be too dogmatic about the percentage of alcohol the "fruit of the vine" must contain to be used in the Lord's Supper.

A number of solutions are possible to the problem you pose in your question. Many people who have a problem with alcohol abuse state that receiving wine at the Lord's Supper in the sacrament of forgiveness does not contribute to their problem, and they receive it regularly. The quantity of wine can be small, and it can be diluted with water as it often was in ancient times and as it sometimes has been done in the Lord's Supper. I believe these are the best solutions since they better preserve the symbolic unity of all who attend the Lord's Supper.

If, however, certain communicants are convinced that they cannot use any alcoholic beverage without placing themselves in severe temptation or if such abstinence is a condition of the treatment they are receiving, we do not have to refuse them this exception to our normal practice, since Scripture does not specify that wine must be used. This is a case in which we accept the needs of those who are weak, without passing judgment on disputable matters (Romans 14:1).

The Lutheran Confessions do not mention wine to specify that a certain percentage of alcohol is necessary in the fruit of the vine used in the Lord's Supper, but simply mention the commonly used elements in their discussion of such issues as the real presence of Christ's body and blood in the Sacrament. See the parallel discussion in the section on the Lord's Supper.

Your
Question **We have no clothing laws in our church, but I have been told that dresses and heels are the only way. Are there clothing laws in the Bible? I am a disabled person and can't stand dresses and only wear three-piece suits and Sassies [orthopedic-type] shoes, also usually cotton socks because I'm allergic to wool, nylon and metal.**

We want to dress for church in a way that shows we regard it as special, but what that means varies with time, place, wealth, health, and so on. No one should criticize anyone who is doing the best he or she can under the circumstances. Read James 2 concerning the attitude we should have about such things.

You don't say who it is that is telling you that dresses and heels are the way to go. If their actions are hindering or discouraging some from attending worship, someone needs to talk to them about their attitude.

Your
Question **What is the WELS stance on fund-raisers? Are they wrong at all times? Or can they be a good thing to get the congregation involved together for a specific purpose?**

The WELS does not have an official statement on this issue. It does not flatly condemn all fund-raisers. There is no reason members cannot contribute their goods or their labor rather than money. Our teachers, however, have quite consistently warned against the danger that fund-raisers for the church may undermine the stewardship of the congregation or may give the impression that church members are seeking the help of outsiders to support programs of the church, which the members themselves are unwilling or unable to support.

Fund-raisers by groups within the congregation, such as a project by a youth group to earn money for a camping trip or retreat together, would be less subject to these objections than fund-raisers that are intended to raise support for the essential mission of the church, which should be supported by the freewill offerings of its members.

If church members want the joy and satisfaction of working together on a project, couldn't they just as easily accomplish this by participating in an effort to help the needy, rather than in a project to raise money for their own needs or desires? Even fund-raisers for the needy or the sick should not be seen as a substitute for our responsibility to give freely to those in need.

Your
Question **Should laypeople who have been given the talent and honor to help in the worship service be paid? I don't think they should be, since the gifts they have received from God should be given back willingly.**

Scripture says, "The worker deserves his wages" (1 Timothy 5:18). Certainly those who devote their lives to serving the church should receive adequate wages, whether their work is preaching, teaching, musical performance and direction, or administration.

The situation is not so clear-cut when we consider part-time service by individuals who earn their living in some other profession. The types of service under discussion might include directing the choir, playing the organ, teaching Sunday school, secretarial work, keeping financial records, or cleaning and repairing the church. All of these services could be performed by members of the congregation as freewill offerings. Some of these services could be performed by individuals who are called to part-time, paid positions. Some services, such as janitorial work, could be performed by nonmembers hired to do the job.

Congregations are free to decide how to fill these needs. Whether or not they offer pay for specific services will usually depend on the amount of time and commitment needed to fulfill such an assignment in a given congregation. When deciding whether to compensate those who serve in part-time positions, congregations should be wary of arbitrary distinctions, such as paying organists but expecting teachers or custodians who do an equal amount of work to serve without pay. Church boards and voters' assemblies should make a careful evaluation of the requirements of all of the various positions they ask members to fill so that there is fair treatment of all who serve.

Your
Question **I would like to join a Bible society which is producing a new translation. I have not found anywhere they claim anything but the**

Bible as their sole purpose, unlike the Gideons. Can WELS members join this Bible society?

WELS members can support Bible societies whose only work is to translate and distribute Scriptures. WELS members have been involved as advisors on the translation projects of such Bible societies, but we do not have a controlling voice in any of them. This can at times result in embarrassment and disappointment. For example, at the last stages of the preparation of the *God's Word* translation, the final editors introduced some rather serious errors into the translation, even on some key passages about justification. Membership in such societies is not without some risk.

Your Question Why isn't Edgar Elgar's "Pomp and Circumstance" played as the march for graduation exercises at our area Lutheran high schools and its worker training schools?

Since our graduation ceremonies are usually worship services, those who are planning the service normally choose a hymn or other religious music that will contribute to the spiritual message of the service as the processional. For the same reason we prefer spiritual music rather than secular music as a wedding processional.

There is, however, no rule against "Pomp and Circumstance," and it has been used in connection with graduation services of WELS schools.

Your Question Why do we, as Lutherans, not participate in the "Catholic" tradition of abstaining from meat on Fridays? What is their purpose in doing so?

There is nothing wrong with people freely choosing to fast or to abstain from certain foods or pleasures as a spiritual exercise reminding them of Christ's suffering or as a spiritual discipline.

The Bible frequently mentions fasting, that is, abstaining from food for a time, as a form of spiritual discipline. God commanded the people of Israel to "deny themselves" on the Day of Atonement, which was the great day of repentance (Leviticus 16:29). This was interpreted as a command to fast. To this the Jews added a number of set dates for fasting, such as the day when they mourned the destruction of the temple (Zechariah 7:5). Special fasts were declared at times of national calamity (Joel 1:14). Individuals also fasted on days of personal mourning or repentance.

God warned the Israelites that fasting was not a substitute for good behavior, nor was it a way to earn merit with God (Isaiah 58:2-8). Fasting was to be an expression of true repentance and a sign of devotion to spiritual concerns.

Jesus' disciples did not fast as regularly as John the Baptist's disciples did, because they had joy in the presence of Jesus (Matthew 9:14,15). Jesus condemned the fasting of the Pharisees because it was done as a show to impress people (Matthew 6:16,17). But Jesus implied that his disciples would fast at the right time and in the right way. The early Christians practiced fasting in connection with special times of prayer and devotion (Acts 13:2; 14:23).

Christians have no command to fast, but Luther recommended fasting as a spiritual discipline. In his comments on preparation for the Lord's Supper in the Small Catechism, he stated that fasting and bodily preparation are fine outward training. On another occasion he said, "There should be a general spiritual fast for us Christians to observe. It would be a good arrangement to observe a general fast for a few days before Easter, before Pentecost, and before Christmas, to distribute fasts over the year. But on no account dare it be done for the purpose of making it an act of worship or a means of meriting something." Luther also recommended fasting as a bodily discipline. "I would also be glad if at certain times, once a week or as often as might seem best, there were no evening meal, except a piece of bread and something to drink, to keep everything from being used up with the kind of incessant guzzling and gobbling that we Germans do, and to teach people to live a little more moderately" (Plath, *What Luther Says*, p. 507).

Christians, therefore, may fast if it helps them focus their attention on special occasions of prayer or repentance. Fasting may also serve as a reminder of the need for bodily self-discipline.

We object to the Catholic type of fasting or abstinence in two circumstances: when it is made a rule of the church binding on everyone and when it is seen as a way of obtaining forgiveness. Though the rule against meat on Friday has been modified in the Catholic church, it is on the authority of the church that this law was changed. To make such abstinence a law was unbiblical. Fasting still remains a rule of the church (the so-called fourth precept), and it is still associated with obtaining forgiveness of sins (*Catechism of the Catholic Church,* par. 1434 and 2043). These are the aspects of such practices to which we would object. Such practices are permissible as a voluntary spiritual exercise with no thought of earning merit.

Your Question My family is trying fasting to clean out poisons and lose weight. I'm concerned about this health fad. What is the WELS position on this?

The Bible frequently mentions fasting, that is, abstaining from food for a time, as a form of spiritual discipline. See the preceding question.

The Bible has nothing to say about fasting as a health benefit. Here a person would have to depend on sound medical advice to avoid excessive fasting, which could be harmful to health.

Your Question Is it legalistic for a congregation to require its confirmation class students to attain a certain level of church attendance as a prerequisite for confirmation?

One of the promises a confirmand makes is to attend church faithfully. If there is no evidence that the person will do this, how can we encourage him or her to stand before God and the congregation and solemnly promise that they will attend faithfully? How can we receive someone as a member who is already flagrantly disobeying God's command to hear his Word regularly?

Certainly, a congregation can expect that someone who wants to become a member of the church will have shown the evidence of that desire in his or her life. It would be best for the congregation, however, to handle poor church attendance by counseling with each individual rather than by simply setting a percentage requirement of attendance, which is mechanically applied.

Your Question What possible reason could there be for changing the last stanza of "A Mighty Fortress" from the powerful "take they our life, goods, fame, child, and wife, let these all be gone, they yet have nothing won" to the colorless, meaningless "do what they will, hate, steal, hurt, or kill"? Aren't Luther's words relevant anymore?

Usually the most unpopular thing about any new hymnal is changes to the wording or melodies of familiar, well-loved hymns, especially sentimental favorites associated with important holidays. When I was serving a congregation that included many Lutherans from a non-WELS background, the version of "A Mighty Fortress" in *The Lutheran Hymnal* was initially one of the least-liked hymns because the people had been used to different music for this hymn (CW, 201) and to a different translation. For them the WELS version (LH 262, CW 200) took some getting used to.

With time, the new versions of old favorites in *Christian Worship* will become "old favorites" too. In the meantime, those of us who have been around long enough to have known and loved *The Lutheran Hymnal* for many years are entitled to a few cases in which we feel "they should've left well enough alone." The changes in *Christian Worship* were attempts by the hymnal committee to make the old favorites clearer and more beautiful for the next generation. At times, a desire for appropriately inclusive language may have been a factor, such as here. Finally, such changes are a matter of opinion.

In this case, I agree with you that the new version is not an improvement over the old, which is a more literal rendering of Luther's thought. Luther's words reflect on what for many would be the supreme sacrifice for the faith, greater even than their own death, that of losing their family. An example of this occurred when the Catholic archbishop of Salzburg expelled Lutherans from his land and forced them to leave their children behind to be raised as Catholics. For them Luther's words had great relevance.

Adiaphora in Daily Life

Your Question **Is Halloween the devil's holiday as some say? How should we feel about children wearing costumes and trick-or-treating?**

All Hallows Evening (Halloween) was a special night because it preceded All Saints Day, an important festival in the medieval church. The crowds expected for this festival may well have been a factor in Luther's choosing October 31 as the day to post his Ninety-five Theses on the door of the Castle Church.

All Saints Day, established in the 7th century, may have been placed on November 1 because this was the New Year's Day for the Celts of the British Isles. By the year 1000, November 2 had become All Souls Day. The Celtic Festival of Samhain (pronounced *sow-een*) on about October 31 was concerned with the return of the souls of the dead and marked the completion of the harvest and the onset of winter's gloom. The connection of elements of witchcraft or the occult with October 31 was thus in competition with All Hallows Evening and All Saints Day, not properly a part of it. In countries where Christianity and superstition coexisted, however, elements of the two often became entangled. Jack-o'-lanterns and masks may be remnants/adaptations of efforts to guard against demons. Trick-or-treating may be a remnant of "souling," the practice of children asking for cakes on All Souls Day as incentive for them to pray for the souls of departed relatives of those who provided the treats.

Standard encyclopedias say that Halloween became a secular holiday in America. It apparently was introduced by the Irish and other immigrants. The emphasis is now on costumes and trick-or-treat, with the treat always given and the trick seldom played.

Halloween now is regarded as a secular holiday that descended from both heathen and medieval Catholic observances. It has often had unsavory elements, such as occult symbols and vandalism, associated with it. The question then is whether these elements have been sufficiently detached from Halloween and it has become a secular holiday that can be observed without offensive features. There certainly has been a concerted effort to make it so. Many public schools ban certain types of costumes that are considered too gross or offensive. Secular groups such as UNICEF have tried to replace the emphasis on getting treats for oneself with a concern for raising money to help the needy.

The fact that some people celebrate Halloween in offensive ways does not in itself rule out the holiday. If this were so we could not celebrate New Year's Eve or even Christmas. The fact that Halloween occupies the day of a heathen holiday is not unique. Many Christian holidays like Christmas and Easter in a sense compete with heathen holidays since both were associated with key points of the astronomical calendar. This is also true of the Old Testament holidays prescribed by God. Some of our Christmas and Easter customs have some similarity to heathen customs just as the Old Testament sacrifices had points of similarity with those of the heathen. Some Christian holidays have become more secularized even while they remain important festivals of the church year (Christmas and Easter). Other minor religious festivals have almost entirely lost their religious connotation (Valentine's Day). For most people St. Patrick's Day has become more of an Irish ethnic fest than a religious holiday.

Whether or not Lutheran Christians should participate in holidays like St. Patrick's Day and Halloween is a question of judgment. Such holidays may have different meaning and different customs attached to them in different times and places. Whether Lutheran Christians should or should not participate depends on the meaning of the holiday in the context in which they live and on the impression their participation will give to others. Naturally, they should refrain from objectionable practices if they participate. Some good arguments can be made against Halloween, but individuals should be convinced in their own consciences of what is best for them to do and should be cautious about judging others.

Your Question Our WELS school library has been asked by several parents within the school to remove the Harry Potter books from circulation on the basis that they promote witchcraft. As the school librarian, I have read these works of fiction and find them entertaining, well written, and extremely popular. The concerned parents are not members of our church body. These parents say that since Harry Potter is a witch-in-training, the books glorify witchcraft and lead children away from Jesus. They also claim that the author is a Satanist—an accusation that cannot be substantiated. I am convinced that the children these books are intended for can tell the difference between fantasy and reality. Do we pull the books in obedience to the Second Commandment, pull them in consideration of the faith of weaker Christians, or instruct on the real dangers of Satan and leave the books on the shelf?

The Harry Potter books, perhaps the most popular children's books ever published, are surrounded by controversy because witchcraft is central to the theme and plot of the book. The battle over Harry Potter books is not limited to Christian schools. A number of public school systems have removed the books from their reading lists or libraries. The Internet is loaded with material attacking and defending the books.

Evangelical Christian opinion is divided. Warnings against the books seem to be the majority opinion, but a minority views the books as harmless fantasy. A review in the November/December 2000 issue of *Lutheran Parent* points out some pitfalls that parents and readers should be alert to.

Because of the extreme popularity of these books, which now are also movies, our schools should help students evaluate them and recognize the dangers in them. Part of the process of Christian education is to help children critically evaluate the media so that they can form judgments about the materials that bombard them, keeping the good and rejecting the bad.

Concerning the question of which books should be in the library: this should be determined by the parties to whom the congregation has entrusted this responsibility, whether it is the librarian, faculty, or some other committee. Ultimately, the school board and congregation have the final responsibility.

The possibility of offense and the feelings of people inside and outside the congregation are certainly factors that should be taken into consideration. But we should also be aware of the danger of letting people impose their views on the church in matters that are matters of opinion and judgment rather than clear principles of Scripture.

In selecting books for church and school libraries, I personally would lean in the direction of not including dubious or doubtful books. If people want these books, they can buy their own or get them from a public library. But in the case you are asking about, we also have to ask whether these protesters are really weak Christians for whose good we will yield our rights, or are they legalists who are trying to impose their will on everyone else? They also seem to be relying at least in part on rumor. I do not know anything about the quality of faith of the author, but she is a member of the Church of Scotland, not a Satanist. We do not help legalists by letting them have their way all the time. The only way to determine what category these people fall into is to talk with them. If these books are not in the curriculum but only available in the library, if these parents do not want to have their children exposed to them, they have a rather simple solution to their concern—tell their children not to read them.

Your
Question I know my pastor is fully capable of answering this question, but since a person of the Baptist faith has asked me, I would like to give him a synod-as-a-whole response.

There is a graveyard here, and many graves have been forgotten through the years. The one in charge of the cemetery has asked a water witch to come in and find these graves. Through this means he has located many lost graves. He asked me what I thought of this process. I told him I don't believe confessional Lutherans are allowed to use these means even to find water. Be it by willow sticks or metal rods, it still is divining, putting trust in something other than God. But I know it is a common practice here in the dry southwest. He then said modern machines do the same thing but not as well. He further stated he believed nothing good can come from the devil, so it must be okay. And God has helped him find these graves through this method. May we use divining rods or the people that use them to find water sources or graves as long as we do not place our faith in them? Some understand it is some natural law God has put into place that draws these devices to the ground though we may not understand this law.

Your question gives us an opportunity to comment on the nature of the answers on our Web site and in this book. These answers are no different than answers you would receive from your pastor in Bible class. They are simply a pastor's response to a question. Sometimes Scripture provides God's answer to the question. Sometimes the questions simply call for information or an opinion. The only time they are "synod answers" is if they quote official statements the synod has made.

Concerning water witching:

1. Any use of witchcraft is wrong even if the results are apparently good. So-called white magic is still idolatrous witchcraft.

2. It would be wrong to use the services of a witch even if we did not become directly involved in the witchcraft ourselves.

3. We can use natural means to "have dominion over" the world God has created for us.

The key question, of course, is whether water witching is witchcraft or a natural process. There is considerable conflicting information and testimony about this. An Internet search on water witching, or dowsing, reveals nearly three hundred sites with information on the topic. The sites fall into three distinct categories. Some advocate dowsing as a human skill enhanced by practice, which has a physical basis. Some advocate dowsing as a psychic skill and associate it with other occult practices. Some either debunk dowsing as unscientific or attack it as occult.

There is no doubt that a rather high percentage of the sites teaching dowsing teach it as an occult practice linked with other occult practices. Some Christians argue that it is a natural skill, which only incidentally is linked with occult practices. Have you asked this particular practitioner how he learned his art?

Certainly Christians should not indulge in doubtful practices. Unless there is clear evidence that water witching is not occult, one should stay away from it.

Your Question

My son has some jewelry with the Yin/Yang symbol on it. What does the symbol mean? Should my son be wearing that kind of jewelry?

First of all, what are Yin and Yang? A Yin and Yang Web site offers this answer: "Yin and Yang express a basic principle of Chinese religion and philosophy, the flow and balance of opposites. Yin and Yang describe the world as a relationship between complementary opposites.

 Yin and Yang are not two separate things. They are one thing expressed in two ways, like two ends of one stick or the two sides of a coin. The 24-hour cycle expresses itself as day and night. This is symbolized as the dark half and light half of the Yin-Yang symbol, which is enclosed in a circle. Yin and Yang become each other. Day belongs to Yang but after reaching its peak at midday, the Yin gradually begins to unfold until it is night. And, in turn, when Yin reaches its peak at midnight, the Yang gradually unfolds until it is day again. This cycle is true for all opposites. The world is neither hot nor cold, it is hot on its way to becoming cold and cold on its way to becoming hot. Thus, any phenomenon may belong to either Yin or Yang, but it contains the seed of its opposite. This is symbolized as the small black and white dots in the Yin-Yang symbol."

The principle of Yin and Yang can be applied to any area of life: Chinese medicine and other forms of holistic healing, martial arts, the study of history, and even Chinese cooking. Today the symbol is often associated with New Age ideas and is widely used as a marketing tool for New Age products and seminars. (It is hard to understand how this symbol can be popular in New Age since Yin is dark, negative, and feminine; Yang is bright, positive, and male. People use it without understanding it.) The symbol is sometimes associated with heathen or spiritist concepts, but some people think of it as simply a symbol of balance in life. It is no longer a distinctly heathen symbol, but I wouldn't use it because of its association with Chinese religion and New Age spirituality.

Your Question

What guidance does God give us in regard to smoking? Since smoking is harmful to one's health and perhaps to others, can the Fifth Commandment be applied? Where does the WELS stand on cigarette smoking? Since it is known to cause heart disease and cancer directly and through secondhand smoke, I have been telling my kids that it is a sin to smoke, since our bodies are the temples of the Holy Spirit. But in recent travels around the surrounding states, I have seen WELS members smoking after the church service. My husband also told me the last conference he attended there were several WELS pastors smoking. Have I been telling my kids the wrong thing?

The Bible does not address this issue directly. It does teach us that we should be good stewards of the life and health God has given us and that we should look out for the welfare of others (secondhand smoke). Christians should carefully weigh whether these considerations permit them to smoke at all or if they only set limitations on it. How does the risk of smoking compare with other risks, such as hazardous sports, being overweight, and so on? Some very strong medical judgments can be made against smoking, but where Scripture does not give us specific guidelines on such issues, we should prayerfully and conscientiously make decisions for ourselves and be cautious in passing spiritual judgment on the decisions of others. WELS has no doctrinal position on this issue.

Your Question

I have worked for a grocery store over 22 years where cigarettes are sold. Sometimes it bothers me to sell tobacco products to people because I know what it will do to them. Especially when I have to sell them to people who are on oxygen because they've been smoking for so many years. I would never dream of working for a tobacco company, but yet is what I do any better? I've been told I have an overactive conscience. I've prayed that if it is God's will that I leave this job, that he help me find another one. I have tried to get another job but haven't been able to. So most of the time I assume this is where God wants me to be. It seems to me that leaving a job when I don't have another one would be testing God. But I'm not really sure.

On smoking see the preceding question.

What about your job? There are many products that can be abused: alcoholic beverages, drugs, guns, food, equipment for hazardous sports, and certainly cigarettes. There seems to be overwhelming evidence that cigarettes are harmful to health, but they are not illegal, nor can we say there is a direct scriptural statement that they are inherently sinful. You are not promoting them or encouraging their use. They are not the principal business of your company. You are selling food. Even there you may not be doing much more than processing people's purchases. Do you have a responsibility to insist that everyone follow a healthy diet? Is not this their responsibility? You do not have a responsibility to regulate people's purchases. The information on cigarettes is well-known. If the government, the cigarette companies, merchants, and the customers choose to ignore this, how does it become your responsibility to regulate this for them? You should not do things that are against your conscience, but in this case you are putting a burden on yourself that is not yours to bear. A sensitive conscience is good, but in this case the person who said you have an overactive conscience on this particular issue seems to be on target.

Your
Question   **Question: If I am walking in the path to follow my Lord, is it wrong for me to go into a bar—not to drink but to listen to a band that is playing? Am I then showing God I am not following him, just because I was in the building? I was listening to music and drinking a pop. I was not degrading my body with alcohol. And also in the Bible it talks about Jesus drinking wine (wine for the wedding he attended). Is it wrong to drink occasionally? I was referred to a book once, *Sipping Saints*—I have not read it yet. Just looking for a few questions answered. Thank you.**

Since the Bible does not condemn the use of alcoholics drinks in moderation, neither going into a bar nor drinking are wrong in themselves. We find many examples of wine being used by believers in the Bible. Drinking and going into bars could be wrong if our actions were leading people into sin. You focus entirely on the drinking, but you would have to ask the same questions about the other things going on in the bar—the type of music, the type of bar, the type of dancing, any sexual misconduct, and so on.

The passages to read about this are 1 Corinthians 8, Romans 14, and Galatians 5. The two principles are best summarized by comparing Galatians 5:1 and 13. I should not do something that will lead a weak person into sin. For example, I should not act in a way that will tempt alcoholic friends to drink. Also we should not act in a way that would lead a reasonable observer to conclude that we were sinning, for example, living together without being married. On the other hand, if there is truly nothing wrong with our actions, for example, using alcohol in moderation, we should not let someone who insists that this is wrong deprive us and others of our freedom.

Your Question

Some of my relatives are getting tattoos and body piercings. They are otherwise model citizens in the church and community. How should we respond to this?

The Old Testament law commanded the Israelites not to disfigure or tattoo their bodies (Leviticus 19:28). This command was a warning to the Israelites not to adopt mourning practices like those of the heathen. God's people were to be different.

Christians should not adopt styles of dress or adornment that will identify them with a false religion or with immoral attitudes. Tattoos, certain types of jewelry and clothing, and certain hair styles have sometimes had such meaning in some cultural settings. Christians obviously should not adopt such styles.

But what if tattoos have no such meaning? Many commentators believe that the biblical prohibition against tattoos and cutting was also aimed at preserving the body intact, as God created it. The biblical text, however, does not state this. We, therefore, cannot recognize this claim as any more than a personal opinion.

We, therefore, have to leave the decision to use or to avoid such styles to the judgment of the individual, but with two warnings: Christians should be very careful not to adopt styles that will cause offense to others, especially during the time when a style that was once offensive has progressed only part way to respectability. Christians who regard certain styles with distaste should be careful about judging fellow Christians by their outward appearance.

Your Question What about dancing and gambling?

Scripture does not explicitly deal with gambling, but it does warn against greed and trying to benefit at the expense of others (Luke 12:15-21; 1 Timothy 6:6-10; Hebrews 13:5,6). In gambling there cannot be winners without losers. In participating in organized gambling, Christians have to also consider the effect it has on society and especially on the weak and those who fall victim to it. A Christian should not gamble if greed or a get-something-for-nothing spirit is involved. Isn't it very difficult to separate gambling from these motives? We are to be good managers, or stewards, of all that God has given us (Matthew 25:14ff.). God's Word promotes the work ethic for obtaining the necessities of life (2 Thessalonians 3:10). Is gambling even in moderation responsible stewardship of what God has given us? Even if a Christian can say that none of this applies to him or her and that gambling is only a form of entertainment, a Christian still must consider the effect on others. For these reasons we warn against gambling. There is not, however, a scriptural basis to say dogmatically that every wager is in and of itself sin.

However, there are a number of biblical principles that apply. Therefore a Christian will seek to apply these principles in analyzing motives for gambling. Christians will also not judge the motives of others and accuse them of sin when they lack any clear evidence that those who gamble are violating these principles. When there is evidence that these principles are being violated, a Christian will lead the sinner to repentance and the assurance that all sins are forgiven through Christ. This same gospel will also provide the power to avoid this sin in the future, especially when we consider that Christ has made us eternally rich (2 Corinthians 8:9).

Lutheran teachers and other Christians often have warned against dancing because of the danger of sexual temptation, which they believed was involved. Some believed such temptation was inseparable from dancing and made a rather sweeping condemnation of dancing.

Scripture makes no blanket condemnation of all forms of dancing. Certain forms of dancing were closely associated with the religious festivals of Israel. Many forms of dancing can be expressions of joyful celebration, which does not necessarily involve sexual temptation.

To my knowledge the WELS has never had an official position on dancing. Nevertheless, it can be said that sweeping condemnations of dancing would be heard much less frequently today than they were in the past. Dances are much more widely accepted in connection with school events and weddings, for example, than they would have been in the past.

This is an area in which Christians should exercise good judgment by recognizing the difference between wholesome fun and exercise, on the one hand, and suggestive or intimate dancing that may promote sexual temptation, on the other. Christians have a responsibility to avoid creating temptation for themselves and others.

Your Question

I am a member of a WELS church and I am also an avid hunter. I have several questions about hunting. When does hunting become a sin? Is predator hunting, shooting animals like prairie dogs, fox, coyotes, etc., a sin? Is trapping or shooting animals for their fur a sin? Is shooting furbearers for fun and turning them in for their furs a sin? Is deer hunting a sin? I would be grateful for any input on these questions or related topics.

The Bible specifically authorizes the use of animals for food (Genesis 9:3). Game animals were among the clean animals permitted as food for Israel. God clothed Adam and Eve with animal skins, and animal skins were used in the construction of the tabernacle. Animals were sacrificed to God.

There is no biblical basis for saying that any of the activities that you list are in themselves sin. The Bible does, however, reflect a concern for animals and that they be treated humanely.

Your Question

Is cremation a God-pleasing way to lay to rest the body of a Christian? Words like "in its narrow chamber keep my body safe in peaceful sleep until your reappearing" (CW 434:3) make me wonder.

It is very clear that burial was the regular treatment of the body by believers during Bible times. Christ's body was buried to await the resurrection. The Bible also compares burial to planting a seed in the ground with the confidence that new life will spring from it (1 Corinthians 15:35-38). We, therefore, prefer to bury the dead in order to follow the custom of Scripture and for the symbolism of burial. Man who was taken from the ground returns to the ground.

Scripture, however, does not forbid cremation. Sometimes during plague or war Christians cremated the dead in order to prevent the spread of plague and disease. Sometimes people who die in a distant land are cremated because it is impossible or very costly to ship their bodies back to their home, but their ashes can be sent to their family for burial. Cremation does not necessarily involve scattering the ashes, but may be a prelude to burial. Burning of the remains was condemned in Amos 2:1 because it was done to desecrate the dead. It was not condemned in 1 Samuel 31:12,13, where the intention was to protect the dead from desecration. If cremation is intended to express unbelief or scorn of God's promise of the resurrection, we would condemn it. This is not necessarily the intention of cremation. As several traditional funeral rites express it, it will make no difference to God whether the body has gone "dust to dust or ashes to ashes."

It will make no difference to God on judgment day whether bodies have been buried, burned, lost at sea, or eaten by animals. He will raise the bodies of all, believers and unbelievers alike, but for two different results. No shameful desecration of the bodies of the martyrs by unbelievers will prevent their resurrection to glory. No arrogant scattering of their ashes by unbelievers will prevent their resurrection to damnation.

Your
Question I'm curious why usury is rarely (if ever) mentioned in churches today. If we look at passages such as Luke 6:34; Psalm 15; Ezekiel 18:13; Leviticus 25:35-37; and Deuteronomy 23:19,20, one can see that we are warned against the dangers of usury. We are especially warned against the practice of usury against other Christians, which causes me to wonder why there are organizations that are connected to the WELS (for example, Thrivent) that focus on insurance policies and investment opportunities. I imagine, you might respond with the claim that usury is the lending of money at excessive interest rates (which is the main dictionary definition). However, that does not seem to be the definition that is used in the passages above (specifically Luke and Deuteronomy). My concern is that the WELS seems to claim that the Bible is inerrant and that it's morality is absolute (excluding Old Testament ceremonial law). The practice of usury is clearly spoken against in several places in the Bible and seems to go against Jesus'

basic message. Yet, the WELS allows its members (and probably many pastors) to participate in the stock market, CD's, 401k's, insurance policies, car loans, house loans, and even saving accounts (which are all forms of usury). How then does the WELS avoid sounding hypocritical, when it accepts usury as an acceptable practice, but at the same time, claims that homosexuality is wrong? Does God's law change? Is it dependent on the current culture (for instance, a capitalist economic structure)? How do you decide to ignore certain laws of God, while holding up others? This issue has been bothering me for quite some time now. I look forward to hearing what you have to say on the matter and thank you (in advance) for your response.

Loaning money for interest has sometimes been controversial among Christians, who have debated whether passages such as Psalm 15:5 and similar verses in Scripture forbid all receiving of interest or only the receiving of usury, that is, excessive, oppressive interest. The Hebrew of Psalm 15:5 literally says, "He does not give out his money with a bite" (*neshek*). This suggests to some that this passage is directed primarily against oppressive, loan-shark interest. The term *bite* is paralleled by *bribe*. It is, however, possible that the term *bite* may simply mean that the interest was paid as a deduction from the loan up-front at the time it was received. The other Hebrew word for interest means "increase" and may refer to interest that was added to the principal. This does not seem to give us much help in determining if the reference is to *interest* or *usury*.

It is very clear that Israelites were not to receive any interest from poor neighbors who had to borrow for the necessities of life. Helping a fellow member of God's people was to be an act of charity, not a business deal:

> Do not take advantage of a widow or an orphan. If you do and they cry out to me, I will certainly hear their cry. My anger will be aroused, and I will kill you with the sword; your wives will become widows and your children fatherless. If you lend money to one of my people among you who is needy, do not be like a moneylender; charge him no interest. If you take your neighbor's cloak as a pledge, return it to him by sunset, because his cloak is the only covering he has for his body. What else will he sleep in? When he cries out to me, I will hear, for I am compassionate. (Exodus 22:22-27)

If one of your countrymen becomes poor and is unable to support himself among you, help him as you would an alien or a temporary resident, so he can continue to live among you. Do not take interest of any kind from him, but fear your God, so that your countryman may continue to live among you. You must not lend him money at interest or sell him food at a profit. (Leviticus 25:35-37)

Do not charge your brother interest, whether on money or food or anything else that may earn interest. You may charge a foreigner interest, but not a brother Israelite. (Deuteronomy 23:19,20)

Notice that these passages specify loans to the needy and to fellow Israelites. If a regulation applies only to Israelites, it is civil or ceremonial law, not moral law. "He who increases his wealth by exorbitant interest amasses it for another, who will be kind to the poor" (Proverbs 28:8). Proverbs 28 refers to the second kind of interest (*tarbit*), which means "increase." This may refer to interest that was added on at the end in addition to what had been deducted at the beginning. Notice that the same word combination, which the NIV translated "interest of any kind" in Leviticus 25, is here translated as "exorbitant interest."

These passages put the prohibition on interest into the context of helping the poor fulfill their bodily needs. They also point out there is a special responsibility toward fellow believers.

The same principle applies today. "As we have opportunity, let us do good to all people, especially to those who belong to the family of believers" (Galatians 6:10). When people have suffered severe hardships or losses and cannot provide the food, shelter, and medical care their families need, we should gladly loan or give them money without hope of financial gain. Jesus says, "If you lend to those from whom you expect repayment, what credit is that to you? . . . Do good to them, and lend to them without expecting to get anything back" (Luke 6:34,35).

Most loans today, however, are not used to obtain the necessities of life, but are used by the borrower as capital for making profit or for raising one's standard of living. The Bible does not specifically deal with loans of this kind, but they are mentioned without disapproval in one of Jesus' parables (Matthew 25:27). Although we have an obligation to help those in need, we do not have an obligation to give our family's money to other people so that they can use it to make a profit for themselves. In fact, Scripture warns against rash loans to others (Proverbs 6:1-3). On this basis, it is valid to recognize a difference between business loans and charitable loans when we are considering the propriety of receiving interest.

Another factor that enters into the equation is the fact that a large part of modern interest is not "increase" at all. It is maintaining the value of the loan against the inflation present in modern economies. Many of the investments you cite in your question don't fall into this category of interest at all. Owning stocks, for example, is not lending money. It is becoming a financial partner in the company, assuming part of the risk in exchange for part of the profit. A person who gives a loan has no right to profits, but a lender is not responsible for the losses as a shareholder is. The risk the lender assumes in return for the interest received is the risk of not getting the loan back. Neither of these situations is the same as loans or gifts for the needy.

Your
Question **Our congregation, like many, is struggling financially and has been for several years. We are conducting maintenance ministries at best, all to the glory of God. As the financial picture becomes more and more bleak, God provides us with a way to meet our expenses that typically comes in the form of an anonymous gift or funds from an estate. God's answer to our financial problems may not always be these kinds of gifts, and we will have to be prepared to meet our expenses in a different fashion. When the financial discussions turn towards borrowing money to meet expenses, there are individuals who insist that borrowing money for this purpose is unscriptural. I have not heard the specific scriptural references and therefore I cannot share them with you for your opinion. What does Scripture say in regards to this topic? I look forward to your response.**

Nothing in Scripture forbids us to borrow to meet immediate needs. Virtually no one buys a house or builds a church without borrowing. It is, of course, unwise to keep borrowing for ongoing expenses, except to meet emergency needs, because those bills are going to come due. A church cannot keep expanding its programs on borrowed funds without a reliable plan to eliminate the debt. The day of reckoning will come.

Given that some businesses exploit human and natural resources as well as consumer covetousness and products that we as Christians would not morally support, how can we as individuals and as church units invest money to earn money in a way that pleases God?

The meaning of the word *exploit* in your question is unclear. Every business uses and to some degree consumes human and natural resources, so there is nothing wrong with that. Every worker is motivated at least in part by a desire to earn. "Exploitation" is only wrong if it means "misuse," not if it means "use."

Christians should not invest in a business that is inherently evil, such as the production of pornography. Beyond that, it is not possible to make a list of permissible or nonpermissible businesses. The fact that a business or profession can be practiced in a wrong way does not mean that a Christian cannot be in such a business. If that were true, a Christian could not work or invest in any business. The fact that wine, for example, can be misused does not mean a Christian can't run a vineyard. The fact that some banks may be unscrupulous in their lending practices does not mean a Christian cannot be a banker. Some Christians even invest in companies that have dubious ethical practices to try to change those practices. In short, a Christian should seek to promote honest dealing and useful service in any business he or she is involved in.

A group of investors forms a corporation that has a twofold purpose: (1) to provide cable television service, and (2) to foster innovations that may improve education at all levels in the community it serves. The investors offer shares of corporation stock as a gift to a WELS Christian day school, along with other institutions (some church related) and foundations. The shareholding institutions are also given video equipment for producing their own programs and preferred time slots for airing them on the company's system. Should the WELS school accept the stock?

There is no reason a church cannot accept a gift of stock or property if it could accept a gift of money from the same source. It should know if there are any strings attached. Does the stock, for example, become the school's property, which it can sell if it chooses? Does the stock involve any obligations to the business? Will it entangle the school in obligations to the business that it will regret?

Scripture Index

Genesis—23
1–3—2
4:21—22
8:21—60
9:3—350
9:6—274
11:7—152
15:18-21—197
17:8—197
17:14—13
19:37,38—16
25:4—13
25:29-34—12

Exodus
4:24—13
4:25—13
18:2—13
20—275
21—275
21:12-14—274
22:2,3—279
22:8—32
22:22-27—352
23:31—197
31:17—47
32:9-14—47

Leviticus
16:29—337
19:28—348
25:35-37—351, 353

Numbers
6:3—131, 334

Deuteronomy
4:2—2
6:4-9—183
8:17,18—283
13:1-3—242
23:19,20—351, 353
25:5,6—27

Judges—17
4:5—15
4:8,9—17
13:14—131

1 Samuel—15
16:1—205
28:6—205
31:12,13—351

1 Kings
22—51
22:20-22—51

2 Kings
11:12—321

Ezra
6:8-10—264
7:13-26—264

Job
1,2—51
38:6,7—50, 51

Psalms

5:5—57
8:2—117
14—281
15—302, 351
15:5—352
19:12—62
19:13—59, 62
47:1—321
51:5—59, 60, 112
58:1-6—272
75—20
76:5—192
82:6—32
98:8—321
103:8-11—113
104:3—20
104:4—19, 20
110—209
110:1—259
144—270
146:4—208
148:1-4—20

Proverbs

6:1-3—354
28:8—353

Ecclesiastes

9:5,10—208

Song of Songs—291

Isaiah

9:6—230
13–34—272
14—22, 24
14:1—23
14:12—23
35:1-7—25
40:25-31—47
52,53—6
52:13—7
53:1—7

55:12—321
58:2-8—338
63:16—194
65:17,19—26
65:17-25—25
66:18-24—25

Jeremiah

7:31—208
31:18—43, 66

Lamentations

2:15—321

Ezekiel

12–32—272
16—200
18:5-18—60
18:13—351
25:6—321
28—21, 22
28:12-19—21
28:13—21, 22
40–48—149

Daniel

1—246
2—200
6—25
7:17—200
9—24
11—200
12:2—193

Joel

1:14—338

Amos

1,2—273
2:1—351
9:11,12—198

Nahum

3:13—321

Zechariah

3—51
7:5—337
14—197
14:4—195

Matthew

1—27
1:16—27
3:11—116
3:16—109
5:18-20—154
5:32—310
5:39—279
6—30
6:16,17—338
7—147, 148
7:1-5—296
7:15-20—146
8:28-32—51
8:29—38
9,10—48
9:14,15—338
10:32-39—166
10:37—174
11:11—209
11:17—22
11:22—207
12:32—30
12:46—28
13:18-23—42, 56
13:55—34
13:55,56—28
16—148
16:18—228
17—210
17:3—25
18:5,6—114
18:15-18—160
18:18-20—126
19:9—310
19:28-30—211
20:1-16—211

22:21—264
22:23—210
23—97
23:2,3—154
23:7-12—96
23:9,10—223
23:23—154
23:24—31
24:15,16—32
24:21,22—32
25—254
25:14—349
25:14-29—211
25:27—353
25:31-46—205
26:20,26—140
26:23—33
26:26—141
26:26,28—143
27:45—36
27:51—36
28:18,19—204
28:19,20—108, 262

Mark

1—110
1:10—109
3:29—29
10—310
10:11,12—309
10:13-16—108
14:20—33
15:33—36
15:34—38
15:38—36
15:43—39
16—10
16:16—114
16:19—39

Luke

1—232
1:41-44—112

1:44—59
3—27, 270
6:34—351
6:34,35—353
7—226
8:11-15—56
8:13—56
10:18—52, 204
11—30
12—207
12:14—264
12:15-21—349
12:47,48—207
13—60
13:1-5—31, 283
13:35—8
16—26, 38, 210
16:22—191
16:22,23—205
16:27,28—191, 194
18:15-17—117
20:35,36—194
21:24—198
22:19—127
22:21—33
22:36—279
22:41—33
23:43—191, 205, 210
23:44,45—36
23:46—37
24—39
24:33—39
24:42-48—39

John

1:1-18—26
3:5—64
3:13—209
3:16—57, 147
4—172
5:17—47
5:19-23—46
6:44—43

6:69—254
6:70—255
8—10
8:39,44—198
9:4—208
10:27-29—42, 56
10:33—32
12:31—52
12:32—204
13:5—324
13:26-30—33
13:27—205
14:6—226
15:5—40
17:15—195
18:36,37—262
19:11—208
19:39—39
20:17—37
20:23—87

Acts

1—39
1:4—39
1:11—195
2:13—132
2:17—192
2:27—9
2:34—209
2:42—173
2:46—248, 318
3:21—8
5:29—280
6—80, 82, 83, 84, 287
8—116
8:38,39—110
10:44-48—116
13:2—338
14:23—215, 338
15—198, 203
16,24,25—279
16:37-40—39
20:17,28—80

20:28—215
22:23-28—39

Romans
1:18—45, 208
1:18-31—296
1:18-32—53, 299
1:20—208
2:6-8—254
2:11,12—208
2:12-15—54
2:28—208
3—58
3:23-26—223
3:28—222
4—24
4:11—115, 117
4:16—223
5—60, 61
5:1,2—61, 121
5:12—60
7—66, 297
7:14-25—62
8:6-8—66
8:7,8—40
9–11—198, 282
9:1—281
9:6-8—198
10:1—282
10:1-3—46
11:6—224
11:11,25,26—198
11:16—223
11:33-36—113, 114
12:6-8—104
13—270
13:1—279
13:1-7—262
13:4—274
14—22, 158, 316, 348
14:1—174, 327, 334
14:1-23—327
14:5,6,10—248, 318

14:13—331
16—148
16:16—324
16:17—165, 182
16:17-19—147

1 Corinthians
1,2—26
2:1-4—323
2:13—2
3—148
3:10-15—211
4:1-4—85
4:15—96
5:9-12—284
5:12—262
6:2—209
6:9,10—296
6:9-11—295
6:11—296
7—308, 309
7:15—310
8—316, 348
8,10—278
8:4-8—327
8:9-13—331
8:10—169
9:11—85, 86
9:12,19-23—63
9:19-21—74
10:12—42, 56, 239
10:13—42, 56, 181
10:14-21—170
10:16—143
10:16,17—34, 129, 134
11—122, 316
11:3,5,8,9,13,15,16—317
11:17-32—129
11:23—128
11:24—127
11:26-32—34
11:27-31—164
11:29-32—205

12:3—66
12:5—104
12:28—104
14—100
14:34—98
14:34,37,38—317
15—193
15:24-28—192
15:35-38—350
15:50—193
16—316
16:2—248, 319

2 Corinthians

3:4-6—63
4:7—63
4:13-14—254
5—61
5:18-21—71, 72
6:3-10—63
6:18—256
8:9—349
10:4-6—262

Galatians—158

1:1-9—163
3:18—223
4:24-31—198
5—316, 348
5:1,13—348
5:1-12—163
5:3,4—224
5:4—223
5:6—40
6:6—85, 86
6:10—353
6:16—198

Ephesians

1—55, 239
1:3-14—55
1:4,5—55
1:11-14—57
2:3—60, 112

2:4-6—202
2:8,9—5, 68, 222
2:8-10—223
4:11—104
4:11-15—149
5—305
5:18-20—173
6:4—183
6:10-18—262

Philippians

2:9-11—259
2:13—40, 66
3:2,3—198

Colossians

2:11,12—115
2:13-16—318
2:13-17—247
2:15—38, 52, 55, 204
2:16—316
2:16,17—74

1 Thessalonians

2:6-12—97
4—26, 193, 196, 197
4:3-5—292
4:13-18—195, 210
4:15-17—196
5:21,22—23

2 Thessalonians

2—200, 242
3:10—43, 349

1 Timothy

1:3—316
2—16, 18
2:3-6—56
2:4—55
2:12—157
2:12-14—317
3—79, 105
3:1-12—106
3:2—104

3:5—104
3:6—21
4:3—158
4:10—56, 71
4:11—104
4:13—104
4:14—80
5:8—42
5:17—80, 104
5:18—2, 3, 87, 336
5:22—182
6:2—104
6:6-10—349

2 Timothy
2:2—215
2:18—158
3:16—1, 2

Titus
1—105
1:5—215
1:5,6—105
1:6-9—106
1:9—80
2:10—64
2:15—100
3:5—112, 117
3:9—158
3:10—165

Hebrews
1—20
1:2—192
1:7—19, 20
2:14-17—256
4:12—53
6—56
6:4-6—56
8:13—197
9:26-28—192
10:25—248, 318
10:26—56, 62
10:26,27—42

10:26-31—239
11:6—40
11:31—14
12:16—12
13:5,6—349
13:17—215

James—155
2—335
2:25—14
5:7-9—192
5:14—80
5:14,16—87
5:16—48, 126

1 Peter
1:23—41, 64
2—270
2:9—102
2:13-17—262
3—304, 308
3:18—38
3:18,19—54, 204
3:18-20—37
3:19,20—191, 205
3:21—115
4:7—192
4:10,11—215
5:8—51

2 Peter
1:4—149
1:19-21—1
2:1-4,13-20—158
2:4—21, 51
3—38, 52
3:8,9—192
3:16—2, 3

1 John
1:8-10—42
2:18,22—40, 41
2:23—46
3:8—204

3:9—41, 42
3:20—57
5:1—64
5:16—205

2 John
10—173
10,11—163, 182
10–11—165

Jude—38
3-10—158
4—8
6—51

Revelation—202
1—203
1,2—201
1:3—192
1:10—248, 319
2,3—158
2:7—210
3:9—198

3:10—195
3:20—43
5:10—209
6—204
6:10—191, 194, 272
12—197, 200, 201, 204
12:7-10—52
12:13,17—51
12:17—230
13—201
16:16—199
17—200
17:5,6—200
20—197, 202, 204
20:4—191
20:6—209
21,22—2, 210
22:10,12—192
22:16—23
22:18—2
22:20—274

Subject Index

A

abortion, 113–114, 274–279, 305–307

absolution, 60–62, 120–121, 126

accountability before God, 163

adiaphora, 21–23, 158–159, 315–355

admonition in termination of fellowship, 217–220

adoration of the Sacrament, 139–142

adultery, 302, 309–313

age of accountability, 59–60

agreement on doctrine, 121–122, 128–130, 148–152, 155–159, 165–177, 213–214, 217–220

aid, government, 263–266

alcohol, 130–134, 136–137, 333–335, 347–348

All Saints' Day, 340–342

altar, 138–139

angels, 50–51, 52–53, 194

Anglo-Catholic beliefs, 93–94

annulment, 311–313

"anonymous Christians," 226–228

anthropopathism, 47

antichrist, 40–41, 195–197, 199–201, 228–229

Antichrist, 5, 40–41, 195, 199–201, 224, 228–229

anti-Semitic, 280–282

apartheid, 280

Apostles' Creed, 251–253, 255, 258–259

apostolic succession, 93–96

applause in church, 321–323

Arianism, 251, 253

Armageddon, 199

Arminian theology, 7–8, 66, 135, 238–239, 241, 283–284

art, Christian, 52–53

ascension of Jesus, 38–39

Asian religions, 58, 249, 345–346

Assemblies of God, 49, 65–67, 241

Athanasian Creed, 46, 251, 253–254

atheism, 45–46

atomic warfare, 271

attendance, church, 339

attitude toward Catholicism, 234–237

Augsburg Confession, 49–50, 94–96, 263, 269, 279

Authorized Standard Version, 40–41

B

Babylon, 199

Baptism, 64–65, 99, 107–119, 126–128, 227, 245

submersion in, 110–111

baptism of Jesus, 28–29, 109–110

Baptists, 43, 49, 109–110, 114, 168–169, 239
Bartimaeus, 38–39
beasts of Revelation, 201–202
Bible (as book), 1–12
Bible codes, 6
Bible society, 336–337
Bible translations, 7–12, 19–20
Billy Graham, 237–238
birth control, 305–307
bishops, 93–94
body and blood of Christ, 119–120, 121–123, 124–125, 128–130, 132–134, 139–143
born again, 64–65
borrowing money, 351–354
Bosnia, 271–274
boycott of secular items, 283–284
bread in Communion, 130–134, 136–137, 334
Buddhism, 249
Byzantium, 11–12

C

call, divine, 83–96, 103–105
Calvinist beliefs, 55–58, 123–124, 135, 241–242
canonical, 2–3
capital punishment, 274–275
catholic, 258
Catholicism, 4–5, 68–70, 93–94, 97, 118, 122, 134–136, 139–142, 152–154, 169–170, 199–201, 207–208, 216, 221–237, 253, 269, 280–282, 303–305, 311–313, 337–339
ceremonial law, 74
chanting, 320–321
chapter and verse divisions, 6–7
charismatic churches, 242–243
children in marriage, 304–305

children, sin in, 59–60, 112–114
Christian art, 52–53
Christian Democrats, 266–267
church attendance, 339
church discipline, 105–106, 157–158, 159–160
church government, 81
Church of the Lutheran Confession (CLC), 217–220
circumcision, 13, 115–116
civil government, 261–287
clapping in church, 321–323
CLC, 217–220
closed Communion, 128–130, 164, 214
clothing in church, 335
codes, Bible, 6
commercial arrangements with heterodox churches, 175–176
common chalice, 132–134, 137–138
Communion, 33–34, 107–109, 119–143, 159–160, 164, 311–313
  closed, 128–130, 164, 214
  officiants of, 125–128
  real presence in, 121–122, 124–125, 128–130, 132–133, 139–140
  recipients of, 128–130
community service, 176, 285–287
confession, 60–62, 120–121
confessions of faith, 251–259
conscience, 53–54, 59, 62, 315
consecration of Communion elements, 136–137, 139, 142–143, 319–320
consubstantiation, 123
conversion, 43, 62–68
Council of Trent, 68–70
courtship, 291–293
Covenant Church, 220–221

creation of angels, 50–51
creeds, 251–259
cremation, 350–351
cross, 34–36
crucifixion, 34–37
cults, 244–249

D
dancing, 349–350
dating, 291–293
David, 27–28
deacon/deaconess, 79–81
death, 191–194, 205
death of Jesus, 36–37
death penalty, 274–275
Deborah, 16–18
deception, 14–15
decision theology, 43, 65–67,
    330–331
descent into hell, Jesus', 37–38,
    52, 54–55, 207
desertion, marriage, 302, 309–
    313
devil, renunciation of, 111–112
discipline, church, 105–106,
    157–158, 159–160
discipline, spiritual, 337–339
discrepancies in Bible
    translations, 19–20
distribution of Communion,
    132–134, 136–137
divine call, 83–96, 103–105
divine providence, 58–59
divining, 344–345
divorce, 105, 301–303, 309–313
doctrinal agreement, 121–122,
    128–130, 148–152, 155–
    159, 165–177, 213–214,
    217–220
Dominus Iesus, 227–228

E
early Communion, 136
Easter, 326–328

education, 178–183, 263–266,
    342–343
Eighth Commandment, 14–15
ELCA, 93, 124–125, 128–130,
    152, 153, 156–157, 215–
    217, 240
elder, 79–81, 105–106
election, doctrine of, 55–58
elements used in Communion,
    130–132
Eleven, the, 38–39
end times, 191–211
Epiphany, 325–326
Episcopal beliefs, 122
Esau, 12
eschatology, 191–211
ethnic cleansing, 271–274
Eucharist, 123
Evangelical Covenant Church of
    America, 220–221
Evangelical Lutheran Church in
    America (ELCA), 93, 124–
    125, 128–130, 152, 153,
    156–157, 215–217, 240
evangelists, 237–238
evidence of God's existence,
    45–46
evil angels, 21, 51–52
exaltation of Jesus, 38, 55
excommunication, 106, 159–160,
    228
existence of God, evidence
    45–46

F
faith alone, 222–226, 229
fall from faith, 41–42, 56–57
false prophets, 146–148
family, providing for, 42–43
fasting, 337–339
fatalism, 58–59
father (as a religious title), 96–98

fellowship, 145–189, 213–214, 217–220, 221–222, 251–252, 254–255, 284–285, 330–331
fetal tissue in medical research, 275–279
Fifth Commandment, 274–275, 346
Fifth Petition, 87–89
figurative language, 31
first Communion, 221–222
forgiveness, 60–62, 67–68, 71–73, 120–121
fraternities, 186–187
free will, 43, 65–67
fruits of faith, 40, 70–71, 74–77, 253–254
fund-raisers, 335–336
funeral practices, 164–166, 350–351

G
gambling, 349–350
genealogy of Jesus, 27–28
Gethsemane, 33
gods, men as, 32
good works, 40, 70–71, 74–77, 211, 222–226, 253–254
gospel, 58, 61, 62–65, 67–68, 74, 76–77, 83–85, 120–121, 224–226, 295–299
government, church, 81
government, civil, 261–287
government aid, 263–266
grace, 60–62, 67–70, 71, 115, 223, 224–226, 232
grammatical-historical interpretation method, 5
grape juice/wine in Communion, 130–134, 136–137, 333–335
Greek manuscripts, 10–12, 40–41

greetings in church, exchange of, 323–324
guilt, 75–77

H
"Hail Mary," 231–233
Halloween, 340–342
Harry Potter books, 342–343
hatred of sinners, God's, 57–58
heaven, 25–26, 51–52, 191–194, 205, 207, 209–211
Hebrew Bible, 6–7
hell, 37–38, 51–52, 72–73, 191–193, 205–209
helping others, 31
hermeneutical interpretation method, 5
hierarchical structure of a church, 81
Hinduism, 249
Holy Spirit
    in conversion, 43, 62–68, 116
    inspiration of Scripture by, 1–12
    sin against the, 29–30, 56–57, 60–61, 205–206
home schooling, 179–183
homosexuality, 295–300
hunting, 350
husband and wife, roles of, 307–308

I
immaculate conception, 231
immersion in Baptism, 109–111
immunizations, 275–279
inclusive language, 255–256
inerrancy of the Bible, 152–154
infallibility, 4–5
infant Baptism, 107–109, 112–114, 117–119
infant Communion, 107–109
injustice, worldly, 271–274, 279–280

Inner Light, 243–244
innocence, 59
inspiration of Scripture, 1–12
interest on loans, 351–354
interfaith wedding ceremony, 303–304
interpretation of Scripture, 5, 150–151, 201–202, 203–205
investments, 355
invisible holy Christian church, 152–154, 166, 176–177
Isaac, 12
Islamic belief, 58, 177
Israel (Jacob), 12
Israel (the land and its people), 197–198

J
Jacob, 12
Jerusalem, 18–19
   destruction of, 32–33
Jesus' descent into hell, 37–38, 52, 54–55, 207
Jethro, 13
Jews, 280–282, 328
Joint Declaration, 68–70
joint prayer, 156, 171–175, 213–214, 251–252
Joint Statement, 217–220
Joseph, 27–28
Judaism, 177
Judas, 33–34, 205
judges, 15
Judgment Day, 32–33, 191–193, 194–206
judgment on sin, 16, 148, 205–206
juice in Communion, 130–134, 136–137, 333–335
justification, 60–62, 67, 68–70, 71–73, 223

K
keys, ministry of the, 87–89
King James Version (KJV), 7–12, 40–41, 82–83
King of Tyre, 21–23
kiss of peace, 324
KJV, 7–12, 40–41, 82–83
Kokomo Statements, 72–73

L
landlords, 293–294
Last Day, 32–33, 191–193, 194–206
last names, 305
Last Supper, 33–34
last things, study of, 191–211
Latter Day Saints (Mormons), 32, 40, 244–246
law, 58, 67–68, 73–74, 75–77, 154, 295–299
law, natural knowledge of the, 53–54, 299
lay readers in church, 99–101
Lazarus, 192–193
LCMS, 16–18, 73–74, 95–96, 99–105, 117–118, 128–130, 132–133, 153–154, 156–159, 178–179, 213–215, 251–252
Left Behind, 243
living together before marriage, 105–106, 289–291, 293–294
loans, monetary, 351–354
Lord's Prayer, 30
Lord's Supper, 33–34, 107–109, 119–143, 159–160, 164, 311–313
Lot's daughters, 16
Lucifer, 23–24
Luther, Martin, 14, 98–99, 101–103, 113–114, 127–128, 140–142, 155, 228, 237, 259, 268–269, 270, 274, 279–282, 339–340

Lutheran Church—Missouri
   Synod (LCMS), 16–18, 73–
   74, 95–96, 99–105,
   117–118, 128–130, 132–
   133, 153–154, 156–159,
   178–179, 213–215, 251–252
Lutheran Confessional Church,
   46
Lutheran Confessions, 49–50,
   216, 228, 229, 263, 269
Lutheran Pioneers, 183–185
lying, 14–15

M
Mariolatry, 229–233
mark of the beast, 201–202
marriage, 170–171, 289–295,
   300–313
   ceremony, 28
   desertion of, 302, 309–313
   different faiths in, 300–301
   reconciliation of, 309–313
Mary (Jesus' mother), 28, 229–
   233
   veneration of, 229–233
Mary of Magdala, 37
mass, 234
means of grace, 49, 77, 94–96,
   102, 114, 116
medical research and treatments,
   275–279
meditation, 249
Megiddo, 199
membership in nonreligious
   organizations, 183–189
Methodist church, 238–239
military efforts, 271–274
millennialism, 194–205
minister, 81–83
ministry
   doctrine of the, 79–106, 156–
   157, 215

offices of the, 79–81, 101–
   105, 156–157, 215
   pastoral, 81–83, 85–106, 156–
   157, 215, 285–287
ministry of the keys, 87–89
Missouri Synod (LCMS), 16–18,
   73–74, 95–96, 99–105, 117–
   118, 128–130, 132–133,
   153–154, 156–159, 178–
   179, 213–215, 251–252
Mormonism, 32, 40, 244–246
Morning Star, 23–24
morning stars, 50–51
Moses, 13
music in church, 20–23, 165–
   168, 234, 320–321,
   328–331, 337
Muslim beliefs, 58, 177

N
NASB, 9–10, 40–41
natural knowledge of God, 26–
   27, 45–46, 53–54, 208
natural knowledge of the law,
   53–54
Nazis, 280–282
New American Standard Bible
   (NASB), 9–10, 40–41
new birth, 64–65
New International Version
   (NIV), 7–12, 19–20, 40–41
Nicene Creed, 46, 251–252, 253,
   254–257
NIV, 7–12, 19–20, 40–41
nondenominational, 65–67
nonmember Baptism, 118–119
nuclear weapons, 271
numbers in Revelation, 201–202

O
oaths, 284–285
objective justification, 57, 71–73
obstacles to faith, 62–64

occult, 342–345
offices of the ministry, 79–81,
     101–105, 156–157, 215
officiants of Communion, 125–
     128
Old Testament Christians, 24,
     207, 209
oppressors, worldly, 271–274
oral sex, 294–295
organizations, nonreligious, 183–
     189, 284–285
original sin, 59–60, 152–154
Orthodox beliefs, 93
overseer, 79–81

P

pagan religions, 326–328
Palestinians, 18–19
papacy, 5, 93–94, 199–202, 222,
     224, 228–229, 269
paradise, 210
Passover, 328
pastoral ministry, 81–83, 85–106,
     156–157, 215, 285–287
pastors, 80–81, 81–83, 85–106,
     285–287
patriotism, 283
Paul, 17–18, 39–40, 96–98
Pentecost, 116
Pentecostals, 46, 242–243
persecution, 48–49
Peter, 228–229
Pfarramt, 101–103
Pharisees, 154
piercing, body, 300, 348
Pioneers, Lutheran, 183–185
poetic language, 25
political involvement, 261–263,
     266–267, 286
pope, 5, 93–94, 199–202, 222,
     224, 228–229, 269
prayer, 30, 47–48, 49

prayer fellowship, 156, 171–175,
     213–214
prayers for the dead, 49–50
predestination, 55–58
Predigtamt, 101–103
prejudice, 280–282
premarital sex, 289–295
prenuptial agreements, 301
priesthood of believers, 99–101,
     102
prophecy, 25
providing for family, 42–43
psalm music, 20–21, 320–321
public ministry, 81–85, 94–96,
     99, 103–105, 126–128,
     156–157
punishment in hell, 207–209
purgatory, 207–208, 223, 224–
     226

Q

Quakerism, 243–244

R

racial separation, 280
Rahab, 14–15
rapture, 193, 194–197, 203–205,
     243
real presence in Communion,
     121–122, 124–125, 128–
     130, 132–133, 139–143
recipients of Communion, 128–
     130
reconciliation of marriage, 309–
     313
redemption factor (abortion),
     277–278
Reformed theology, 7–8, 24–25,
     122, 124–125, 128–130,
     135, 152, 241–242, 269
rejection of salvation, 26–27,
     29–30, 71, 72–73, 87–88
relationships in heaven, 210

remarriage, 309–313
"renegade Lutherans," 220–221
renunciation of the devil, 111–
    112
repentance, 31, 60–62, 67–68
reproductive techniques, 301
rest for God, 47
resurrection from death, 191–
    193, 197, 204–205, 350–351
resurrection of Jesus, 257
return of Jesus, 194–206
revenge, 279–280
reverend, 97
Reverend Father, 96–98
Revised Standard Version (RSV),
    40–41
Roman citizenship, 39–40
Roman crucifixion, 34–36
Romanizing Lutherans, 93–96
rosary, 231–232
RSV, 40–41

S
Sabbath, 74, 246–248, 317–319
sacraments, 107–143
sacrifices for faith, 162–163,
    179–183
saints, 72–73
    praying to, 233–234
Samson, 16
sanctification, 66–68, 70–71, 75–
    77, 223
Satan, 21–24, 29, 51–52, 54–55,
    202, 204
schools, 179–183, 263–266,
    342–343
Scouts, Boy and Girl, 183–185,
    284–285
Scripture, inspiration of, 1–12
second coming of Jesus, 194–206
second marriages, 309–313
secondhand smoke, 346–347
secular society, 283–284

segregation, 280
self-defense, 279–280
separation of church and state,
    261–266, 268–269
service to others, 324–325
Seventh-day Adventists, 246–
    249
70 weeks of Daniel, 24–25
sex
    oral, 294–295
    premarital, 289–295
sex change, 300
sexual morality, 289–313
shareholders, 355
sheol, 206–207
siblings of Jesus, 28, 34
sign of the cross, 319–320
sin, original, 59–60, 152–154
sin against the Holy Spirit,
    29–30
sin in children, 59–60, 112–114
sinful nature, 53–54, 59–60
sinners' prayer, 65–67
666, 202
Sixth Commandment, 310
smoking cigarettes, 346–347
sola scriptura, 4–5, 222–224
Solomon's temple, 19
sororities, 186–187
soul and spirit, 53
soul sleep, 192–193
spies, 14–15
spirit and soul, 53
sports leagues, 189
state churches, 268–269
stem cells, 275–279
stocks, 355
subjective justification, 71–73
submersion in Baptism, 110–111
Sunday worship, 317–319
surrogate motherhood, 301
symbols in Revelation, 201–205
synergism, 66

Synodical Conference, 159, 251–252

T

tattoos, 348
temple, 19
  destruction of, 32
Temple Mount, 19
temptation of Jesus, 29
temptation, sexual, 291–293, 349–350
Ten Commandments, 74
Textus Receptus, 11–12
theology of glory, 48–49
theology of the cross, 48–49
Third Commandment, 317–319
Third Use of the Law, 73–74, 76
Thomas, doubting, 37
thousand-year reign of Jesus, 194–205
titles in the church, 96–98
translations, Bible, 7–12, 19–20
transubstantiation, 123
tribulation, 195–197, 203–205
trick-or-treating, 340–342
Trinity, 46, 245, 253–254
tunes of psalms, 20–21
tyrants, worldly, 271–274

U

unbaptized children, 112–114
unborn children, 59–60, 112–114
unforgivable sin, 29–30, 56–57, 60–61

unit concept of church fellowship, 145–146
universalism, 71–73
usury, 351–354

V

vaccines, 275–279
veneration of Mary, 229–233
verse and chapter divisions, 6–7
virgin birth, 215–216
visible Christian church, 176–177
vouchers, government, 263–266

W

war, 269–271
washing disciples' feet, 324–325
wedding practices, 165–171, 303–304
will of God, 47–48, 51–52, 58–59
will, free, 43, 65–67
wine in Communion, 130–134, 136–137, 333–335
witchcraft, 342–345
woman and man in marriage, roles of, 307–308
women in the church, 16–18, 98–101, 126–128, 157–158, 160–162, 316–317

Y

Yin-Yang symbol, 345–346
yoga, 249

Z

zazen, 249
Zipporah, 13